Lincoln's Political Generals

Lincoln's Political Generals

DAVID WORK

UNIVERSITY OF ILLINOIS PRESS

Urbana and Chicago

Frontispiece and Lincoln portrait on opening chapter pages from
the Library of Congress, Rare Book and Special Collections Division,
Alfred Whital Stern Collection of Lincolniana.
Illustrations after p. 138 from the Brady Collection,
National Archives.

Library of Congress Cataloging-in-Publication Data
Work, David K.
Lincoln's political generals / David K. Work.
p.   cm.
Includes bibliographical references and index.
ISBN 978-0-252-03445-9 (cloth : alk. paper)
1. Lincoln, Abraham, 1809–1865—Military leadership.
2. Generals—United States—History—19th century.
3. United States—Politics and government—Civil War, 1861–1865.
4. Patronage, Political—United States—History—19th century.
5. Command of troops—History—19th century.
6. United States—History—Civil War, 1861–1865—Campaigns.
I. Title.
E457.2.W875   2009
973.7092—dc22   2008055269

This book is dedicated
to the memory of my sister, Amy.

Contents

Acknowledgments

I would like to thank my mother and father,
Peggy and Harry Gault, Dr. Joseph Dawson,
Dr. Walter D. Kamphoefner, Dr. Charles E. Brooks,
and Dr. Henry C. Schmidt.

Lincoln's
Political Generals

The Necessity of the Time

Let me lead this charge. Why, with a success like this, governor
be damned, I could land in the White House.
—Col. Phil Secord, *The Horse Soldiers*

In John Ford's 1959 Civil War film, Colonel Secord is an ambitious Northern politician seeking to win glory on the field of
battle that will translate into victory at the polls when the war is
over. The character is portrayed as a selfish, pompous, and incompetent officer
who evaluates every military action for its potential impact on his political
career. Although overdrawn, the character captures an important truth: the
presence of politicians within the officer corps of the Federal army. At the
beginning of the war, politics influenced the selection of nearly every officer,
regardless of their grade, since all officers were either elected by the men in
their commands or appointed by state governors and the president. As a result,
it was perfectly natural, commented Maj. Gen. Jacob Cox, himself a political
appointee, that politicians should hold army positions. They, after all, "called
meetings, addressed the people to rouse their enthusiasm, urged enlistments,

and often set the example by enrolling their own names first." Politicians in uniform, Cox concluded, "were the necessity of the time."[1]

Among the most famous politicians to wear Union blue were the political generals, men elevated to the highest ranks and granted important commands primarily on the basis of their political influence. Before the war, men who became political generals either had served in political office or represented an important constituency or ethnic group. Some of them had military experience, but they were not West Point graduates or career military officers, and military ability was a secondary consideration when deciding whether to grant these men commissions. They received their appointments from President Abraham Lincoln, who deliberately placed politicians from both political parties and various ethnic groups in the army. In appointing them, Lincoln sought to secure their and their constituents' support for the war effort and ensure that the war became a national struggle, waged by all political factions and ethnic groups for the common goal of reuniting the Union.

It is important to emphasize that political generals had not been trained at West Point. Because politics affected nearly every appointment and played an influential role in making promotions, it can be argued that generals such as George McClellan, Ulysses Grant, or William Sherman were also political generals. Lincoln knew that McClellan was a Democrat and took this into account when dealing with him, but the president initially appointed McClellan as a general and then as commander of the Army of the Potomac for military reasons: his West Point education, prior military service, and early success in the West Virginia campaign. McClellan's political standing became important only later. Men such as McClellan, Grant, Sherman, and others educated at the military academy owed their appointments to their military credentials and not to their party affiliation. None of them was appointed in order to secure their or their supporters' loyalty to the war effort. Political generals owed their appointments to this consideration.

Several political generals served in important positions and gained notoriety for their lack of military ability, but others, notable in the 1860s, have slipped into relative obscurity. Higher-profile officers such as Nathaniel P. Banks, Benjamin F. Butler, John C. Frémont, John A. McClernand, and Franz Sigel all held prominent commands and seemed to fail as combat generals, earning them reputations for incompetence that branded most political appointees as failures who hindered the Union war effort. These officers represented only a small sample of the citizen generals in the army. Just how many political generals served in the Union army is difficult to determine, often depending on how one decides to classify individuals who pursued several different occupations before the war. Perhaps well over one hundred men potentially may be classed as political generals. Most of these men have been forgotten by all but the most enthusiastic Civil War students, and, in most cases, their careers have not been evaluated. Thus, the overall effectiveness of the political generals as a group remains understudied and unappreciated.[2]

Although Lincoln's policy of making political generals is well known, few historians have attempted to evaluate the president's plan and the overall performance of these generals. In two separate studies, Bruce Catton takes a favorable view of Lincoln's policy. Catton argues that by using political generals, Lincoln prevented the war from becoming a solely Republican Party conflict and that "final victory came more *quickly*, rather than more *slowly*, because he did use them." In the end, Catton concludes that the "use of the political general was justified." More recently, in three works, James McPherson argues that "these appointments made political sense but sometimes produced military calamity." Nevertheless, McPherson concludes that the policy "was essential." On the other hand, Brooks D. Simpson condemns Lincoln's policy of appointing politicians to high command. These officers, Simpson argues, made "costly military mistakes" that "outweighed whatever political benefit their retention may have realized" and "ultimately incurred political costs."[3]

These studies suffer for two reasons. Each one examines only political generals who commanded armies and briefly mentions only one or two other generals who served as division or corps commanders. As a result, these studies offer a narrow focus on only a handful of generals and fail to analyze the wider implications of Lincoln's policy. Even more important, these studies restrict themselves to an examination of the battlefield impact of political generals, seeking to evaluate these generals strictly on how well they performed in campaigns and battles. Generals during the Civil War dealt with a vast array of tasks, from politics to military administration to dealing with African Americans, and evaluations of political generals need to take into account these features of their service along with campaigns and battles.

Finally, Thomas Goss presents a favorable view of political generals that examines a variety of different issues. His study briefly surveys their impact on the battlefield, toward slavery, on politics, and on military administration, but the primary focus of his work is the "conflict between U.S. Military Academy graduates and political generals," especially their diverging views on what was "required for successful generalship." As a result, Goss's work, which studies only Banks, Butler, Frémont, John A. Logan, McClernand, and Sigel, does not provide a full and detailed evaluation of Lincoln's policy.[4]

The present study seeks to provide a closer evaluation of a selected sample of citizen generals—a term often used by some political generals to distinguish themselves from West Pointers—that takes into account all of their activities. It will cast a wider net, looking at sixteen generals—eight Republicans and eight Democrats, including two Germans and two Irish—to provide a larger field from which to draw conclusions about the overall effectiveness of Lincoln's policy. These generals are Banks, Francis P. Blair Jr., Butler, James W. Denver, John A. Dix, Frémont, Stephen Hurlbut, Logan, McClernand, Thomas F. Meagher, Robert Schenck, Carl Schurz, James Shields, Daniel Sickles, Sigel, and James S. Wadsworth. Such a small sample is necessary for practical reasons; to study every political general in more than superficial detail would be infeasible.

Several factors led to the selection of these particular men. These include political affiliation, as an effort was made to have an equal number of Republicans and Democrats. It was also necessary to examine generals representing several different geographic regions—New England (Banks and Butler), the middle states (Dix, Sickles, and Wadsworth), the Midwest (Hurlbut, Logan, McClernand, and Schenck), and the trans-Mississippi (Blair, Denver, and Frémont)—and the most important immigrant groups, the Germans (Schurz and Sigel) and the Irish (Meagher and Shields). The sample, therefore, represents every region, though New York State is overrepresented since four generals (Dix, Meagher, Sickles, and Wadsworth) came from that state alone. This occurred because of the state's large population, presence of the largest city, and the fact that many Irish settled there. In the Midwest, Illinois is slightly overrepresented because it was Lincoln's home state and contained the important southern section of Egypt. Some of these generals were chosen because of particular actions they took during the Civil War that have not received attention. Finally, an effort was made to include generals who commanded various army units, ranging from regiment to brigade, division, corps, and army, and compare well-known commanders with lesser-known individuals in order to place their actions in a larger context.

Campaigns and battles were important and will receive considerable attention, but the present study seeks to look beyond these already well-covered aspects of the conflict. Other areas of the war effort discussed include operating military administrations, enforcing the draft, determining commercial policy, running for elective office, stump speaking during political campaigns, shaping Federal policy toward blacks, and implementing Reconstruction. How the citizen generals exerted political influence to advance their careers will also be covered. All of these topics must be studied in order to evaluate the full effect that political generals had on the war.

The sixteen political generals surveyed in this study exerted a considerable amount of influence over the Federal war effort, though some individuals had more of an impact than others. They served in virtually every theater of the conflict and fought on dozens of battlefields, commanded units of different sizes, and compiled uneven combat records, though only a few of these generals could be called outright failures. On other aspects of the war, they often had great sway. Lincoln placed several of them in positions of military government from which they played major roles in exerting Federal control over the South, determining Federal trade policy, and charting the early course of Reconstruction, to list just three areas where their influence was important. A few generals made their greatest contribution in helping to form the Union's policies toward African Americans, beginning with the issue of fugitive slaves and including emancipation, black labor, and black soldiers. Finally, most of these generals spoke at public rallies or wrote letters that urged their constituents to support the war effort, even if they did not agree with all of Lincoln's policies.

These political generals were not the failures often depicted in the historical literature and popular culture, but instead compiled mixed records. Though few of them were great battlefield generals, they proved to be good administrators and popular speakers and made important contributions to the Union war effort. Lincoln's decision to use them was wise, though he did not always employ them effectively and often allowed generals to remain in command after they had demonstrated their incompetence. The overall impact of political generals, however, benefited the Federal cause.

CHAPTER 2

Hunting
for Generals

A s the Civil War began in April 1861, President Abraham
Lincoln needed generals to command his growing army
of volunteer soldiers. One problem he faced was that the
U.S. Army possessed few general officers. At the beginning of the year, there
were only five generals in the army: Winfield Scott, John E. Wool, David E.
Twiggs, Frederick Harney, and Joseph E. Johnston. Three of them were over
seventy years old, and none were under fifty, the youngest being fifty-three. By
the end of April, two of these officers had resigned and joined the Confederate
army (Twiggs and Johnston), leaving Lincoln with only three septuagenarians
to lead his rapidly organizing volunteer army.[1]

Thus, Lincoln, as one of his secretaries wrote, had to go "hunting for
generals"; he had to find men to lead the army he was trying to create. To
fill many of these positions, he turned to politicians, granting them appointments because they represented politically important groups. Many of these
men lacked both military education and experience and seemed to possess no
qualifications other than their political prominence. In 1861 alone, Lincoln
made forty-four political generals, though only sixteen of them possessed no

military experience. Many of them had served in either their state's militia or the Mexican War. But military experience was just a bonus and not the primary reason for appointing politicians to high rank in the Union army. As Lincoln wrote during the war, "In a purely military point of view it may be that none of these things is indispensable, or perhaps, advantageous; but in another aspect, scarcely less important, they would give great relief."[2]

Appointing politicians to high rank within the new volunteer army made perfect sense to Lincoln and his contemporaries for a variety of reasons. For one thing, there was no one else to turn to. There were not enough men in the United States with a military education to officer the new volunteer army. In 1861, the Regular army had 1,105 officers, but 296 of them resigned to either join the Confederacy or take no part in the conflict, leaving 809 to serve in the Union army. Of those 1,105 officers, 824 were graduates of West Point. Of them, 184 joined the Confederacy, leaving Lincoln with 640. Finally, there were another 900 U.S. Military Academy graduates in civilian life, but only 114 rejoined the Federal army. Thus, there were 754 West Point–educated officers that Lincoln could draw on when commissioning generals as well as colonels, majors, captains, and lieutenants. There were not enough professionals to fill all of these positions, meaning that the president had to use civilians, no matter what prewar occupation they pursued.[3]

None of these potential generals, including professional military men, had any experience leading large field armies. Even General Scott, the most experienced commander in America, had never commanded an army larger than 14,000 men, the size of the force he led during the Mexican War. In the spring of 1861, none of the 754 West Pointers then in or rejoining the army had directed a unit as large as a brigade. Their careers in the Regular army had revolved around duty with small forces at isolated posts, usually on the frontier, where they rarely saw any unit larger than a company. Even their education had not prepared them for high command, as the West Point curriculum focused primarily on engineering and training cadets to be lieutenants. Some officers had supplemented their education by reading military texts and serving in the Mexican War, but as one historian points out, in 1861 none of these men "was capable of efficiently administering and fighting a large army." Thus, Lincoln had no experienced officers whom he could commission as generals, and politicians, with their backgrounds in party organization, election campaigning, and administering state, local, and federal governments, seemed to possess many of the qualities necessary for running an army.[4]

The policy also had strong historical precedent. In every American war to that time, civilian generals had played prominent roles. During the American Revolution, such civilians as Benedict Arnold, Henry Knox, and Nathanael

Greene all became excellent generals despite their lack of military training. The War of 1812 also witnessed a similar use of civilian generals. Many of these appointments went to politicians. William Hull had served as the governor of Michigan Territory, and Stephen Van Rensselaer was a powerful Federalist from New York. Both of these generals proved to be failures, but their failure did not prevent future generations from adopting this policy, primarily because Americans remembered only the successful civilian generals of this war, Andrew Jackson and William Henry Harrison.

The most important precedent for the Civil War came from the Mexican War, during which President James K. Polk appointed civilians to all thirteen of the generalships created by Congress. Polk, a Democrat, made appointments that were openly political. He was disdainful of most senior Regular army officers, believing that they were "all Whigs and violent partisans" who sought to inhibit his "prosecuting the Mexican War successfully." To offset this perceived Whig bias, every one of the volunteer generals the president appointed was a Democratic politician. Polk wanted to win the war and ensure the supremacy of the Democratic Party. Thus, he needed Democrats to command the army and win the prestige that came with victory. Not all of Polk's appointees performed well, but Polk's policy of making political generals in order to serve political needs was a powerful precedent that would influence Lincoln.[5]

The ideology of the nineteenth century also encouraged the policy, as it enforced the notion that specialized training was not necessary for success in war and common citizens could become successful generals. Any talented man might possess the genius necessary to command an army. Lincoln and his contemporaries all came of age during the Jacksonian era, which embedded in them this belief in the common man. The editors of the *New York Times* drew directly on this notion when they praised Lincoln's selection of political generals, arguing that "military talent or genius for command are [not] confined to the graduates of our military schools." They believed that success in any field depended on genius, something that education "strengthens" but "cannot create." Other newspapers, such as the *New York Tribune* and *Harper's Weekly*, agreed with the *Times*. The key, according to these newspapers, was to find the men of genius to fight the war.[6]

This notion was also reflected in the hostility directed against West Point. During the antebellum period, many politicians had attacked the military academy because they viewed it as a citadel of aristocracy, and several attempts by Congress to eliminate the institution nearly succeeded. Similar attacks continued during the Civil War. One senator dismissed West Point as an engineering school and called for the resignation of every engineer and for "the men of the North, with their strong arms and indomitable spirit, [to] move down upon the rebels." This view was widely held in the North. One of Senator Lyman Trumbull's Illinois constituents wrote him that West Point graduates are "totally unfit for any practical results." He suggested that the Regular army and volunteer army be separated, allowing the volunteers to put down the rebellion, while assigning the professionals the task of taking "care of the old ladies who are held prisoners at Washington."[7]

Lincoln harbored some of these antimilitary sentiments. On the one hand, he never made any hostile comments about West Point and said once that "a man educated in military affairs was better fitted for military office than an uneducated man." On several occasions, however, he disparaged his own military service during the Black Hawk War. He also had no interest in military values, ideas, and practices and displayed little understanding of the military profession and what those professionals valued. These sentiments led the president to undervalue military professionals and to believe that civilians could become successful generals.[8]

All of these factors underlay Lincoln's policy, but it was the president's desire to build a national coalition to wage civil war that was the driving force behind the commissioning of politicians. Lincoln realized that the North was divided into different factions, between Republicans and Democrats, antislavery and proslavery, nativists and immigrants, high tariff and low tariff, and many other competing interest and ethnic groups. Not all of them viewed the war favorably. As president, it was Lincoln's primary task to unite these often hostile groups behind the war effort. One of the tools he used to effect this was to appoint the leaders of these competing factions to high positions within the army. By doing so, he sought to cement their allegiance to the war effort, hoping that their constituencies would follow the example of their leaders and enlist in the army or vote to continue the struggle, without which it would be impossible to win the war. This was the "great relief" that Lincoln hoped to create by using politicians in the army. Essentially, appointing generals was a tool he used to solidify support for the Union.

This fact distinguished Lincoln's political generals from those commissioned by President Polk during the Mexican War. Polk sought only to promote the Democratic Party; he was motivated solely by partisan politics. Lincoln, though never ignoring partisan politics, was also motivated by a patriotic desire to create a united front to oppose the rebellion. His actions also were driven by necessity, as they reflected the fact that he was the leader of a divided nation. Polk could afford to ignore the opposition party, since most Americans supported his war policies. Lincoln could not. There were too many potential opposition groups that might not support him. Thus, Lincoln appointed generals in ways designed to secure the loyalty of three basic groups: his own

Republican Party, the rival Democratic Party, and ethnic groups, specifically the Germans and the Irish.

The Civil War proved to be an excellent source of patronage for a president harried by job seekers. It provided Lincoln, as well as state governors and the Republican Party in general, with a vast number of new jobs that they could use for patronage. The spoils system quickly became an important instrument for filling all military offices, from commissioned officers to paymasters and provost marshals. As one observer commented, the most important factor in determining who received a commission was which candidate "would produce the more agreeable consequences at the next election time." Another critic was former Democrat Edwin M. Stanton, who complained that "army appointments appear . . . to be bestowed on persons whose only claim is their Republicanism."[9]

Inevitably, the spoils system was extended to the appointment of generals. Lincoln and the state governors all used patronage to reward Republican officials, though this system often gave the president unnecessary headaches. After one governor demanded that one of his favorites be granted a major general's commission in the Regular army, Lincoln replied that "you must know that major-generalships in the regular army are not as plenty as blackberries." Lincoln from the beginning of the war realized the potential benefits that could be reaped by using generals' commissions to win the favor of important Republican officials. It was an excellent way to secure the loyalty of Republicans who had not received a patronage position before the conflict. By making them generals, Lincoln expected to garner the support of both them and their constituents.[10]

The most important Republican whom Lincoln had to commission was Nathaniel P. Banks. Born into a working-class family in Waltham, Massachusetts, in 1816, Banks as a youth worked in a textile mill, earning the nickname the Bobbin Boy, before entering politics in his early twenties. As a Democrat, he won election to both the Massachusetts legislature and the U.S. House of Representatives, but he left the party after the passage of the Kansas-Nebraska Act, which he opposed. He flirted with the Know-Nothing Party before helping to form the Massachusetts Republican Party, opening the way for him to become the first Republican Speaker of the House of Representatives and then the governor of the Bay State. By 1860, Banks was one of the most prominent Republicans in the country.[11]

Banks was a logical candidate to fill one of the cabinet positions in Lincoln's administration. Lincoln sought to achieve regional balance in his cabinet, and the Bobbin Boy seemed ideal for the New England slot. Many important Republicans, including David Davis, George Boutwell, and Isaac Arnold, personally recommended Banks, and Lincoln himself favored the appointment. The president-elect left the final decision to his vice president, Hannibal Hamlin, who disliked Banks and thus rejected him, choosing instead Gideon Welles. Denied a cabinet post and no longer holding political office, Banks took employment with the Illinois Central Railroad, a position that he held when the Civil War began.[12]

The former governor of Massachusetts was high on the list of prospective generals. Once again, Lincoln received several recommendations for Banks's appointment, and his cabinet viewed the appointment favorably. Secretary of the Treasury Salmon P. Chase believed that Banks "will make a first rate officer." This debate took place even though the Massachusetts politician, as Banks admitted, was "not acquainted with details of military matters." Despite this, Lincoln granted Banks a commission as a major general of volunteers, dated May 16, making the Massachusetts politician the second-highest-ranking Union volunteer general of the war.[13]

After Banks, the most distinguished Republican whom Lincoln had to satisfy was John C. Frémont. Frémont, born in 1813 in Savannah, Georgia, was a romantic figure to mid-nineteenth-century Americans due to his exploits in the West, where he commanded four expeditions that explored the region and helped to open it to settlement. During the Mexican War, Frémont led a revolt in California against the Mexicans that added further luster to his reputation. These exploits and his marriage to the daughter of Senator Thomas Benton allowed him to become one of California's first senators. Frémont's opposition to slavery led him to join the new Republican Party and become its first presidential candidate in 1856. Though he lost the election, Frémont remained influential in the party. After Lincoln's election in 1860, he became a candidate for a post in the cabinet. William Seward recommended Frémont for secretary of war, and Lincoln briefly considered appointing him either to a cabinet post or as the minister to France. In the end, Lincoln made neither appointment, and Frémont found himself with no position in the new administration.[14]

With the onset of the Civil War, Frémont immediately was placed on the list of potential generals. Unlike Banks, Frémont seemed to have extensive military experience that justified his appointment. The Pathfinder was a former Regular army officer and had briefly commanded troops in California during the Mexican War, but this experience was deceptive. His army career was spent leading exploration parties across the American West, not commanding troops, and his exploits in California did not entail much active campaigning.

Such facts were overlooked by the powerful interests pushing Lincoln to grant Frémont a commission and appoint him to a command in the West. These groups included Horace Greeley; Governor Richard Yates of Illinois; Gustave

Koerner, a powerful figure in the German American community, a group that greatly admired Frémont; and, most important, the Blair family. The Blairs had tremendous influence within the Republican Party and on Lincoln. The family included the old patriarch Francis P. Blair Sr., who had advised every American president since Andrew Jackson, and his two sons, Montgomery Blair, the postmaster general in Lincoln's cabinet, and Francis P. Blair Jr., a congressman from Missouri. They were also good friends of Frémont and his wife.[15]

Lincoln himself had no objection to commissioning Frémont because it would allow him to grant the Pathfinder a position and it solved the political problem of whom to assign to the Western command. The Blairs' first choice for this job, Nathaniel Lyon, was considered to be too radical by the conservative Unionists of Missouri, led by Lincoln's attorney general, Edward Bates. The conservatives would accept Frémont. The only opposition to the appointment came from Lincoln's cabinet, where Chase objected because he feared that Frémont would "be surrounded by unworthy men who would plunder the public." Lincoln ignored Chase's fears and commissioned Frémont as a major general in the Regular army, ranking third on the list of Regular generals, and placed him in command of the Western Department.[16]

Banks and Frémont were major figures in the Republican Party, but Lincoln also had to satisfy the desires of party members who were important at the state and regional levels but were not powerful nationally. One of the most prominent of these men was Robert C. Schenck of Ohio. Born in Franklin, Ohio, in 1809, he graduated from Miami College, practiced law for a time, and won election as a Whig to the Ohio legislature and then to the U.S. House of Representatives, an office he held throughout the 1840s. After his wife died in 1849, Schenck retired from politics. He spent much of the 1850s working as a lobbyist for various railroads and did not reenter politics until 1859 when he joined the Republican Party.[17]

Schenck actively campaigned for Lincoln during the 1860 presidential election, speaking throughout the Midwest and New York, and fully expected to be rewarded for his efforts. Lincoln was particularly eager "to provide for" Schenck and gave some thought to offering him a position in the cabinet. Schenck also had the backing of Senator Benjamin Wade of Ohio, but the cabinet position went to Ohio's other senator, Chase. Unable to grant Schenck a position in the cabinet, Lincoln made an effort to have Schenck fill Chase's vacant Senate seat, but the Chase faction in Ohio objected because they felt that Schenck was a latecomer to the Republican Party and not deserving of such a reward. Lincoln also thought of recommending Schenck for a diplomatic post. This, too, failed to materialize, and by the end of March Schenck was without a position within the administration.[18]

The Civil War gave Lincoln the opportunity to reward Schenck for his help during the 1860 election. Schenck, who had no previous military experience, let it be known that he would like an appointment as a brigadier general, writing to both Lincoln and Ohio governor Merriam Dennison requesting such a commission. In mid-May, Lincoln met with Schenck in the White House and offered him the appointment, commenting that he was sure Schenck would "succeed at it." According to Chase, Schenck was "the Presidents personal preference" to receive one of the first brigadier general appointments, an appointment that was formally tendered on June 5.[19]

Lincoln was especially anxious to reward politicians from his home state of Illinois, an attitude that explains why he commissioned Stephen A. Hurlbut. Born in Charleston, South Carolina, in 1815, Hurlbut practiced law there until a family scandal forced him to flee the state. He eventually settled in Illinois, resumed practicing law, was elected to the second Illinois State Constitutional Convention, and in 1848 actively campaigned for Whig candidates with Lincoln. After the passage of the Kansas-Nebraska Act, Hurlbut helped to form the Illinois Republican Party. He served in the Illinois House of Representatives and became an important figure in state politics, earning the loyalty of such Republicans as Yates, Trumbull, Representative Elihu Washburne, and Lincoln.[20]

Hurlbut sought some form of patronage following Lincoln's election, and specifically requested the office of U.S. district attorney for northern Illinois. He failed to obtain this position because Lincoln had another assignment for Hurlbut to undertake. Taking advantage of Hurlbut's South Carolina past, Lincoln asked him to return to Charleston and collect intelligence on the political strength of Unionist sentiment in the city. The outbreak of the war ended this assignment.[21]

Returning to Illinois following the attack on Fort Sumter, Hurlbut formed a company of volunteers and then sought election as a colonel in one of the newly formed regiments. He lost this election, but Lincoln took note of Hurlbut's recruiting actions, commenting that Hurlbut was "especially worthy of attention. In anything further done for Illinois, let him not be neglected." Hurlbut's powerful Illinois Republican friends worked hard to get him appointed as a brigadier general. Yates met with Lincoln to discuss Hurlbut, and Washburne telegraphed the president that Hurlbut's appointment "would gratify friends." Both Illinois senators, Trumbull and Orville H. Browning, sought to secure his commission. Also working in Hurlbut's favor was his service in the state militia. Though he commanded only a company and never engaged in any activities other than drill and parade, Hurlbut was viewed by many, including Lincoln, as "one of the best military men in Illinois." These influences plus Lincoln's desire to reward Hurlbut led to his appointment as a brigadier general on June 14.[22]

Lincoln did not base all of his selections solely on the need to reward the services of individual Republicans; he also wanted to ensure that the commissioning of generals recognized all factions within the party. This desire motivated the selection of James S. Wadsworth. Wadsworth was born in 1808 in Geneseo, New York, to a family of wealthy landowners, graduated from Harvard, and was admitted to the bar. Eschewing the law, he instead became active in state politics, supporting Democratic candidates until bolting from the party after the Wilmot Proviso made slavery a national issue. Wadsworth, a supporter of abolition, helped to form the Free-Soil Party in New York and then in 1856 led it into the Republican Party. The Republicans of New York were divided between his radical Free-Soil–Barnburner wing and the moderate William Seward–Thurlow Weed wing. In 1860, Wadsworth, an absentee delegate, wrote "pungent letters" to delegates at the Republican presidential nominating convention attacking Seward in a successful effort to deny Seward the party's nomination.[23]

After Lincoln's election, Wadsworth and his fellow Free-Soilers attempted to keep Seward out of the cabinet. Some of them pushed Wadsworth as the New York representative, but Lincoln never seriously considered this suggestion and selected Seward as his secretary of state. By the time of Lincoln's inauguration, Wadsworth's faction had received no patronage, leading Wadsworth and several other prominent Free-Soilers to meet with Lincoln to discuss their being left out of the distribution of offices and express their fears that Seward was deliberately excluding them. Lincoln promised to examine the matter.[24]

By the time the Civil War began, Lincoln had still not acted on his promise, but the opening of the war provided him with an entirely new means of looking out for Wadsworth. It was New York governor Edwin Morgan who first commissioned Wadsworth. Wadsworth was one of the two major generals of volunteers Morgan chose to command the state forces, though he accepted only on the condition that no graduate of West Point or officer of the Regular army was available. These appointments aroused controversy with Washington because only the president had the authority to designate generals, and as a result Secretary of War Simon Cameron insisted on accepting only one of the New York generals. Wadsworth ended the argument by resigning his commission. He instead took a position as a volunteer aide on the staff of Gen. Irvin McDowell, fought at Bull Run, and won praise for his performance during the battle. As a result of this action and in an effort to appease the Free-Soil wing of the Republican Party, Lincoln offered Wadsworth a general's commission in August, and the New Yorker accepted with the stipulation that he serve without pay.[25]

Lincoln's appointment of Francis P. Blair Jr. was based on his desire to use Blair's influence to aid the war effort. Blair, born in 1821 in Kentucky, was the youngest son of one of the most powerful political families in America. He graduated from Princeton College and migrated to St. Louis, Missouri, where he began practicing law and entered politics, becoming an active member of the Democratic Party. After the 1848 election, he committed himself to the Free-Soil doctrine. He was elected to the Missouri legislature and during the 1850s became one of the most powerful Republicans in the state, winning election to the U.S. House of Representatives, a position he still held when the Civil War began.[26]

The Blair family was rewarded by Lincoln for their efforts on his behalf during the 1860 presidential election, as Montgomery Blair received the cabinet position of postmaster general. Frank Blair Jr. did not seek any patronage for himself and remained in the U.S. Congress, but returned to Missouri during the spring of 1861 to accept a commission as a colonel in the state militia. He played a decisive role in helping to prevent Missouri's secession from the Union and then returned to the House of Representatives to serve as the chairman of the Committee on Military Affairs, assisting in the organization of Union forces during the early months of the war.[27]

Despite several efforts on his behalf to obtain him a general's commission, Blair preferred to remain in Congress until the summer of 1862. At that time, Secretary of War Edwin Stanton asked the congressman to return to Missouri and raise troops that he would himself lead into the field. There was little doubt that Lincoln was behind this suggestion, as the president desired to apply Blair's speaking abilities to the critical need of enlisting more soldiers. This time Blair accepted the appointment and received his commission as a brigadier general in August 1862.[28]

If rewarding Republicans was one reason for making political generals, an even more important rationale was to secure the loyalty to the Union's cause of members of the Democratic Party. In the 1860 election, the party won 44.7 percent of the Northern vote. The North was divided politically, a division that could prove fatal if the Democrats chose not to support Lincoln's war policies. The president realized that he could not ignore the Democratic Party after the attack on Fort Sumter. "The administration could not even start in this," Lincoln wrote in 1862, "without assistance outside of its party. It was mere nonsense to suppose a minority could put down a majority in rebellion." Many Republicans understood this fact. Republican congressman Albert Riddle of Ohio argued that some Democrats had to receive commissions because the war was a "purely national, not a Republican, contest; justice

15

to the Democrats, as well as sound policy, demanded that they should not be discriminated against."[29]

Fortunately for Lincoln and his party, large numbers of Democrats agreed with his course of action immediately following the opening of hostilities and rushed to the defense of the Union, but Lincoln wanted to ensure their continued support for the war effort after this initial burst of patriotism dissipated. To do so, he conferred generals' commissions on many prominent Democrats. It was an important method used by Lincoln to unite the North behind the war effort.

At the time the Civil War began, one of the most prominent Democrats in the North was John A. Dix of New York. Born in 1798 in New Hampshire, Dix entered the army during the War of 1812, though he did not see any combat, and remained in the service until 1828. He spent most of his military career studying law, an occupation he entered upon leaving the army. Over the next three decades, Dix accumulated a stellar résumé of public service. He served as New York's adjutant general, secretary of state, and postmaster; spent one term in that state's legislature; and also served a term in the U.S. Senate. Following the election of Lincoln, Dix, a Southern sympathizer but staunch Unionist, entered President James Buchanan's cabinet. He served as the secretary of the treasury in the waning months of that administration, and became a national hero for his order to Treasury Department officials in New Orleans: "If any one attempts to haul down the American flag, shoot him on the spot."[30]

Dix's service as the secretary of the treasury won him the praise of many prominent Republicans, including Governor Morgan, who praised Dix for his "valuable services rendered to both state and country." The governor was so impressed with Dix that following the attack on Fort Sumter he commissioned the Democrat as one of New York's two major generals, placing Dix in command of the state forces. These appointments aroused controversy between Washington and Albany. In order "to relieve the president from all embarrassment," Dix offered to decline the position, but Lincoln decided that the prominent Democrat could be of service. On June 14, he commissioned Dix as a U.S. major general of volunteers, ranking from May 16, and made Dix the highest-ranking volunteer officer of the war.[31]

Another prominent Democrat Lincoln appointed in the spring of 1861 was Benjamin F. Butler. Butler, born in 1818 in Deerfield, New Hampshire, earned his wealth by practicing law in Massachusetts and became active in politics at an early age. He won a reputation and a seat in the Massachusetts legislature as both a representative and then a senator for supporting radical causes that favored the working class. At the 1860 Democratic Party convention in Charleston, Butler demonstrated his unorthodox thinking by voting fifty-seven times for Jefferson Davis to be the party's presidential nominee because he believed that Davis was the only man who could reconcile the two sections.[32]

Though Butler sympathized with the South, he did not support secession and pledged his loyalty following the attack on Fort Sumter. Before the war, Butler had been a member of the Massachusetts militia, holding the rank of brigadier general. The militia did little except participate in holiday parades and in 1861 was woefully underequipped and poorly trained, but Butler's high position within it meant that he had an excellent chance of commanding its first troops that went to Washington. In order to secure the appointment, Butler brought pressure upon Governor John Andrew, asking Massachusetts senator Henry Wilson to telegraph the governor that Butler should be given the command. This pressure, and Andrew's desire to create a united front by appointing a prominent Democrat to command the state troops, led to Butler's appointment. Butler's aggressive actions in Annapolis and Baltimore in April, as well as his Democratic credentials, impressed Lincoln, who commissioned Butler into the national service, making him the third-highest-ranking volunteer general of the war.[33]

Securing the support of Illinois Democrats, especially those from the region of southern Illinois known as Egypt, was of particular concern to Lincoln, explaining why he commissioned John A. McClernand. McClernand was born in 1812 in Kentucky, and shortly thereafter his family migrated to southern Illinois. After serving in the militia during the Black Hawk War, he entered politics, winning three terms in the Illinois legislature and five terms in the U.S. House of Representatives. McClernand was a Jacksonian Democrat who opposed abolition, supported Stephen Douglas, and disagreed with Lincoln when they served together in the Illinois legislature. Nevertheless, even before the Confederacy fired on Fort Sumter, he pledged his loyalty to Lincoln and the Union.[34]

In the spring of 1861, McClernand worked with Governor Yates to secure southern Illinois and prepare the state for civil war. Egypt, which was important strategically because the Mississippi and Ohio rivers converged there, had strong Southern sympathies, and there was even talk that it might leave the Union. To help secure the region, McClernand and John Palmer were sent to Cairo to gain control of all commercial traffic and prevent stores from being shipped to the South. After successfully completing this task, McClernand urged its citizens to remain loyal. He also traveled through the rest of the state calling on people to rise above partisanship until the war was over, helped to raise several regiments, and journeyed to Washington to confer with Lincoln about various war-related issues.[35]

These activities made McClernand a leading candidate for a general's commission. He had the support of the Illinois congressional delegation and Lincoln, who viewed favorably McClernand's "great energy, and industry" as well as his influence in the crucial region of southern Illinois. On the advice of a friend, the president delayed the appointment, so that McClernand could return to the House of Representatives and use his influence and vote on key issues that could be helpful in organizing Union forces for the war effort. Finally, at the beginning of August, Lincoln conferred on McClernand the appointment of brigadier general, personally informing McClernand of the commission. He also reminded the new general why he had been appointed: "Keep Egypt right side up."[36]

Some Democrats were completely surprised when Lincoln selected them as generals. Such was the case with James W. Denver. Born in 1817 in Winchester, Virginia, Denver's family migrated to Ohio, where he studied law before moving to Missouri. During the Mexican War, he served as a captain in the Twelfth U.S. Volunteer Infantry Regiment, participating in Scott's campaign from Vera Cruz to Mexico City, though he saw no combat due to an attack of yellow fever. After the war, Denver moved to California, won election to the state senate, served as California's secretary of state, and then won a term in the U.S. House of Representatives. He also gained notoriety for killing a newspaper editor in a duel. Despite this action, he was appointed commissioner of Indian affairs and then governor of Kansas Territory, activities that made Denver one of the most prominent Democrats living west of Missouri.[37]

Denver was from the South, generally supported that region, and, like many Democrats before the attack on Fort Sumter, pledged that he "would not engage in fratricidal strife." Following the assault on Fort Sumter, Denver decided that war was necessary to preserve the Constitution, but he made no effort to join the army. In August, Lincoln commissioned Denver a brigadier general, an action that completely surprised the new officer. The "appointment," he wrote, "was given to me without my knowledge or solicitation." Lincoln sought to take advantage of Denver's popularity among Democrats in the West, hoping that he could raise and organize troops in California with the intention that they might be used in an invasion of Texas.[38]

The most notorious Democrat that Lincoln appointed was Daniel Sickles. Born in 1819 in New York City, he dropped out of college to become a lawyer, studying in the law offices of a powerful Tammany Hall politician. After entering politics, he served in the New York state legislature, as a delegate to the Democratic Party convention in 1848, as first secretary to James Buchanan when the latter was minister to the Court of St. James, and in the U.S. House of Representatives. While serving as a congressman, Sickles shot and killed

18

his wife's lover in broad daylight within sight of the White House, but he won acquittal in court and returned to Congress. He was a strong Southern supporter who in December 1860 defended peaceful secession and promised his Southern friends that the city of New York would never wage "war against any State of this Union."[39]

Early in 1861, after Southern states had seized federal property and fired on U.S. ships, Sickles changed his mind about secession and promised that New Yorkers would go "anywhere to protect the flag." Immediately following the surrender of Fort Sumter, Sickles pledged to the secretary of war that New York "will sustain the Government. . . . Democrats are no longer partisans. They are loyal to the Government and the flag." Shortly thereafter, Sickles, angling for a general's commission, asked for and received permission to raise a brigade. The prospect of Sickles becoming a general terrified many of his political opponents, including Thurlow Weed, who wrote one letter to Seward and two to Lincoln urging them not to appoint the Tammany Hall politician. Neither Seward nor Lincoln acted on Weed's advice; the need for Democratic support was too great to ignore even someone like Sickles.[40]

Sickles spent the spring and summer raising his brigade, but problems arose when the governor of New York refused to accept Sickles's brigade because it put New York over its troop quotas. Determined to receive a commission, Sickles descended upon Washington and met with Lincoln, arguing that the president should accept his brigade into federal service. Lincoln, anxious to maintain the political support of Democrats, agreed to Sickles's proposition, accepted his brigade, and commissioned Sickles as a brigadier general.[41]

Another Democrat Lincoln appointed was John A. Logan, but Lincoln's decision to grant Logan a general's commission was based on both political and military considerations. Logan was born in 1826 in Brownsville, Illinois, located in Egypt, and served as a second lieutenant in an Illinois volunteer infantry regiment during the Mexican War without seeing any combat. Following the war, Logan earned a law degree and became active in Democratic politics, winning election as his county's prosecuting attorney, then to the Illinois state legislature, and finally in 1858 to the U.S. House of Representatives. By 1861, Logan had become one of Egypt's most important politicians.[42]

Logan reluctantly came to support the war effort. Initially, he viewed the secession of the South with despair, blamed extremists in both the North and the South, and called for compromise throughout the winter and spring of 1861. Even after the attack on Fort Sumter, he expressed no enthusiasm for war and made no effort to enlist, leading some observers to label him a secessionist. It was not until June that Logan broke his silence and began openly supporting the Union, speaking in southern Illinois on several occasions. After returning to Congress in July, Logan witnessed the debacle at Bull Run and then told his wife that he intended "to join the army." In a meeting with Lincoln, Logan discussed raising and commanding a regiment, but the president was unenthusiastic. He preferred that Logan remain a civilian and use his oratorical skills to convince Democrats to support the conflict. Logan ignored the president and, after the congressional session adjourned, left for Illinois to join the army and recruit a regiment.[43]

After Logan returned home to recruit, Governor Yates gave him command of the Thirty-first Illinois Infantry Regiment, but there was no talk of granting him a general's commission at that point. Colonel Logan led his regiment into battle at Belmont, Fort Henry, and Fort Donelson, gaining the favorable notice of Gen. Ulysses S. Grant, who recommended that Logan be promoted. Grant was aware that Logan was a prominent Democratic congressman and explained that his proposal was based "solely on grounds that the service would be benefited" by Logan's promotion. Logan, Grant wrote, was "eminently qualified . . . his gallantry having stood the test" of battle. When Lincoln received this recommendation, he wasted no time in promoting Logan to general, though he was motivated as much by Logan's political qualifications as by his military ability.[44]

Lincoln had to secure the support of not only both Republicans and Democrats but also the many ethnic groups that lived in the North. In 1860, 13 percent of the persons living in the United States were foreign born, and more than 90 percent of them lived in the Northern states. By far the two largest immigrant groups were the Germans and the Irish. Before the war, these two communities had played influential roles in politics, as both the major parties sought to win their votes, a fact that Lincoln understood, having lived in a state with more than three hundred thousand immigrants. The president realized that the support of these groups would be crucial for successfully prosecuting the war.[45]

In the spring of 1861, the loyalty of both the Germans and the Irish was impossible to predict. The Irish had been staunchly Democratic as well as pro-Southern and antiblack before the war, and though they generally rallied to the Union cause immediately after Fort Sumter, maintaining this loyalty would be difficult in a protracted conflict. Like the Irish, the Germans in the early 1850s had tended to vote Democratic, but by 1860 many of them had begun to support the Republican Party. Nevertheless, as the war began, significant numbers of Germans remained loyal Democrats and uncertain about the war. To win the support of these ethnic groups, Lincoln gave some of their leaders generals' commissions, hoping that this would convince these groups to fight for the Union.[46]

Of all the Germans that Lincoln selected, by far the most popular among Germans was Franz Sigel. "I fights mit Sigel" became a legendary phrase used by German troops under his command that demonstrated their enthusiasm and devotion toward the general known as the "Yankee Dutchman." Born in 1824 in the village of Sinsheim in the Grand Duchy of Baden, Sigel received his education at the Karlsruhe military academy, graduated near the top of his class, and then served in the army of the grand duke of Baden for four years. In 1848–49, he fought with the revolutionary forces in Germany against Prussia, rising to the rank of general in the Rebel army and commanding more than five thousand soldiers in battle on several occasions. The revolutionary army did not stand a chance against the Prussians, and Sigel lost every engagement in which he fought. After fleeing to the United States, he settled in St. Louis, where he was a professor of mathematics and history at the German American Institute and became involved in politics, actively campaigning for the Republican Party. He joined a local military unit and in the spring of 1861 played an important role in pro-Union activities in Missouri. For his role in these events, Nathaniel Lyon, who commanded the Union's military forces in the state, promoted Sigel to colonel.[47]

At the beginning of the Civil War, Sigel could make a strong argument for being one of the most experienced military officers in the United States. Only Winfield Scott, during the War of 1812 and Mexican War, could claim to have commanded more troops in battle. Sigel's campaigns in Germany may have ended in defeat, but they gave him more practical experience in commanding an army than most Americans possessed. This fact and the uncritical praise heaped upon him by the German press, which acclaimed him a military genius, made Sigel a leading candidate to receive a general's commission. Several important Republicans, including Charles Sumner and Thurlow Weed, who called Sigel "the strongest German in the Union," also recommended him. All of these factors led Lincoln to commission Sigel as a brigadier general at the beginning of August.[48]

Another prominent German that Lincoln elevated to the rank of general was Carl Schurz. Schurz was born in 1829 near Cologne, Prussia, graduated from the University of Bonn, and then was swept up in the revolutionary fervor of 1849, joining the revolutionary army and serving as a lieutenant. He fought in several battles and was slightly wounded. Following the defeat of the revolution, Schurz immigrated to the United States and settled in Wisconsin where he became active in politics. He joined the Republican Party, ran unsuccessfully for several offices, formed a friendship with Lincoln, and in 1860 campaigned throughout the North for the Republican ticket. Schurz and many other Republicans, including Lincoln, believed that the Germans had played an important, perhaps decisive, role in securing Lincoln's victory, and Schurz was rewarded with an appointment as minister to Spain.[49]

Immediately following the attack on Fort Sumter, Schurz attempted to secure a military command. In late April, he journeyed to Washington, where he "talked war" with Lincoln. The German proposed that he travel to New York City and raise a brigade of cavalry from among the city's German population, and Lincoln eagerly assented, granting Schurz a three-month leave from his diplomatic post and promising him that if he succeeded, "you shall be Brigadier General." Schurz raised his brigade, but Lincoln was unable to fulfill his promise because Seward insisted that Schurz undertake his mission to Madrid.[50]

By the beginning of 1862, Schurz, tired of diplomacy, was back in the United States. Lincoln would have preferred that Schurz return to Spain, but the German insisted on going into the army, and, with the support of Chase, who believed Schurz's appointment would be "a decided benefit," the president relented. Lincoln may have preferred to see Schurz return to Spain, but he also did not want to antagonize the influential German. So, hoping to retain both Schurz's and German support for the war, Lincoln granted him his commission.[51]

Looking to another significant immigrant community, Lincoln named as one of the first Irish generals an old political opponent from Illinois, James Shields. Shields was born in 1806 in Altmore, Ireland, and immigrated to the United States in 1826, eventually settling in Illinois. He became a lawyer and was then elected to the Illinois General Assembly as a Democrat. The Irishman served only one term in the assembly but remained active in politics and held several other state offices. In 1842, he challenged Lincoln to a duel because of several letters Lincoln wrote that impugned Shields's reputation, but the duel was not fought because at the last moment Shields accepted Lincoln's apology. During the Mexican War, President Polk gave him a general's commission, and Shields fought with distinction in Mexico and received a near-fatal wound. He used this service to win election to one term in the U.S. Senate from Illinois and one term from Minnesota, where he moved in the mid-1850s. By 1861, Shields was living in San Francisco.[52]

When the Civil War began, Shields was a logical candidate to receive a volunteer general's commission, but the effort to appoint Shields met with several obstacles. The first attempt was initiated by several prominent men, such as Thomas F. Meagher, Senator Milton Latham of California, James Denver, and John McClernand, all of whom supported Shields's selection. Lincoln agreed and issued the appointment in August. Shields, now living in Mexico, did not receive notice of his commission until October. He pledged his "devotion and loyalty to the constitution and government," but declined the appointment because his old war injuries prevented him from performing the tasks it required.[53]

By December, Shields's health had improved and he accepted the appointment, but comments he had made the year before almost denied him a commission. Shields had stated publicly in the fall of 1860 that if a "sectional struggle" occurred, "my part will be taken with the South." These comments led several important individuals, such as Senator James McDougall of California, former congressman Edward Stanly, and the editor of the *Sacramento Union*, to oppose Shields's appointment because they believed he was disloyal. With these charges swirling about, in early January 1861 Shields arrived in Washington determined to prove his loyalty. He met with Lincoln and Seward and convinced them that he was willing to provide "his earnest, intelligent, and self-sacrificing cooperation with the Government" to save the Union. Lincoln and Seward came away from the meeting with "hearty and unreserved confidence" in the Irishman, and the president reappointed him.[54]

Thomas F. Meagher was one of the most prominent Irishmen Lincoln commissioned. Born in 1823 in Waterford, Ireland, Meagher participated in the 1848 Irish uprising against British rule. He was captured by the British, tried for high treason, and sentenced to death, but instead was exiled to Tasmania. After escaping and making his way to the United States, he studied law and became a popular speaker. Politically, Meagher was a Democrat who, even after the firing on Fort Sumter, still confessed that "my sympathies are entirely with the South!"[55]

Meagher shortly thereafter changed his mind and pledged his loyalty to the Union, chiefly because he believed that only by aiding the United States in this hour of crisis could the Irish hope to win the help of Americans in freeing Ireland. He raised a company of Zouaves and fought at Bull Run, where his gallantry brought him the favorable attention of the archbishop of New York, John Hughes, a friend of Seward. Hughes believed that Meagher would make a "worthy" general. Despite this recommendation, Lincoln did not consider commissioning Meagher until the Irishman offered to raise an Irish brigade. His recruiting efforts were astonishing. After speaking in New York City and Boston, he convinced three thousand Irishmen to enlist, demonstrating, as the *Irish American* newspaper wrote, that his name was "a word of talismanic power." Meagher intended for Shields to command the brigade, but when Shields declined Meagher became the logical choice. After several officers of the Irish Brigade, Senator Preston King, and Frank Blair Jr. urged the appointment, Lincoln commissioned Meagher in February 1862.[56]

These were among the most significant political generals Lincoln appointed in 1861–62. Although their backgrounds were often quite different, they all had in common the fact that they owed their generals' commissions primarily to political factors. Only a few had military experience that entailed commanding troops in combat or practical maneuvers, but the motivation for appointing even these veterans was political. Their military capabilities were just a bonus.

These men brought with them a vast amount of political experience, as only four of them (Meagher, Schurz, Sigel, and Wadsworth) had not held a state or federal office. Among the rest of the group, ten had served in their state legislature or senate, one had filled numerous state offices, and two had been governors (one of a territory). At the federal level, seven of them had won election to the House of Representatives, three had been appointed to the Senate, and one had served as the secretary of the treasury. This service gave these men unique experience in administering large organizations, dealing with a variety of issues, and working with a diverse group of individuals.

The amount and type of military experience within this sample varied greatly. Six had no previous military experience, whereas ten had served in some military capacity, whether it was in their state militia, wartime volunteer units, or the Regular army. Two of these political generals had held commissions in the peacetime U.S. Army. Of the other eight, three had been in state militias without gaining any extensive military knowledge and three had fought in the Mexican War, but only two saw combat. The final two had participated in the German revolution of 1849. Only two of these new generals had previous experience in high command; the rest had served only as junior officers or enlisted men.

The amount of actual command experience, commanding troops in the field or in battle, varied greatly among those ten political generals with previous military service. Only two of these politicians had experience as generals. During the German revolution, Sigel served either as a corps commander or, at the end of the conflict, as an army commander. In these capacities, he participated in combat operations, though all of them ended in failure, and gained more experience than any other political general possessed. Shields was a volunteer general during the Mexican War. Taking part in Scott's campaign as a brigade commander, Shields demonstrated battlefield courage and leadership ability. His experience was not as extensive as Sigel's, since he never directed an army, but it nevertheless provided him with command knowledge that few Civil War generals enjoyed in 1861.

The other eight political generals had significantly less practical experience. Both Dix and Frémont had served as captains in the Regular army, but Dix spent his career as an aide to Gen. Jacob Brown and Frémont commanded only exploring expeditions of the American West and participated only in the revolt in California. Neither of these men had much command experience. Those men who had served in the state militias had even less experience. McClernand had spent three unproductive months in the militia during the Black Hawk War, whereas Butler and Hurlbut both spent a decade in their respective state militias, but their experience was limited to drill and holiday parades. The Mexican War provided both Denver and Logan with the opportunity to command a volunteer company, but neither man saw combat. Finally, Schurz had fought as a lieutenant in the German revolution of 1849. This service was so brief that he had little time to acquire anything but the most rudimentary command experience.

Regardless of what previous military service they had, Lincoln hoped that these political generals would be able to accomplish several different tasks, from controlling units in the field to administering departments and convincing their constituents to support the war effort. Some generals would be expected to perform several of these duties, whereas others might be assigned to execute only one. Lincoln did not expect all of these politicians to become field commanders. Thus, their lack of military experience was not necessarily a liability. The president intended to employ them in ways that would make the best use of their talents and do the most to help win the war.

CHAPTER 3

The
Opening
Campaigns

I n 1861, some of Lincoln's political generals included in this study engaged in their first military operations. Their record was mixed, with some generals performing well while others struggled, but one theme emerged during these first battles that continued to be true throughout the rest of the war. Political generals serving under professional officers, men trained at the U.S. Military Academy, tended to function creditably, but those who received independent commands invariably failed.

Virtually no general in 1861 possessed the experience to command the large armies that dominated the Civil War. West Point–trained officers had received the training and knowledge and the basic practical experience of working with smaller bodies of soldiers from companies to regiments. Thus, they knew, even if only at a rudimentary level, the requirements for maintaining troops in the field, supplying armies, and fighting battles. Most political generals possessed none of these necessary qualifications, forcing them to learn on the job. When placed under West Point–trained officers, they could learn the basics of army command under the watchful eye of professionals who knew what mistakes to look for and how to correct them. This allowed the novice officers to learn more about their new and complex profession. No politician was qualified to hold an independent command, as they lacked both the training and the experience. When placed in such a position, the new commanders floundered, failing badly with harsh repercussions for their reputations, their troops, and the Union cause.

Political generals sought to receive a combat position, and most of them were so employed. Few politicians obtained independent commands at this early stage of the conflict. Only Frémont, assigned to command of the Western Department, and Butler, delegated to Fortress Monroe, attained independent assignments. The War Department detailed the majority of citizen generals to the command of a regiment, brigade, or division. Banks, in 1861, and Shields and Schurz, in 1862, received divisions, but most politicians first led a brigade. In 1861, brigade commanders included Hurlbut, McClernand, Schenck, Sickles, and Wadsworth and, in 1862, Meagher, Denver, and Blair. The first assignment for both Logan and Sigel was command of a regiment.

Finding a proper assignment for an appointee often proved to be a difficult task. For instance, Denver did not receive a permanent command for the first ten months of his Civil War service. Lincoln appointed Denver in August 1861 with the intention of assigning him to California, where he would raise troops and then invade Texas. In September, Denver journeyed to Washington, D.C., to consult with General Scott, but while in the capital his orders to California were canceled because political enemies from that state objected to Denver's assignment to the West Coast. Two months later, Denver was ordered to Kansas, a post he seemed qualified for since in the late 1850s he had served as governor of the territory. Once again, old political foes, namely, James Lane and other Kansas Republicans, forced his recall, and in January 1862 Denver found himself reassigned to West Virginia.[1]

His stay in West Virginia was brief. Gen. William Rosecrans, in command of the department, could find no suitable duty for Denver, and in March the politician reported to Gen. Henry Halleck, commanding the Western Department. Halleck made the mistake of placing Denver in charge of Union activities in the Indian Territory, arousing the opposition of the same political foes that had forced Denver out of Kansas only three months before. Finally, in May, he took command of a brigade in the division of Gen. William T. Sherman, then participating in the campaign to take Corinth, Mississippi. Denver never became angry over his treatment, viewing it instead with a touch of humor. Nevertheless, his case demonstrated the difficulty Lincoln often faced when trying to find assignments for his political generals.[2]

Dix never received a combat assignment. The president refused to assign him to a frontline unit because the president preferred to use Dix in administrative positions. At the beginning of the war, Dix almost received command of the Union field army assembling outside of Washington. Scott intended to place Dix in charge of the Department of Alexandria and Arlington, then held by Gen. Irvin McDowell, a duty that would have given Dix command of McDowell's army. Shortly after his arrival in the capital, Dix lost this assignment because several cabinet members preferred that McDowell retain it.[3]

This was the closest that Dix came to receiving a combat command. Shortly after the first battle at Bull Run, he was selected to head the Department of Pennsylvania, where he remained until the spring of 1862, when Lincoln transferred him to Fortress Monroe. Both of these positions were essentially administrative, involving only limited combat duties, and Dix never took the field at the head of an army. He disliked not having an independent combat command, especially when men he outranked received these assignments. His complaints to Lincoln fell on deaf ears. The president believed Dix to be "a wise man," but thought him too old for active service. More important, he preferred to take advantage of Dix's thirty years of administrative experience gained while in government service by assigning the general to posts that would best utilize these abilities. In doing so, Lincoln made the greatest use of Dix's talent in ways that advanced the Union cause.[4]

The sagas of Denver and Dix were the exception, because most of Lincoln's political generals received military commands that allowed them to participate in operations against the Confederacy. Adjusting to the requirements necessary for combat absorbed the energies of most generals during their first months of service. They had to learn the basics of military life, such as how to move large bodies of troops, build camps, and enforce discipline, as well as gain a working knowledge of the rules and regulations that governed how their units operated. This study was a difficult task. One officer in Banks's division, after watching Banks struggle, commented that the general was "oppressed somewhat with a position novel and untried, and full of responsibilities of a character so different from those he has had heretofore that he feels ill at ease."[5]

Political generals struggled with mastering the essential procedures for army administration. For instance, the granting of furloughs caused aggravation for several generals. Banks was rebuked for liberally allowing furloughs "based on surgeons certificates of disease." McClernand upbraided Logan for granting too many furloughs and lectured the colonel on the proper way to issue such documents. Ironically, just a few months later McClernand was castigated for improperly granting furloughs.[6]

Most political generals had difficulty exercising command in the field. They usually failed to accurately determine the amount of supplies their men needed. On one training march, Sickles, commanding a brigade in northern

Virginia, was reprimand by his division commander for taking along too many wagons. In January 1862, McClernand, while leading an operation in Kentucky, failed to provide adequate supplies for his men, forcing him to write to his superior, Grant, requesting such articles as axes, shovels, hatchets, and even bread, because "many officers are absolutely destitute of provisions." The failure to provide these articles irritated the West Point graduate. He reminded McClernand that "it is the duty of the commanding General to see that proper supplies are furnished for the soldiers." In this one instance, Grant agreed to provide the requested items, but warned McClernand that "this permission is not to be regarded as a precedent for future action."[7]

Problems such as these were not unusual. New generals had no experience with such matters and had to learn how to operate their units before they could become efficient commanders. To gain this knowledge many generals read military texts. For example, Schurz read the works of Antoine-Henri Jomini and Carl von Clausewitz; Banks studied the campaigns of Napoléon; both Logan and McClernand read William J. Hardee's *Rifle and Light Infantry Tactics;* and Sickles spent hours studying the signals that governed troop movements on the battlefield. Other political generals had read military texts before the war. Butler had studied the campaigns of Caesar and Napoléon, Sigel had read extensively about Napoléon and other military commanders, and Meagher was familiar with the exploits of Irish soldiers at battles such as Fontenoy.[8]

A few tried to overcome their inexperience by asking for professional assistance. At least two officers, Wadsworth and McClernand, asked that graduates of the U.S. Military Academy be assigned to their staffs. Such requests were not always granted. Wadsworth received an officer who resigned from West Point one year before graduating, and the War Department refused McClernand's attempt to have Capt. James Wilson assigned to his staff. By asking for such help, these officers recognized that to succeed they needed the aid of professionals, men who had received military training and gained some practical experience in the Regular army.[9]

One military matter that caused special difficulty for political generals early in the war was discipline. This issue plagued all new officers, regardless of their prewar occupation. Their troops were civilians and continued to think and act as such after enlisting, demonstrating little respect for military discipline and often violating the rules and regulations established by officers. Furthermore, many officers had received their positions by election, leading many of them to feel beholden to their soldiers and reluctant to enforce discipline. This was a problem for politicians, who were used to catering to their constituents to win elections. Currying favor with soldiers was not conducive to good discipline. All officers, even professionals, had difficulty keeping discipline within the ranks of the new volunteer army, but political generals were particularly poor at this necessary duty.[10]

Most former politicians in 1861 had problems enforcing discipline. Logan, who despite having commanded a company during the Mexican War, struggled to control his volunteers and was once rebuked for the "careless use of fire arms by soldiers in your command." His men, many of whom knew him before the war, also continued to address him as "John" rather than "Colonel Logan," as required by regulations. Wadsworth, commanding a brigade near Arlington, Virginia, faced similar difficulties, as he was unable to "put a stop" to "contests & firing between the pickets" in his brigade and nearby Confederates. In Virginia during the fall of 1861, Sickles completely failed to control one of his regimental commanders, a colonel who so desired action that he raided a Confederate outpost without authorization. Sickles expressed his pleasure with the colonel's actions, but Gen. George McClellan was infuriated and ordered the immediate arrest of the offending officer.[11]

McClernand struggled for three months with the major disciplinary issue of his command: excessive drinking by the officers and men in his brigade at their camp outside of Cairo, Illinois. The soldiers spent most of their off-duty hours in the city's saloons where, one citizen complained, "rows, fights & murders are almost daily occurrences." This carousing also spilled into McClernand's camp, where all semblance of discipline and order often vanished. The trouble was so acute that local citizens sent complaints to Frémont, then in command of the Western Department. Frémont referred the matter to Grant, who ordered the Illinois politician to deal with it.[12]

McClernand's efforts to stop this behavior floundered because he refused to establish a method to enforce discipline. He first ordered all drinking activity to stop and placed responsibility for enforcing these instructions with the regimental commanders. The colonels, many of whom were themselves political appointees, proved unable to enforce these orders, and within a month fresh complaints were being made about the "liquor & beer-houses." McClernand next issued instructions that closed all of the drinking houses in Cairo. The liquor, however, continued to flow. Three weeks later McClernand "absolutely" prohibited the sale of alcohol, which also had no effect on the situation. None of these orders provided a way to enforce them, such as arrests and punishments, making them ineffective. Finally, in December, McClernand at last directed that "sufficient force" be used to "break up effectually all" drinking establishments. With this order, McClernand actually began enforcing discipline within his command, and no more complaints were made about drinking.[13]

Another of Lincoln's political generals, Hurlbut, nearly ruined his entire career because of his inability to control his drinking. During a trip to Chicago in July, Hurlbut spent most of his time consuming alcohol. One witness complained to Senator Trumbull that "he has been so far intoxicated as to . . . make himself generally ridiculous." Such conduct led powerful Illinois Republicans, like Joseph Medill, the editor of the *Chicago Tribune*, to recommend that the Senate not confirm Hurlbut's appointment as a brigadier general. Hurlbut temporarily saved himself by promising Senator Browning that he would stop drinking. The general was unable to keep his pledge. Now assigned to Missouri, in early September 1861 Hurlbut proceeded to get drunk, forcing his immediate superior, Gen. John Pope, to arrest the Illinois general and send him to St. Louis in a cattle car. Frémont then ordered him to return home.[14]

This final indignity led Senator Browning to write to Lincoln that "Genl Hurlbut is a failure. . . . Let him go." Although Lincoln suggested that Browning convince Hurlbut to resign, the senator refused, as he did not think Lincoln was "in earnest." The matter was allowed to drop. After letting Hurlbut stew in Illinois for a few months, Lincoln recalled the general to active service in December, hoping that he had reformed himself. Hurlbut's intemperance nearly cost him his commission, and it was only Lincoln's forgiving nature that saved the general from a humiliating end to his army career.[15]

These escapades were only a prelude to the real business for which political generals were being trained. Military operations against the Confederacy began almost immediately after the war commenced, and political generals were involved in many of these early engagements. The first two such operations in which politicians played prominent roles were both Union defeats and led many people to question the policy of giving politicians major commands.

The first engagement occurred at Big Bethel, Virginia, on June 10 when Union troops in Butler's department, though not under his immediate command, suffered a humiliating repulse. Butler had earned fame in Maryland for his actions that secured Union control of Baltimore, a city with strong secessionist sentiment, and opened communications between Washington and the rest of the North. These acts angered Scott, who in mid-May sent Butler to take command of Union forces at Fortress Monroe, a strategic position that controlled the mouth of the James River. Scott ordered Butler to undertake actions only "within a half-day's march of you." Under these restraints, designed to keep the political general from committing any blunders, Butler seized Newport News, giving him control of the Lower James River. This operation convinced Scott that Butler was reliable, and he removed the restriction on the general's actions.[16]

Butler determined to attack two Confederate positions midway between Fortress Monroe and Yorktown. The first was a Rebel outpost at Little Bethel, a church the Southerners used as a base to raid Union positions, and then strike at Big Bethel, a larger church where the Confederate forces were constructing breastworks. The general's plan, which was based on poor intelligence, was to march several regiments in different columns under cover of darkness to Little Bethel, quickly take this position, and, if successful, capture Big Bethel and then destroy both the Bethels. Gen. Ebenezer W. Pierce was given command of fifteen hundred troops to carry out the operation.[17]

This plan was too complex for the green officers and soldiers to carry out effectively at this stage in the war, and the result was a Union defeat. Despite precautions taken to allow the troops to identify one another in the dark, the columns mistakenly fired on each other, suffering twenty-one casualties and alerting the Confederates to their presence. Pierce managed to capture Little Bethel, but only after the Rebels abandoned it and concentrated four thousand troops at Big Bethel. Despite being outnumbered, Pierce attacked and was defeated, suffering eighteen killed and fifty-three wounded. Although Butler was not in immediate command during the battle, his flawed plan, especially his inability to provide adequate intelligence, underlay many of Pierce's mistakes.[18]

The defeat caused outrage throughout the North. Edward Baker, inspecting Fortress Monroe for Lincoln, reported that it was "discreditable" and "shameful." The *New York Times*, whose editors on May 31 had called Butler a "great soldier," now blasted the Massachusetts politician for lacking "the simplest exhibition of prevision, practical judgement, and soldierly conduct." The *Times* concluded that he must be "dismissed" or "at once placed where such qualities shall be less mischievous." For the moment, Butler was retained at Fortress Monroe, but in August Gen. John Wool, a Regular army officer, was placed in command. Butler remained as his subordinate.[19]

Only a week after the skirmish at Big Bethel, a second of Lincoln's political generals met with a humiliating defeat. On June 17, a small force commanded by Schenck was ambushed at Vienna, Virginia, and forced to retreat. Schenck was in command of a brigade in McDowell's army. McDowell ordered the political general to send a regiment by train toward Vienna, a small village north of Fairfax Court House, and scout the region, guard railroad bridges, and inspect track. The order admonished Schenck to proceed "with caution."[20]

Schenck advanced by train as instructed. As the train moved down the rail line, he left detachments behind to guard bridges and conduct patrols. At one stop, a local citizen informed Schenck that there were Confederate troops at Vienna. Schenck disregarded this information and failed to place scouts in advance of his main force. Thus, as the train approached Vienna it was surprised by several Confederate batteries that opened fire on the exposed cars. The train came to a sudden stop, the engineer fled, and Schenck and his men retreated into the woods and then marched back to the Union lines. The affair at Vienna cost the Union twelve casualties and reflected badly on Schenck, who committed amateur mistakes such as ignoring intelligence and failing to properly reconnoiter the area.[21]

The Northern press castigated Schenck, but Lincoln took a more charitable view of the affair. The editors of the *New York Times* commented that "the simplest knowledge of military matters must condemn so heedless a movement as to the last degree reckless and unscientific." They called Schenck an "incompetent" commander who completely lacked any qualification that "entitles him to lead troops to battle." Lincoln, on the other hand, studied the matter and concluded that Schenck should not be removed because of his actions, writing that "not one officer, or private, who was present at the disaster, has ever cast a word of blame upon" Schenck, and "they are all anxious to have another trial under" him.[22]

The results of Big Bethel and Vienna led many newspaper editors to question the policy of bestowing on politicians military assignments and to call for the use of professionally trained soldiers. The editors of the *New York Times*, who originally praised the use of political generals, now believed that it would be "too costly" to educate such men in military matters. The *New York Evening Post's* editors commented that defeat "shows the great importance of having as leaders . . . men who are by education and experience familiar with warlike operations." A U.S. Military Academy graduate, the editors concluded, "is clearly more trustworthy than a civilian." The editors of the *Boston Daily Advertiser* argued that these battles demonstrated that "in military life . . . education, regular training, and experience must surely count for something." Only West Point–trained officers, they determined, possessed these attributes.[23]

Whether Lincoln read these comments is not known, but he certainly ignored the advice. He continued to appoint political generals and place these individuals in important commands throughout the rest of the war. Neither the battle of Big Bethel or Vienna nor the criticisms of Northern newspaper editors had any effect on his policy. The political benefits gained by retaining these generals in the army were too valuable to abandon the concept after only two minor defeats. In fact, both Schenck and Butler would again lead soldiers in combat before the summer was over.

Having been cleared by Lincoln, Schenck participated in the first battle of Bull Run on July 21. His brigade was assigned to the division of Gen. Daniel Tyler, a West Point graduate who was directed to demonstrate against the Stone Bridge on Bull Run. By doing so, it would pin down Confederate troops in that area and allow McDowell's main force to strike the Rebel flank. The nature of this assignment prevented Schenck's brigade from participating in the main battle. Aside from occasionally exchanging rifle and artillery fire with Confederate troops, Schenck's men did relatively little once they took position next to the bridge. Significantly, when Tyler sent troops across the bridge to attack the Southerners, he chose the two brigades commanded by Gen. William T. Sherman and Col. Daniel Keyes, both West Point graduates, and left Schenck, the politician, to guard the bridge. Tyler had little faith in Schenck's ability.[24]

The first battle of Bull Run did not provide much evidence to judge Schenck's competence. Schenck handled his troops well, but then he was not called upon to do much with them. In his report, McDowell praised Schenck for his "most effective service" and "gallant manner," but admitted that the politician did not participate in the main action. Thus, after one small skirmish and limited action in the first major battle of the war, Schenck's capacity to command troops in combat was still unknown. In August he was transferred to the Department of the Ohio, where he received command of a brigade.[25]

Just as Schenck was able to redeem himself at First Bull Run, so was Butler able to revive his military fortunes by participating in the capture of Hatteras Inlet on August 27. This combined land and naval operation was designed to capture the entrance to Pamlico Sound, North Carolina, and tighten the Union blockade. Butler commanded 850 soldiers, but they played no role in the battle because, after a brief artillery duel, the superior Union navy forced the small Confederate fort into submission. The army then occupied the fort. Though Butler's military contributions were negligible to achieving victory, his minor role in the success restored his superiors' confidence in his abilities. He was shortly thereafter transferred to New England to recruit new regiments to be used in another amphibious operation against an as yet undetermined target.[26]

As major military campaigning in the East came to an end for the year, the war in the West witnessed its first operations. Lincoln's top political general in this region, Frémont, commanded the Western Department. This department encompassed Illinois and all of the states and territories west of the Mississippi River to the Rocky Mountains. It also included Kentucky, but, because that state had declared itself neutral in the conflict, the president refused to allow Union troops to operate there, fearing that the state might secede if Federal units violated its supposed neutrality. Frémont's primary mission was to raise and equip an army to descend the Mississippi River, thus cutting the Confederacy in two. The general recognized that "who held the Mississippi would hold the country by the heart" and "control the result of the war."[27]

Before Frémont accomplished this task, he first needed to secure control of the state of Missouri, the key to gaining possession of the Mississippi River. The state was bitterly divided between unionists and secessionists. The Union forces had succeeded in preventing Missouri's formal secession and driving the organized Confederate military into the southern parts of the state, but disorder reigned over much of the region and St. Louis was considered to be "insurrectionary." Adding to the confusion were reports of large Rebel units operating throughout the state. Furthermore, Frémont's command consisted of hastily assembling raw recruits who lacked arms, equipment, and the money to pay for these items. The general faced a herculean task. He had to organize and equip a new army, prevent Confederate incursions into the state, build defenses for key positions on the Mississippi, and begin planning for and then undertake offensive operations. This was perhaps the most daunting task faced by any Union general in 1861.[28]

On July 3, 1861, Frémont was formally appointed to his post, but instead of immediately leaving for St. Louis and assuming command of his new department, he went to New York City. The Pathfinder remained there for three weeks. During this time, Frémont was out of touch with his command and unable to personally review the situation and direct operations, leaving his subordinates to deal with the chaos in Missouri. The purpose of this delay was to obtain arms and equipment, matériel Frémont felt he must acquire in person because Lincoln's "expressed desire to me was, to organize at once the Illinois force." These must have seemed like orders to the Pathfinder, and he dutifully sought to carry them out. Nevertheless, the failure of Frémont to immediately leave for the West was a mistake that would have dangerous repercussions. Frémont was needed in the West as soon as possible in order to evaluate and gain control of the situation. The purchase of supplies in New York was best left to subordinates. When Frémont finally arrived in St. Louis on July 25, he found a much more disorganized situation than he had previously imagined.[29]

During the month of July, the fighting in Missouri had shifted into the southwestern part of the state as the Union forces maneuvered the Confederates out of central Missouri. One of the engagements that occurred during this movement was on July 5 at Carthage and involved Col. Franz Sigel. Sigel, marching west from Springfield with 950 men, determined to attack a superior Confederate force, but he did not know the terrain or adequately scout the area to discover the intentions of the Rebels. The Southerners, with 6,000 men, already knew of Sigel's presence and were awaiting his attack when his troops finally arrived at Carthage. Despite the odds, the German launched an assault. The Union troops were overwhelmed, as Rebel cavalry swept around their flanks and into the Federal rear. Sigel remained calm and managed to extricate his unit and retreat in good order back to Springfield. The skirmish demonstrated that Sigel was aggressive and willing to take chances but that he was prone to mistakes such as failing to reconnoiter to obtain information about the terrain and the enemy.[30]

Following Sigel's defeat, Gen. Nathaniel Lyon, the Union commander in southwestern Missouri, rushed to Springfield in order to prevent the Yankee Dutchman's force from being destroyed. Lyon found himself in a precarious position. At Springfield, he was at the end of a long and tenuous supply line that stretched from St. Louis to Rolla by rail and then from Rolla to Springfield by wagon. His army consisted of about 7,000 men, half whom were only three-month volunteers whose term of service was about to expire. The men had not been paid, their clothing was dilapidated, and their morale was low. Lyon feared that many would not reenlist, and he begged for reinforcements. To the south, a large Confederate army was gathering, which he erroneously estimated at 30,000 men, that threatened to imperil not only his own army but also the entire Federal position in southwestern Missouri.[31]

This was Lyon's situation when Frémont arrived in St. Louis on July 25. Lyon on four separate occasions sent emissaries to explain his predicament and ask for reinforcements, but Frémont also confronted menacing military developments to the southeast. Reports arrived that a large Confederate army of approximately 11,000 men had occupied New Madrid, a strategic position on the Mississippi River, and was threatening other key points along the river, including Bird's Point and Cape Girardeau in Missouri and Cairo in Illinois. All of these locations needed reinforcements as well as other places within Missouri's interior. Frémont did not have enough troops to adequately reinforce every one of these positions and provide Lyon with what he was demanding.[32]

Frémont decided that protecting the Mississippi, upon which, as he wrote, "depended the descent and control of the Mississippi Valley," was his primary duty. He personally led 3,800 men to Cairo and ordered further reinforcements to Cape Girardeau and Bird's Point as well as to Ironton and Rolla, key towns in the interior that lay on the railroad. He also instructed that fortifications be constructed at these locations and St. Louis. These were all sound strategic decisions that ultimately benefited the Union war effort.[33]

Dealing with Lyon proved much more difficult, made worse by Frémont's late arrival in Missouri. Lyon, a headstrong and independent Regular army officer, would have given Frémont trouble no matter what the circumstances, but during the three-week delay while the Pathfinder was in New York, Lyon had advanced beyond Frémont's ability to control him. Springfield placed

Lyon more than two hundred miles from St. Louis, only half of which could be traversed by train. Communications between the two men took time, and Lyon was not always disposed to obey his orders when he finally received them.

The Pathfinder issued sensible directives to Lyon. Frémont instructed Lyon that if he *"was not strong enough to maintain his position as far in advance as Springfield, he should fall back toward Rolla until reinforcements should meet him."* These orders did leave some room for discretion, as Frémont directed Lyon to retreat only if facing a superior enemy, but since Lyon reported that he faced that situation, Frémont clearly intended that Lyon should withdraw to Rolla. Again, the Pathfinder proposed a sound strategic move, as it would shorten Lyon's supply line, make it easier to reinforce him, and buy Frémont more time to organize his army.[34]

Lyon, however, did not receive these orders until three days after Frémont wrote them, and during that time the strategic situation changed. A Confederate army of about 10,000 troops advanced to within ten miles of Springfield. Lyon decided to disobey Frémont's order to retreat and instead attack the Confederate army because he did not want to abandon southwestern Missouri to the Rebels. He then adopted a daring plan proposed by Sigel. The Union army would be divided into two parts. Lyon with the main force would strike the Rebel center, while Sigel took 1,100 men and attacked the Confederate rear.[35]

Nearly all of Lyon's officers opposed this plan. The idea of dividing a smaller force in the face of a superior enemy was dangerous, and all military textbooks advised against it. The superior enemy army would be able to take advantage of interior lines, allowing it to shift its forces to meet first one threat and then another. The large number of inexperienced troops in the Union army increased the risk. Lyon did have a small contingent of Regular army units in his force, but the majority of his men were volunteers who had been in the service for only a few months. Their lack of training, discipline, and experience made it difficult to control them in the best of conditions. Despite all of these drawbacks, Lyon decided to go ahead.

Lyon accepted Sigel's advice because, as John Schofield, Lyon's aide, later wrote, Lyon had "great confidence in Sigel's superior military ability and experience." At this point in the war, Sigel's education at a top German military school and the fame he had won during the revolution in 1848 and 1849 were imposing credentials and suggested that Sigel was a capable military officer. Lyon had no reason to question these credentials. Furthermore, Sigel's defeat at Carthage could be ascribed to superior enemy numbers. Thus, the German's plan and the confidence with which he proposed it impressed Lyon, who then accepted it despite the opposition of the rest of his officers.[36]

Late on the evening of August 9, Sigel and his little force of 1,100 men left Springfield and by daybreak, August 10, had marched to within a mile of the Confederate camp, approaching it from the southeast. Miraculously, they reached this point without being discovered by the enemy. Sigel took position on a hill overlooking the valley, where the Rebel camp lay, and then waited for Lyon's attack to begin. At about five thirty in the morning, musketry fire could be heard to the north, and Sigel ordered his artillery to commence firing, which had "a stirring effect on the enemy." As the Confederate camp descended into chaos, Sigel led his infantry off the hill, crossed Wilson's Creek, and attacked the encampment, compelling the remaining Rebels to retreat into the woods. He now had his force across "the principal line of retreat of the enemy."[37]

Shortly after taking the camp, the firing to the north died off, and Sigel paused to rest for a half hour. He made a tactical mistake at this point by not placing enough troops to guard his right flank on the Wire Road, running through the middle of the valley and the most likely avenue of a Confederate counterattack. Sigel did not worry about this because the cessation of gunfire to the north led him to believe that Lyon's assault had been successful and that Lyon now pursued the retreating Rebels. Sigel's greatest concern was that his troops might fire on fellow Union soldiers, some of whom wore gray uniforms.[38]

At this moment, sentries reported Federal units coming down the Wire Road, and Sigel ordered his men not to fire on the advancing soldiers. These troops were not Lyon's. They were Confederates launching a counterattack, an error that Sigel did not realize until it was too late. The Rebels struck Sigel's exposed right flank and dispersed the artillery units positioned there. The flight of this artillery caused panic in the ranks of the infantry, and the soldiers broke and ran, "followed and attacked incessantly by" Confederate cavalry. The rout was complete. Sigel tried to rally his stampeded troops, but his efforts were in vain and he was swept up in the widespread panic. Pursued by Rebel cavalry, the Union troops fled across the valley. Sigel eluded capture by wrapping a blue blanket over his uniform and putting on a yellow slouch hat, a disguise similar to the uniforms worn by a Texas unit at the battle. Although recognized and briefly chased, he managed to reach Springfield safely.[39]

As Sigel fled the battlefield, the Confederates defeated the rest of Lyon's army and forced it to retreat. Lyon had been killed, placing Sigel in command of what was left of the army when it trickled into Springfield, a situation not favored by many of the American-born soldiers, who did not like Sigel and "were all afraid of his generalship." Sigel and the other officers agreed to retreat to Rolla, a retreat that led to a mutiny. The German placed his own troops at the head of the column and left the Regulars in the rear guard, which, as

Schofield reported, "would be kept on the road until late in the night, and then, unable to find their wagons, be compelled to lie down without food." This treatment led several Regular army officers to insist that Sigel relinquish command to the next ranking officer. At first, Sigel refused, but he eventually yielded on the grounds that he had no commission from a recognized authority (Sigel's commission was given to him by Lyon).[40]

Sigel performed wretchedly at Wilson's Creek. He began well enough, successfully maneuvering his troops to within a mile of the Confederate camp and then taking the campsite, but after that things began to fall apart. He failed to secure his flanks, neither placing enough troops to guard them nor sending out scouts to ascertain the location and possible intentions of the Confederates. His overconfidence led him to assume that Lyon's assault had also been successful, an assumption not based on any facts. The final rout resulted from both these failures and the overly ambitious battle plan, a strategy that placed Sigel and Lyon in positions from which they could neither support nor communicate with one another. Thus, neither officer knew the other's situation.

Despite his poor record at Wilson's Creek, the defeat enhanced Sigel's reputation, especially among Germans, although not everyone approved of this praise. The *Janesville Daily Gazette*, a Wisconsin newspaper, believed that Sigel was the only general qualified to fill Lyon's place "and to whom we now all turn with hope and confidence as a leader able [to] sustain the Union cause in Southwest Missouri." On the other hand, several American officers who fought at Wilson's Creek criticized Sigel. The most perceptive of these critics was Schofield. He wrote that Sigel was well educated in military affairs and "familiar with the duties of the staff, but in tactics, great and small logistics, and discipline he is greatly deficient. These defects are so apparent as to make it absolutely impossible for him to gain the confidence of American officers and men, and entirely unfit him for a high command in the Army." These criticisms went unheeded by the Lincoln administration, and Sigel remained in the service.[41]

The battle of Wilson's Creek drove the Union army out of southwestern Missouri, gave the Confederates control of the region, and allowed them to threaten the rest of the state. Frémont, laboring at his headquarters in St. Louis, reacted to the defeat by increasing his requests for reinforcements, arms, and money. Writing directly to Lincoln and Montgomery Blair, he complained that his department was "very weak in men and arms" and was in immediate need of "aid in fixed artillery and men with arms in their hands." These appeals resulted in the arrival of more troops, but many of these soldiers lacked tents and other camp equipment. Frémont spent much of the month of August working hard to obtain needed arms and equipment, becoming bogged down in these details and doing little to deal with the military situation in western Missouri.[42]

By this time, Frémont had developed a basic strategy. He intended to strengthen and fortify all of the key points in Missouri and along the Mississippi River so that they could be held by small forces, "leaving me free to concentrate our whole force for operations against the enemy." He hoped to use a field army to move down the Mississippi and, to accompany this expedition, ordered the construction of thirty-eight mortar boats and eight steam tugs.[43]

In early September, events along the Mississippi forced Frémont to concentrate his attention on the river. On September 1, Confederate forces occupied Columbus, Kentucky, violating that state's supposed neutrality. Frémont was not caught by surprise. He had already prepared for a possible movement into Kentucky, having at the end of August placed Grant in command in southeastern Missouri with instructions to organize such an expedition. Four days after the Southerners acted, the Pathfinder ordered Grant to take Paducah, Kentucky, a city that commanded the junction of the Ohio and Tennessee rivers, "if you feel strong enough." Grant occupied the city that day.[44]

Frémont hoped to exploit this operation by continuing to move down the river. His plan was to combine his units already on the river and take Columbus. At the same time, another force would use the railroad to advance into the interior of Tennessee and occupy Nashville. These two separate wings would then combine for an attack on Memphis. The plan was sound and somewhat similar to the strategy that ultimately led to the capture of these strategic points, but Frémont would not have the chance to undertake it.[45]

The deteriorating military situation in western Missouri, which Frémont had done little to rectify, finally exploded and eclipsed the events occurring on the Mississippi. The defeat at Wilson's Creek had left southwestern Missouri in the hands of the Confederates, but they were initially too weak to exploit their victory. In mid-September, a Southern army of eighteen thousand men advanced northward toward Lexington, defended by three thousand Federal troops. Frémont ordered Col. Jefferson C. Davis and Gen. Samuel Sturgis to send reinforcements to the threatened city. Gen. John Pope also promised to dispatch reinforcements. Despite Frémont's efforts, no reinforcements ever reached Lexington, and the city fell after a two-day siege. His field commanders refused to march to its relief.[46]

Frémont was heavily criticized for allowing Lexington to fall to Confederate forces. It symbolized to his growing body of critics his ineptness and unfitness to command. This criticism began after Wilson's Creek and came from many important individuals, including the Blair family, who blamed Frémont for that defeat, believing that he had not done enough to help Lyon. In fact, some of these critics thought that the Pathfinder had deliberately withheld reinforcements from Lyon. Another consequential foe was Attorney General Edward Bates. Bates feared that Frémont would "ruin our state [Missouri] utterly and endanger our cause" and fumed that he "sits like a nightmare upon the nation's breast."[47]

Much of this criticism was preposterous, but some of it was based on problems that Frémont caused for himself. For one thing, Frémont had a big staff that included a large number of foreign officers. Their presence, according to Pope, "with their strange appearance and not too good manners, gave a foreign tone and look to everything about his headquarters, which was offensive to Americans." Most of these foreigners were conscientious men who volunteered their services to aid the Union cause, but their arrogant manners and difficulty with the English language made working with them troublesome.[48]

Furthermore, Frémont's staff cut him off from outside contact. Many visitors commented on the number of guards around Frémont's headquarters, guards who made it difficult for people, even senior officers and government officials, to see the general. One officer, bearing important dispatches, had to wait for three days before Frémont saw him. Sherman had to badger staff officers for two days before finally being admitted into Frémont's presence, and Gen. Lewis Wallace was not allowed to see him at all. Just how detrimental this situation was is difficult to assess. On the one hand, Frémont does not seem to have been denied important information, but on the other hand, it angered influential politicians and many of his subordinates, adding more difficulties to his mounting troubles.[49]

Accompanying these criticisms were several others. Critics condemned Frémont for his extravagant purchases of equipment and payments to construction companies building fortifications. There was talk of corruption, though no substantial proof was offered. He then began feuding with the Blair family, his onetime benefactors. The dispute began over his role in the Wilson's Creek campaign and refusal to grant contracts to friends of Frank Blair Jr. to provide clothing and other equipment to the army. In September the hostility flared into the open after Frémont arrested Blair for insubordination and Blair began actively striving to cause the Pathfinder's removal. To further complicate matters, at the end of August, Frémont issued a proclamation that declared martial law and ordered the slaves of Rebels freed. This announcement upset Lincoln, who wanted to avoid making slavery an issue at this stage in the war and did not want one of his generals seizing the initiative on this topic, and the president ordered Frémont to retract the sections dealing with slavery.[50]

By this time, Lincoln was beginning to worry that Frémont was in over his head. He feared that the general was "losing the confidence of his men" because "he isolates himself, & allows nobody to see him; and by which he does not know what is going on in the very matter he is dealing with." In order to aid Frémont, he sent Gen. David Hunter, a Regular army officer, to supply the political general with professional advice. Hunter provided no help and by mid-October had come to the conclusion that "Frémont was utterly incompetent."[51]

Throughout the rest of September and October, Lincoln sent a steady stream of officials to investigate the situation in Missouri. These included Montgomery Blair, Adj. Gen. Lorenzo Thomas, Secretary of War Simon Cameron, and Lincoln's private secretary, John Nicolay. Their reports painted a picture of incompetence, confusion, and hopelessness. Nicolay wrote Lincoln that "everything in the worst possible condition, with no hope for reform." Many officers, Nicolay continued, have no "faith that Frémont will or can accomplish anything" and "are quite convinced that he will not." Lincoln also received unsolicited reports. Ward Lamon, a longtime friend of the president, told Lincoln that Missouri was "in a terribly unorganized state . . . and I find great complaints about the Commanding General. . . . He certainly knows but little of his command, i. e. about its organization and capacity."[52]

Such reports were impossible to ignore. On October 7, Lincoln asked Gen. Samuel Curtis whether he should relieve Frémont. Curtis's answer was yes. Still, Lincoln hesitated, and it was not until October 24 that the president finally decided that Frémont had to go, though he did hedge his bets. Frémont was in the field at the time, and Lincoln decreed that if he was engaged in battle, "or shall then be in the immediate presence of the enemy, in expectation of battle," the order was not to be delivered.[53]

As Lincoln agonized over what to do about his controversial general, Frémont had finally assumed command of an army. Following the disaster at Lexington, the Pathfinder was forced to abandon his proposed operations on the Mississippi and instead proceed into the interior to confront the Confederate army in western Missouri. He arrived at Jefferson City, located in central Missouri, on September 27 and began marching west with an army of twenty-one thousand effectives, but he failed to obtain adequate transportation. As a result, the march was slow because Frémont had to pause frequently to wait for supplies or to gather food to feed his men. Another problem was the hostility of many of his generals, as Curtis, Hunter, and Pope (all West Pointers) held Frémont in contempt and severely criticized his conduct of operations. By the end of October, the army had reached Springfield. A cavalry charge routed the Confederate garrison, a victory that Frémont eagerly reported to Lincoln, but it was too late. On November 2, the order relieving Frémont from command reached the army, and he stepped down.[54]

Frémont's military performance as commander of the Western Department was mixed. He successfully held and fortified key points on the Mississippi River as well as ordered the occupation of strategic sections of Kentucky. These steps, and his beginning the construction of a riverboat fleet, laid the foundation for the Union successes on the western rivers in 1862 and 1863. They also demonstrated that Frémont was a sound, if not original, strategist who understood where and how the Union would have to strike in order to defeat the Confederacy.

43

He failed, however, to adequately control his generals and manage his troops so as to prevent the Confederate victories in western Missouri in August and September. Whether it was Lyon, Sturgis, Davis, or another subordinate, Frémont had difficulty getting his generals to carry out his orders. Many of them did not respect him, believing he lacked the necessary qualities for command, and Frémont was unable to do anything to change their minds. He spent too much time secluded in his headquarters and not enough time out among his troops. This also cost him the respect of his soldiers, some of whom viewed the Pathfinder as "an empty, spread-eagle, show-off, horn-tooting general" who "had no abilities of any kind." Finally, Frémont never gained mastery over the situation in western Missouri, primarily because he did not understand the requirements necessary for maneuvering troops in such a vast space where it was hard to supply soldiers and communicate effectively. The military failures there, when combined with his poor administration and controversial slavery policy, led to his removal.[55]

Almost immediately after Frémont's dismissal from command, the first significant combat action occurred along the Mississippi River at Belmont, Missouri. On November 1, Grant, commanding the Union forces along the Mississippi, received orders "to make demonstrations with your troops along both sides of the river." Grant sent out various detachments to demonstrate against Rebel positions, and then, on November 6, he proceeded south on steamboats with three thousand soldiers to attack the Confederate camp at Belmont. His force was divided into two brigades, with McClernand commanding the largest one, consisting of three regiments. Logan commanded one of these regiments. This battle was the first combat engagement for both of these politicians.[56]

On the morning of November 7, the Union soldiers debarked from their transports, assembled in a hollow a short distance from the river, and then began marching toward Belmont with skirmishers well in advance. McClernand dispatched two cavalry companies to scout ahead of the main force to seek out enemy units and discover the lay of the land. About a mile and a half from the enemy camp, McClernand deployed his three regiments into a line of battle, placing Logan's regiment on the left, and began advancing upon the Rebel forces. The soldiers struggled through woods and undergrowth, making it difficult for the officers to keep their men in proper battle lines. The troops' inexperience contributed to this problem, as they became temporarily disordered, but were "rallied under the gallant example" of Logan. During the fighting, Logan feared the Confederates would try to outflank the Federals, and he extended his line farther to the left to block any such attempt. The Union troops continued to advance, slowly pushing the Southerners back. McClernand then ordered a charge by his entire line, driving the remaining Confederates from the field and allowing the Federals to occupy the Rebel encampment.[57]

All discipline melted away as the Union troops entered the camp. The men, as Grant later wrote, "laid down their arms and commenced rummaging the tents to pick up trophies." McClernand did not help matters by leading the soldiers in "Three cheers for the Union," causing the men to applaud their general and contributing to the breakdown in discipline. Logan, though not leading any cheers, did nothing to help restore order. Few of Grant's officers were of any aid to him at this moment, as most of them "galloped about from one cluster of men to another and at every halt delivered a short eulogy upon the Union cause and the achievements of the command." Having won the engagement, the Federal army was on the verge of disintegration.[58]

To bring the situation under control, Grant ordered the troops to set the camp on fire. This occurred just as the Confederates launched a counterattack. McClernand, Logan, and Grant's other officers rallied their men and prepared to retreat. During the celebration, Southern units had moved between the Federal army and its transports, forcing the Union soldiers to fight their way out of the trap. To counter this situation, McClernand ordered his artillery turned around to face the new threat. The cannon fire blasted the Rebel troops, and Logan exploited the situation by charging, which forced the Southerners to give way without firing a shot and allowed the Union troops to reach and embark on their transports, leaving the battlefield to the Confederates.

The battle of Belmont was at best a draw for the Union, but it provided valuable combat experience to the soldiers involved and Grant's officers. Both McClernand and Logan demonstrated exemplary courage under fire. They remained near the front during the entire battle and showed a fearlessness that was encouraging to their troops. Grant praised McClernand in his official report, writing that the politician "was in the midst of danger throughout the engagement, and displayed coolness and judgement." In a letter to his father, Grant wrote that McClernand "proved that he is a soldier as well as a statesman." In his report, McClernand praised Logan's tactics and admitted that they "largely" contributed "to the success of the day."[59]

In some important ways, the leadership of both McClernand and Logan was deficient. Neither officer handled their troops well. Logan admitted that at times he got his "men in line poorly," and McClernand had difficulty moving his command in the face of enemy fire. The inexperience of both officers and men and the difficult terrain accounted for their difficulties. An even more important problem was their inability to control their troops after capturing the Confederate camp. The major culprit was a lack of discipline. Neither officer enforced discipline, and, in fact, by their own acts both of them encouraged such behavior. Despite these flaws, both McClernand and Logan demonstrated at Belmont that they could become good combat officers if they were given time to learn their trade and placed under experienced officers who could properly direct them.[60]

As 1861 came to a close, the generalship of Lincoln's political generals in combat was mixed. Those exercising independent commands—Butler, Frémont, Schenck at Vienna, and Sigel at Carthage and Wilson's Creek (his flanking movement placed him in such a position)—failed, oftentimes badly. They all demonstrated similar command deficiencies. These included the failure to reconnoiter properly, incapability to discipline their troops, poor planning, and inability to handle troops in battle. Those political generals who fought under West Point professionals functioned well. Schenck, at Bull Run, operated his brigade efficiently, if unspectacularly, and both McClernand and Logan, although guilty of mistakes, displayed personal courage and battlefield leadership ability at Belmont.

Lincoln retained all of these generals, no matter how poorly they may have performed, because at this stage in the war he still needed their political backing. Frémont had lost some of his initial support, specifically from the Blair family, but his proclamation freeing Missouri's slaves earned him the praise of Missouri's Germans, abolitionists, and the Radical Republicans in Congress. Lincoln could not afford to alienate the latter group and, at their urging, granted Frémont a second command in 1862. The president faced a similar situation with Sigel, who, despite his terrible combat record, remained a popular figure in the German community. Paradoxically, the defeats at Carthage and Wilson's Creek actually increased Sigel's political importance because most Germans, and many Americans, believed that only Sigel fought well at those battles. Even Hurlbut was not formally dismissed. Though Hurlbut's drinking alienated most of his political supporters, Lincoln was fond of him and hoped that the general would reform himself and make a positive contribution to the war effort.

As for Schenck, McClernand, and Logan, they also continued to be consequential politically. Schenck retained Lincoln's personal friendship, which protected him from the early blunders he made at Vienna and allowed him to continue in command. McClernand remained politically important because of his significance both as a war Democrat and as an influential Illinois politician. Nothing had changed to upset the basic reasons for his appointment. Finally, Logan's combat performance enhanced his political credentials. In 1861, as Lincoln made his first political generals, Logan had not been important enough to receive one of these commissions, but battlefield success would make Logan a national figure and thus politically consequential, a fact that Lincoln would eventually recognize.

As 1861 ended, all of the basic factors that compelled Lincoln to adopt the policy of commissioning politicians as generals remained in play. The generals examined in this study nearly all retained the same political importance that they possessed when first commissioned. Most of these generals had not participated in combat operations, but they still contributed to the war effort through recruiting, administration, or providing the political backing sought by Lincoln. In the new year, most of Lincoln's political generals would have their military capabilities tested.

The Campaigns of 1862

The year 1862 witnessed military operations in every theater of the war, and political generals played major roles in all of these campaigns. Two generals, Banks and Frémont, held independent commands during the Shenandoah Valley campaign, but the rest of them served in subordinate positions, some under West Point graduates and a few below Banks or Frémont. As in 1861, almost every political general that occupied an independent command failed on the battlefield, whereas those in a subordinate position, especially those under West Pointers, performed adequately, as politicians were better generals when supervised by men with a military education.

A dangerous trend emerged during this year. Conflict between graduates of the U.S. Military Academy and civilian political appointees regularly occurred. Many factors contributed to this conflict. The primary motivator was that most West Pointers resented that incompetent or unproven politicians were receiving important commands, while many political generals believed that professional soldiers hogged the important assignments and prevented citizen generals from obtaining high command. Some conflict had nothing to do with this reason, but this growing hostility was clearly hazardous because it adversely affected Union military performance in several campaigns.

Following Frémont's removal, Lincoln divided the Department of the West into the Departments of Kansas and Missouri and placed Gen. Henry Halleck in charge of the latter. Halleck's department was subdivided into several districts, and Sigel commanded the District of Southwestern Missouri. At the end of December 1861, Gen. Samuel Curtis superseded Sigel in command of this district. This change prompted Sigel to resign, but in early January 1862 Sigel agreed to withdraw his resignation and serve under Curtis. To appease the German, Curtis arranged his command along ethnic lines. He named Sigel second in command of the army and placed him in charge of two divisions; in each more than one-third of the soldiers were foreign born. The army's other two divisions were composed of mostly native-born soldiers.[1]

Ordered to pursue and destroy the Confederate army operating in southwestern Missouri, Curtis, throughout January and February, maneuvered the Rebels into northwestern Arkansas. By early March, Curtis, with two divisions, had established a fortified position behind Little Sugar Creek, just south of Elkhorn Tavern on the Telegraph Road, running from Fayetteville, Arkansas, to Springfield, while Sigel and his two divisions stationed themselves twelve miles to the south at Bentonville. In response, the Confederate army, located south of Fayetteville, advanced around Curtis's position and placed itself in the Union army's rear. Late in the afternoon of March 5, reports of this movement reached Curtis, who sent a courier to Sigel with orders to retreat to Little Sugar Creek. This order did not reach Sigel until late in the evening, arriving at the same time that scouts reported enemy forces coming up the road from Fayetteville.[2]

Delaying the retreat until two o'clock on the morning of the sixth, Sigel then sent only part of his two divisions to Little Sugar Creek. He retained six hundred infantry and one battery of artillery as a rear guard under his personal command at Bentonville. This decision violated Curtis's orders, since they directed the Yankee Dutchman to retreat with his entire force, and nearly caused the destruction of his tiny rear guard. Shortly after ten o'clock in the morning, Sigel evacuated the town, but Confederate forces advanced around his flanks and threatened to surround his force as they marched north. The Union soldiers repelled three attacks. Sigel remained cool throughout and directed the troops so they could meet each threat as it appeared. At three thirty in the afternoon, reinforcements sent by Curtis met Sigel's column and escorted it to the main Federal position.[3]

The next morning, the battle of Pea Ridge began, but Sigel played no role during the action on the first day. Most of the fighting occurred toward

Elkhorn Tavern, north of the location assigned to Sigel on Little Sugar Creek, but Sigel's actions at the end of the day reduced Curtis's confidence in him. Curtis ordered the Yankee Dutchman to reinforce the Federal units at Elkhorn Tavern. Sigel diligently advanced, but when darkness fell he halted his command and, so as not to expose his position to the Confederates, instructed his men to build no campfires or move about. At two o'clock in the morning, Sigel decided that his men needed proper rest and food and directed them to return to their former camps. Curtis realized that this march would take the entire night, leaving the soldiers with no time to eat or rest before the battle recommenced. He "urged" Sigel "to rest the troops where they then were." Sigel complied with this request.[4]

Sigel redeemed himself when the battle resumed in the morning. Curtis deployed his forces across the Telegraph Road, facing north toward Elkhorn Tavern, with Sigel's two divisions on the left flank, west of the road. Sigel established two lines, placing the First Division in the first line and the Second Division in reserve, but it was his use of artillery that won the battle. Personally sighting the guns, Sigel directed a barrage against the Confederate positions, destroying enemy guns and disrupting their infantry formations. Sigel then ordered forward his infantry and drove the Confederate forces from the field.[5]

The battle of Pea Ridge ended in Union victory, and Sigel, despite his erratic performance, deserved much of the credit. His foolhardy actions on March 6, when he disobeyed Curtis's orders, nearly resulted in the loss of six hundred soldiers. The fact that Sigel conducted a masterful retreat does not excuse this fact. Given little to do on March 7, Sigel nevertheless managed to place the Union army in a perilous situation by marching his troops too much and not allowing them to rest and eat. It was only Curtis's intervention that prevented Sigel from exhausting his soldiers. Sigel's actions on the final day of battle were his finest as a Union general. He used his artillery brilliantly, displaying gifts as an artillerist that he did not possesses as a commander of infantry, though on this day he did deploy his infantry in the positions from which they could easily exploit the artillery barrage. His conduct played a decisive role in achieving victory.

For his role in the battle, and to appease the German community, Lincoln promoted Sigel to major general, but controversy soon made it impossible for Sigel to remain in the theater. Newspaper accounts of the battle portrayed Sigel as responsible for the victory and even claimed that Curtis had wanted to surrender before the decisive actions on March 8. Officers in Sigel's divisions wrote many of these accounts, without the Yankee Dutchman's knowledge, and this fact, as much as the false accounts of the battle, irritated Curtis. In his first report of the engagement, Curtis had singled out Sigel for praise, writing that the German had acted "gallantly" and "drove back the left wing of the enemy," but in his final report he made no special mention of Sigel. In a private letter to Halleck, Curtis complained that "I cannot understand [Sigel] and I do not wish to have the honor of commanding him." Consequently, Sigel's usefulness in the trans-Mississippi was at an end, and the War Department transferred him to Virginia.[6]

The battle of Pea Ridge had great strategic consequences for the war in the West. It reduced the Confederate threat to Missouri and allowed Halleck to transfer men and resources to the operations being conducted in Tennessee and along the Mississippi River. These maneuvers already had commenced in early February, when Grant advanced down the Tennessee River to attack Fort Henry and Fort Donelson on the Cumberland River, bastions that prevented Union gunboats and transports from sailing into middle Tennessee. The capture of these forts would allow the Federals to advance into Tennessee, threaten Nashville, and outflank Confederate positions on the Mississippi River. Political appointees McClernand and Logan accompanied Grant in these operations.

The attack against Fort Henry occurred on February 6. Grant ordered McClernand, commanding the First Division, to land on the east bank of the river at eleven in the morning and assume position astride the roads from Fort Henry to Fort Donelson, prevent all reinforcements from reaching the fort, and ensure that the garrison did not escape. Grant directed the Second Division, commanded by Gen. Charles F. Smith, to land on the west bank and attack the fort directly, supported by the riverboat fleet commanded by Flag Officer Andrew Foote.[7]

These instructions upset the citizen general because Grant sent a West Point officer, Lt. Col. James McPherson, to guide McClernand's advance. The Illinois politician feared that this order might place McPherson in command of the division and demanded to know whether the orders were "intended to interfere with my authority." They did not, but McClernand was growing suspicious of West Point graduates, as he believed that there existed in the army "a professional military jealousy of citizen generals." Early in January, he wrote to Logan, "I feel the influence of this jealousy."[8]

The army played no role in the battle of Fort Henry because, after a two-hour artillery duel, the riverboat fleet forced the fort to surrender, but the Confederate garrison escaped. McClernand failed to move his troops into position in time to block the road. Grant had admonished McClernand to advance with "celerity," but neither he nor McClernand took into account the effects of the weather on the division's movements. Heavy rains fell the night before, swelling streams and turning the roads into a sea of mud. Thick woods further hindered the divisions' movements. The Confederates overcame the mud and other difficulties and slipped by McClernand's division.[9]

McClernand's failure to block the Confederate escape did not deter the politician from trumpeting his exploits. On the day the fort fell, McClernand wrote triumphantly to Grant that his division "was the first of the land forces to enter the Fort," a dubious honor since he did not prevent the enemy garrison from escaping. Two days later, the politician provided Lincoln with an account of the battle. This letter focused on McClernand's own exploits, and, though he did praise Foote for disabling the enemy guns, he portrayed his actions as being the chief reason for the Union victory and contended that this was "the most complete victory achieved during the war." Neither Grant nor Lincoln responded to this self-promotion.[10]

Immediately after the fall of Fort Henry, Grant decided to "take and destroy Fort Donelson," located eleven miles east of Fort Henry. On February 11, he met with his division and brigade commanders to discuss whether to advance upon Fort Donelson. All of these generals agreed that the army should attack. When asked for his opinion, McClernand read a paper that proposed a plan of campaign, most likely the same strategy he described in a letter to Grant two days before. In it, McClernand recommended that his division both lead the advance and invest the fort; he assigned no duty for either the Second Division or Grant himself. According to Gen. Lew Wallace, "the proceeding smacked of a political caucus" and irritated Grant. The meeting ended with no comments being made upon McClernand's proposal, and it was forgotten.[11]

On February 12, Grant's army of fifteen thousand men marched unopposed to Fort Donelson, and, over the next two days, the Union forces invested the fort. Fort Donelson lay on a bend in the Cumberland River east of the town of Dover. McClernand's division took position on the right flank, south of the Confederate stronghold. He carefully established his three brigades on a series of wooded hills that overlooked the center and right of the fort, placing his division astride two roads leading south from Dover. To the left of McClernand's division stood Lew Wallace's division and then Smith's division. By the morning of February 15, reinforcements allowed Grant to place twenty-five thousand men in line, facing approximately fifteen to twenty-one thousand Confederates.[12]

McClernand positioned his men well and ensured that he was able to guard his entire line with infantry. On the other hand, McClernand did not have any reserve and failed to dig entrenchments. The reasons for the latter omission lay in part with Grant, who decided that the "nature of the ground was such that" there was no need to entrench. The general was thinking offensively and did not believe that the Confederates would attack. Furthermore, at this early stage of the war, few commanders bothered to entrench their troops.[13]

On February 13, McClernand disobeyed orders and directed that Col. William Morrison's brigade attack a Confederate position. Grant wanted to avoid any action that might bring on a general engagement, but McClernand desired to eliminate a Confederate battery annoying his troops. The Southerners repulsed this assault, and Grant rebuked McClernand for making the unauthorized attack. Earlier in the day, however, Smith had ordered a similar assault that met with the same result. Grant did not reprimand Smith, who was a fellow military academy graduate and the commandant of cadets when Grant attended West Point. This double standard convinced McClernand that Grant favored West Point graduates and only tolerated the political generals under his command.[14]

Other than these unauthorized assaults, no major fighting occurred until February 14, when the riverboat fleet attempted to pound Fort Donelson into submission. This bombardment failed, and Grant concluded that the fort would fall only after "a protracted siege." The enemy's strong breastworks deterred him from attempting a general assault because he feared "the result of attempting to carry the place by storm with raw troops." Despite the defeat of the riverboat fleet, the Union forces remained confident, so much so that Grant assured McClernand that the Confederates would not attack.[15]

The Southerners realized the precariousness of their position and in the early morning hours of February 15 launched an assault against McClernand's lines in an attempt to break out of the Federal siege and retreat southward. The Confederates achieved both surprise and numerical superiority at the point of attack. Massing their troops against the Federal right flank, they gained a four-to-one advantage. Federal pickets detected the offensive, allowing McClernand's four brigades to form lines of battle. On the extreme right, McClernand had posted Col. John McArthur's brigade; next to it rested brigades commanded by Col. Richard Oglesby, Col. William Wallace, and finally Colonel Morrison.[16]

The Union forces mounted a stout defense that initially blunted the attack, but by eight in the morning McClernand faced a grave situation. The overwhelming Confederate numbers forced McArthur's brigade to retreat, exposing Oglesby's right flank. Furthermore, Oglesby's soldiers were nearly out of ammunition. McClernand realized that he lacked sufficient forces to hold back the Southerners and requested reinforcements from both Grant and Lew Wallace. Wallace eventually sent one brigade (commanded by Col. Charles Cruft), and McClernand placed it in reserve behind his battle line, but Grant was nowhere to be found. Earlier that morning, the commanding general had traveled to the river to consult with Foote and would not arrive on the battlefield until one o'clock. Lacking direction from Grant, McClernand ordered Oglesby to "hold his ground as long as possible" and continued his efforts to find reinforcements.[17]

After another hour of fighting, the Southern attack forced Oglesby's entire brigade to fall back to new positions except for Logan's Thirty-first Illinois, located on Oglesby's extreme left flank next to William Wallace's brigade. Logan remained in line and, to secure his exposed right flank, ordered the right flank of the regiment to fall back on its center, at a right angle to the left flank. This maneuver established a new front to face the Confederate flanking attack. Cruft's brigade then moved into line on the right of the Thirty-first. With Rebel troops striking at both front and flank, Logan rode behind the line, shouting encouragement to his soldiers. He received two serious wounds, but refused to leave the field. Finally, after holding out for more than an hour, the regiment exhausted its ammunition and retreated. Wallace's and Cruft's brigades stood their ground for a short while but then fell back, and McClernand established a new line at a right angle to his old one. The Confederates had gained control of the roads leading south and now had the opportunity to escape.[18]

At this moment, the Southern attack stalled because the Confederate commanders began arguing among themselves about what action they should take next. This delay proved fatal. Grant finally arrived on the battlefield, met with his subordinates, and determined to counterattack. He ordered Smith on the left flank to assault the Confederate works and told Lew Wallace and McClernand to retake the ground lost in the morning. McClernand, his division having suffered fifteen hundred casualties and still low on ammunition, was "not ready to undertake" the assignment. As a result, Wallace's division recaptured the lost ground. By the end of the day, the Union assaults had driven the Confederates back into the fort and even captured some of the outer fortifications. The next day, the garrison surrendered.[19]

Both McClernand and Logan rendered valuable service during the battle on February 15. The nature of the fighting, primarily a brigade and regimental action, precluded McClernand, as a division commander, from playing a direct role in the engagement. He did take constructive actions, such as continually asking for reinforcements and attempting to keep his units in line of battle as long as possible. When the Confederates broke his line, he formed a new one that helped to check the attack and protect the Union army. The *Illinois State Journal* praised McClernand and printed a letter that described him as "continually with his command, exposing his person day and night" to enemy fire. More important, Lincoln promoted McClernand to major general.[20]

At the regimental level, Logan performed brilliantly, demonstrating that he was an excellent combat officer. His maneuver to form a new flank helped to blunt the Confederate attack, giving the Federal forces more time to create a

53

new battle line. The colonel also demonstrated personal courage that inspired his troops and contributed to the Union victory. Grant heaped praise on Logan in letters to Secretary of War Stanton and Representative Washburne. He recommended that Logan be appointed to brigadier general and requested that if Logan "be promoted I want him left with the Division of the Army I may have the honor of commanding." Shortly thereafter, Lincoln granted Logan a commission as a brigadier general, but due to his wounds Logan could not participate in the spring campaign.[21]

Just as after the capture of Fort Henry, McClernand worked hard to advertise his feats. He published a congratulatory order to his division that portrayed the fall of both Forts Henry and Donelson as the result of his division's efforts alone. In two letters to Lincoln, McClernand sent the president copies of both his official report and the congratulatory order. In these letters, he inflated his own exploits, while subtly denigrating those of Grant and the other division commanders, claiming, "I was not properly supported; hence my great loss." Lincoln's reaction to these letters was not recorded. Although unaware of these letters, Grant did not like what McClernand wrote in his official report. In a note attached to it, the commanding general commented that it was "a little highly colored as to the conduct of the First Division." Grant disliked McClernand's grandstanding, but could do little about it since the Illinois politician enjoyed the favor of the president.[22]

The Union victories at Forts Henry and Donelson had major strategic consequences for the war in the West. The triumphs allowed Union forces to outflank the Southern defense on the Mississippi in Kentucky, Missouri, and Tennessee and opened up middle Tennessee to Federal invasion. On February 25, Nashville fell to Union forces and shortly thereafter the Confederates abandoned two key positions on the Mississippi, Columbus and New Madrid. The Southerners retreated to Corinth, Mississippi, the site of a railroad junction, and began concentrating available forces for a possible counterattack.

By the end of March, Grant had advanced south as far as Pittsburg Landing, Tennessee, located on the west bank of the Tennessee River, twenty miles north of Corinth, where the Union army was assembling before continuing its penetration of the Confederacy. Grant's army, now called the Army of the Tennessee, consisted of six divisions, approximately thirty-eight thousand men. It awaited the arrival of Gen. Don Carlos Buell's Army of the Ohio. The Army of the Tennessee placed itself in a strong defensive position, with its left flank secured by the Tennessee River and right flank resting on Owl Creek.

McClernand remained in command of the First Division, and Hurlbut commanded the new Fourth Division. Hurlbut returned to duty in December 1861 and held in the winter of 1862 a number of administrative positions before being assigned to his first field command since Frémont had relieved him for drunkenness the previous summer. Many officers in Hurlbut's division disliked serving under a drunkard, and a petition circulated throughout the unit demanding his resignation, but the general remained in command. This pleased the enlisted men, who had confidence in Hurlbut due to his hard work and considered him to be "a brave and efficient officer."[23]

As at Fort Donelson, Grant failed to prepare his army for a possible Confederate attack. He and many of his generals believed that the war was nearly over, assuming that the defeats at Forts Henry and Donelson and the loss of Nashville had so demoralized the Confederates that they would soon surrender. As a result, the Union forces concentrating at Pittsburg Landing did not dig entrenchments or prepare for a possible Confederate attack. Only McClernand feared that such an event might occur. Showing considerable insight for a novice, on March 27 he suggested to Grant that the army "should be formed upon some general and connected plan" in order "to avoid confusion and self destruction in case of a possible night attack." McClernand had obviously learned from the surprise assault at Fort Donelson and believed that the Federal forces should prepare for a possible Confederate offensive, though he failed to recommend that the Union forces entrench.[24]

The Union army, as McClernand feared, was not positioned to meet an attack. Three brigades of Gen. William T. Sherman's division had been placed around Shiloh Church with their right anchored on Owl Creek, but the second brigade was stationed to the east on the opposite side of the Union line, next to the Tennessee River. In between Sherman's division, but forward of it, rested the division commanded by Gen. Benjamin M. Prentiss. Directly behind Sherman lay McClernand's division, with its three brigades encamped in a line perpendicular to Sherman's brigades. To the east of McClernand and behind Prentiss were Hurlbut's three brigades. Gen. William Wallace's division was stationed behind Hurlbut's division, and Lew Wallace's division was several miles to the north at Crump's Landing.

In the early morning hours of April 6, a Rebel army of forty thousand men attacked and achieved complete surprise. On the right, Sherman's division struggled to meet the onslaught. McClernand responded to Sherman's request for support by promptly providing his third brigade, but even with this reinforcement Sherman was forced to give ground. While this occurred, McClernand assembled his other two brigades and established a defensive position three hundred yards behind the front. When Sherman's division fell back, establishing itself on McClernand's right, the Confederates launched an assault against McClernand. The Illinois politician's left flank was uncovered, allowing the Southerners to strike his exposed flank and force him to retreat another two hundred yards, where he and Sherman attempted to establish a new defensive line.[25]

The Confederate attack had nearly destroyed Prentiss's division in the center of the Union line, thus accounting for why McClernand's left flank was so exposed, and the survivors of Prentiss's division took position in a sunken road. To their east, in a peach orchard, Hurlbut moved two of his brigades (the Third Brigade was sent to support Sherman) to shore up the Federal army's left flank. He positioned his brigades at nearly right angles, with the Second Brigade posted next to Prentiss facing west and the First Brigade to the left facing south. In this position, Hurlbut's division repelled repeated Confederate charges and held its position for five hours. In the afternoon, Rebel forces threatened to turn his left flank, forcing him to move the Second Brigade from its station next to the remains of Prentiss's command to the left. This maneuver blunted another Southern assault. Shortly thereafter, Hurlbut realized that he could no longer hold this line against the increasing enemy pressure and ordered his division to retreat. It fell back in good order to a new line near the river established by Grant, which Hurlbut held throughout the rest of the day.[26]

While Hurlbut held the Union left flank, McClernand and Sherman struggled to maintain a defensive line on the right. After retreating another two hundred yards, McClernand ordered a charge that drove the Rebels back a half mile. Sherman, who joined in the Union counterattack, called it a "fine charge," but the Federal forces could not hold the retaken ground. For the rest of the afternoon, the Confederates slowly forced back what remained of McClernand's and Sherman's divisions. Finally, near the end of the day, the two generals managed to piece together a final defensive line that repulsed the Rebel assaults. The new position anchored the right flank of the line established by Grant earlier in the day.[27]

During the night, the troops remained in line as Buell's Army of the Ohio arrived on the battlefield. The next day, April 7, the combined Union armies counterattacked. The Confederates gave way grudgingly, but the superior Federal forces pushed the Rebels back across the battlefield. Hurlbut took no part in the fighting this day, but McClernand, commanding the remains of his division and fragments of other units, eventually retook his camp and then advanced against Southern troops fighting from behind a hastily constructed breastwork. The Rebels temporarily stopped McClernand's attack, but the Federals eventually broke through. Following this action, McClernand continued to advance, eventually retaking Sherman's camp, until the Southern army abandoned the field. Grant was satisfied to regain the field, and, exhausted by its efforts, the Union army made no effort to pursue the Rebels.[28]

McClernand fought well at Shiloh. On the first day of battle, he did a good job of moving his troops on the battlefield, managing to conduct several retreats in the face of a superior enemy, always a difficult maneuver to perform. He again demonstrated battlefield courage that helped to rally his troops at critical moments. On the second day, the former congressman performed adequately, but he acted rashly on several occasions and thus exposed his troops to Confederate counterattack. On both days McClernand worked successfully with other generals, especially Sherman, who later wrote that they acted "in perfect concert." This allowed the Union forces on the right flank to establish successive defensive lines that eventually stalled the Rebel assault.[29]

Hurlbut performed magnificently on the first day. He moved quickly to secure the Union left flank and saved the Union army, since his division prevented the Confederates from sweeping around that exposed flank and into the Federal rear. This action also gave Grant time to form a final defensive line. Hurlbut did a good job of maneuvering his troops to meet new Confederate threats, thus allowing him to hold his line for more than five hours. Finally, he demonstrated personal courage that inspired his men. One enlisted man hailed Hurlbut for handling "his troops with more skill" and showing "greater personal bravery" than any other officer on the field.[30]

The battle of Shiloh had important consequences for the war. For one thing, it stopped all talk among Union generals of the Confederacy quickly submitting. It became obvious to many that the Union would have to conquer the South. The Federal victory ended any immediate attempt by the Confederates to retake middle and western Tennessee, thus helping to secure the Federal occupation of that region. Shortly after the battle, Union forces took Island No. 10 on the Mississippi River and in June occupied Memphis.[31]

The huge casualties at Shiloh played a major role in ending further Union advances. Shortly after the battle, Halleck arrived at Pittsburg Landing and assumed command of the Federal army. Grant, heavily criticized for allowing the Confederates to surprise him, was demoted to second in command. At the end of April, Halleck began a slow advance against Corinth, as he stopped to entrench his soldiers every night, and took a month to cover the twenty miles between Pittsburg Landing and Corinth. The Confederates evacuated the city as soon as the Union army drew near. Halleck then dispersed the huge Federal force of one hundred thousand men, using it to occupy various cites and towns and guard the railroad in western Tennessee and sending a large part under Buell to advance into eastern Tennessee. By the middle of June, the Union offensive in the West had ground to a halt.

At the end of April, the Union achieved another victory in the West when the city of New Orleans capitulated to a combined army and navy operation.

57

Butler led the land forces, but the navy, commanded by Flag Officer David Farragut, won the victory. In late January 1862, the Lincoln administration ordered Butler to capture New Orleans, using the five thousand soldiers the general had recruited in the fall of 1861. Arriving off the mouth of the Mississippi River in April, the Union forces proceeded to bombard the two Confederate forts guarding the approaches to the city. Farragut grew impatient with this tactic and determined to run past the forts. He successfully accomplished this on April 24, steamed up the river to New Orleans, and forced the city to surrender. Butler's troops played no role in the battle except to occupy the city. The general assumed command over New Orleans and remained there until December, but during this time no important military operations occurred outside the city. By the end of 1862, Butler's abilities as a field commander remained untested.[32]

As Union offensives pushed the Confederates out of West Tennessee and gained control of New Orleans, dramatic events transpired in the East. Following the battle of Bull Run, the eastern theater settled into a period of inactivity as the rival armies spent the fall of 1861 and winter of 1862 training and organizing their forces. As spring approached, the armies began to stir. Gen. George McClellan, the commander of the Army of the Potomac, planned to attack the Confederate capital at Richmond by shifting his army by water from northern Virginia to Fortress Monroe, situated on the peninsula between the York and James rivers. The Lincoln administration agreed to this plan, but ordered McClellan to provide enough troops to secure Washington, D.C., and also protect the Baltimore and Ohio Railroad, a task that required him to occupy the lower Shenandoah Valley. McClellan assigned this mission to Banks, who commanded a corps of twenty-five thousand men.[33]

Beginning in February, Banks advanced south from Maryland into the Shenandoah Valley. In mid-March, his lead division, commanded by Shields, occupied Winchester. Shields, whose recent assumption of command pleased the enlisted men because "he was a good general in the Mexican War," reported that the Confederate army had fled the valley, leaving only a small cavalry force to harry the Union forces. Acting on Shields's dispatch, the War Department ordered Banks to take all of his forces except Shields's division and march east of the Blue Ridge Mountains, anticipating that Banks would participate in McClellan's offensive on the peninsula.[34]

The Irish general quickly realized that his original report was wrong. The Confederate army under Gen. Thomas Jackson had not evacuated the valley and was in fact marching north. After falling back on Winchester, on March 22 Shields fought an engagement with Rebel cavalry, but made sure to mask the size of his force so that the Southerners did not know how large it was.

During this skirmish, a shell fragment fractured Shields's right arm above the elbow, forcing him to remain in bed for several days. Anticipating a Southern attack the next day, the Irishman posted two brigades three miles south of Winchester on a ridge overlooking the village of Kernstown that commanded all approaches to Winchester. He kept his third brigade in reserve. The next day, March 24, the Confederates attacked. The bedridden general was unable to direct the battle, and his immediate subordinate took command.[35]

The Federal army achieved a tactical victory at Kernstown, forcing the Confederate army to retreat, but the South won a strategic triumph. Banks, instead of proceeding to the peninsula, returned to the valley with orders to drive the Rebels out and prevent them from returning. Furthermore, Lincoln detained a second of McClellan's corps, commanded by Gen. Irvin McDowell, at Manassas in order to cover the capital. These decisions deprived McClellan of two corps, weakened his peninsular campaign, and opened up a new area of operations.[36]

In the valley, Banks cautiously pursued the Confederates, marching at a leisurely pace of three miles a day. This pace pleased Secretary of War Stanton, who preferred that Banks not advance recklessly, but the slow pursuit allowed the Confederate army to escape. By the end of April, Banks, now at Harrisonburg, reported that "there is nothing more to be done [here] by us." The War Department ordered him to fall back to Strasburg and send one of his two divisions (Shields's) to Manassas. By this time, Shields had so completely alienated most of his command that many of his officers petitioned the War Department for transfers to other units. These officers thought that he "must at times be crazy" and complained that he "abuses everyone." Despite these complaints, Shields retained command of his division.[37]

Meanwhile, a second Union army was operating in western Virginia. Shortly before the battle of Kernstown, Lincoln had established a new department in this region for Frémont. The Pathfinder's dismissal in November 1861 had aroused a storm of protest from the Radical Republicans, who supported Frémont because of his strong antislavery views. These protests forced Lincoln to create a new command for the general, to be called the Mountain Department. Lincoln intended for Frémont to march into eastern Tennessee and capture Knoxville, a movement that would cut the Virginia and Tennessee Railroad and relieve the Unionists living in that region. The president's desire was not feasible. The area was mountainous, possessed few roads, and had no north-south railroads or major rivers. Supplying an army there would be a logistical nightmare. Furthermore, of the twenty-five thousand men Frémont commanded, he could put maybe fifteen thousand in the field, and the Confederates, controlling the railroad, could at any time transport reinforcements to oppose Frémont.[38]

Frémont accomplished little in his first month in command. He spent most of April begging for more men, money, and supplies and did not begin his movement into eastern Tennessee. In May, General Jackson derailed Frémont's plans when he attacked one of the Pathfinder's brigades. Frémont's troops were spread throughout western Virginia, with Gen. Robert Milroy commanding one brigade of four thousand men at the town of McDowell. On May 7, Milroy reported the approach of Jackson's army and asked for help.[39]

Schenck, commanding a brigade of two thousand soldiers, responded to Milroy's appeals by marching from Franklin to McDowell, a distance of thirty-four miles, in twenty-four hours. As the senior general, Schenck assumed command and decided that the Union defensive position "was entirely untenable." Before retreating, the Union force attacked the Confederate army in order to "check or disable" the enemy's ability to pursue. Following a successful assault, that night Schenck pulled the combined force out of McDowell without losing a man or any supplies. Over the next three days, the Federals fell back to Franklin, where Frémont met them with reinforcements and supplies. The battle of McDowell, though a tactical standoff, effectively removed Frémont from the campaign for nearly a month, as he remained in the vicinity of Franklin, licking his wounds.[40]

With Frémont temporarily neutralized, Jackson reentered the Shenandoah Valley and pushed northward, seeking to destroy Banks's army. After reaching Harrisonburg, Banks had withdrawn as ordered to Strasburg, on the valley pike, where with one division he remained in mid-May. Strasburg was not a good defensive position because an enemy force could attack it by advancing directly up the pike or by crossing over to the south side of Massanutten Mountain, which ran down the middle of the valley, capturing Front Royal, and striking from the southeast. Banks believed that the Confederates would advance directly up the valley pike, though he had no evidence to support such a judgment because he had not bothered to scout the region. To complicate matters, Stanton ordered Banks to place one thousand men at Front Royal to guard the railroad that ran to Manassas. This directive reduced Banks's force at Strasburg to seven thousand.[41]

On May 23, Jackson attacked Front Royal and eliminated the two regiments stationed there. This movement confused Banks. He still believed that the main Confederate army was on the valley pike, leading him to conclude that a small detachment carried out the attack on Front Royal. As a result, he failed to recognize the threat to his flank, and, though he did order his supply trains to Winchester, he refused to retreat and intended to "stand firm" at Strasburg. In fact, Banks feared the political repercussions of retreating more than he feared the enemy. As he told one of his generals, "We have more to fear from the opinions of our friends than from the bayonets of our enemies."[42]

Early in the morning of May 24, Banks realized that the Rebel army at Front Royal was larger than originally presumed and intent on striking his rear. Abandoning his intention to remain at Strasburg, the general fled to Winchester. It took several hours for the troops to organize, and the movement did not begin until midmorning, giving the Confederates more time to fall upon him. As the Federal column scurried north toward Winchester, the Southerners struck its flank, inflicting casualties and capturing stores. Fortunately for Banks, the Rebel troops delayed to scavenge the captured wagons, allowing the Union army to escape to Winchester. Once at this town, Banks felt secure. He resisted advice to retreat farther up the valley, maintaining his theme that "the enemy is not as remorseless as the public!" Instead, the general retired to his room and took a bath, leaving Gen. Alpheus Williams to arrange the town's defenses.[43]

As the new day dawned, it became clear that the Confederates intended to attack Winchester. Inexplicably, Banks decided to resist the assault, even though he believed that the enemy outnumbered him eight to one. Unfortunately, Williams had placed the two Union brigades in a mediocre position: a hill just south of the town that could be easily flanked. The Rebels succeeded in turning the Union right flank, and the Federal regiments gave way. Banks's and Williams's efforts to prevent a stampede failed, and the men poured back into Winchester in "a confused mass." All hopes of an orderly withdrawal evaporated, and what remained of Banks's army fled northward, not stopping until it crossed the Potomac River into Maryland. In a dispatch to Lincoln, Banks portrayed this retreat as a successful withdrawal in the face of superior numbers, when in fact he had been completely routed and barely managed to escape. Furthermore, the Rebel offensive had taken Banks out of the campaign.[44]

These battles had major strategic implications. Upon receiving news of Banks's retreat to Winchester, Lincoln suspended the planned operations of both Frémont (still at Franklin) and McDowell (at Manassas) and ordered both generals to immediately march into the valley to relieve Banks. This decision arrested the movement of McDowell's army (including Shields's division) toward Richmond and Frémont's intended offensive into eastern Tennessee. The president hoped to do more than rescue Banks. He also sought to destroy Jackson's army. To do so, he ordered Frémont to march on Harrisonburg and McDowell to advance on Front Royal, seeking to catch the Confederate army between these Federal forces and crush it. Success, as Lincoln told Frémont, depended "upon the celerity with which you can execute" these orders.[45]

A race ensued in which the Union armies attempted to close the trap before the Rebels could escape. Shields, leading McDowell's forces, was unable to leave until May 27. He reached Front Royal at the end of the month, but, though he knew that the Confederates were marching south on the valley pike, he chose not to advance and capture Strasburg, a move that might have enabled him to cut off the Southern army's retreat. His excuse for not acting was that he "dare not interfere with what was designed for Frémont."[46]

Lincoln had initially ordered Frémont southeast to Harrisonburg, but the Pathfinder instead marched north to Moorfield, about thirty miles west of Strasburg, because, he explained, the Rebels had obstructed the roads to Harrisonburg. Hoping to take advantage of this blunder, the president ordered Frémont to Strasburg. Delayed by the need to bring up reinforcements, bad roads, and terrible weather, the Pathfinder failed to reach Strasburg before the Confederates, who thus slipped between Frémont and Shields.[47]

Over the next week, the Union forces pursued the Rebels, Frémont down the valley pike and Shields on the other side of Massanutten Mountain, as thunderstorms drenched the troops, turning roads into mud and causing rivers to flood. Frémont, following directly behind the Confederates, claimed to be "in rapid pursuit of the enemy," but proved unable to catch them and force a major engagement. Shields also failed to move quickly enough to get ahead of the Confederates. The Rebels slipped through Lincoln's noose.[48]

The Shenandoah Valley campaign reached its climax in early June when Jackson's army turned and attacked its pursuers in two separate battles. The first battle occurred at Cross Keys on June 8 when Frémont engaged the Confederates. The Pathfinder deployed three brigades in line of battle, with Schenck's brigade on the right, and held a fourth brigade in reserve. He mistakenly advanced his left against a Rebel position on a ridge, exposing his left flank. After making these initial dispositions, Frémont played little role in the battle, remaining at his headquarters, although from there he could not follow the course of the engagement. Thus, there was no central direction to the Union effort.[49]

On the left, after three hours of fighting, the Confederates managed to force back the Federal brigade, but in the center and on the right Frémont's troops had more success. The two brigades here drove the Rebels back, but failed to turn the exposed Confederate flank. The primary reason for this disappointment lay with Schenck, who was more worried about protecting his own flank than he was about attacking the enemy. Schenck did advance slowly, but these movements ended when Frémont ordered the Ohio general to fall back. The battle of Cross Keys concluded in a tactical standoff, but Frémont became even more cautious than usual.[50]

The next day, the Confederates attacked Shields's lead brigade at Port Republic. The Irish general had made two mistakes as he approached this town. First, he allowed his brigades to become separated so that they could not support one another if attacked. Second, he ordered his lead brigade commander not to burn a crucial bridge over the North River, a bridge that the Rebels captured. This provided them with an avenue of escape southward. On June 9, the Southern army crossed the bridge and attacked Shields's lead brigade, easily brushing the Union troops aside before continuing its retreat. The Union might have prevented this if Frémont had come up and posted his artillery on the hills overlooking Port Republic, but the Pathfinder inched toward the sounds of battle and arrived too late. The inability of Frémont and Shields to communicate with one another and coordinate their movements contributed to this failure. As it was, Jackson inflicted yet another defeat on the Union forces and sped south to reinforce the Confederate army at Richmond.[51]

Not one of the four selected political generals who participated in the Shenandoah Valley campaign performed well. In fact, their dismal showing was the primary reason the campaign was such a disaster for the Union. Their errors ranged from poor reconnaissance and tactical ineptitude to overly cautious behavior and a failure to cooperate, and provided their Confederate opponent with ample opportunities to defeat and embarrass them. Some of the blame must also be laid on Lincoln, who failed to provide adequate strategic direction and establish a unified command. As a result, confusion often reigned among the Union's generals.

The level of ineptitude varied from general to general. Banks fared the worst. He was too timid, displayed a dangerous inability to gather intelligence or understand the information he did obtain, and generally failed to properly handle his troops. Finally, politics excessively influenced his military decision making to a degree exhibited by no other general during this campaign, placing his soldiers in needless peril because Banks feared the political ramifications of retreating. Frémont shared some of Banks's faults, such as too much caution and a failure to maneuver his units. He also showed an inability to follow orders or communicate with other generals. At times, Frémont seemed not only uncertain but also lost and unable to comprehend the military situation he faced.

The performances of Shields and Schenck were mixed. At Kernstown, Shields demonstrated superior tactical ability, as he successfully fooled the Confederates into thinking he had few troops. He performed less well later in the campaign. The Irish general failed to vigorously pursue the Rebels and at Port Republic allowed his brigades to become dangerously separated and missed the significance of a key bridge, a result of poor reconnaissance and communication. Finally, Schenck also had a jumbled record. At McDowell, he successfully relieved Milroy and conducted a retreat in the face of superior numbers, but at Cross Keys he was timid when he needed to be aggressive. This resulted from his inability to understand the shifting fortunes of the battlefield. Schenck's lack of military experience served as the primary reason for this mistake.

As the Confederates whipped the various Union forces in the Shenandoah Valley, Generals Meagher and Sickles served as brigade commanders in McClellan's peninsular campaign. McClellan intended to land the Army of the Potomac at Fortress Monroe, advance up the peninsula, and capture Richmond. The first units of McClellan's army arrived on the peninsula in mid-March, and by early April most of the Army of the Potomac had disembarked. After a monthlong siege, the army captured Yorktown and the Confederates retreated to Richmond. At the beginning of May, the Union army followed.

McClellan reached Richmond in late May, drawing within five miles of the Rebel capital. Most of McClellan's army lay north of the Chickahominy River, which flowed to the southeast before emptying into the James River, as the commanding general sought to protect his communications on the York River Railroad. He positioned two corps in an exposed position near Seven Pines, south of the Chickahominy. On May 31, the Confederates attacked these isolated corps.

The Rebel attack fell upon the Federal Fourth Corps at Seven Pines, where a brutal battle ensued. Reinforcements soon began arriving, notably the Third Corps, containing Sickles's brigade, and the Second Corps, including Meagher's Irish brigade. Neither Meagher nor Sickles participated in the fighting on the first day. On June 1, Meagher's brigade served primarily as a reserve and saw little action, save to prevent stragglers from running away. Sickles's brigade, taking position north of the Williamsburg Road, became involved in the thick of the fighting. Sickles maneuvered his troops well, successfully carrying out orders to throw part of his brigade to the south side of the road, and ordered a charge that drove Rebel resistance out of a grove of woods. By the end of the day, he had recovered some of the Federal camps lost the day before. Sickles's strong performance earned the praise of Gen. Joseph Hooker, Sickles's division commander, who called the New York general a "gallant leader."[52]

The battle of Seven Pines forced McClellan to shift most of his army south of the Chickahominy River, but he left one corps north of the river at Beaver Creek Dam. McClellan remained confident and throughout June prepared to place Richmond under siege. By the last week of June, the general was ready to begin the final segment of the campaign. As part of this operation, on June 25 Hooker's division launched an offensive to capture an important hill, where McClellan hoped to place artillery for use against Richmond. Sickles's brigade played a prominent role in this engagement.[53]

Tactical mistakes characterized Sickles's performance during the battle of Oak Grove. Hooker placed Sickles's brigade on the right and the First Brigade on the left. Sickles advanced seven companies of skirmishers, but the First Brigade put out two full regiments. This meant that as the Union forces moved forward, Sickles's brigade fell behind. To make matters worse, as the brigade engaged the enemy one of Sickles's regiments panicked and fled, forcing the New York general to delay his advance as he rallied the broken regiment. After re-forming his line, Sickles pressed forward, forcing the Rebels back, when orders arrived canceling the offensive. Apparently, Sickles's problems alarmed McClellan, who stopped the assault.[54]

The battle of Oak Grove was the first engagement in the series of battles that became known as the Seven Days. The next day, June 26, Gen. Robert E. Lee, commanding the Army of Northern Virginia, in an attempt to break the siege and drive McClellan's army away from Richmond, attacked the exposed Union corps at Beaver Creek Dam. The Federals repulsed the assault and fell back to Gaines Mill, just north of the Chickahominy River. The attack unnerved McClellan, who already believed that the Confederates outnumbered him, and the next day he decided to retreat southward to the James River, thus abandoning his campaign.[55]

As McClellan made this decision, the Confederates attacked the Union position at Gaines Mill. One of the brigades sent to aid the Union defense was Meagher's Irish brigade, which arrived at dusk just as a Rebel assault broke the Federal lines. Forcing their way through fleeing stragglers, Meagher's men established a final defensive position and helped to rally parts of several retreating regiments. Meagher himself was drunk, having fortified his courage by consuming alcohol. The inebriated general, as one observer noted, tried to rally every soldier he met and even struck one "over the head with his sword, knocking him down." Fortunately for Meagher, this performance went unnoticed by his superiors and he escaped censure.[56]

Over the next four days, the Union army retreated toward Harrison's Landing on the James River, fighting battles on each day. Neither Meagher nor Sickles saw much combat. On June 28, the Irish brigade fought at the battle of Savage Station, but Meagher did not command the brigade during this engagement. For some unknown reason, he had been arrested, and the senior colonel led the unit. This arrest continued until June 30, when he resumed command of the brigade at the battle of White Oak Swamp. During this action, the Irish regiments guarded several Union artillery positions. As for Sickles, at Savage Station his brigade marched from one threatened point to another without actually engaging the enemy. Otherwise, his brigade spent most of its time protecting Union artillery batteries and supplies.[57]

On July 1, the Union retreat temporarily stopped at Malvern Hill, where McClellan established a formidable defensive position. Nonetheless, Lee ordered the Confederates to attack. Neither Meagher nor Sickles participated in most of the battle, but each provided assistance near its conclusion. Meagher's brigade took position on the Union left. As it arrived, one of Meagher's regiments struck the Southerners head-on while a second regiment hit them in the flank, forcing the enemy to fall back and allowing the Irish brigade to establish a defensive disposition slightly forward of the main Federal line. Sickles initially supported Union artillery, but his brigade eventually went to the relief of Gen. Darius Couch's division on the Federal right flank. Each of his regiments went forward individually to relieve one of Couch's regiments, leaving Sickles with little to do but direct troop movements and bring up ammunition. That evening, after repulsing the Confederate assaults, at McClellan's direction the Union forces abandoned Malvern Hill and retreated to Harrison's Landing.[58]

During the peninsular campaign, both Meagher and Sickles began to learn the ropes of command and performed effectively as brigade commanders, though each was guilty of mistakes. They demonstrated courage under fire and the capacity to rally not only their own troops but also soldiers from other units. Each conducted successful retreats in the face of the enemy. Meagher demonstrated tactical ability, as shown by the success that he had maneuvering his soldiers at Malvern Hill. Sickles had more trouble conducting his troops on the battlefield, exemplified by the problems that he encountered at Oak Grove. The Irishman, owing to heavy drinking, performed disgracefully at Gaines Mill. Consuming alcohol before combat was common among Civil War soldiers, for both officers and enlisted men, but at Gaines Mill Meagher was drunk and incapable of adequately commanding his unit. Overall, both of these generals showed that they could become excellent brigade commanders, though, at least in the case of Meagher, they demonstrated little capacity for higher command.

After the Seven Days, which ended McClellan's campaign against Richmond, the fighting in the East once again shifted into northern Virginia, as part of the Confederate army under Jackson moved northward to oppose a new Union army. In late June, following the Federal defeats in the Shenandoah Valley, Lincoln decided to consolidate the forces in northern Virginia into three corps (commanded by Frémont, Banks, and McDowell), placing them in the new Army of Virginia and putting Gen. John Pope in command. All three corps commanders outranked Pope, but only Frémont demanded to be relieved, complaining that his new position was "inferior to those hitherto conceded me." The Pathfinder must have been particularly galled by the fact that he was placed under a general whom he had previously commanded in Missouri. The War Department accepted his resignation.[59]

A West Pointer, Pope had little confidence in the political generals serving as two of his corps commanders, Sigel and Banks. Sigel, recently transferred from the West, succeeded Frémont, a fact that Pope regretted. He was aware of Sigel's lackluster performance in the West and feared that the German would fail in his new command. Even before the campaign ended, Pope came to believe that Sigel was "perfectly unreliable," but political considerations demanded that Pope retain him. Sigel also had little respect for Pope, commenting that the commanding general's strategy does not come "from sound courage or judgement, but from mere . . . desperation." As for Banks, Pope told the Massachusetts general that he had "great confidence" in Banks's "judgement," but Pope clearly had little respect for him, believing that the former politician lacked aggressive instincts. Throughout July, he chided Banks "to dismiss any idea" of retreating or "to await any attack of the enemy."[60]

During the month of July and into early August, Pope maneuvered his army in northern Virginia and by August 7 had most of it assembled at Sperryville, a few miles north of Culpeper Court House. Learning the next day of a nearby enemy force, Pope decided to advance upon Culpeper Court House. Pope and Banks's corps arrived at Culpeper Court House on August 8, but only one of McDowell's divisions also reached the town and Sigel's corps was nowhere to be seen. For some unknown reason, Sigel became confused while marching from Sperryville and asked Pope what road to take. This request bewildered the commanding general since there was only one road between Sperryville and Culpeper Court House and he could not understand Sigel's mixup, except for the fact, as he said, that the German was "slow and stupid." Sigel further infuriated Pope by failing to have his men prepare two days' cooked rations, so when he arrived at Culpeper Court House on the afternoon of August 9, his men were without food and, instead of going forward, had to prepare and eat a meal. Thus, the Yankee Dutchman would not participate in the battle fought in the afternoon, leaving Banks to engage the enemy alone at the battle of Cedar Mountain.[61]

On the morning of August 9, Pope issued Banks ambiguous orders, telling the political general to advance to Cedar Run, take up a strong position, and stop the movement of the enemy while determining their strength. He further told Banks to deploy "skirmishers if the enemy approaches and attack him immediately as soon as he approaches." Finally, Pope sent a staff officer to show Banks the ground "you are to hold." These orders made it unclear whether Banks was to hold his position while engaging only the enemy skirmishers, delaying the Rebels until reinforcements arrived, or attack the entire

Confederate force immediately upon making contact. Banks interpreted these orders to mean the latter.[62]

Banks took position with approximately eight thousand men, but made two mistakes that influenced the battle. First, he positioned his troops poorly, placing them behind a small stream called Cedar Run that was dominated by Cedar Mountain, a commanding terrain feature occupied by the Confederates. From atop the mountain, Rebel artillery could either support a Southern attack or pound Union troops as they advanced. Banks compounded this mistake by failing to properly reconnoiter the enemy positions. He failed to send out any scouts and made no effort to ascertain what kind of enemy force opposed him. Thus, he did not know that he confronted Jackson's corps of twenty thousand troops. As late as two thirty in the afternoon, Banks still believed he faced only cavalry, reporting to Pope that "no infantry seen and not much artillery."[63]

Despite these errors, Banks nearly achieved a victory. Throughout the afternoon, the armies lobbed artillery at each other and advanced snipers to harry one another. Around four o'clock, Banks decided to silence the enemy batteries and snipers and ordered a general advance. Unknowingly attacking superior numbers, Banks's assault on the Rebel center quickly stalled. Undeterred, the Massachusetts general ordered an attack against the Southerners' left flank. Banks used only Samuel Crawford's brigade, minus its largest regiment, in this assault, but it caught the Confederates by surprise and rolled up their line, causing panic among the Rebel ranks and threatening to break their line.[64]

Banks made another mistake by not committing any reserves to support this successful attack. By itself, Crawford's brigade could not sustain the assault, and when the Confederates regrouped and counterattacked, the brigade retreated back across the ground it had captured. The Rebels now attacked along the entire front, driving back the numerically inferior Union troops. At this point, Banks had no hope of achieving victory and should have retreated, but instead he tried to hold his ground by launching two separate unsupported assaults that the Rebels cut to pieces. After these failures, the Union army finally withdrew to Culpeper Court House. Only five thousand men remained in the corps.[65]

Responsibility for this defeat rested with many individuals. Pope failed to ascertain the size and intentions of the enemy and sent Banks forward with ambiguous orders and no reinforcements. Sigel did not arrive at Culpeper Court House on time and was unable to aid Banks. Primary responsibility rests with Banks, who once again performed poorly. He failed to properly position his troops, adequately reconnoiter the enemy positions, and reinforce a successful attack. Under the pressure of command, he did not handle his troops properly and never understood what was occurring on the battlefield. Perhaps the worst aspect of this affair was Banks's failure to realize that he had been beaten and how miserably he had performed. He was proud of his conduct and believed it was "the best fought battle" of the war. An officer in Banks's corps best summed up Banks's performance, calling the battle "about as great a piece of folly as I have ever witnessed on the part of an incompetent general." Regardless of his performance, Banks, because of the heavy casualties his corps had suffered, played no further role in the campaign.[66]

For the next two weeks, Pope maneuvered in northern Virginia, operating in the triangle formed by the Rapidan and Rappahannock rivers. The Union was withdrawing the Army of the Potomac from the peninsula to northern Virginia, a situation that the Confederates exploited by shifting the entire Army of Northern Virginia from Richmond to face Pope, seeking to destroy his army. Pope retreated behind the Rappahannock. For several days, he strove to prevent the Confederates from crossing the river while also seeking an opportunity to strike a blow.

On August 23, Pope ordered Sigel to march on Sulphur Springs and attack Rebel units reported to be there. Once again, Sigel moved slowly and did not arrive in time to prevent the Confederates' escape. Forty-eight hours later, Sigel followed this fiasco by failing to follow instructions owing to confusion over orders, leading Pope to rebuke the German general. On August 25, the two generals had an angry confrontation, during which Pope used "such offensive language that Sigel asked to be relieved." Pope refused, but, inexplicably, later that evening asked Halleck, now commanding the entire Union army, to relieve the Yankee Dutchman. Halleck, due to political reasons, could take no such action, and Sigel remained.[67]

In the last week of August, the campaign came to a dramatic conclusion. Lee sent Jackson's corps on a long march around Pope and into the Union army's rear, forcing Pope to retreat to Manassas. The Union commander hoped to advance quickly and destroy Jackson's corps, but Sigel moved so slowly that he delayed the entire Union army. The Yankee Dutchman took five hours to get his troops moving, and, though originally on the correct road, he then began marching toward the wrong route. This ineptness cleared the main avenue and allowed the rest of the Union army to begin marching toward Manassas. There on August 28, it discovered Jackson's corps.[68]

The main action began at dawn the next day, as Pope ordered Sigel to "attack the enemy vigorously." Attacking west against Confederate positions along a railroad cut, Sigel placed Schurz's (he recently joined the corps) division on the right, the brigade of Gen. Robert Milroy in the center, and Schenck's division on the left. At dawn, the commands formed lines of battle and advanced into the woods, engaging the Rebel troops. Schurz led the assault, pushing the enemy back about a mile and a half before the Confederates counterattacked, striking his center twice. On the second charge, two of Schurz's regiments broke and ran, allowing the Rebels to advance to the edge of the forest before Schurz brought up a battery of artillery that blasted the Southerners' flank and stopped their assault. On the left flank, Schenck's division also had trouble, advancing slowly until Rebel fire forced it to terminate its attack. Schenck did not bring his entire division into the battle and failed to make a meaningful contribution to the assault.[69]

At this point, reinforcements from the Army of the Potomac arrived. Sigel placed these forces in positions where they bolstered the Union line and provided support for a renewal of the assault. Sensing that an opportune moment had arrived, Sigel ordered his reinforced corps to attack, requesting that Gen. Phil Kearny support the offensive with his division. Schurz immediately advanced, meeting with initial success as his troops pushed the Confederates back to the railroad embankment and then swarmed over and captured the position before Rebel rifle and artillery fire brought the assault to a conclusion.[70]

The attack failed to dislodge the Rebels because Schurz attacked alone. Kearny refused to support Schurz's assault. Even though the two men had never met, Kearny disliked Sigel because, earlier that summer, the Yankee Dutchman had published a letter by Kearny in which Kearny criticized the performance of German troops. This act outraged Kearny, who considered Sigel to be "extremely arrogant." For his part, Sigel viewed Kearny "as a man of extraordinary egotism" who "disregarded the rights of others." The end result of this feud was that Kearny refused to obey Sigel's orders, leaving Schurz's division to fight alone against Jackson's corps. Schurz held out until two o'clock, when Sigel finally removed his troops from the line, replacing them with Gen. Joseph Hooker's division.[71]

The fighting resumed the next day, August 30, but Sigel's corps did not participate in the Union offensive. It remained in reserve until a Confederate counterattack struck the Federal army, which then began a precipitous withdrawal. Sigel's division played an instrumental role in the rear guard, helping to delay the Rebel onslaught and allow the Union army to retreat. During this fighting, Sigel's flank became uncovered when the division guarding it retreated, allowing the Confederates to strike the exposed flank. Schenck ordered his division to change front to meet the assault and then counterattacked, pushing the enemy back, only to run into a second Rebel column as it launched an assault. Schenck, in the middle of the fighting, attempted to rally his troops when he was wounded, forcing him to abandon the field. Shortly thereafter, Sigel realized the hopelessness of retaining his position and ordered his entire corps to retire, thus ending the second battle of Bull Run. The next day, Pope decided to retreat to Washington, a decision that Sigel protested, leading to one final confrontation between the two generals that ended when Pope reprimanded the German general for questioning his orders.[72]

Sigel performed ably during the battle, though in the days leading up to the engagement he again proved to be an inept general. He repeatedly moved too slowly, disobeyed or failed to comprehend orders, and disrupted the Union army's movements. Pope was right to ask that Sigel be relieved, though why he did not accept Sigel's resignation when the German general offered it remains a mystery. During the second battle of Bull Run Sigel operated efficiently. He placed his division in good positions, attempted to launch coordinated assaults, and capably handled the rear guard on August 30. The failure of his assault on August 29 lies with Kearny's refusal to follow orders. Sigel received no recognition for his fine generalship during the battle, probably because his overall conduct in the campaign was so poor.

As for Sigel's division commanders, each had their positives and negatives. Schurz demonstrated excellent command qualities, managing to launch a successful, unsupported assault against superior numbers. He handled his troops properly in this engagement and proved to be a courageous commander. Both Stanton and Lincoln personally congratulated Schurz, with Lincoln commenting, "I hear you fought first rate." Schenck again displayed too much caution on the first day of fighting and was never able to engage fully his division, contributing to the failure of Sigel's offensive. On the second day, Schenck fought ably as he attempted to stabilize the broken Union line with a series of maneuvers and charges, but the Rebels overwhelmed him. His wound served as a testament to his personal courage. Lincoln, shortly after the battle, promoted Schenck to major general "for gallant and meritorious service."[73]

After the defeat at Second Bull Run, the Union army retreated into the defenses of Washington, D.C., to reorganize, refit, and repair the soldiers' wounded morale. By the beginning of September, the entire Army of the Potomac had arrived from the peninsula and was integrated with the remains of Pope's army. Lincoln placed McClellan in command of the combined force and sent Pope to Minnesota to fight the Sioux. Two weeks later, McClellan marched out of the capital, moving northwest to confront the Confederate invasion of Maryland, initiated by Lee after his victory at Second Bull Run. Banks and Sigel remained in Washington with their commands to man the city's defenses. Marching north with the Army of the Potomac was Meagher, still commanding the Irish brigade.

On September 17, McClellan and Lee confronted one another at Antietam. Meagher's brigade, the second brigade of Israel Richardson's division,

Edwin Sumner's corps, participated in the fighting in the center of the battle, where the Union assaulted the Confederate position in the Sunken Lane. After crossing Antietam Creek, Meagher's brigade formed a line of battle, marched through a cornfield in good order, and, while under fire, crossed a fence, approximately 150 yards from the Sunken Lane.[74]

Once over the fence, Meagher intended to fire two volleys and then charge, but Confederate rifle fire stymied the advance. After exchanging a half-dozen volleys, Meagher finally ordered a charge. The Rebels repulsed this assault, but Meagher managed to maintain his battle line, and the soldiers continued to fire volleys until they ran low on ammunition, at which point the brigade retired to replenish its cartridges. This accomplished, Meagher again advanced his brigade, but was then thrown from his horse, disabled, and carried off the field. Meagher claimed that his horse had been shot, but several eyewitnesses reported that the Irish general was drunk and unable to control his animal.[75]

Meagher fought adeptly at Antietam, displaying great courage that won him the praise of his superiors. Sumner commended the Irishman, and McClellan singled out the Irish brigade for bravery, though he made no mention of Meagher. The Irish general handled his troops well under fire, maneuvering them over difficult terrain and sustaining a battle line against punishing Confederate fire. It seems likely that, as at Gaines Mill, Meagher had imbibed too much alcohol before the battle and lost control of his horse, resulting in his fall and retirement from the field. His conduct caused outrage among some members of the press, one of whom wrote that Meagher "was too drunk to keep the saddle." Irish newspapers defended his conduct. Once again, Meagher's drinking habits did not bring him an official reprimand, and he retained his command.[76]

The battle of Antietam forced the Confederates to retreat into Virginia and allowed Lincoln to issue the Emancipation Proclamation. Though the battle was a Union victory, the president believed that McClellan had failed to vigorously pursue the fleeing Rebels. Lincoln relieved McClellan and placed Gen. Ambrose Burnside in command of the Army of the Potomac. In mid-November, Burnside marched his army to Fredericksburg, hoping to cross the Rappahannock River and advance on Richmond before Lee could react. Speed was essential for this operation to succeed, but unfortunately miscommunication foiled the plan because no pontoon bridges were sent to Fredericksburg, preventing Burnside from crossing the river. As the Federals waited for their bridges, the Army of Northern Virginia took position on the hills overlooking the town.

On December 13, Burnside decided to launch a frontal assault against the formidable Confederate position on Marye's Heights, during which Meagher's Irish brigade played a prominent role. As the brigade formed at eight in the morning, Meagher went before each regiment and gave a speech, promising them that "I will be with you when the battle is the fiercest." The brigade then marched across the river (the pontoon bridges having finally arrived) and through Fredericksburg, all while under artillery fire. Once outside of town, Meagher formed his brigade into a line of battle and then ordered the men forward up the hill at double time. After passing through the remains of Federal units that had previously assaulted the Rebel positions, the Irishmen advanced against the enemy breastworks, only to be slaughtered by Confederate rifle and artillery fire.[77]

Meagher, despite his promise, was not with his brigade as the Rebels butchered it below Marye's Heights. As the brigade began its advance, the Irish general returned to Fredericksburg to retrieve his horse because, as he wrote in his report, of "a most painful ulcer in the knee-joint." Apparently, Meagher's injured knee prevented him from walking any great distance and made it impossible for him to lead his brigade into the carnage.[78]

Correspondent Henry Villard accused Meagher of cowardice, writing that Meagher's retreat "was nothing but a piece of arrant cowardice." Gen. Winfield Scott Hancock, Meagher's division commander, defended the Irishman against these charges, writing that Meagher had "a serious lameness" that made "it difficult to either ride or walk." No soldier of the Irish brigade criticized him. Once again, Meagher's conduct raised questions about his command abilities. If his injury was so serious that he could not accompany his brigade, then before the battle he should have relinquished command to another officer who could have provided the leadership the brigade needed during the engagement.[79]

The Federal catastrophe at Fredericksburg ended most of the active campaigning in 1862. Nearly all of those political generals who served under West Point–trained officers rendered satisfactory and at times excellent service. Some of them demonstrated that they could be effective combat generals. McClernand, Logan, and Hurlbut all fought well as division, brigade, and regimental commanders in the western campaigns, and Schenck, Schurz, and Sickles showed similar attributes in the eastern campaigns. At times these generals were erratic and made mistakes, but this was a reflection of their lack of military experience and not a serious problem as long as they remained under professional officers.

Only Meagher's and Sigel's records raised serious questions about their continued usefulness. Meagher's alcoholism impaired his ability to command troops in combat and provided evidence that he probably should have been relieved. When under the firm leadership of Curtis at Pea Ridge, Sigel made positive contributions to Union victory, but under Pope in Virginia he proved to be a liability. Only the continued political usefulness of both men allowed them to keep their commands, as Lincoln still needed to retain the support of both the Irish and the German constituencies.

The campaigns of 1862 demonstrated that giving independent commands to politicians who lacked military training was a recipe for disaster. Both Banks and Frémont performed miserably while leading armies in the Shenandoah Valley campaign, and Banks, while directing a corps under Pope but operating independently, suffered a second humiliating defeat at Cedar Mountain. Two other generals also had autonomous commands. Shields, acting on his own, technically won the battle of Kernstown, but the engagement was actually fought by a subordinate. Furthermore, Shields's actions before Port Republic contributed to that Federal defeat, and he managed to alienate most of the officers and soldiers in his command. Butler led the army during the operation against New Orleans, but played no direct role in the city's capture. He had become a political liability by the end of the year, when Lincoln relieved him from command in New Orleans over his controversial administration of the city. Butler's abilities in the field remained untested.

These various engagements should have illustrated to Lincoln how fool-hardy it was to give military amateurs separate commands. In 1863, however, the president would give Banks and McClernand important autonomous assignments. Despite his wretched performance, Banks retained Lincoln's confidence, as the president considered him to be "one of the best men in the army." As a result, Banks received command of New Orleans, replacing Butler in an assignment that was primarily administrative and political, but with orders to open up the Mississippi River. McClernand, using his political connections, convinced the president to back his scheme to lead an independent command down the Mississippi River to capture Vicksburg. Thus, in the fall of 1862, Lincoln placed the important mission of opening the Mississippi in the hands of two citizen generals.[80]

Lincoln rewarded several other political generals for their generalship during 1862. Schenck received a promotion to major general and command of the Middle Department, Sickles was promoted to major general and placed in command of a corps in the Army of the Potomac, and Hurlbut and Schurz also obtained promotion to major general. The president compensated these generals for both their battlefield experience and continuing political significance. All of these generals retained important political credentials and constituencies that Lincoln still could not ignore.

For three of Lincoln's political generals the war was over. Denver, who never saw any combat, resigned his commission early in 1863, primarily because of his opposition to the Emancipation Proclamation. In 1863, Shields also resigned his command. The Irishman had been criticized by some subordinates, and there was a consensus of opinion among officers and enlisted men that he was insane, and none of them, as one private wrote, "want an insane man to lead us." Although Lincoln promoted Shields to major general, Congress refused to approve the appointment, and Shields's political usefulness ended. At his own request, Lincoln transferred him to California, where the Irishman tendered his resignation during the summer of 1863.[81]

Frémont was the biggest casualty among the political generals during 1862. After Lincoln placed Frémont under Pope, the Pathfinder asked to be relieved from command, and the War Department granted his request. Despite his continued popularity among many Republicans, Frémont never received another command because Lincoln could safely ignore him for three reasons. First, he had given Frémont two chances to prove himself, and the Pathfinder had failed on both occasions; second, Frémont had voluntarily resigned; and third, the Emancipation Proclamation lessened Lincoln's need for Frémont, since the president no longer required Frémont's credentials as a supporter of emancipation. Thus, Lincoln gained no political benefits for retaining Frémont in command.

Finally, during the campaigns of 1862 conflict between West Point graduates and political appointees significantly influenced military operations. As a result, military operations began to suffer. In the West, McClernand and Grant had clearly come to dislike one another, though they still managed to work together. In the East, the hostility that existed between Pope and both Sigel and Banks influenced that campaign, as did the feud between Kearny and Sigel. This strife had a negative impact on the campaign and the battles of both Cedar Mountain and Second Bull Run. This growing conflict posed potential dangers for future operations.

CHAPTER 5

The Vicksburg Campaign

I n 1863, Lincoln's political generals played major roles in several campaigns. The most vital of these aimed at regaining control of the Mississippi River, specifically, the operations to capture Vicksburg and Port Hudson. Of the two, Vicksburg was the most important to the Rebels because of its size, position on a sharp bend in the river, and location astride two railroads that permitted connections between the eastern half of the Confederacy with the trans-Mississippi. The capture of this Rebel citadel by the Union would cut the Confederacy in two and deny to the eastern half essential recruits and supplies.

Though possessing great strategic significance, Vicksburg also held important economic and political implications for the Midwest. As long as the Confederacy controlled lengthy stretches of the Mississippi River, midwestern farmers could not ship their harvests down the river to market, a fact understood by all midwestern politicians and military professionals. The longer this situation prevailed, the more chance there existed for a political upheaval in the region that might seriously undermine the war effort. Opening the great river to commerce as quickly as possible was thus a major goal for Lincoln,

McClernand, Blair, Logan, and other midwestern politicians as well as Grant and Sherman.

With the political stakes so high, it was inevitable that bitter discord between professional soldiers and political generals would hamper the Vicksburg campaign. West Point graduates sought to control the operations against the fortress, contending that citizen generals lacked the training necessary to lead the campaign. Political generals sought to participate in these operations, realizing the political benefits that would accrue from taking part in such an important victory. Some of them had little patience and much contempt for West Point generals and, in the case of McClernand, hoped to command the army that captured Vicksburg. Lincoln did little to resolve the ensuing discord and inadvertently encouraged it. In the end, he supported the military professionals. Nevertheless, throughout the entire campaign, tension between West Pointers and political generals impeded the conduct of operations against Vicksburg.

In the fall of 1862, the offensive against Vicksburg was in the hands of Grant, who commanded the Union forces in western Tennessee and northern Mississippi. Grant was unable to undertake operations against the river bastion because his forces were spread out to guard the railroad and garrison important towns and cities, protecting them against Rebel cavalry raids. Furthermore, in September and October, he fought off Confederate attempts to recapture western Tennessee that also impeded any immediate movement against Vicksburg. These Rebel forces attacked Corinth, only to be repulsed and forced to withdraw.

Hurlbut played a minor part in Grant's efforts to destroy this retreating Southern army. Grant ordered Hurlbut to march to the Davis Bridge (spanning the Hatchie River on the Tennessee-Mississippi border) and prevent the Rebel army from escaping. Hurlbut arrived at the bridge by dusk on October 4, where he encountered Confederate forces. At this point, Gen. Edward O. C. Ord arrived and assumed command of the Federal units, relegating Hurlbut to a subordinate position during the engagement fought on October 5.[1]

As the battle ended, Ord was wounded and Hurlbut resumed command. He demonstrated both bravery and good tactical sense when he led a charge against the Confederate right flank that compelled the Rebels to flee the battlefield, but over the next several days he failed to vigorously pursue the fleeing Confederates and allowed them to escape. The reason for this failure was that, immediately following the battle, Hurlbut drank himself into a drunken stupor, stumbled across the battlefield, and challenged a teamster to a brawl. The general was thrashed and forced to spend the next day and a half in bed recovering from his "wounds." Demonstrating his unsuitability for high command, Hurlbut's incapacity prevented any swift pursuit of the Rebels.[2]

Fortunately for Hurlbut, neither Lincoln nor Grant learned about his disgraceful actions following the battle at Davis Bridge. Nevertheless, Grant was disappointed in Hurlbut's performance and entertained no thought of placing Hurlbut in another field command. Instead, Grant banished Hurlbut to Memphis, where he commanded the Sixteenth Army Corps, an administrative position that required no duties that might place Hurlbut on a battlefield. Quite simply, Grant removed Hurlbut from commands involving military operations because he lost confidence in the political general's abilities.[3]

As Grant stymied the Confederate offensive in northern Mississippi and turned his attention to Vicksburg, McClernand journeyed to Washington, D.C., seeking to gain command of his own independent operation against the Rebel fortress. His quest for this assignment began in the fall of 1861. At that time, the Illinois politician had sought the creation of a new military department "embracing the immediate valley of the Lower Mississippi," lobbying friends in Congress and sending to Washington Logan to discuss the matter with Lincoln. McClernand hoped to gain command of this new department, but these efforts failed because, as Logan reported, of "too much West Point controlling things." McClernand blamed the failure of this initiative on "a professional military jealousy of citizen generals" and became suspicious of West Pointers.[4]

Following the conclusion of the spring campaign in 1862, McClernand determined to speak personally with Lincoln about receiving an independent command. At the end of August, he obtained leave and traveled to Washington, D.C., stopping in Chicago to make a speech demanding the appointment of officers "on account of merits, and not because he is a graduate of West Point." McClernand arrived in the capital near the end of September and met with Lincoln and Stanton. At this meeting, the citizen general proposed to raise an army of sixty thousand men and lead them on an expedition down the Mississippi River to capture Vicksburg. In his proposal, the former congressman expounded upon the project's economic and political significance, reminding the president that the closure of the Mississippi had made midwestern agricultural products "comparatively valueless." The capture of Vicksburg would be met with "gratitude and joy" and end the political discontent brewing in the Midwest.[5]

Several other factors also weighed heavily in the proposal's favor. For one, it promised to raise a large number of new soldiers, something that was especially significant since McClernand expected to recruit these troops from among his Democratic constituents. Further buttressing McClernand's appeal was the simultaneous request from eight governors that Lincoln assign McClernand to "an independent command" in the Mississippi Valley. It is not known whether

McClernand arranged to have this petition made, but this political pressure certainly did not hurt his cause.[6]

Confronted with military stalemate in every theater of the war, a stalemate that the West Pointers seemed unable to break, Lincoln decided to back McClernand's proposition. Several factors influenced the president's decision. The former congressman presented a persuasive plan and argued it forcefully. The president also understood the political benefits to be gained from appointing a prominent Democrat to such a command. The appeal by eight governors undoubtedly influenced Lincoln, providing further evidence of McClernand's political standing. Finally, at this point in the war, Lincoln retained a favorable opinion of the citizen general's military capabilities, commenting that McClernand was "brave & capable."[7]

Lincoln, however, hedged his bets in the orders given to the political general. At first glance, McClernand seemed to have achieved his goal of an independent command, but the directives issued by Stanton and approved by Lincoln did not quite give him what he wanted. They authorized the former congressman to organize troops throughout the Midwest and forward them to several points along the Mississippi River that all lay within Grant's department. The orders then read that after "a sufficient force not required by the operations of General Grant's command shall be raised, an expedition may be organized under General McClernand's command against Vicksburg."[8]

These orders did not create a separate department for McClernand and placed under Grant's authority all of the troops he was raising. McClernand was authorized to undertake a river expedition only after Grant decided that he had enough troops for his own operations. Lincoln was not going to give the citizen general complete control of the campaign against the Rebel fort, primarily because he feared McClernand lacked the tact and patience to work with military professionals. These orders failed to state who was in charge of what. Although the orders stated that McClernand was to command any campaign on the river against Vicksburg, they did not state whether McClernand fell under Grant's authority. The former congressman believed these orders gave him an independent command and returned to Illinois to commence raising troops for his enterprise.

Gen. Henry Halleck grasped that these orders did not give McClernand a separate command, but feared that McClernand might seize on the orders' ambiguity to create a new command. Halleck detested political generals. The appointment of "incompetent and corrupt politicians," he believed, had "almost ruined the Army, and . . . will soon ruin the country." To prevent this, he swore "to do all in my power to sustain the military officers against this political pressure." Assigning McClernand to command of the Vicksburg campaign disgusted him, for he viewed the former congressman as another incompetent citizen general, wholly unfit to lead such an operation. The problem facing Halleck was how to prevent the political general from assuming his command without offending the president.[9]

The occasion presented itself in early November when Grant asked whether he had authority over the regiments being raised by McClernand. Halleck jumped at the opportunity to derail the political general's appointment, telegraphing Grant that "you have command of all troops sent to your Dept., and have permission to fight the enemy when you please." By telling Grant, who hoped to undertake an overland campaign against Vicksburg, to ignore McClernand and proceed with his plan, Halleck sought to capture the river citadel before the political general could undertake the campaign approved by Lincoln.[10]

Grant immediately moved to carry out his operation, hastily preparing to move south from Oxford, Mississippi, where his army was encamped. Speed was essential. Grant, like Halleck, hoped to capture the city before McClernand arrived because he had no confidence in the political general's military skills. After the war, he wrote that the former congressman had neither "the experience [n]or the qualifications to fit him for so important a position." Thus, Grant had no compunctions about undermining McClernand's proposed command, even if this violated the spirit, if not the letter, of Lincoln's intentions. Despite his efforts, by early December Grant's expedition, delayed by railroad repairs, had not moved south.[11]

At this point, Grant realized that a river expedition, probably under McClernand's command, was inevitable. In order to forestall this, Grant ordered Sherman, then at Memphis, to organize all of the troops in the city, proceed down the river, and capture Vicksburg. Grant promised to support this action by moving south from Oxford. Halleck approved all of these arrangements, perceiving correctly that if successful they would prevent McClernand from exercising any command over the operations against Vicksburg. These actions clearly violated Lincoln's orders, but the West Pointers, determined to prevent McClernand from participating in the campaign, paid no heed to such considerations and went ahead with their plans.[12]

Though unaware of what Halleck and Grant were doing, McClernand feared that he was about to lose his independent command. At the end of November, McClernand forwarded the last of the new regiments raised in the Midwest, but no orders arrived directing him to proceed to Memphis and assume command of his expedition. Growing suspicious, the former congressman turned to his political allies for help. He wrote letters to Governor Yates and Senators Trumbull and Browning requesting that they inquire into the status of his operation. Browning talked with Lincoln and Stanton, and assured McClernand that no move had been made to supersede him.[13]

This reply did not put McClernand at ease, primarily because he still received no orders to proceed to Memphis. During the first two and a half weeks of December, McClernand sent two letters to Lincoln, three to Stanton, and one each to Halleck and Browning begging to be sent forward, but received no reply. Finally, on December 17, Stanton informed him that there was "no order superseding you," but then told the citizen general that the War Department was organizing all of the troops in Grant's department into three corps, with McClernand commanding the First Corps and assigned to operations on the Mississippi River. Stanton made no mention of an independent command, and these orders plainly and finally placed the citizen general under Grant's authority. McClernand ignored this significant omission and hurried off to Memphis to assume command of what he still believed was his independent campaign against Vicksburg.[14]

Lincoln accepted McClernand's subordination below Grant, though he ensured that McClernand acquired "the immediate command" of the river expedition. The president insisted on this arrangement after he heard rumors that "there was a combination to prevent [McClernand's] having that command." Visibly angered by this news, Lincoln said, "it should not be so," and received assurances from Stanton and Halleck that they had arranged for McClernand to command the river operation. As already related, Halleck and Grant conspired to prevent the political general from directing even this expedition, as Grant ordered Sherman to proceed against Vicksburg with the troops McClernand relayed to Memphis, an expedition that left before the citizen general arrived to assume command. Thus, Halleck and Grant had outmaneuvered McClernand and successfully prevented him from attaining an autonomous command.[15]

Sherman left Memphis on December 19, and Blair, commanding a brigade, accompanied him. Blair entered the army at the end of the summer and spent most of the fall recruiting troops for his brigade. Keenly interested in opening up the Mississippi River, Blair applied for assignment with McClernand's river expedition, a request that Lincoln granted. This assignment pleased neither Grant nor Sherman. Grant later wrote that he "dreaded" Blair's coming because he feared that the politician would interfere with Sherman's authority. Sherman, who had known Blair in Missouri, hated politicians and disliked Blair in particular.[16]

On Christmas Day, the expedition arrived at Milliken's Bend, Louisiana, and the next day proceeded up the Yazoo River to near the mouth of Chickasaw Bayou, where the troops disembarked. From there, Sherman hoped to move inland and fall on Vicksburg from the northeast. He expected Grant, marching south from Oxford, to support his operation by drawing off the main Confederate army, leaving Vicksburg vulnerable to his movement. Unbeknownst to Sherman, Rebel cavalry raids stalled Grant's advance by destroying Union supply depots and communications, allowing the Rebels to concentrate against Sherman.[17]

For two days, Sherman scouted the Southern positions on Chickasaw Bayou, and then on December 29 he attacked the strong Confederate trenches. Blair led his brigade, which was attached to Gen. George W. Morgan's division, against the Rebel right flank. After sending out skirmishers, Blair moved the brigade forward, struggling through heavy timber, cottonwoods, and a large pool of water and up a steep bank. The political general managed to get his men through these barriers and then formed his brigade into two battle lines. The brigade charged the Rebel breastworks and forced its way through the first and second lines, but the men could not carry the last line of enemy entrenchments. Realizing that further effort was useless, Blair halted the assault.[18]

The frontal attack was a complete failure, ending Sherman's attempt to capture Vicksburg, though Blair did fight well and received praise for his efforts. Blair led his brigade through extremely difficult terrain, kept it together, and then formed it into a battle line in the face of Confederate fire. His assault failed due to the strength of the Rebel positions, not through any fault of his own. Gen. Frederick Steele, Blair's division commander, praised the citizen general for leading his brigade "with intrepidity," and, early in the spring, the congressman was rewarded with command of a division.[19]

Blair refused to accept the defeat and sought to find a scapegoat. In a private letter to his brother, Frank complained that the "troops were rushed into the fight" and the army attacked with "divided forces and incompetent commanders." He directed his anger at Morgan. In a letter to his father, Blair accused Morgan of "skulking," and in his official report he claimed that Morgan failed to adequately scout the region and thus missed a road that, if discovered before the battle, would have allowed the Union forces to strike the Confederate flank and perhaps win the day. Both Morgan and Sherman denied this charge, asserting that they knew about the road before the battle and that it provided no military advantage for the Union. This dispute signaled the beginning of a controversy between Sherman and Blair.[20]

Sherman's failure to capture Vicksburg derailed Halleck and Grant's plans to deny McClernand an independent command. On January 2, 1863, McClernand arrived at the Yazoo River and, as the ranking officer, assumed command of the river expedition. Publicly, Sherman submitted gracefully, but in private he complained that "it was simply absurd to supercede [*sic*] me by McClernand." At a meeting held on January 3 with Adm. David Porter (commanding the naval forces), Sherman proposed that the expedition steam northward and attack Arkansas Post, a Confederate fort on the Arkansas River that threatened Union commerce and communications. McClernand understood the importance of reducing this fortress and agreed to the proposal. During the conference, a confrontation occurred between the former congressman and Porter. Just what caused this showdown remains obscure, and the meeting concluded with no punches being thrown, though it was clear that neither Porter nor Sherman had much respect for McClernand.[21]

Shortly thereafter, the Union fleet steamed up the Mississippi toward Arkansas Post. On January 8, McClernand sent Grant a dispatch explaining the reasons that this expedition was being undertaken. Due to communication difficulties, Grant did not receive the dispatch until January 11, the same day that the Federal forces attacked the fort.[22]

Now in charge of an operation, McClernand efficiently accomplished his goal. On January 10, after ascending the Arkansas River to the fort, the troops disembarked and, after reconnoitering the area, invested the post. The next day, the Federal attack commenced. After a thirty-minute naval bombardment, Union infantry stormed the Rebel works. The fighting was intense but never in doubt, as the combination of naval gunfire and numerically superior infantry overwhelmed the Confederate garrison, forcing it to capitulate after three hours of combat. Upon receiving news of the surrender, a jubilant McClernand shouted, "Glorious! glorious! my star is ever in the ascent!"[23]

The political general made few mistakes during this operation. He issued clear and precise orders and ensured that his army executed them properly, while carefully adjusting to changing circumstances. Despite his earlier confrontation with Porter, McClernand worked well with the admiral during the battle, a victory that resulted from the coordination of naval gunfire and an infantry assault. In private letters, Sherman claimed that he, not McClernand, deserved all the credit for the victory, but, though Sherman undoubtedly assisted the political general, McClernand planned the operation and ensured that it was carried out correctly. The former congressman deserved the credit for the victory, and praise was not long in coming. Lincoln told the citizen general that his success "was both brilliant and valuable, and is fully appreciated by the country and government."[24]

Grant, however, did not approve of an action that diverted men and resources from the primary objective—Vicksburg. When he finally received McClernand's dispatch informing him of the intended operation, Grant telegraphed Halleck that McClernand was off "on a wild goose chase." In response, Halleck gave Grant permission either to relieve McClernand or to assume

83

command of the river expedition himself. That same day, January 11, Grant wrote to the political general, voicing his disapproval of the operation and berating him for undertaking the expedition. He ordered McClernand to return to Milliken's Bend and resume operations against Vicksburg.[25]

This response shocked McClernand. Defending the operation, for which he took full responsibility, he complained that he had "anticipated your approval" of the victory "rather than your condemnation." McClernand then appealed to Lincoln for help, claiming that "the clique of West-Pointers" was oppressing "citizen soldiers" by depriving them of opportunities to command. Lincoln counseled McClernand to be patient and focus his attention on the capture of Vicksburg. Ironically, it was Sherman who calmed down Grant. Sherman, who originally proposed the attack on Arkansas Post, wrote to Grant, "We were compelled to reduce it." This letter persuaded Grant that the attack on Arkansas Post was not just a "wild good chase," and he dropped his opposition to the enterprise.[26]

The entire episode provided further evidence to Grant that McClernand was incompetent and could not be allowed to conduct the campaign against Vicksburg. In mid-January, Grant journeyed to Napoleon to review McClernand's situation and discovered that "there was not sufficient confidence" in the citizen general by either the army or the navy "to insure . . . success." Both Sherman and Porter begged Grant to replace McClernand. Grant realized that, though he had the authority, he could not relieve the former congressman outright because Lincoln still supported the Democratic politician, nor could he place another general in command because McClernand was the senior major general after Grant in the department. The only way for Grant to resolve the dilemma was to assume personal command of the river expedition, an action he took on January 29, relegating McClernand to command of the Thirteenth Army Corps.[27]

This act infuriated an already fuming McClernand, who still believed that he commanded an independent army. He decided to challenge Grant's authority. McClernand wrote two insubordinate letters to Grant in which he questioned Grant's authority over him and issued a formal protest against what he believed to be an unjust order. He sent copies of these two letters to Lincoln and asked the president to intervene. Grant countered by writing to the adjutant general, explaining that he assumed command because he lacked confidence in McClernand's ability to conduct the operations against Vicksburg. He also asked the president to resolve the dispute. Lincoln, exhausted by the constant bickering, refused to intercede and, in doing so, sustained Grant. When confronted with the question of whether to support a professional soldier or a political general, the president chose the former, signaling that his policy of promoting politicians had its limits.[28]

Throughout the winter and spring, the controversy between Grant and McClernand continued to simmer. McClernand bombarded Lincoln with letters critical of Grant, attacking Grant's current conduct of operations as well as the failed attempt to capture Vicksburg in December 1862. In March, the former congressman accused Grant of being "gloriously drunk" and offered to send the president more evidence of Grant's drunkenness. Lincoln did not respond to these communications, leading McClernand to appeal to Governor Yates. "The Republic is dying of inertia," McClernand wrote. "Can't you prevail upon the president to send some competent command?" Nothing came of this petition.[29]

Grant and the rest of his staff were aware of McClernand's machinations and often discussed in private McClernand's "intriguing." The commanding general characterized the former congressman's conduct as "highly insubordinate," but could do nothing about it because the political general enjoyed Lincoln's patronage. Nevertheless, by the end of April, it was clear that Grant and most of his top subordinates, including Porter, Sherman, and McPherson (both corps commanders), and John Rawlins (Grant's chief of staff), all distrusted and disliked the commander of the Thirteenth Army Corps. Furthermore, they managed to convince Charles A. Dana, an assistant secretary of war sent to report on Grant's operations directly to Lincoln and Stanton, that McClernand was incompetent. Throughout the spring, Dana's dispatches to the president and secretary of war became increasingly critical of the citizen general.[30]

The Grant-McClernand feud was not the only controversy raging in Grant's army between West Pointers and citizen generals. Ill will also existed between Sherman and Blair. In late January, Blair talked with several newspaper reporters, who published stories portraying Blair as the hero of the battle at Chickasaw Bayou, attacking Sherman's conduct of the operation, and also divulging sensitive military information. This incensed Sherman, who held no love for either newspapers or politicians. Sherman demanded that Blair answer twenty-two questions, essentially asking the political general to report exactly what he had told the correspondents, especially whether Blair said anything critical of Sherman. Blair replied immediately, admitting that he had met with the reporters but denying that he had censured Sherman or divulged any classified information. These answers mollified the corps commander, but in private he continued to describe Blair as "a disturbing Element."[31]

The only political general who aroused no animosity from the regulars was Logan, commanding a division in McPherson's corps. Logan worked well with McPherson and won the confidence of Grant, who considered Logan to be "brave, ambitious, and competent." Even Sherman called Logan a "good" soldier. In a letter to Stanton, Dana praised Logan as "a man of remarkable qualities. . . . [F]ew can serve the cause of the country more effectively than he, and none serve it more faithfully." Despite this praise for Logan, dangerous tensions existed in Grant's army between the military professionals and the political generals.[32]

In spite of the constant bickering, Grant continued to search for a solution to the Vicksburg riddle. His army was encamped northwest of the Rebel citadel in and around Milliken's Bend on the west bank of the Mississippi River. Vicksburg lay atop a high bluff that commanded a sharp bend in the Mississippi, making it impossible to attack the city directly from the river. Grant concluded that the best way to take the fortress was by assaulting it from the east, forcing him to find a way to get his army onto dry ground east of the city. He ruled out as politically unacceptable returning to Memphis and resuming the overland campaign that had failed in December. Throughout February and March, he attempted a variety of different schemes designed to bypass the fortifications. None of them succeeded. Finally, in April, he decided to march his army south down the west bank of the Mississippi River to a point opposite Grand Gulf, run the navy past the Vicksburg batteries, and then ferry his troops to the east bank of the river, placing them on dry ground south of Vicksburg.

Despite their differences, Grant chose McClernand to lead this operation for several reasons. One was practical. McClernand's corps was encamped closest to the only overland route down the west bank of the Mississippi River, making his corps the logical choice to lead the advance. Second, of all Grant's senior commanders, only McClernand supported Grant's plan. Sherman was critical of the proposed operation, describing it as "hazardous in the Extreme" and predicting that it "will fail must fail." McClernand resolutely backed it and lobbied to lead the advance. Finally, Grant did not trust McClernand and believed he could not leave the politician in command of the forces outside Vicksburg while he took part of the army south. Grant could trust Sherman, despite his opposition to the plan, to watch over Vicksburg. As a result of these reasons, Grant gave McClernand command of the operation, though he intended to watch his subordinate closely.[33]

Grand Gulf proved too strong for the navy to assault, forcing Grant to march farther south to Bruinsburg, where on April 30 McClernand's corps crossed over to the east bank of the Mississippi River. The landing proceeded without any major difficulties, but a series of events occurred in the days before it that led Dana to castigate McClernand in his dispatches. On April 25, confusion among McClernand's staff caused a slight delay in the march southward. On April 26, the citizen general occasioned further delays so his wife, her servants, and her baggage could be brought up, in direct violation of Grant's orders that officers leave their baggage behind. That same day he held a review for Governor Yates, complete with speeches from the two politicians, a mock battle, and a fifteen-gun artillery salute, fired in violation of another order issued by Grant to use no ammunition except against the enemy. These delays infuriated Grant.[34]

Upon debarking at Bruinsburg, McClernand advanced northeast against Port Gibson, a small town that commanded Grand Gulf's communications and held a bridge spanning the Bayou Pierre. On May 1, McClernand encountered a Confederate army of seven thousand men defending the two roads leading into Port Gibson and holding strong defensive positions on a series of ridges divided by ravines. McClernand sent one division down the Bruinsburg Road, ordering it to strike the Rebels' right flank, while he directed the units on the Rodney Road assaulting the Confederate left flank at Magnolia Church. At ten in the morning, after massing two divisions, McClernand attacked and drove the Rebels from their position at the church.[35]

Dense terrain slowed the Union advance, and it was not until the early afternoon that McClernand encountered the Confederates' new position atop another ridge. Blindly moving up this rise, the Federal troops received a blast of Rebel canister that staggered the Union line. A firefight broke out that lasted for about ninety minutes, during which time McClernand continually requested reinforcements, leading Grant to send a brigade from McPherson's corps. At two o'clock, the former congressman concentrated three and a half divisions, about sixteen thousand men, on a front of only eight hundred yards, and ordered a frontal assault. Despite this massing of troops, the attack floundered through the underbrush and made only slow progress against the Rebel defenders. Finally, shortly after four o'clock, the Union force overwhelmed the Southerners and forced them to flee the field.[36]

As McClernand drove the Rebels on the Rodney Road, the Union advance up the Bruinsburg Road ran into trouble. For five hours, the lone division McClernand assigned to the task of striking the Confederate right flank struggled through the woods and underbrush while skirmishing with Rebel defenders. Sometime after two o'clock, Logan arrived with one brigade, positioned it on the Federal left flank, and ordered the brigade to advance, dislodging the Rebels from their first line. Logan pressed the enemy, pursuing them to a second line atop a hill and ordering a charge that "drove the enemy in wild disorder from the field." The day after the battle, the Union forces occupied Port Gibson.[37]

The battle of Port Gibson ended in Union victory and secured Grant's bridgehead, a victory achieved primarily under the direction of McClernand

and Logan. McClernand struggled throughout the engagement. He had trouble maneuvering his troops in the difficult terrain and failed to properly scout the region and Confederate defenses. As a result, he never understood how large the enemy force was, allowed his troops to blunder into Rebel fire, and launched unimaginative, uncoordinated frontal assaults. Logan, in a limited role, performed much better. Immediately upon arriving on the field, he put his troops into a position from which they could inflict the most damage on the enemy and then aggressively pursued the Rebels until they abandoned the battlefield.

In the aftermath of the engagement, McClernand wrote Lincoln another self-serving note. He briefly described the battle, inflated the size of the enemy force, and claimed almost total responsibility for the victory. On the other hand, Dana, who made no report of the engagement, wrote in a dispatch on May 5 that if not "for the exceeding incompetency of General McClernand," the Union army would have captured "5,000 instead of about 700 rebels." More important, Dana's dispatches from late April led Stanton, almost certainly with Lincoln's approval, to send Grant the "full and absolute authority . . . to remove any person who, by ignorance, inaction, or any cause, interferes with or delays his operations." This order was directed at McClernand and served as a clear signal that Lincoln would not object to the former congressman's removal. Grant did not receive this directive until May 14 and took no action at that moment, carefully pocketing the order for use at a later time. In the meantime, he resolved, somewhat contradictorily, to closely watch and control the political general's future actions while refraining from meeting with McClernand in person unless absolutely necessary.[38]

Until the successful crossing of the Mississippi River, Grant intended, once he got below Vicksburg, to dispatch a corps southward to join with Banks against Port Hudson. Halleck expected the two generals to cooperate in the reduction of both Confederate river bastions, but, once across the river, Grant received word that Banks would be unable to reach Port Hudson before May 10. As a result, he abandoned his efforts to cooperate with Banks and resolved to strike on his own against Vicksburg. By doing so, he would retain both the initiative against the Confederates and, perhaps even more important, the command of the operation since, if Grant and Banks linked up, Banks would assume command of the combined army because he outranked Grant.

Grant determined to cut loose from his supply lines and move northeast into the interior of Mississippi, seeking to destroy the Confederate forces defending Vicksburg and capture the city. The main Rebel army, commanded by Gen. John Pemberton, was located between Vicksburg and Jackson, but Grant decided to ignore this army and strike at Jackson, where a second Rebel army was assembling. By doing so, he hoped to eliminate from the campaign one Confederate army, destroy Pemberton's supply depot, and cut off Vicksburg from outside assistance. Grant reasoned that the river citadel would then fall into the hands of the Union army.[39]

On May 7, the three corps of the Army of the Tennessee began marching northeast toward Jackson, with McClernand's corps forming the left flank, closely hugging the Big Black River. From this position, the former congressman's corps protected the army's left flank. Though the march proceeded smoothly, McClernand and Grant continued to snipe at one another. The citizen general whined about a lack of transportation that prevented his men from carrying all of the equipment they needed. An exasperated Grant pointed out that the Thirteenth Corps owned more than enough wagons and mules to carry the corps' equipment if the "officers, soldiers, and negroes" stopped riding on them. Despite this constant strife, the two generals managed to work together, probably because they rarely saw one another.[40]

On the morning of May 12, Logan's division, spearheading the army's advance, moved toward the town of Raymond. As his skirmishers advanced, they encountered a Rebel force of about five thousand men. Logan immediately ordered his lead brigade to deploy and attack, but the Confederates struck first, hitting the Federals as they attempted to organize themselves in dense undergrowth and throwing the Union troops into confusion. At that moment, Logan galloped up, rallied the staggered brigade, and helped to stymie the Rebel attack. Logan brought up a second brigade to form on the right and ordered an immediate advance, driving the enemy to a creek, where the Rebels took up position behind the creek bank.[41]

The Union troops moved across a wide-open field to engage the Confederates, steadily advancing against rifle and artillery fire. Finding cover behind a fence and timber, Logan's two brigades exchanged fire with the Rebels as the citizen general brought forward his third brigade, placing it on his right flank. For two hours, the battle raged. Then Logan, on the advice of an enlisted man, sent the Eighth Illinois Infantry onto a small rise on his left that flanked the Rebel position. The regiment arrived at this location just as the Twentieth Illinois Infantry broke the Confederate line. Together, the two regiments charged the enemy with bayonets, forcing the Rebels to retreat over the creek and allowing the rest of the Union line to surge forward and wade across the water. The Rebels gave ground grudgingly, but by three thirty they were retreating to Jackson.[42]

Logan once again demonstrated excellent command abilities during the battle of Raymond. His inspiring leadership rallied his troops after the initial Rebel attack, and he then displayed good tactical judgment. The citizen general committed two brigades to his attack, carefully keeping his third brigade in reserve until he discovered the Confederates defensive position and basic strength. Finally, he wisely listened to the advice of an enlisted man and placed a regiment on a key hill that allowed him to flank the Rebel line. After less than two years of service, Logan was growing into a fine combat commander.

Following the victory at Raymond, Grant pushed his army into Jackson. On May 14, he sent McPherson's and Sherman's corps into the city, where they routed the small Rebel army and destroyed railroad equipment and much of the city's manufacturing capacity. Next, Grant ordered McClernand to advance one division to Clinton and two near Raymond to demolish the railroad and guard the army's western flank. His fourth division, with Blair's division, which had been guarding the army's supply wagons, remained in the army's rear near New Auburn. This task required McClernand, whose corps was at Edward's Ferry confronting Pemberton's army, to withdraw in the face of the enemy. The political general easily accomplished this assignment. The maneuver was so successful that Grant later praised it, writing that McClernand withdrew "with much skill and without loss, and reached his position . . . in good order."[43]

The next day, after learning that Pemberton was marching to attack his rear, Grant ordered McClernand (with Blair's division) to advance toward Bolton Station. McClernand promptly moved forward and seized this town. For the rest of the day, the political general concentrated his troops on the three roads that ran west from Bolton and issued orders for the next day's westward movement to Edward's Station. New orders issued by Grant directed McClernand to advance toward Edward's Station and feel for the enemy. If he encountered the Rebels, the commanding general admonished McClernand not to bring on a battle "unless you feel entirely able to contend with him."[44]

Early in the morning of May 16, McClernand's corps marched west toward Edward's Ferry with one division on the northern road, two on the middle road, and two on the southern road. McPherson's corps followed on the northern road (Sherman's remained at Jackson). The Union forces expected to encounter Rebel forces, but the terrain—heavy woods covering ravines and hills perfect for defense—through which they marched made coordination difficult and necessitated a cautious approach. At seven in the morning, the lead units on the southern road encountered Rebel skirmishers, and a sharp engagement broke out, while a similar action occurred on the middle road.[45]

With two of his lead divisions now engaged, McClernand hesitated. Mindful of his orders not to bring on a battle, he ordered Gen. A. P. Hovey (commanding the division on the northern road) to "move forward . . . cautiously but promptly" and then sent messengers to Grant, who was accompanying McPherson, asking whether he should "bring on an engagement." After sending these dispatches, the former congressman connected his divided forces on the middle and southern roads and then, reluctant to exceed Grant's orders and initiate a major battle, sat down and waited for Grant's reply.[46]

As McClernand wavered, Hovey, advancing on the northern road, became engaged with Rebel units posted on Champion's Hill. Hurrying forward shortly after ten o'clock, Grant directed McPherson's two lead divisions, including Logan's, to move rapidly to the front, positioning Logan on the right of Hovey. Grant then ordered McClernand to support Hovey and McPherson, while reminding the former congressman to act cautiously, but he did not direct the citizen general to attack.[47]

Logan placed two brigades in line of battle, keeping his third brigade in reserve, and then ordered the division to advance. His two lead brigades moved across the broken terrain, driving the fleeing Rebel skirmishers before them. The division then encountered the main Confederate line. For several moments, a battle raged as the Rebels firmly stood their ground, but Logan broke the impasse when he ordered his entire line to charge. At the same moment, recognizing that the enemy's left flank was exposed, Logan directed his reserve brigade into line on his right flank, where it struck the Rebels' dangling flank. This combined assault on the Confederates' front and flank destroyed the Southern battle line and compelled them to withdraw. This success placed Logan across the enemy's only avenue of retreat, but the Union was unable to exploit this superb position because Hovey, pressed by Confederate attacks, called for reinforcements. Grant ordered Logan to move to Hovey's relief, uncovering the Rebels' escape route.[48]

As Logan and Hovey struggled successfully with the Confederates, McClernand continued to dither. Despite the fact that he commanded four divisions, he refused to seize the initiative and undertake any offensive action. McClernand realized that an engagement was under way to the north, but, facing forbidding terrain, an indeterminate number of Rebels in his front, and with orders directing him to act cautiously, he preferred to abide strictly with Grant's dispatches and not risk advancing into the unknown. At 12:35, Grant, upset with McClernand's inaction, finally issued explicit orders to the former congressman, authorizing him to attack the enemy and promising that McPherson's corps would cooperate with the assault.[49]

This directive did not reach McClernand until sometime after two o'clock, and the political general did not launch his attack until two thirty. At that time, McClernand's four divisions, including Blair's, moved forward only fitfully. On the middle road, the movement advanced slowly until the lead division encountered the Union assault descending from the north. On the southern road, the attack never transpired because the two divisions (including Blair's, but commanded by A. J. Smith) remained inactive until after five o'clock, when the Rebels were in full retreat. McClernand's assault occurred just as the Confederates began to withdraw, rendering the advance meaningless because, as one private wrote, the Rebel army "vanished before us like snow beneath the summer sun."[50]

The battle of Champion's Hill was a major Union victory that sent Pemberton's army reeling back toward Vicksburg, but the record of the citizen generals in the engagement was mixed. Once again, Logan performed brilliantly. He moved his division quickly into line and then made a series of superior tactical decisions that helped to secure the victory. Finally, his personal charisma and courage provided inspiring leadership. Blair played no role in the battle, as his division failed to engage the enemy, a result that occurred through no fault of his own but was the outcome of McClernand's hesitation and Smith's refusal to attack.

In his second battle as a corps commander, McClernand turned in his worst performance of the war. After the initial contact with the enemy, he essentially went into a shell and refused to demonstrate any initiative or imagination, following his orders to the extreme, despite the fact that he knew an engagement was occurring just north of his position. When he finally attacked, his assault was uncoordinated and developed so slowly, when it developed at all since McClernand failed to get all of his units into the battle, that it was useless. For all practical purposes, McClernand sat out the contest and thus missed a golden opportunity to destroy Pemberton's army. Quite simply, McClernand was proving to be an ineffective corps commander.

Over the next two days, the Union army pursued the fleeing Rebels into their defenses at Vicksburg. On May 17, McClernand's corps routed a Confederate rear guard at the Big Black River, captured an important railroad bridge, and defeated the last Rebel army outside of Vicksburg. Two days later, Grant's army completed the investment of the fortified city and moved into position for an assault. Grant stationed Sherman's corps on the north, McPherson's in the center, and McClernand's to the south. At two o'clock, the Federal army attacked Vicksburg in a series of uncoordinated and fruitless charges that failed to dent the city's defenses.[51]

Undeterred, Grant decided to attack again on May 22, hoping that a coordinated, carefully planned assault would carry his army into Vicksburg. Only McClernand objected to this plan. He argued that the Union army could not take the city if it attacked across a broad front, as Grant proposed to do. Instead, the citizen general contended, the army should mass its forces against one or two specific points, seeking to overwhelm the Confederate defenses at those points and break into the town. Grant rejected this advice.[52]

At ten o'clock in the morning, the Union infantry left their trenches and proceeded against the Vicksburg entrenchments. The attack was a bloody failure. In the north, Blair's division led Sherman's assault. A storming party of 150 men preceded his advance up a road that led straight into the Rebel defenses and managed to plant a flag on the outskirts of the Rebel trenches, but no one else got any closer. Confederate fire cut down dozens of men and forced the rest to falter and dive for cover. Despite the pleadings of their officers, the enlisted men refused to renew the assault, and Blair's attack limped to a halt. In the center, the attack of Logan's division fared no better, as his assault completely failed. By noon, both Sherman and McPherson had largely ended their attacks.[53]

To the south, McClernand's storming parties achieved several local successes. Parts of several of his regiments managed to carry "the ditch, slope, and bastion" of one fort and the first line of entrenchments in a second section of the Rebel line. Despite their gallantry, McClernand's troops achieved only limited and precarious gains that needed to be immediately reinforced if the Union army was to obtain a larger success, a fact that the corps commander understood. The citizen general had no reserves on hand to exploit the success. Throughout the early afternoon, McClernand sent a series of messages to Grant, who first observed the attack with McPherson and then rode on to Sherman's headquarters, asking for reinforcements. In these dispatches, he made clear that his corps had taken "part possession of two forts" and "gained the enemy's entrenchments on several points," but he did not claim to have taken any of the Rebels' forts. The political general requested that McPherson renew his assault.[54]

Grant hesitated to grant McClernand's request, believing that the former congressman exaggerated his success. While at McPherson's headquarters, where he received the first of McClernand's dispatches, Grant later claimed that he could see that McClernand had not taken "possession of forts," but he nonetheless sent one division to aid the Thirteenth Corps. Later in the afternoon, while at Sherman's headquarters, the commanding general received another message from McClernand calling for help. He scoffed at this message, remarking, "I don't believe a word of it," but Sherman lectured Grant that the message could not be ignored and must be treated as credible. If the assault were not renewed, then McClernand could claim that the attack failed because Grant refused to provide him with proper support, validating his claims that a West Point conspiracy was directed against him. Sherman offered to renew the assault.[55]

With Sherman's encouragement, Grant ordered both Sherman and McPherson to again attack the Confederate earthworks in support of Mc-

Clernand. These attacks, like those in the morning, also failed and did nothing to help the Thirteenth Corps, which was unable to exploit its earlier, limited successes. The day ended with the complete repulse of the assault and 1,500 Union casualties. The failure of this second assault convinced Grant that Vicksburg could "only be taken by a siege," and the army set about the business of accomplishing this task.[56]

Just why Grant renewed the assault when he did not believe McClernand's reports is a mystery. Neither Grant nor Sherman respected the former congressman and had no reason to believe him at this crucial moment. Yet on this occasion, both West Pointers inexplicably acted on the reports of a man they despised and distrusted. The best explanation was that Grant feared the political fallout if he failed to support McClernand. On May 24, Grant blasted McClernand in a letter to Halleck, writing, "McClernand's dispatches misled me as to the real state of facts, and caused much of this loss." This was not true, since McClernand never reported that he captured any forts, as Grant, in his official report, claimed the former congressman had told him.[57]

Nevertheless, Grant and Dana battered McClernand in their dispatches to the high command in Washington. Grant claimed that the citizen general "is entirely unfit for the position of corps commander. . . . Looking after his corps gives me more labor and infinitely more uneasiness than all the remainder of my department." Dana asserted that "McClernand's report was false, as he held not a single fort, and the result was disastrous." The next day, Dana telegraphed Stanton that McClernand "has not the qualities necessary for a good commander, even of a regiment."[58]

Despite his dislike of McClernand, Grant chose not to use this controversy as an excuse to relieve him. Instead, he decided to leave the former congressman in his current position until the siege concluded and then ask the citizen general to take a leave of absence. In the meantime, Grant determined to carefully watch McClernand and double-check all of his reports. The political general's military career with the Army of the Tennessee was essentially over.[59]

McClernand sensed that the controversy aroused by his actions during the May 22 assault threatened his position, and he attempted to secure support by writing letters to Yates and Lincoln. His letters glorified his role in the campaign, arguing that the success of the operation rested on the actions of himself and his corps. In a letter to Yates that the *New York Times* later published, he described in great detail the role played by his corps in the assault of May 22 and warned the governor that Yates was certain to hear "rumors which would fix upon me the responsibility of the failure of the assault." These rumors are, McClernand claimed, "the spawn of petty, prejudiced partisans." To Lincoln, he defended his actions during the May 22 attack and implicitly cast blame for the assault's failure on Grant, writing that "the plan of attack was incapable of successful execution." Any rumor to the contrary, McClernand asserted, merely indicated "a disposition to shirk responsibility" for the failure.[60]

Finally, McClernand appealed to Grant in an attempt to defend himself. The tone of his letter did not help his cause. He complained that "a systematic effort to destroy my usefulness as commander" was under way and listed several false rumors that were finding their way up the river. These included reports that he attacked without orders, was to blame for the failure of the assault, and had been arrested. Then the political general bragged that, despite all of the obstacles, his attack was "in a larger measure more successful than any other." This sentence must have outraged Grant, but he offered no response.[61]

Neither Lincoln nor Yates replied to McClernand's letters, and events quickly made any response irrelevant. Early in June, McClernand, in a loud outburst in front of James Wilson, refused to follow one of Grant's orders. When Wilson told Grant of the citizen general's insubordination, the army commander resolved to "get rid of McClernand the first chance I get." The opportunity arose in mid-June when the *Missouri Evening Bulletin* and *Missouri Democrat* published one of McClernand's congratulatory orders. The order praised the accomplishments of the Thirteenth Corps while subtly indicting the other two corps for failing to do their duty.[62]

Even though publishing the order in the newspapers violated army regulations, nothing would have come of this incident if not for the hostile reaction of Sherman and McPherson. Both corps commanders responded with indignation, protesting what Sherman called the "catalogue of nonsense—such an effusion of vain-glory and hypocrisy." The thrust of their complaints was that the order, as McPherson wrote, cast "insinuations and criminations against the other corps." The order and the venomous response it generated provided Grant with the opportunity to act on the authority granted him by Stanton and relieve McClernand. He previously held off doing so because Lincoln appointed the political general to command, but now, with "almost the entire army under my command" demanding it, he could no longer refrain from sacking the former congressman. On June 18, the blow fell when Grant dismissed McClernand and directed him to report to Illinois.[63]

Grant was justified in dismissing the political general. Although McClernand recognized the political and strategic significance of Vicksburg and successfully captured Arkansas Post, as a corps commander he turned in a barely adequate performance. He continued to provide courageous and inspiring leadership and exhibit good tactical sense, as exemplified by his objections to Grant's May 22 assault plan. On the other hand, the citizen general struggled with the complexity of his assignment, demonstrating a marked inability to maneuver such a large body of troops in combat and acting cautiously and unimaginatively at key moments. More important, he feuded constantly with Grant, Porter, and the other corps commanders in the Army of the Tennessee. He detested serving under Grant and working with West Pointers, feelings that he made no attempt to conceal. The West Pointers felt the same toward the Illinois politician, but McClernand actively worked to undermine Grant's authority. The strife this caused threatened to undercut Union operations, and it is one of the miracles of the Vicksburg campaign that it did not. Though the final reason for his removal was trivial, McClernand deserved his fate.

None of McClernand's protestations of innocence persuaded Grant to change his mind. As a result, the former congressman returned to Illinois. He tried to plead his case with Lincoln, asking the president to "hear me," and also solicited the aid of both Halleck and Stanton, demanding, "in justice, that I may be restored to my command" and calling for an investigation of the circumstances that led to his removal. He again turned to Yates for help, but the governor only asked Lincoln to place McClernand in command of Pennsylvania. None of McClernand's efforts bore any fruit. Lincoln refused to intercede, and Halleck and Stanton, acting under the president's authority, also declined to take any action. McClernand watched from Illinois as Grant took Vicksburg on July 4.[64]

McClernand's military career was not at an end. Lincoln allowed the former congressman to stew in Illinois for the rest of the year, but the president remained mindful of McClernand's political importance. Early in 1864, he reassigned McClernand to command of the Thirteenth Corps, then stationed in the Department of the Gulf, the dumping ground of discredited generals.

Ironically, one of the individuals instrumental in McClernand's downfall was another political general: Blair. It was Blair who brought to Sherman's attention McClernand's congratulatory order, a "most audacious & detestable string of falsehoods," as Blair angrily referred to it, and first demanded the latter's removal. By this point, the bickering between Blair and Sherman had receded because they both had come to respect one another. As Sherman wrote, "Blair and I are on the very best of terms."[65]

Even Grant, who originally feared Blair's assignment to his command, now held a high regard for the political general and, in late May, entrusted the congressman with an independent command. Grant sent Blair's division up the Yazoo to drive out any enemy forces in the region, strip the area of all its supplies of food and forage, destroy bridges, and make the roads impassable. Blair successfully carried out these orders. His command destroyed five hundred thousand bushels of corn and immense quantities of bacon, burned every gristmill in the area, confiscated and burned cotton, and drove into the

Union lines more than a thousand head of cattle. This was the last major action involving a political general before the surrender of Vicksburg.[66]

Both Blair and Logan turned in superior performances during the campaign. Blair, as a brigade and then division commander, showed ability as a combat commander, maneuvering his troops successfully and providing inspiring leadership. Logan was quickly becoming one of the army's best generals. As a division commander, he handled his troops extremely well, demonstrated excellent tactical ability, and remained an inspiring battlefield general. Just as important, both of these generals managed to serve under West Pointers, followed orders, and submerged some of their personal ambition for the good of the cause. The intense strife that existed between McClernand and the military academy graduates did not infect the relationship of Blair and Logan and those same officers.

Thus, Blair and Logan emerged from the Vicksburg campaign as rising stars in the western Union army, gaining the backing of both Grant and Dana. In his memoirs, Grant wrote of Blair that "there was no man braver than he, nor was there any who obeyed all orders of his superior in rank with more unquestioning alacrity" and that Logan "ended the campaign fitted to command [an] independent" army. Dana, in a letter to Stanton that Lincoln undoubtedly read, seconded this praise. He explained that Blair "is intelligent, prompt, determined . . . [and] a brave fighter." As for Logan, Dana was effusive in his adulation. He could not find enough superlatives to describe the citizen general, labeling Logan "remarkable," "heroic," "brilliant," "inspiring," and "splendid," and concluded by commenting, "Few can serve the cause of the country more effectively than he." Both of these political generals had bright military futures before them.[67]

CHAPTER 6

Battles
in the West
and the East

In 1863, political generals played key roles in four other campaigns besides Vicksburg. Banks received an independent command in Louisiana, where he undertook an important operation to open a section of the Mississippi River. In the East, Sickles, Schurz, and Wadsworth fought at Chancellorsville and Gettysburg, making significant contributions to Union defeat in one battle and victory in the other. Finally, at Chattanooga, Tennessee, Blair and Schurz both participated in the Federal attempt to secure control of that town. In these campaigns, once again those citizen generals who served as brigade or division commanders performed well, whereas those promoted to army or corps command failed, indicating that they were promoted above their capability.

In the fall of 1862, Lincoln decided to employ Banks in Louisiana and placed him in command of the Department of the Gulf. Two motives lay behind the president's decision. One was his desire to replace the current department commander, Butler, whose management of New Orleans caused a series of headaches for the president. More important, Lincoln intended to use Louisiana as a laboratory to experiment with Reconstruction, and he needed a commander whom he could trust to carry out his designs. The president trusted Banks's political skills and judgment. Thus, Lincoln assigned Banks to the Department of the Gulf primarily for political reasons.[1]

Political considerations in no way diminished the military importance of Banks's assignment, a fact that Lincoln made clear in his orders. Banks was directed to sail for New Orleans with ten thousand men. His first duty was "the opening of the Mississippi," a task the president regarded "as the first and most important of all our military and naval operations." All other field operations were secondary. To accomplish it, Banks was to cooperate with Grant, though no line of demarcation was made between their departments. In fact, the orders made it clear that Banks was the ranking officer and could assume authority over "any military forces . . . which may come within your command."[2]

Banks arrived in New Orleans in mid-December. He first sent troops up the Mississippi River to occupy Baton Rouge, a city that Butler seized following the capture of New Orleans but abandoned in August because he lacked the troop strength to hold it. Banks promised Lincoln that as soon as he consolidated his forces, he would attack Port Hudson and open communications with the forces operating against Vicksburg. He told Halleck that "whatever may happen we shall not be idle."[3]

Banks failed to follow through on this pledge. Intelligence reported that twenty-three thousand Confederate troops defended Port Hudson, causing Banks to cancel his plans to immediately attack the fortress. The Gulf Department contained thirty thousand Federal solders, but the former governor had to use a significant number of his troops to garrison forts, cities, and towns, leaving Banks with a small field force. Another problem was that most of his men were raw recruits who barely knew how to use their weapons and had trouble performing the simplest maneuvers. Furthermore, Banks lacked adequate numbers of horses, leaving him with only six companies of cavalry, and water transportation, making it difficult to convey a single division. Banks complained to his wife that he had "nothing that is required for the work expected of me." Several weeks passed before his army was adequately trained and organized.[4]

Adding to his difficulties was the complexity of the assignment. Upon his arrival in New Orleans, Banks discovered that he had to deal with a vast array of civil functions. These included the assessment of taxes and fines, regulation of charities and churches, conduct of trade, and working of plantations. The political general whined to Halleck that "the precise nature of the duties devolving upon me . . . were not explained to me in detail." As a result, Banks was unable to undertake any military operations throughout the winter of 1862–63 because he had to focus his energy on solving the other problems confronting him in Louisiana. His failure to promptly advance up the Mississippi brought a slight censure from Halleck, but the commanding general tempered this by admitting, "The obstacles you have had to contend with are not fully appreciated."[5]

In mid-March, Banks, working with Farragut, who commanded the naval forces in the department, finally moved against Port Hudson. Farragut concluded that the only way to cut the fort's supply lines was to block the Red River by running naval forces past Port Hudson and then patrolling the Mississippi River from above the Rebel bastion. The army's role in this action was to support the navy by demonstrating against Port Hudson. Banks failed to carry out his assignment. Leaving Baton Rouge on March 13 with about twelve thousand men, Banks arrived in the vicinity of Port Hudson at daybreak the next day. The political general proposed to demonstrate on the Ross Landing Road, a point clearly marked on his maps but reconnaissance conducted in the afternoon proved did not exist.[6]

After this, the Union plan unraveled. Banks successfully marched to Port Hudson's rear, but was not in position until five o'clock in the afternoon and was unable to bring up any artillery until late in the evening. To make matters worse, Banks and Farragut failed to properly communicate with one another. Banks assumed that Farragut would not attempt to run past Port Hudson until early the next morning, but at five the admiral informed Banks that he intended to run the batteries at eight that evening. The former governor realized that he could not be ready by that time and retired to his tent. As a result, Farragut's attempt to run past the batteries was almost a total disaster. Of his seven ships, only two managed to slip past Port Hudson, all of them suffered heavy damage, and one blew up.[7]

Responsibility for this fiasco lay with both Farragut and Banks: the admiral for his insistence on running the fort regardless of the situation and the political general because he failed to support the navy. This was a result of poor reconnaissance on Banks's part and dismal communication between the general and the admiral. On March 15, the former governor, lacking the strength to safely invest Port Hudson, marched away from the Rebel fort, a decision that cost him the respect of many of his men. "Banks will never do anything," one soldier griped. "He will conduct another campaign of glorious retreats as he did in the Shenandoah Valley."[8]

After spending ten days fruitlessly trying to contact Farragut, Banks returned to Baton Rouge to ponder his next move. Having failed to make any substantial progress against Port Hudson, the former governor decided to shift his attention to the west bank of the Mississippi River in order to destroy a small Confederate army, located at Fort Bisland on Bayou Teche, west of New

Orleans, command by Gen. Richard Taylor. Banks undertook this operation to find a route to the Red River by way of the Atchafalaya River and open communications with Grant. He intended it to be a quick strike and hoped to return to Baton Rouge as quickly as possible.[9]

By doing so, Banks disregarded his orders, explicitly decreeing that the opening of the Mississippi River was the primary mission, and committed himself to a program barren of any strategic significance. Even if he reached the Red River, the former governor still had to deal with Port Hudson in order to secure Federal communications. Any delay in attacking this fort just gave the Confederates the chance to improve the bastion's fortifications, and the Southerners took full advantage of the opportunity. Finally, the Rebels at Fort Bisland had only three thousand men and posed no immediate threat to New Orleans, but by moving west Banks gave the Confederates the opportunity to transfer troops from Port Hudson to more threatened areas, specifically Vicksburg. Gen. Edmund Kirby Smith, the Confederate commander in the trans-Mississippi, was delighted by Banks's decision, later writing that it was "one of the most desirable events of the campaign."[10]

None of these objections occurred to the citizen general as he approached Fort Bisland on April 12. Banks's plan of attack called for the former governor to strike the Rebel works, aiming to pin down the Confederates. A second division, commanded by Gen. Cuvier Grover, would embark on transports and then land in the Southerners' rear. Banks intended to crush the Rebel army between these two pincers. The plan depended on coordination between the two forces and sound reconnaissance, but potentially it could eliminate the Confederate army in central Louisiana.[11]

On the afternoon of April 12, the citizen general's army drove in Rebel pickets and took position within sight of Fort Bisland, using the rest of the afternoon to scout the enemy works. The next day, the Union troops skirmished with the Confederates, but Banks made no effort to launch an assault as he waited in vain for sounds that Grover's division was in the enemy's rear. Fog and a gunboat running aground delayed Grover's attack, but a landing finally occurred late in the afternoon, too late to attack that day. At daylight the next morning, Banks ordered an assault, only to discover that the Confederates had evacuated Fort Bisland during the night. Over the next several days, Banks pursued the Rebels farther into central Louisiana, covering fifty miles and occupying Opelousas, a move that opened the safe water route to the Red River.[12]

Knowing that he disobeyed orders by advancing into central Louisiana, the political general sought to justify his actions to his superiors in Washington. To Lincoln, Banks boasted that he had "completely" dispersed the Rebel army and claimed that "the Enemy cannot reorganize his forces, here, again." These statements were not entirely without foundation, since Banks's army captured eleven guns, one steamer, and large amounts of ammunition and other equipment; they destroyed the saltworks at New Iberia and confiscated three million dollars worth of property, including ten thousand bales of cotton, ten thousand head of cattle, and large amounts of sugar and molasses. He did not, despite his extravagant claims, destroy the Rebel army, but his troops captured one thousand enemy soldiers and chased the Rebels out of central Louisiana. The problem with this campaign was that, no matter how successful the outcome, it delayed the conquest of Port Hudson.[13]

At this moment, the political general should have resumed his operations on the Mississippi, but this did not happen. Instead, Banks continued his pursuit of the Confederates into northwestern Louisiana, advancing all the way to Alexandria, captured on May 7, and pushing his lead units west as far as Lawson's Ferry, a forty-one miles farther up the Red River. Seeing the Rebels scampering toward Shreveport, on May 10 the citizen general told Lincoln that he was contemplating seizing this town. A week earlier, he lectured Grant that the key to control of the Mississippi lay in western Louisiana and begged him to send a corps so "we can expel the enemy from Louisiana," an event that if successful would mean "Vicksburg and Port Hudson must fall." Banks was losing all sense of reality.[14]

The high command in Washington, from Lincoln to Stanton to Halleck, boiled over with rage when they learned of Banks's campaign, a rage expressed by Halleck in a dispatch sent to Banks. With barely concealed disgust, the commanding general wrote that he regretted the "divergent" operation to Alexandria. "If these eccentric movements," Halleck continued, "do not lead to some serious disaster, it will be because the enemy does not take full advantage of his opportunity." He concluded by reminding Banks that the "*opening of the Mississippi River* has been continually presented as the *first* and *most important* object to be attained"; all other operations "are only of secondary importance, to be undertaken *after* we get possession of the river." Banks did not receive this letter until after he had invested Port Hudson at the end of May, but it must have shaken him to read that his campaign elicited such harsh condemnation.[15]

After occupying Alexandria on May 7, the political general spent a week debating his next move. He determined that it was "not practicable for me to follow" the Rebels to Shreveport, but wavered between moving on Port Hudson and joining Grant at Vicksburg. Banks changed his mind on three occasions before deciding to move against Port Hudson. The final decision was made on the evening of May 16, when Banks received a report that the Rebels had evacuated all of their troops from Port Hudson save for one brigade. The former governor now felt confident that he could capture the Rebel bastion.[16]

Banks concentrated all available forces against Port Hudson, assembling an effective army of about fourteen thousand men and ninety pieces of artillery. On May 23, the Federals completed their investment of the fortress. Port Hudson's fortifications extended for four and a half miles in a semicircular sweep from the Mississippi River at Ross Landing, located below Port Hudson, to an impassable swamp above the fort. Though strong on their own, the surrounding terrain of thick forests and undergrowth made the works truly formidable. Any attack would have to proceed through this rugged terrain, making careful reconnaissance absolutely necessary.[17]

On May 26, Banks determined to assault the fort, but his vaguely worded battle plan almost guaranteed the assault's failure. It ordered the artillery to open fire at dawn. Banks then instructed Thomas W. Sherman, whose division held the Federal left flank, resting on the Mississippi River south of Port Hudson, and Christopher C. Augur, next to Sherman, to support this bombardment by taking "instant advantage of any favorable opportunity" to attack the enemy. The plan also directed Godfrey Weitzel, commanding a brigade on the right, north of Port Hudson, to attack while holding in reserve Grover's division, located between Augur and Weitzel, but Banks's instructions to Grover were unclear. The former governor provided no definite orders to Gen. Halbert Paine's division. Except for the artillery bombardment, Banks set no specific time for any division to advance, leaving this decision at the discretion of the division commanders, men who barely understood their role in the upcoming battle. Worst of all, the orders made no attempt to coordinate the assaults, meaning that Banks's attack could break down into a series of unsupported assaults struggling through unknown terrain, a recipe for disaster.[18]

The attack began as planned, but then descended into a nightmare as the individual assaults bogged down and Banks and his officers squabbled. On the right, Weitzel and Paine both attacked at ten in the morning, only to see their assault grind to a halt owing to the difficult terrain and Confederate rifle and artillery fire. Banks waited nervously for the rest of his divisions to attack, but he heard no sounds of battle coming from either Sherman's or Augur's direction. At noon, the citizen general rode over to Sherman's headquarters, where he found the division commander sitting down to lunch. Apparently, Sherman believed that he did not have to attack. Upon hearing this, Banks became furious and demanded that Sherman attack, but the division commander retorted that any assault would be suicide. Banks angrily left and, as he rode to his headquarters, decided to replace Sherman with Gen. George Andrews.[19]

The result of this scene was a series of idiotic, uncoordinated assaults that wasted the strength of the army. By the time Andrews reached Sherman's command, Sherman was drunk but still preparing to lead his division against the enemy works. Irresponsibly, Andrews allowed the intoxicated general to retain command, and he promptly led his men into Confederate fire that cut the division to pieces. Undeterred, Banks turned next to Augur, who was waiting for specific orders from the former governor before launching any attack. Augur's assault failed as well, and Banks directed Grover to throw his uncommitted division into the maelstrom. Grover's troops fared no better, and the cruel day came to an end.[20]

Thus concluded one of the worst-planned and -executed attacks of the entire Civil War, accurately characterized by one observer as "a miserable repulse" and "useless waste of life." Banks alone bears responsibility for this disastrous result. His failure to properly scout the enemy positions and poor planning were compounded by the foolish unsupported assaults he launched throughout the day. Banks's stupidity cost the Union 293 killed, 1,545 wounded, and 157 missing. The only bright spot that the former governor found on this miserable day was the performance of two black regiments, who charged the enemy works with great courage, though they too suffered heavy casualties. This was the first major engagement in which black soldiers participated, and Banks called their performance "heroic" and believed it "answered every expectation." Despite this, the assault demonstrated that Banks failed to learn anything from the reverses he sustained in Virginia. He made many of the same errors in Louisiana, including the failure to learn from his mistakes.[21]

Undeterred, the political general determined to attack Port Hudson again, bringing up reinforcements and siege guns to support the second assault. At eleven on the morning of June 13, the Union artillery opened a bombardment on the Rebel positions that lasted for one hour. Then Banks sent out a flag of truce asking the garrison to surrender. The post commander refused to capitulate. This answer confused Banks, who expected the enemy to surrender, and the citizen general wavered, uncertain whether to attack. Finally, at eleven thirty Banks made his decision and ordered an assault for the next day. These orders did not reach the various Federal units until after one in the morning.[22]

This decision disgusted the Union soldiers, who realized the folly of attacking after demanding that the enemy surrender, a demand that signaled Banks's intentions. One soldier commented that the surrender demand "looked to us like boys' play." Though the planning and execution for the assault on June 14 were better than for the earlier attack, the result was the same. The Confederates correctly guessed Banks's intentions, and the assault columns made no headway against the Rebel defenders. The action cost Banks another 400 dead and 1,400 wounded.[23]

Following this defeat, Banks settled in for a siege, though he still harbored hopes of launching a successful assault sometime in the future. It was fortunate that he did not because his troops had lost all confidence in him. The soldiers of a Connecticut regiment, after listening to one of his speeches, declined to cheer the political general, and the officers of the 173rd New York Infantry refused to go into battle under Banks. One soldier complained, "We are poorly led and uselessly slaughtered, and . . . the brains are all *within* and not *before* Port Hudson." The siege finally ended on July 9 when the Confederate garrison capitulated, primarily because they received word of the surrender at Vicksburg.[24]

Although Lincoln thanked Banks for the victory, the Port Hudson campaign ended in Union victory despite the presence of the Bobbin Boy. Though handicapped by the modest size of his field force, he nevertheless handled it badly. He spent too much time on a divergent and useless campaign in central Louisiana and then launched poorly planned, uncoordinated assaults at Port Hudson that needlessly bled his army, demonstrating that he possessed a poor grasp of both strategy and tactics. Equally important, he completely lost the respect of many of his officers and enlisted men, who viewed him as little more than a politician seeking glory at their expense. Banks was now a military liability for Lincoln, but political considerations, and the fact that he managed to capture Port Hudson, kept him in command.[25]

As the campaigns in the West secured control of the Mississippi River for the Union, equally violent and dramatic battles occurred in the East, during which political generals made conspicuous contributions. Following the disaster at Fredericksburg, Lincoln relieved Ambrose Burnside and replaced him with Joseph Hooker. During the winter and early spring of 1863, Hooker restored the morale of the Army of the Potomac and prepared to lead it against Robert E. Lee's Army of Northern Virginia. The Union force was encamped in and around Falmouth, across the Rappahannock River from Fredericksburg, where the Rebel army watched the Federals. Hooker realized the futility of conducting another frontal assault against this Confederate position. Instead, he planned a turning movement, intending to march three corps westward, cross the Rapidan River, turn south, ford the Rappahannock River, and advance eastward through the Wilderness to strike Lee's army in the flank.

On April 27, the campaign began that resulted in the battle of Chancellorsville. Hooker's turning movement proceeded smoothly, as his lead units successfully crossed the Rapidan and then marched south to the Rappahannock, forded on the evening of April 29. By May 1, Hooker had three corps in the Wilderness on Lee's flank, a force that was increased to five corps by the next day. Despite this success, Hooker refused to attack the Confederates and instead assumed a defensive position in the woods around the Chancellorsville House.[26]

The decisive events of the battle of Chancellorsville occurred on May 2 and directly involved two political generals, Schurz and Sickles. Schurz retained command of the Third Division in the Eleventh Army Corps, now directed by Gen. Oliver O. Howard, a West Point graduate who in early April replaced Sigel. Sigel submitted his resignation in mid-February, primarily because he felt that his command was too small for a general of his rank. The War Department did not accept his resignation, and the German instead took a leave of absence. He attempted to return in April, but Halleck ordered the citizen general to report to New York, ending his career with the Army of the Potomac. After Sigel's departure, Schurz temporarily commanded the corps and resented the promotion of Howard to this post. No overt hostility existed between the two generals, but Schurz did not respect Howard, characterizing him as "intellectually" weak, a man with "a certain looseness of mental operations, a marked uncertainty in forming definite conclusions."[27]

Sickles now commanded the Third Army Corps, having enjoyed a meteoric rise to corps commander. The New York politician rose from brigade to division commander by the end of 1862 and in March 1863 received command of the Third Corps. Though his military performance was not inadequate, Sickles owed his promotion entirely to the political support of Lincoln and his friendship with Hooker, who served as Sickles's division commander on the peninsula, corps commander at Fredericksburg, and drinking companion. As a result, Sickles was promoted to corps command over several higher-ranking generals. He quickly became Hooker's favorite corps leader and the only non–West Pointer in the bunch.[28]

During the opening operations of the campaign, Sickles's corps supported the demonstration against Fredericksburg while the Eleventh Corps participated in the turning movement, but by May 2 both units were positioned in the Wilderness. Hooker had five corps surrounding the Chancellorsville House. At the extreme western end of the line, holding the army's right flank along the Turnpike, stood the Eleventh Corps. Directly next to it, on the Orange Plank Road, was Sickles's corps and then the Twelfth Corps. The Union line then veered slightly to the northeast, where the Second and Fifth corps lay, with the latter's left flank resting on the Rappahannock River.

A major flaw in this disposition placed the Eleventh Corps' right flank in the air. It was not anchored against any natural barrier, nor did Hooker or Howard face any appreciable number of troops to the west. At the extreme end of his line, Howard positioned his First Division, commanded by Charles Devens, but only two regiments faced westward. Schurz's division stood next in line, and finally the Second Division. Except for two regiments, Howard's entire corps faced southward, a dangerous disposition since it opened the vulnerable right flank of the Union army to attack. As May 2 dawned, no one seemed concerned about this situation. Hooker inspected Howard's lines and pronounced the breastworks to be strong, but neither he nor any other officer feared that the Rebels might attack the exposed flank.[29]

Early in the morning of that fateful day, Lee decided to take advantage of this situation. The Confederate general reacted decisively to Hooker's turning movement, transferring the bulk of his army westward to confront the Union menace developing on his flank. In one of the war's great gambles, Lee decided to retain only a small force to oppose Hooker directly along the Turnpike and Orange Plank Road and sent Thomas Jackson with about thirty thousand men on a long march west through the woods and past the Union line. Jackson was ordered to strike the vulnerable Federal flank.

This movement did not go unnoticed by the Federals. The Third Corps' lead division pushed south about two miles to a small hill called Hazel Grove and late in the morning reported the movement of large enemy forces across its front. Sickles rode out to see for himself and observed a long line of infantry, artillery, and wagons moving off to the southwest, heading for either Orange Court House or Louisa Court House. Whether the Rebels were retreating or preparing to attack, he could not ascertain, but Sickles sensed that the exposed Rebel column made an inviting target. He reported this development to Hooker, also sending notice of it to Howard, and asked for permission to attack.[30]

This information convinced Hooker that the Rebels were withdrawing. He ordered Sickles to cautiously advance and harass the enemy retreat, hoping that the political general might capture the Confederate artillery. As the morning wore on, Hooker began to fear for his defenseless right flank. He sent a dispatch to Howard, warning the general to strengthen the vulnerable flank and send out pickets to scout for enemy movements.[31]

Within Howard's command, only Schurz feared that the Confederates might attack the Union right flank. Throughout the morning, Schurz received reports of the Rebel movement and rode forward, where he "observed them plainly" as they marched past his positions. Worried about the safety of the Federal flank, he proceeded to Howard's headquarters and discussed the situation with the corps commander, recommending that the corps form at a right angle to the Turnpike and place strong infantry and artillery reserves behind the line. Howard rejected this advice. He insisted that the Rebels were retreating and voiced no apprehension for his dangling flank.[32]

Shortly before noon, Howard retired to his tent to catch some sleep and left Schurz to tend to the corps' headquarters. Hooker's letter arrived shortly thereafter, and Schurz took it to Howard. While the two generals conversed, a staff officer delivered a second message from Hooker, essentially repeating the warning contained in the earlier missive, and Schurz and Howard argued about the importance of these documents. The German implored Howard to reinforce the two regiments guarding the flank, but the corps commander dismissed this advice with the comment that they "will have to fight."[33]

Schurz returned to his headquarters and decided to act on his own. He detached three of his regiments and placed them behind his line, turning them ninety degrees to face westward. The political general also ordered several reconnaissances to be made along the Orange Plank Road and into the wooded country to the south. Then he asked Devens to help him awaken Howard to the approaching danger, but to his astonishment he found this officer to be in agreement with the corps commander. Schurz did confront Howard one last time, but Howard refused to take any action. A sullen Schurz returned to his headquarters, hoping that his fears would not be realized.[34]

As Schurz worked to shore up the imperiled Union flank, Sickles moved to attack the Confederate column. He pushed forward two divisions, keeping his third division in reserve, supported by two battalions of sharpshooters, who engaged the enemy skirmishers and drove them back before encountering stiffer resistance at Catharine Furnace. At this point, Sickles demonstrated his military inexperience by calling for cavalry to pursue the Rebels. The terrain was heavily wooded and full of dense underbrush, making it completely unfit for cavalry operations. Furthermore, late in the afternoon Sickles reported that his movement had been a complete success because his troops gained the road and "poured a destructive fire on the retreating column of the enemy." The political general never realized that he engaged only the Rebel rear guard and that Jackson had slipped by him.[35]

Shortly before five thirty that evening, the soldiers of the Eleventh Corps were sitting down to supper when frightened deer, rabbits, squirrels, quail, and other wildlife suddenly burst into the Union camp. Right behind them came Jackson's troops. Caught completely by surprise, Devens's division crumpled under the weight of the Rebel assault. Within minutes, the fugitives of the First Division were pouring into Schurz's command, just as the German general was trying to change front in order to meet the oncoming Confederate wave. Schurz managed to turn about several regiments, but this line dissolved as the guns, caissons, and men of the First Division crashed through, closely followed by charging Rebel troops.[36]

There was nothing that Schurz or any other Union officer could do to stem the rout. What was left of Schurz's first line held for about twenty minutes, mostly because the Rebels advanced cautiously through the undergrowth, but was soon compelled to retreat. The minor changes Schurz fashioned in his line to protect against a flank attack made no difference, because the Confederates simply overwhelmed the three regiments he repositioned. With enemy troops overlapping both flanks, Schurz retreated to a shallow rifle pit. Here the Eleventh Corps made one last futile stand. Schurz tried to rally the confused mass of men milling about and lead them back into line, but enemy fire easily dispersed this formation. Two more such attempts also failed. This position quickly became untenable, and around seven o'clock the remains of the corps fell back to an area near the Chancellorsville House. The corps played no further role in the engagement.[37]

The flight of the Eleventh Corps also swept through the Third Corps. Frantic fugitives ran across Sickles's artillery park located at Hazel Grove, followed closely by Rebels. Using his only available troops, several cavalry regiments, the citizen general managed to create a temporary line that held off the Confederates until the majority of his infantry arrived at the point of battle and established a more secure position. The combination of infantry and artillery blunted the Rebel advance. The falling darkness ended Jackson's assault and allowed Hooker to establish a defensive line just west of the Chancellorsville House.[38]

Sickles, now holding the southern end of the Union line, ordered a night attack in order to recapture several cannons lost at twilight and retake the former Union position along the Orange Plank Road. Beginning shortly before midnight, the assault was badly managed. Attempting to strike northwest, a move that would have allowed Sickles to drive into the Rebel rear, the attack instead veered to the northeast. Units quickly became tangled together in the darkness and the dense woods, and only a few units reached the Plank Road. The bungled affair lasted several hours before Sickles finally called it off. As badly managed as it was, the attack did recover the lost cannons and ended any chance that the Confederates would renew their attack in the dark.[39]

As the sun rose on May 3, Sickles still retained control of one of the key points on the battlefield, Hazel Grove. From there, Union artillery could fire on the flanks of the divided Confederate army, but Sickles's position was exposed itself because only two regiments held the line that connected it with the main Union force. The citizen general grasped the importance of Hazel Grove and urged Hooker to hold it by extending stronger forces to cover the position. By this point in the battle, Hooker was a defeated man and had no desire to undertake any offensive actions. He feared that Sickles's corps was too vulnerable and ordered the citizen general to abandon Hazel Grove and fall back toward Chancellorsville. The Confederates took advantage of this movement by planting artillery on the important hill.[40]

For the next two days, Sickles and the rest of the Union army fought a series of defensive battles. Sickles first held a position at Fairview, but Rebel assaults battered his corps, drained it of ammunition, and forced it to retreat to Chancellorsville. Sickened by this second withdrawal, he begged Hooker to allow him to retake the lost ground, but Hooker refused to authorize offensive action. Instead, the former congressman marched his corps back to the fords near the Rappahannock River where it entrenched with the rest of the army.[41]

On the evening of May 4, Hooker held a council of war with his corps commanders, asking them to vote on whether the army should retreat across the river or stay and fight. Each general was allowed to express his opinion. Sickles, citing his lack of experience, refused to speak on the military aspects of the question and instead argued, on political grounds, that the army should withdraw. Citing the defeats in the fall elections and the growing Copperhead strength in the North, he reasoned that "it will not do to risk here the loss of this army." The final vote was three to two for fighting, but Hooker made the whole proceeding irrelevant by ignoring the poll and ordering the army to retreat. The army crossed the river the next night, ending the Chancellorsville campaign.[42]

The two political generals who fought at Chancellorsville turned in a mixed performance. Schurz correctly feared that the Union flank was in danger and tried to take steps to protect it, but Howard ignored his warnings and his efforts proved ineffectual. His labors to stem the rout on May 2 also failed, but by that time there was little that anyone could do. Sickles was aggressive but struggled to maneuver his units and made several mistakes that resulted from his inexperience. Overall, his actions during this campaign demonstrated that he was not ready for corps command because he lacked the training and experience to handle such a large body of troops.

Howard's Eleventh Corps was universally blamed for the defeat, with most of the criticism falling on the heads of the German soldiers and specifically on Schurz's division. The *New York Times*, whose reporter mistakenly claimed that the attack first struck Schurz's division, condemned the "cowards" for fleeing "almost instantly," and the *New York Herald* belittled their performance as "disastrous and disgraceful." Many in the army shared this opinion, as the derogatory phrase "I fights mit Sigel und runs mit Schurz" illustrated. The German general hoped to correct these abuses by having his official report published or a court of inquiry into his actions, but the War Department refused to allow him to do either. Because of this treatment, his standing among the German American public rose. In early June, they held a large protest meeting in New York City to defend Schurz and his troops, but this vote of confidence did little to improve the citizen general's reputation with the broader public or army.[43]

Following his victory at Chancellorsville, Lee decided once again to launch an offensive into the North. He cited several reasons that this campaign was necessary, but his major goals were to fight a battle of annihilation on Northern soil, destroy the military effectiveness of the Army of the Potomac, and achieve a negotiated peace. In early June, the campaign that culminated in the battle of Gettysburg began when the Army of Northern Virginia started moving north through the Shenandoah Valley. Lee then marched unopposed into Pennsylvania, shadowed by a Federal army that made no effort to attack because it preferred to remain between Washington and the Rebel army. Hooker still retained command but at the end of the month resigned, and Lincoln promoted George Meade to lead the Army of the Potomac. The general never had a chance to settle into his new assignment. On July 1, the two armies collided at Gettysburg, a small town in southern Pennsylvania where ten roads converged.[44]

The battle began at midmorning when Union cavalry encountered two Confederate divisions west of the town. The cavalry gave ground grudgingly until the First Corps arrived, commanded by Gen. John F. Reynolds, who directed the Union army's left wing, consisting of three corps (the First, Third, and Eleventh). Leading the First Corps' advance was Wadsworth's First Division.

At this stage in the war, Wadsworth had no combat experience. In the fall of 1861, he commanded a brigade and then throughout the spring and summer of 1862 the defenses of Washington, D.C., but in the fall of that year he temporarily left the army to run unsuccessfully as the Republican candidate for governor of New York. Following his defeat, Wadsworth returned to active duty and in December received command of a division. He participated in the Chancellorsville campaign, but his division saw no combat. Despite his inexperience, Wadsworth quickly won the respect of his troops. Lt. Col. Rufus Dawes of the Sixth Wisconsin Infantry later commented that Wadsworth was "an intensely practical commander" who looked "closely after details" and "the personal comfort of his men."[45]

Wadsworth immediately advanced his lead brigade to McPherson's Ridge, placing three regiments on the north and two on the south side of the Chambersburg Pike. As soon as these troops reached this position, a Rebel attack fell upon the Union right flank, forcing the regiments north of the pike to fall back to Seminary Ridge. At the same time, a second Confederate assault developed on the left flank.[46]

Just then, Wadsworth's second brigade arrived on the field, and Reynolds, moments before he was killed, immediately ordered these new troops to strike the menacing Rebel force on the left. This attack succeeded brilliantly, catching the Confederates completely by surprise, driving them off McPherson's Ridge, and capturing several hundred prisoners. On the right flank, Wadsworth brought up a reserve regiment and, with the two regiments originally posted south of the pike, launched an assault that blunted the Confederate attack and drove the Rebels back. Despite this success, Wadsworth, betraying his military inexperience, was initially confused by the action and, fearing that his position was about to be overrun, directed his division to retreat to Cemetery Hill. He quickly realized the folly of this order, stopped the withdrawal, and by noon was able to reestablish his original line on McPherson's Ridge.[47]

Shortly before noon, the Eleventh Corps arrived on the battlefield, under the command of Schurz because Howard, after Reynolds's death, assumed overall direction of the Federal forces at Gettysburg. Howard and Schurz surveyed the situation atop Cemetery Hill, south of the town. After receiving a dispatch from Wadsworth, who reported that the Rebels might be preparing to attack his right, Howard decided to hurry forward Schurz with two divisions to form on the First Corps' right, extending the Union line to Oak Hill, and keep the Second Division as a reserve atop Cemetery Hill.[48]

By two o'clock, Schurz's divisions were in position north of the town, though not on Oak Hill because the Rebels already occupied that prominence. Instead, the corps formed in an open plain at an obtuse angle to the First Corps, with the Third Division deployed on the left between the Mummasburg and Carlisle roads and the First Division on the right toward the Heidlersburg Road. Schurz's line was precarious because his force of only six thousand men covered a front of fifteen hundred yards. Worried about his puny command, the German general failed to ensure that his line connected with the Third Division of the First Corps and allowed a dangerous quarter-mile gap to form between the two corps. This line was characterized by Gen. Abner Doubleday, now commanding the First Corps and who also did nothing to close the gap, as "exceedingly faulty."[49]

To make matters worse, the First Division advanced without orders to secure a small hill known as Blocher's Knoll. Schurz originally ordered this division to refuse its right wing, but when faced with a fait accompli, he reluctantly directed the Third Division to extend its right flank to reestablish contact with the First Division. As Schurz later commented, "This made still thinner a line already too thin." Realizing that he lacked the strength to hold this position, the German general sent requests to Howard, imploring him to bring forward a brigade to reinforce the weak Union line.[50]

Before any response arrived, at three o'clock two Confederate brigades burst upon the First Division, launching an assault that struck the division's exposed flank. As the right flank collapsed, fighting engulfed the entire Union line. Schurz attempted to rally the First Division and prayed for the arrival of the requested reinforcements. After an hour of fighting, the Rebels turned the left flank of the Third Division, pushing right through the gaping hole that existed between the First and Eleventh corps and rendering the Federal position untenable. Schurz realized that his only option was to retreat and ordered his divisions to withdraw. As these units fell back, the brigade that Schurz had requested finally reached the field, too late to be of any use except to cover the retreat. This brigade temporarily stalled the Rebel advance, allowing the rest of Schurz's disorganized troops to stream through Gettysburg in a confused attempt to reach the safety of Cemetery Hill. The retreat was not quite a rout, but the Confederates still captured about fifteen hundred of the corps' men.[51]

As Schurz's corps collapsed, a similar event was transpiring on the left with the First Corps. Heavy, enfilading Confederate artillery fire compelled Wadsworth to withdraw the right of his division to Seminary Ridge, a position Howard ordered him to hold "as long as possible." At two thirty a Rebel assault pushed Wadsworth's left flank back to Seminary Ridge, where he attempted to establish a final defensive line. At this point, a little after three thirty, Confederate units, striking through the gap between the First and Eleventh corps, forced the First Corps' Third Division to retreat, exposing Wadsworth's right flank. As this occurred, other Rebel assaults overlapped his left flank and pressed down on his front. Faced with these threats, his ammunition exhausted, and no hope for reinforcements, Wadsworth directed his division to retire, following the rest of the corps in a movement that nearly ended in a rout and resulted in the capture of two thousand First Corps soldiers.[52]

The remains of the First and Eleventh corps retreated to Cemetery Hill, arriving at this position shortly after five o'clock. Wadsworth, his division diminished to about sixteen hundred effectives, placed his troops on the western slope of Culp's Hill, located to the southeast, next to Cemetery Hill. Schurz, reduced to command of the Third Division (it contained only fifteen hundred men), entrenched his troops on Cemetery Hill immediately opposite the town, where, as twilight descended, he watched the enemy movements and waited for reinforcements to arrive.[53]

During the night, three more corps of the Army of the Potomac, including the Third Corps, arrived at Gettysburg, and at one o'clock in the morning Meade reached the field. The commanding general decided to remain and fight at Gettysburg, taking position on the series of hills that lay south of the town. The hills formed a fish hook, with Culp's Hill forming the point; Cemetery Hill the bend; Cemetery Ridge, rolling gently to the south, the stem; and Little Round Top, at the southern end of the line, the loop. Meade placed Sickles at the left end of the line next to Winfield Scott Hancock's Second Corps, positioned on Cemetery Ridge, with orders to extend the Union line to Little Round Top.[54]

By this point in the war, Sickles and Meade did not like one another. Sickles viewed Meade as an overly cautious, stuffy West Point professional lacking in resolve; he was disgusted that Meade had replaced Hooker, especially since he believed that Meade held him in disdain for various unspecified incidents that occurred during the Chancellorsville campaign. Meade harbored a similarly unfavorably opinion of the citizen general, an estimate strengthened by several incidents that had occurred over the previous three days. On June 29, the Third Corps' train suddenly stopped, delaying the movement of all units in the rear, and the next day the corps marched too slowly to satisfy Meade. Finally, on July 1, Sickles, after receiving a message from Howard requesting help, angered Meade by marching from Emmitsburg to Gettysburg without Meade's permission.[55]

On the morning of July 2, Sickles surveyed the position that his corps was ordered to hold and did not like what he saw. The corps held the lower end of Cemetery Ridge, where the ridge tapered off before Little Round Top, forming what he later called a "hole." Sickles described the depression as "unfit for infantry, [and] impracticable for artillery" because of the presence of a swamp, boulders, and a forest that impeded movement and obscured visibility. Making matters worse, his line was twenty-two hundred yards long, but he possessed only two divisions consisting of twelve thousand men, rendering his force "a mere skirmish line utterly incapable of resisting assaulting columns." Sickles, convinced that the Rebels intended to launch an assault against the Union left flank, concluded that it was impossible to hold this spot.[56]

Just two thousand feet in front of him appeared a much more attractive location, a ridge some forty feet higher than the ground he presently held on which ran the Emmitsburg Road that commanded the ground both in front and behind it. Sickles believed it was dangerous to abandon this position to the enemy, since they would be able to place artillery on it that could fire on his vulnerable troops on Cemetery Ridge. The debacle at Chancellorsville, where Hooker relinquished Hazel Grove to the Rebels, obviously influenced Sickles's thinking and convinced him that it was necessary to occupy the Emmitsburg Ridge Road in order to deny this position to the Confederates.[57]

Determined to secure the Ridge Road, Sickles rode over to Meade's headquarters and asked the commanding general for permission to place his troops as he chose. Meade replied that Sickles could do so only "within the limits of the general instructions I have given to you." Meade did send Gen. Henry Hunt, chief of artillery for the Army of the Potomac, to look over the ground. Hunt agreed that the Ridge Road was a superb location, provided it was held by sufficient troops, but refused to give Sickles permission to occupy it. Only Meade could issue those orders. This answer did not please Sickles, who became worried after a reconnaissance reported enemy units moving toward the Union left. Sickles was convinced that he needed to act in order to prevent the Confederates from taking the Ridge Road. On his own authority and without bothering to notify Meade, Hancock, or anyone else, he directed the Third Corps to take possession of the Emmitsburg Road, an event that occurred in full view of much of the army shortly after one o'clock in the afternoon.[58]

Sickles's movement was foolish because it placed his corps in a vulnerable position. The corps now formed a V in front of the main Union line, with David B. Birney's division posted on the left from the Devil's Den to the Peach Orchard and Andrew A. Humphreys's division stationed on the right along the Emmitsburg Road. Although this new line possessed certain advantages, such as good ground for artillery and an excellent jumping-off spot for an advance, Hunt's evaluation was correct: it could not be held without sufficient troops, and Sickles's corps lacked those troops, being too weak to cover the ground by itself. The new line was twice as long as the one previously held by Sickles on Cemetery Ridge, a position he deemed too extensive for his corps. Now he defended an even longer line that was impossible for the Third Corps to maintain by itself.[59]

Moving forward created several other problems. For one, it left both of the corps' flanks in the air. On the right, Humphreys's division no longer connected with Hancock's corps, and a gap of about three-quarters of a mile opened between the two corps. Next, the extreme angle formed where the corps' two divisions came together at the Peach Orchard allowed well-placed enemy artillery to enfilade the line. Finally, by moving forward, Sickles abandoned Little Round Top, a key position that had to be held in order to secure the entire Federal line. Simply put, the political general blundered by advancing to the Emmitsburg Road, a movement that placed the Union position at Gettysburg in jeopardy.[60]

Shortly after three o'clock, an aide informed Meade of Sickles's forward movement, and the commanding general was not happy about it. Just then, Sickles arrived at Meade's headquarters to attend a conference, and Meade angrily ordered the politician to retire to his former position. At that moment, small arms and artillery fire erupted on the left flank, and Meade directed the former congressman to return to his command, promising to follow shortly. No major attack had been launched by the time Sickles returned to his corps, followed closely by Meade. After surveying the dispositions of the Third Corps, the commanding general told the former congressman, "I am afraid you are out too far." He ordered Sickles to withdraw to Cemetery Ridge, but just then a massive cannonade opened on the Peach Orchard. Realizing that an orderly retreat was now impossible, Meade told Sickles to maintain his position and promised to bring up reinforcements.[61]

A little after four o'clock, the Confederates, using nearly half of Lee's army, began an assault that fell on Sickles's exposed corps like a tidal wave. On the left flank, Rebel artillery pounded Birney's division, and infantry attacks threatened to overwhelm the line, forcing Sickles to send a brigade from Humphreys's division to shore up Birney's faltering line. Shortly thereafter, enemy assaults dashed against Humphreys's now weakened division, threatening to destroy the Union position. Fortunately, Meade fed reinforcements into the battle zone as quickly as possible, eventually sending units from five separate corps that allowed Sickles to maintain a precarious hold on the position.[62]

Sickles managed the battle from a farmhouse located in the middle of the V, but made sure to ride forward and inspect the battle lines. Shortly before six thirty, Sickles was returning from an inspection when an errant cannonball tore off his right leg below the knee, forcing the former congressman to be carried off the field. Sickles remained calm despite the searing pain, stuck a cigar in his mouth, propped himself up to demonstrate that he was still alive, and ordered General Birney to assume command of the corps. The Third Corps could not hold its position, and by the end of the day the Rebel assaults pushed the corps back to Cemetery Ridge and Little Round Top, from where the Union forces repelled the final Confederate attacks on the left flank.[63]

As the day ended, the Rebels launched assaults against both Culp's Hill and Cemetery Hill. On Culp's Hill, Wadsworth brought three regiments forward to reinforce the Union line and then offered encouragement to the men as he sat on a rock behind the breastworks. Just as darkness descended on the field, one last Confederate assault fell upon Cemetery Hill. Schurz gathered up two regiments, ordered the men to fix bayonets, and moved double-time to the endangered point, driving back stragglers with his sword. They arrived as Rebel infantry scaled the breastworks and fell upon the battery stationed there. Hand-to-hand combat ensued that ended when Schurz's infantry reinforcements pushed into the melee and drove off the few remaining enemy soldiers.[64]

The next day, the battle of Gettysburg ended when Lee's final assault shattered against Cemetery Ridge, though none of the political generals in this study participated in the third day's fighting. Sickles was in the hospital and played no further part in the campaign, but following the final attack both Wadsworth and Schurz expected Meade to launch a counterstrike to destroy Lee's army, an event that never occurred. Meade believed his army was too weak to risk an assault. Schurz was particularly angry over the failure to attack, later complaining that it was "one of those rare opportunities in war promising of great results," but because there was "no instant resolution the great opportunity was lost."[65]

Nevertheless, Gettysburg was a major Union victory that turned back Lee's last offensive into the North, but political generals engaged in the action turned in haphazard performances. Wadsworth fought well, maneuvering his troops expertly and providing inspiring leadership that helped to maintain throughout most of the first day the Union line west of Gettysburg, only retreating when finally overwhelmed by superior numbers. As for Schurz, he demonstrated bravery under fire, but on the first day he positioned his corps poorly, allowing a dangerous gap to develop between the First and Eleventh corps, and proved unable to control his division commanders. Schurz was handicapped by the small size of his force, but the result was another defeat for the Eleventh Corps. He partly redeemed himself on the second day, bringing forward reinforcements that helped to secure Cemetery Hill.

As for Sickles, he made a tactical mistake that nearly destroyed the Army of the Potomac. The Emmitsburg Ridge Road was a better position than the one he held on Cemetery Ridge, but Sickles blundered by advancing his corps there because he lacked sufficient troop strength to hold it. He compounded this error by failing to tell anyone that he was moving forward; thus, Hancock was not able to adjust his line to the movement, and Meade was unable to bring up reinforcements until after the Confederate attack began. The result of this egregious error was 4,211 Third Corps casualties and the near loss of Little Round Top, a disaster that might have cost the Union the battle.[66]

Another engagement in 1863 involving political generals was the struggle for Chattanooga. During the summer, Union general William Rosecrans, commanding the Army of the Cumberland, maneuvered the Confederate army out of southeastern Tennessee, forcing the Rebels to abandon the strategically important railroad city of Chattanooga and withdraw into northern Georgia. In mid-September, Rosecrans pushed after the Confederates, who turned around and attacked him at Chickamauga. The Army of the Cumberland was defeated and compelled to retreat to Chattanooga, followed closely by the Rebels, who laid siege to the town. In response, the War Department promoted Grant to command of all the troops between the Appalachian Mountains and the Mississippi River and dispatched reinforcements from both the Army of the Potomac and the Army of the Tennessee.

From the Army of the Potomac, Washington sent the Eleventh and Twelfth corps, under the command of Joseph Hooker. This pleased Schurz, who feared that his division, reduced to only 1,500 men, might be eliminated when the army was reorganized. On September 25, 1863, the Eleventh Corps left for Tennessee, arriving in early October. At the end of the month, the corps was at Brown's Ferry, just to the west of Chattanooga and across the Tennessee River from Lookout Mountain, a point occupied by the Confederates. In the early morning hours of October 29, the Rebels attacked Hooker's lead division at Wauhatchie, located in the valley west of Lookout Mountain. Hooker ordered Schurz to reinforce the threatened division, ensuring that the German general understood the directive by sending Schurz two dispatches and then summoning the politician to his headquarters to personally explain the order.[67]

Schurz quickly implemented his orders, marching with one brigade to the sound of gunfire. The brigade encountered little resistance from the Confederates, but problems developed in the rear, where Schurz's two other brigades failed to follow because of Hooker's interference. For some unknown reason, Hooker ordered both brigades to halt, and then compounded this error by sending a staff officer to direct Schurz to attack a hill next to the railroad gap. Inexplicably, Hooker still believed that the German general was marching toward Wauhatchie with his entire division.[68]

Despite Hooker's confusion, Schurz carried out his orders and captured the hill, assuming that the new directive meant "circumstances might have changed." Shortly thereafter, Schurz encountered Hooker, who was shocked to discover that the citizen general had not proceeded to Wauhatchie as originally ordered. A furious Hooker gave the German general a harsh tongue-lashing and again directed him to march to Wauhatchie. This farce ended when Schurz carried out these orders, arriving early in the morning.[69]

Although Schurz's division remained at Chattanooga, it played no role in the decisive battle fought in late November. On November 23, the division skirmished with enemy pickets, an event that summed up its service during the engagement, as Union commanders held it in reserve and allowed it to make no contribution to the Federal victory. In his report, Schurz accurately described his role: "nothing of importance occurred."[70]

Another political general at Chattanooga was Blair, and he too saw little or no action. Grant's promotion to command of all the Union troops west of the Appalachian Mountains elevated Sherman to command of the Army of the Tennessee. Sherman chose Blair to replace him as commander of the Fifteenth Corps, a selection Sherman made because he now viewed Blair as an "able, cool, brave man, somewhat loose and scattering, but nevertheless trustworthy." Blair marched the corps from Corinth to Chattanooga, but, while much of his corps participated in the late-November fighting, the political general did little himself, a circumstance reflected by the fact that he did not even bother to write an official report of his actions during the engagement.[71]

In the battles around Chattanooga, neither Schurz nor Blair distinguished himself. Schurz again fought well when given the opportunity, as on October 29 when he was able to overcome Hooker's ineptness and successfully carry out his orders, but was granted few opportunities. Blair handled his troops expertly and demonstrated a capacity for corps command; Chattanooga provided an easy test of his skills, as he was not called on to do anything particularly difficult.

In January 1864, one last event connected with this campaign occurred when Hooker published his report of the engagement on October 29, a report that damned Schurz for not carrying out his orders. This insult led Schurz to demand a court of inquiry. This time, the War Department granted his request. The court exonerated the German general, finding that he acted appropriately, a verdict that an exultant Schurz found to be "conclusive and emphatic." Despite the victory in court, this affair essentially ended the political general's career with the Eleventh Corps, since the acrimony it created between Schurz and Hooker made it impossible for them to serve together in the same army. In February, the German general went on leave, not to return again until the spring of 1865.[72]

The campaigns of 1863 demonstrated that political generals fought well and made important contributions to Union victory when not promoted above their level of competence. Those generals who remained in command of brigades or divisions—Blair, Hurlbut, Logan, Schurz, and Wadsworth—for the most part capably performed their duties. At this point, these men possessed fewer than two years of experience and were still learning how to operate military units. They were not ready for higher levels of authority. As division and brigade commanders, they served under military professionals who exercised an important level of control over them, allowing these citizen generals to gain experience without placing them in positions that they lacked the ability to hold. As the war progressed, some of them, though not all, might earn the right to command larger units, but at this stage they served most effectively as brigade and division commanders.

Citizen generals who commanded either an army or a corps did not perform well during these campaigns, illustrating that these men lacked the knowledge and experience to lead such units. Banks, McClernand, and Sickles (and Schurz for one day at Gettysburg) all found themselves promoted to positions of authority that their fewer than two years of service left them unprepared to hold. The result was Banks's bungled near disaster of a campaign in Louisiana, McClernand's barely competent record as a corps commander, and Sickles's inept tactical decisions that nearly ruined the Army of the Potomac. Good luck and some hard fighting prevented a catastrophe from occurring. These campaigns showed that at this stage of the war, political generals with no previous military experience were not prepared for army or corps command.

Nevertheless, political considerations kept most of these officers in the army. Because of his wound Sickles's career was over, Schenck resigned to take a seat in Congress, and Schurz went on a lengthy leave, but nearly all the rest of these officers continued to serve in 1864, commanding troops and making important contributions in the campaigns during the last year of the war. Democrats Dix, McClernand, Logan, and Butler and Republicans Banks, Blair, Sigel, and Hurlbut all retained important political connections that made it difficult to permanently remove them, no matter how badly they performed.

Political calculations, made on the eve of a presidential election year, even prevented two generals from voluntarily leaving the army. Meagher resigned as commander of the Irish brigade after Chancellorsville because the War Department refused to allow him to recruit new troops for his depleted brigade, but the army did not allow him to resign his commission. For the rest of 1863, Meagher languished in New York until, in 1864, Lincoln recalled the Irish general to service and sent him to Tennessee. He was too significant as a symbol of Irish commitment to the Union to allow him to quit. After Gettysburg, Wadsworth, disgusted that Lee had been allowed to escape, also attempted to resign. As with Meagher, the War Department refused to accept the resignation and, in the fall of 1863, dispatched Wadsworth to the Mississippi Valley to inspect black troops. By the spring of 1864, he was back in the East commanding a division. The administration could not afford to lose Wadsworth, who remained an important New York Republican.[73]

Finally, discord between political generals and West Point graduates affected the campaigns of 1863 to an alarming degree. The unrelenting conflict that raged between Grant and McClernand constantly interfered with the operations against Vicksburg and made it difficult for the army to function effectively. In the East, similar, if not as virulent, friction also existed, especially between Sickles and Meade, a relationship that was so strained that it was difficult for the two generals to communicate with one another. Fortunately, there were some positive signs. Logan and Blair both worked effectively with the West Pointers in the Army of the Tennessee, and Wadsworth and Schurz also coexisted with the military professionals in the Army of the Potomac. These examples indicated that many citizen generals and West Pointers could set aside their hostilities for the good of the Union cause.

CHAPTER 7

The Western Theater in 1864–65

I n 1864, political generals received commands throughout the western theater of operations. Banks directed an invasion of northwestern Louisiana along the Red River, and Hurlbut, Blair, and Logan all held commands in operations conducted east of the Mississippi River. During all of these campaigns, conflict between citizen generals and West Point graduates occurred, though not always to the detriment of the Union cause. Only Banks's expedition on the Red River ended in defeat, demonstrating that citizen generals who lacked experience or failed in the past should not have been allowed to lead troops on the battlefield. Some of these generals continued to make excellent contributions, proving that when not promoted beyond their abilities, political generals could become good commanders.

In February 1864, Hurlbut participated in Sherman's Meridian operation. Sherman planned to march east from Vicksburg with four divisions to destroy the railroads at Meridian, Mississippi, a move intended to prevent the Confederates from threatening the Mississippi River and free up Union troops currently guarding the river for use in future campaigns. Two of the divisions came from Hurlbut's Sixteenth Army Corps. This forced Sherman, against his better judgment, to allow the Illinois Republican to accompany the operation, since the political general desired to command his troops in the field. Sherman had little confidence in Hurlbut's military abilities, believing that the politician "is too easily stampeded by rumors," but was stuck with the citizen general.[1]

Sherman's expedition left Vicksburg and marched east on February 3. The advance proceeded easily because the Confederates in Mississippi were too disorganized and confused to react properly to the swiftly moving Federal columns. What problems the Union forces encountered, they created themselves. Hurlbut's corps, after spending more than a year in garrison duty, was not prepared for active operations and suffered from straggling. The corps commander and staff were undertrained and lacked the experience necessary to direct such a large body of soldiers in the field. As a result, the corps became stretched out, and on one occasion the corps' train stopped in the middle of the road for no reason, blocking all movement and leading Sherman to rebuke Hurlbut for failing to move his troops along.[2]

The columns overcame these problems, marched 150 miles, and successfully reached Meridian on February 14. Over the next several days, the Union troops destroyed the city's arsenal, storehouses, depots, and the railroad in all directions as well as cotton gins, hospitals, offices, hotels, and private homes. The city was reduced to ashes. The devastation completed, on February 20, Sherman's army marched back to Vicksburg, reaching the Union lines by the end of the month. Hurlbut performed competently during this expedition, but his lack of experience hindered the operation on occasion. Fortunately, the Federal troops encountered no resistance, and Hurlbut's inexperience never became a serious hindrance.[3]

Sherman now had no faith in the citizen general's military capabilities and, by early April, was trying to rid his command of Hurlbut's presence. Throughout March, Hurlbut, back in Memphis, failed to act aggressively against Rebel cavalry raids led by Nathan Bedford Forrest, who rode with impunity throughout West Tennessee. The politician's inability to stop the raids angered both Sherman and Grant, who were fed up with, as Sherman put it, Hurlbut's "apathy & fear to go out of Memphis to fight Forrest." Since Hurlbut refused to resign, Sherman attempted to take "the greater part of the Sixteenth Army Corps out from under General Hurlbut's control" by transferring parts of the corps to other departments. Finally, Grant relieved Hurlbut on April 15. In September, Lincoln returned Hurlbut to active duty, assigning him to command of the Department of the Gulf, an administrative position headquartered at New Orleans.[4]

As Sherman destroyed Meridian, Banks prepared for a major operation up the Red River. The genesis of this expedition lay with Halleck, who, as early as August 1863, was urging an invasion of the Red River country with the goal of capturing Shreveport, the Confederate capital in the trans-Mississippi, and occupying northeastern Texas. In January 1864, Halleck once again pressed Banks to undertake such an adventure. Banks, like Grant, Sherman, and Frederick Steele, the Union commander in Arkansas, all of whom would be expected to cooperate with Banks, remained lukewarm to the idea. Halleck managed to convince Grant, Sherman, and Steele to support his plan, forcing Banks to reluctantly agree.[5]

An expedition up the Red River promised strategic, economic, and political benefits. Strategically, a successful campaign would cripple Confederate power in the trans-Mississippi, capture the Rebel capital in that region, and give the Union a clear foothold in Texas. The economic and political reasons for the operation were even stronger. Northern textile mills lacked a sure supply of cotton, and as a result three-quarters of their spindles were standing idle, leading to unemployment and falling profits. This economic crisis became a political problem for the administration when Northern governors demanded that something be done to obtain cotton. The Red River country provided a solution because it contained thousands of bales of the crop. Thus, capturing this region would provide the North with a source of cotton and solve a political headache.[6]

Halleck, who conceived the operation and drew up its plan, entrusted its conduct to Banks and Steele. Sherman wanted to go, and Grant hoped he would lead the expedition, but since Banks, who outranked Sherman, intended on commanding himself, Sherman "thought [it] best not to go." He simply had no desire to serve under the former governor. As a result, the campaign was left in the hands of Banks, a political general who had proved on more than one occasion that he was not fit to direct such a campaign, and Steele, a West Point graduate and Mexican War veteran who earlier in the Civil War had demonstrated the ability to command larger troop formations.[7]

Once committed to the scheme, Banks threw himself wholeheartedly into carrying out Halleck's complicated plan. Banks, with seventeen thousand men, would advance northwest from New Orleans to rendezvous at Alexandria on March 17 with ten thousand troops from Sherman (commanded by Gen. A. J. Smith) and Admiral Porter's gunboats. The combined force would then proceed up the Red River to Shreveport. At the same time, Steele, with about ten thousand men, would march south from Little Rock, seeking to meet up with Banks, Smith, and Porter somewhere in the vicinity of Shreveport.[8]

Halleck's scheme suffered from a number of flaws that rendered it problematic and dangerous. First, no individual was placed in overall command of the campaign, leaving no clear lines of authority among the three army commands. Second, the distances separating Banks and Steele made it impossible for them to communicate, let alone cooperate, effectively. As a result, the Union forces would be operating separately along exterior lines, leaving them vulnerable to Confederate units who, because they were operating along interior lines, could mass against one of the Federal columns. Finally, although everyone was expected to begin sometime in the middle of March, there was no agreed-upon starting or rendezvous date, meaning that the Union forces would be moving toward an objective with no knowledge of when their support might arrive.[9]

From the beginning, this strategy bred trouble. For one thing, Steele dithered in Arkansas, failed to threaten Shreveport, and essentially took himself out of the campaign, allowing the Rebels to concentrate against Banks. Then a late start delayed Banks's rendezvous with Smith and Porter. On March 12, Smith and Porter advanced up the Red River to the Confederate stronghold of Fort de Russy, captured the fortress two days later, and arrived at Alexandria as planned, but Banks was not there. Rainstorms delayed the former governor's forces, the Thirteenth and Nineteenth corps under the command of Gen. William B. Franklin, while the political general remained in New Orleans to supervise the election and installation of a Reconstruction government. Banks finally arrived in Alexandria on March 19, and his troops filtered into the city over the next week.[10]

Banks lingered in Alexandria for more than two weeks to conduct elections in central Louisiana, hoping to buttress the newly installed government in New Orleans. A more important reason for the delay was the low stage of the Red River, which prevented the gunboats from proceeding upriver. Banks believed that the "fleet was as necessary to the campaign as the army" and refused to advance until Porter could move his boats. In order to do so and then continue steaming upstream, the naval vessels had to be lightened by off-loading the supplies they were carrying and constructing a supply depot at Alexandria to store them. This action not only delayed the Federal advance, thereby providing the Rebels with more time to concentrate against the Union forces, but also necessitated leaving four thousand soldiers behind to defend the town, reducing Banks's effective force to twenty-six thousand men.[11]

Finally, on April 2 Banks resumed the advance toward Shreveport. The army occupied Natchitoches, and the navy pushed on four miles farther to Grand Ecore. Unfortunately, Banks now made a crucial mistake that contributed directly to the failure of the campaign. The citizen general had to decide what road to use for his advance on Shreveport. Maps identified two possible routes.

One ran through barren country so far inland that the gunboats could provide no support, while the second, running along the east side of the river and easily supported by the navy, would require two or three more days to reach the objective. Banks consulted with his subordinates, but refused to reconnoiter the countryside to determine if a more practical route existed. This was an error, since a proper scouting of the terrain would have identified a third road that ran along the west bank of the river through an area full of corn and cattle. Unaware of the third option, the political general chose to advance on the inland route, arguing that it was "the shortest and only practicable road."[12]

Banks's decision carried with it grave dangers. The general himself accurately summarized some of the hazards, writing that the road passed "through a barren, sandy country, with little water and less forage, the greater portion an unbroken pine forest." Thus, the army had to carry all of its supplies. Furthermore, the rugged terrain provided few clearings where a large force could stop and rest, and there were no roads branching off from the main road. As a result, not only would the Union army have to push straight through to Shreveport, since it could neither stop for long nor move cross-country in another direction, but Banks would be unable to maneuver his large army or easily bring forward reinforcements if he encountered resistance. No one expected the Confederates to make a stand before Shreveport, so none of these potential problems troubled Banks, who only worried about reaching Shreveport as quickly as possible.[13]

On April 6, the final movement began, and Banks allowed his forces to become stretched out for more than twenty miles along the narrow road. Leading the advance was the cavalry division, commanded by Gen. Albert Lee, followed by three hundred wagons. Then came the Thirteenth and Nineteenth corps, under Franklin's command, seven hundred more wagons, and, bringing up the rear, Smith's two divisions. The wagons, all one thousand of them, or one for every eighteen men, carried ammunition, food, and other stores and added at least twelve miles to the Union column. It took one full day's march to move from the tail to the head of the Federal army.[14]

Lee, under Banks's conflicting orders "to attack the enemy wherever . . . [he] could find him, but not to bring on a general engagement," pushed ahead of the main column. On April 7, the first signs of trouble arose when Lee encountered unexpected resistance near Pleasant Hill. After a sharp skirmish that lasted about two hours, Lee's cavalry drove off the Rebels, but the appearance of Confederate forces frightened Lee, who requested infantry support. Banks agreed to provide a brigade of infantry.[15]

The next day, Lee continued on to Sabine Crossroads, where the road came upon a large clearing. As the Union cavalrymen advanced, they encountered opposition from eleven thousand Rebels under the command of Gen. Richard Taylor. Taylor had established defensive positions on the edge of a wood at the opposite end of the clearing, a fact that Lee's skirmishers quickly revealed. Sometime between one and two o'clock, Banks, after forcing his way up the congested road, arrived on the battlefield. The citizen general ordered Lee, supported by the one infantry brigade, to hold his ground, and sent dispatches to Franklin directing him to hurry his infantry forward. Lee's three hundred wagons blocked the road and prevented Franklin from moving his infantry to the battlefield. As a result, Banks managed to bring no more than five thousand men onto the field.[16]

A little after four o'clock, Taylor, who now held a two-to-one manpower advantage, began a general attack that overlapped both Union flanks. The Rebels overwhelmed Banks's meager force and compelled the Federals to fall back. Neither the late arrival of one of Franklin's divisions nor repeated efforts by Banks to rally the soldiers could stem the retreat. The Union troops began an orderly withdrawal until they encountered the wagons, which someone had parked far too close to the battlefield. In the face of the Rebel onslaught, panic set in among the teamsters, and they bolted, leaving behind their wagons as they dashed down the already congested road. The panic spread to the rest of the Union army. "Such a babble of confusion I never saw," exclaimed an infantryman, "batteries of artillery rushing on the retreat . . . [t]he large force of cavalry on a perfect stampede. Now it was a *complete rout*."[17]

The stampede was finally stemmed when the defeated units reached Pleasant Grove, three miles east of Sabine Crossroads. Here, Gen. William H. Emory's division, unable to slog its way up the obstructed road, established a defensive line that blunted the Rebel attack and allowed Banks's demoralized forces to regroup. One officer properly termed the engagement a "serious disaster." The army lost 20 artillery pieces, 175 wagons, 11 ambulances, and 1,001 draft animals and suffered more than 2,000 casualties, including 1,500 captured.[18]

Even worse, Banks allowed his officers to talk him into retreating. The former governor believed that he could maintain his position at Pleasant Grove until Smith arrived, then counterattack and destroy Taylor, and finally capture Shreveport. Franklin, Lee, and several other officers, all West Pointers who had little respect for Banks, argued that Smith, seventeen miles behind at Pleasant Hill, could not arrive in time, and anyway there was not enough water to sustain the troops and animals. Faced with this opposition, Banks caved in and ordered the army to withdraw to Pleasant Hill.[19]

The next day, April 9, the entire Union army took position on Pleasant Hill, a small prominence about one mile square, covered in woods, and with open fields to the west that offered good defensive positions. A little before five o'clock, Taylor unleashed an attack against the left flank that staggered the Federal forces, but they managed to hold and beat off the attack. Taylor next launched an assault on the right flank. The battle raged for nearly four hours until Smith brought forward his reserves and counterattacked, throwing the Rebels into confusion and forcing them to withdraw. As the Confederates retreated, an excited Banks rode up to Smith, shook his hand, and shouted, "God bless you, general; you have saved the army." Banks's assessment was correct because, though he rode behind the line rallying the men, he played little role in achieving the Union victory, an honor that lay primarily with Smith.[20]

Following this success, the political general made his second great mistake of the campaign. After consulting with Smith, Banks determined to press his advantage and chase after Taylor's army at dawn, seeking to finish off the wounded Rebel force and enter Shreveport. Smith agreed and returned to his command to prepare for the advance. Once again, Banks's other generals talked him into retreating. At a conference not attended by Smith, Franklin and every general officer in the Nineteenth Army Corps forcefully argued that the absence of water, lack of rations, and heavy casualties sustained in combat (another 1,369 at Pleasant Hill) rendered any advance both impossible and foolhardy. The army had to reestablish communications with the navy, not move on Shreveport. Banks's earlier confidence evaporated, and, unwilling to argue with so many military professionals, he reluctantly acquiesced, effectively abdicating his status as commanding general.[21]

Unspoken at the conference was the real reason Franklin and the other generals wanted to retreat: they had lost all confidence in Banks. "From what I had seen of General Banks' ability to command in the field," Franklin later commented, "I was certain that an operation depending on plenty of troops, rather than upon skill in handling them, was the only one which would have probability of success in his hands." As far as Franklin was concerned, retreat was the only option because Banks could not be trusted to lead the army any further.[22]

The withdrawal destroyed what little confidence the soldiers had left in Banks, who quickly became the most despised man in the army. "Any corporal in the army could have done better," wrote one private. "We lost all respect for Gen Banks and during our retreat he was hooted whenever he came near the 13th corps and would doubtless have been killed by some reckless yank if he had not made himself pretty scarce." Another private commented that Banks "accomplished—the loss of our army." A staff officer expressed the feelings of many when he wrote that it was a "grave, almost fatal, mistake" to make Banks a general. Few, if any, Civil War generals engendered such loathing from their soldiers.[23]

Over the next two weeks, the army linked up with the navy and withdrew to Alexandria, arriving on April 25. The low stage of the river prevented Porter's gunboats from continuing any farther. Although Porter believed that the former governor would "sacrifice my vessels" and leave without the navy, Banks remained at Alexandria to protect the navy and construct a dam that would allow the gunboats to proceed south. The Union forces, augmented by reinforcements to about thirty thousand soldiers, dug in to defend themselves against Taylor's army of six thousand men.[24]

Among the reinforcements was McClernand. Lincoln sent McClernand to the Department of the Gulf in January and gave Banks the authority to "assign him to such duty as you may deem best." Banks returned McClernand to command of the Thirteenth Army Corps and ordered the former Illinois congressman to assume control of the Texas coast. Now with the army at Alexandria, McClernand did little save squabble with Smith and request that Banks turn over command of the army to him so he could "go out, fight and beat the enemy." Nothing came of this appeal. Shortly thereafter, McClernand became ill with malaria and relinquished command of his corps, ending his military career.[25]

The end was also rapidly approaching for Banks. Even as he struggled to save the gunboats, Northerners castigated him for the failure on the Red River. Secretary of the Navy Gideon Welles chastised Banks, saying he is "no general, has no military capacity, is wholly unfit for the position assigned him." He blamed Banks alone for the fiasco, an opinion that was "very unanimous." Even Banks's political supporters told the citizen general that the country "hold[s] you responsible for what is considered an unnecessary and unmilitary disaster." A columnist in the *New York Times* summed up the general consensus when he wrote that "the overthrow in Louisiana has made it plain to everybody that Maj-Gen. Banks is practically no General at all."[26]

One man who agreed with these opinions was Grant, who was disgusted with what he termed Banks's "incompetency." On April 22, he began the task of ending the citizen general's military career, writing Halleck that "the best interests of [the] service demand" Banks's removal. Lincoln, Halleck informed Grant, refused to act on this advice "for the present." A week later, probably after talking with Lincoln, Halleck explained that the president was afraid to offend the former governor's many political friends, but "if you insist upon General Banks' removal as a military necessity," thus providing Lincoln with some political cover, the president would consent.[27]

In the end, Lincoln settled the matter not by removing Banks but by creating on May 8 the Division of West Mississippi and placing Gen. Edward R. S. Canby in command. The new division included Banks's department. Canby's appointment ended the political general's control of military matters because it restricted the former governor's authority to political questions in Louisiana. The next day, May 9, the navy's ships began passing Alexandria, and by May 12 the entire squadron was safe, allowing Banks to continue his retreat down the Red River. The former governor crowed to his wife that rescuing the gunboats "will be one of the most remarkable achievements of the war," but it had no effect on Lincoln's decision.[28]

The Red River campaign was an ill-conceived adventure that went horribly wrong, primarily due to Banks's failures. He repeated previous mistakes, such as failing to properly reconnoiter, quarreling with his subordinates, and acting indecisively, and he made fatal new ones. These included his insistence on taking the navy up the Red River despite the low level of the water and the fact that it was not essential for success; choosing the inland road even though he knew it diverted him from the river, lacked water and forage, and provided no room to maneuver; and allowing his subordinates after the victory at Pleasant Hill to talk him into retreating when his instincts properly told him to continue the advance. The last two proved to be decisive mistakes that doomed the expedition. Other generals committed errors during the enterprise that contributed to the reverse, but Banks, as the commanding officer, bore the primary responsibility. Once again, his blundering resulted in a disastrous defeat that the Union could ill afford at this stage of the war.

Even before Banks limped away from Alexandria, Sherman's advance against Atlanta had begun. This operation was the major effort in the West undertaken as part of Grant's strategy to end the war. The new commanding general was determined to ensure that the various Union armies stopped acting "separately and independently of each other." To accomplish this goal, Grant concentrated "all the force possible against the Confederate armies in the field" and ordered all Federal armies to move at roughly the same time. By doing so, the Rebels would be unable to send reinforcements from one army to the other since Union forces would threaten all of their units at the same time. Thus, as the Army of the Potomac advanced against Lee, Sherman pushed south into Georgia at the head of the Armies of the Cumberland, Ohio, and Tennessee, seeking to destroy the Rebel Army of Tennessee, commanded by Gen. Joseph Johnston, and capture Atlanta.[29]

Two political generals accompanied Sherman on the drive toward Atlanta, Logan and Blair, both corps commanders in the Army of the Tennessee, led by Gen. James McPherson. Logan commanded the Fifteenth Army Corps and participated in the campaign from the beginning. Blair led the Seventeenth Army Corps but, because he spent the winter and early spring in Congress, was unable to join Sherman's force until the second week of June.

On May 7, the Union army moved southward. Sherman ordered the armies of the Cumberland (commanded by George Thomas) and Ohio (commanded by John Schofield) to demonstrate against the main Rebel position at Buzzard Roost Gap while McPherson swung his army around the Confederates' left and into their rear, seeking to capture the railroad junction in Resaca. Two days later, Logan's corps, supporting the Sixteenth Corps, advanced toward the town. Despite the fact that only a small garrison held the town, McPherson refused to assault the Rebel positions, fearing the entrenchments were too strong. As a result, Johnston was able to retreat into Resaca. Logan was "disgusted" at McPherson for this decision because he believed that they could have captured the town.[30]

Over the next week, fighting raged around Resaca. On May 13, Logan assaulted and captured the Camp Creek Hills, an important height that overlooked the Confederate position in Resaca. He placed artillery on the hills and pounded the Rebels in the city. The next day, he made a feint attack, preventing reinforcements from being sent from his front, and then, late in the day, ordered a general assault, hoping to capture a key railroad bridge. Though the Fifteenth Corps managed to capture the next line of hills, fears of a Confederate counterattack led Logan to halt and entrench. This proved to be a wise decision, for shortly thereafter the Rebels fruitlessly assaulted his position. Logan, though unable to capture the bridge, was now close enough to bombard it, forcing Johnston to build a new railroad bridge and on the night of May 15–16 retreat.[31]

After spending a week resting, refitting, and reprovisioning, the Union army moved south and discovered the new Confederate line of defense between Allatoona and Dallas. Once again, Sherman attempted to flank Johnston's position by slipping around the Rebel left and falling on Dallas from the west. On May 25, the Union army collided with the Confederates. Logan's corps took no part in the fighting, but over the next several days, as he advanced toward Dallas, his troops frequently skirmished with the Rebels.[32]

On May 28, as McPherson's army began to withdraw in anticipation of moving eastward to New Hope Church, the Confederates launched an assault against Logan's front. The fighting, according to Logan, was "close and deadly," but the Federal troops sent every Rebel assault "back broken to their works." At one point, the Confederates captured several artillery pieces, leading Logan to gallop up, jump over the entrenchments, and call to the men to recover the guns. This bit of heroics saved the artillery, and the general continued to ride behind his troops, urging them to throw back the enemy until the hourlong engagement concluded.[33]

Once again, Johnston retreated, falling back to a new stronger position anchored on a trio of mountains, Kenesaw, Pine, and Lost. Just before the Union forces moved against these positions, Blair's corps joined Sherman's army on June 8. In the middle of June, the Union army began to take up position opposite the Confederate works. Constant skirmishing occurred over the next ten days as the Federal troops ineffectually probed the Rebel lines for weaknesses. These operations frustrated Sherman, who sought some way to pry the Rebels from their fortified line. Rejecting another flanking movement, the general instead determined to launch a frontal assault, seeking to blast straight through the Confederates. None of his subordinates approved of the plan. Logan for one predicted that it would fail and later wrote that the operation was "universally considered ill-advised," but Sherman refused to heed their advice and ordered the attack for June 27.[34]

At eight o'clock, Logan's assault columns advanced toward the thirty-five-foot precipices his corps was ordered to capture. His two columns stumbled their way up the hill under enemy rifle and artillery fire; the Rebels even threw "rocks, clubs, and every conceivable species of missiles." Despite this fire, the troops managed to capture two lines of the Confederate works, but all attempts to continue the attack failed and Logan halted the offensive before any more men were killed. The corps suffered 80 killed, 506 wounded, and 17 missing to gain a position that Logan did not "regard as important."[35]

The entire engagement was a tactical defeat for the Union, and Sherman never again attempted a frontal assault; instead, he returned to his flanking movements. In the first week of July, McPherson's army swung around the Rebel right flank, forcing Johnston to abandon his line on Kenesaw Mountain and retreat across the Chattahoochee River, the last natural barrier between Sherman and Atlanta. Constant retreating infuriated President Jefferson Davis. Fed up with Johnston's Fabian tactics and refusal to stand and fight, Davis replaced Johnston with John Bell Hood, an aggressive general who, if nothing else, would fight to save the city. On July 20, Hood did just that, attacking Thomas's army at Peachtree Creek. Thomas repulsed the assault, but it was merely a prelude.[36]

Two days later, Hood renewed his efforts to destroy the Union hordes by striking McPherson's army, then operating east of Atlanta on the Atlanta and Augusta Railroad. The Army of the Tennessee tore up the railroad and spent the night of July 21 digging entrenchments, with Logan's corps holding the right flank, just east of Atlanta, and Blair's corps on the extreme left of the Union line. Earlier that day, Blair had captured Bald Hill, an important position that commanded the entire area, placing one division on the hill and a second division on the McDonough Road with its left flank angled to meet any threat from the east.[37]

At noon on July 22, Hood's army launched an assault against these positions, hitting the left flank and rear of the Army of the Tennessee. The attack first fell on the Sixteenth Corps (commanded by Grenville Dodge), which had moved into position just before the Rebels struck, and then barreled into Blair's troops. A second assault then began against the front of both Logan's and Blair's corps.

One of the first casualties was McPherson, killed by Rebel skirmishers as he rode to the battle line, and Logan assumed command of the army. The new army commander galloped over to the weakest part of the Union line, the gap between Dodge's and Blair's corps, and immediately ordered a brigade to fill the hole while directing the two corps commanders to each move reinforcements into the breach. He then told Blair to hold Bald Hill at all costs. The position was the key to the Union line because it commanded the entire area and allowed the Federals to observe Confederate movements.[38]

As Logan made these dispositions, the Rebels launched a second assault against the vulnerable gap, but Blair and Dodge, though giving some ground, managed to hold. Blair was fortunate, for the Confederates failed to coordinate their assaults. Though facing enemy onslaughts against both his front and left flank, the Rebels never attacked both at the same time. Thus, Blair's troops were able to beat off one attack and then "jump over their breastworks" to meet an assault from the other direction. Nevertheless, the attacks eventually compelled Blair to abandon part of his position and form a final line centered on Bald Hill. The Confederates made a last advance on this line, sweeping up the hill and planting their battle flags in the entrenchments, but, after hand-to-hand combat that continued until darkness fell, Blair's corps held.[39]

While Blair struggled on the left, Logan rode back to the army's right flank, also facing Rebel attacks. Taking two brigades with him, Logan arrived to discover that a Confederate column, advancing up a railroad cut, had compelled several units to retreat, captured some artillery, and now threatened to turn the Union right flank. He immediately ordered artillery to pound the Rebel force, an action that blunted the enemy attack and provided Logan with sufficient time to organize a counterattack. With Logan riding behind them, the Union troops chanted, "Black Jack! Black Jack!" drove the Rebels back, and recaptured the lost ground and guns.[40]

The battle of Atlanta ended in another tactical Union victory, though it had no immediate decisive impact on the course of the campaign. Hood's attack inflicted 430 killed, 1,559 wounded, and 1,733 missing on the Union force, but the Confederates failed to destroy the Army of the Tennessee. Although the Rebel army suffered heavy casualties, it was able to retreat back into the works around Atlanta and prepare for another fight. The Southern force was weakened, but Sherman's troops were unable to cripple Hood's army and still faced the same strategic quandary as before: how to draw Hood out of the city where his army could be destroyed.[41]

Both Logan and Blair led their units extremely well during this engagement. Blair captured a key hill and then held it against Rebel assaults while also managing, with the aid of both Dodge and Logan, to prevent the enemy from turning his left flank and driving into the Federal rear. He provided inspiring leadership and displayed sound tactical ability. Logan once again demonstrated superior battlefield abilities. After assuming command of the army, he identified both the weakest and the strongest parts of the Union line and took sensible steps to defend them. He did not neglect other threatened areas and arrived at the imperiled right flank with reinforcements just in time to blunt a Rebel assault and then lead a successful counterattack. These excellent tactical decisions were complemented by his inspiring leadership.

With McPherson dead, the Army of the Tennessee needed a new commanding officer. Logan, as the army's ranking corps commander and acting army commander, was the logical choice, certainly expected to receive the appointment, and many officers and soldiers in the army believed that he deserved the promotion. There was, however, considerable opposition from West Pointers to placing a political general in such a position. Thomas objected to Logan's appointment and said he might resign if such an event occurred; Schofield and several other West Point graduates also voiced hostility. Sherman finally settled on Oliver Howard, currently a corps commander in the Army of the Cumberland, because Howard was a West Pointer. At this moment, Sherman later wrote, he needed "commanders who were purely and technically soldiers," that is, "professional soldiers." Logan, because he was merely a volunteer who "looked to personal fame and glory," was not a professional soldier and thus was not "equal to the command of three corps." Essentially, Sherman passed over Logan because he believed the politician lacked the training, knowledge, and experience to manage an army.[42]

Logan was visibly upset by Sherman's decision, but suppressed his anger for the good of the Union cause and remained in the service. In private, he complained that he received "no credit" for any of his achievements because "West Point must have all under Sherman who is an infernal brute." Both Howard and Sherman acted to soothe the bitterness Logan felt. Howard "took pains" to praise Logan and carefully explained "his own high opinion of him as an officer and the respect in which he was held by the whole army." Immediately after appointing Howard, Sherman wrote a private note to Logan, promising "to give you every credit," assuring Logan that he had "my Entire Confidence," and praising him for "the honourable manner in which you acted" during the battle of Atlanta. The Illinois politician was pacified, though he remained hostile to West Point for the rest of his life.[43]

Logan was denied a command he deserved because he was not a West Point graduate. Sherman's argument that Logan lacked the experience and training to lead such an army rings hollow because Howard possessed little more experience than Logan. Howard graduated from West Point in 1854, but more than half of his antebellum military career was spent as an instructor of mathematics at the military academy. More important, Howard's record as a regimental, brigade, division, and corps commander was lackluster and contained the great debacle of Chancellorsville. Logan's record as a commander of the same size units was superior to Howard's. He also had served with the Army of the Tennessee for three years, knew the officers and men, and had earned their loyalty and respect.[44]

At this point in the war, it is true, the record of political generals who had led armies was dismal. Frémont's two efforts both had miscarried, Banks had failed everywhere save at Port Hudson, and Butler during the spring and summer of 1864 was confirming that he lacked the ability to command an army. These dreary performances should not have been held against Logan, a general who had proved he could capably direct troops at every level of command. Unlike so many of his fellow political generals, Logan had demonstrated that he could lead an army; only Sherman's hostility to citizen generals prevented him from being promoted to a position he deserved.

There was little time for the army to digest these events before the Army of the Tennessee once again found itself in battle. Following the engagement on July 22, Sherman sent Howard's army on a long march to the west of Atlanta to strike the railroad south of the city. On the morning of July 28, the army moved eastward toward Ezra Church, with Logan's corps on the right, Blair in the center, and Dodge on the left. Logan's corps moved forward slowly and gained the summit upon which Ezra Church stood when skirmishing began, leading Howard to halt the advance. Fearing a Rebel attack, Logan's troops hastily threw up a crude barricade of logs, rails, and church pews.[45]

Shortly after eleven thirty, the full weight of the Rebel attack fell upon Logan's corps, seeking to break through with one massive rush. The Fifteenth Corps, as Logan wrote, "stood firm . . . and repelled the assault handsomely." The Confederates continued to throw themselves at Logan's troops, re-forming and coming across the open ground at the crude entrenchments on six separate occasions, only to be repulsed each time. "All we had to do," Logan related to his wife, "was to lay still and kill and wound them."[46]

Once again, the Federals won a complete tactical victory but failed to destroy Hood's army. The battle did bleed the Rebel force, weakening it further and making it more difficult for Hood to defend the city. Logan's corps suffered 50 killed, 439 wounded, and 73 missing in a battle they fought exclusively. Howard praised Logan's conduct, commenting that the politician "was spirited and energetic, going at once to the point where he apprehended the slightest danger of the enemy's success." Nevertheless, despite this success, as July ended, Hood's army remained a cohesive and dangerous force within the fortifications of Atlanta.[47]

Throughout August, Sherman laid siege to the city while he contemplated how to force Hood out of Atlanta. Near the end of the month, Sherman returned to his tried-and-true maneuver of striking the enemy's flank and rear, in this case the town of Jonesboro, near which two railroads ran. By taking Jonesboro, the Union army would sever the last rail link to Atlanta, cutting the city off from supply and reinforcement. Moving south on August 25, Logan's corps led the advance for the Army of the Tennessee, reaching the Atlanta and West Point Railroad two days later, a line the army proceeded to rip apart. With this work, in Howard's words, "remarkably well done," the army moved east toward Jonesboro. Blair took a road on the right, while Logan followed the main route to the town, encountering skirmishers but no major opposition before reaching the Flint River. The Rebels failed to destroy a bridge spanning the water, and Logan rushed troops across, establishing a bridgehead. By the end of the day, Logan's corps had secured the final hill between the river and the Macon and Western Railroad, Atlanta's last rail line.[48]

The next morning, August 31, the Fifteenth Corps worked to fortify its position; an attack was expected at any moment, as trains bearing Rebel reinforcements could be heard pulling into Jonesboro. The onslaught finally came at three o'clock that afternoon when Hood launched an attack against Logan's corps, which once again, with the exception of some reinforcements sent by Blair, bore the brunt of the action. After an hour of combat, the Rebels retreated, only to re-form and come at the Union lines on two more occasions, though, as Logan observed, "evidently with far less spirit and determination than the first." As before, the Fifteenth Corps repulsed the Rebel assaults while suffering only 154 total casualties.[49]

The defeat at Jonesboro destroyed Confederate hopes of defending Atlanta. Sherman's army had captured the last rail link to the city, forcing Hood to evacuate the beleaguered city on September 1 and allowing Federal forces to occupy the prize the next day. "Atlanta is ours, and fairly won," Sherman jubilantly wrote. The strategic victory was the decisive event of the year, lifting Union morale and contributing significantly to Lincoln's winning a second term as president in November.[50]

Logan's generalship was brilliant throughout the campaign. He demonstrated excellent tactical abilities, competent administrative skills, and inspiring battlefield leadership qualities. In every battle in which his corps was engaged, Logan was an aggressive commander who accurately read the nature of the terrain as well as the strengths and weaknesses of the Rebels and his own positions. With the sole exception of Kenesaw Mountain, he successfully maneuvered his corps (and army at the battle of Atlanta) in such a manner as to give it the best chance of achieving victory. The last two engagements, including the decisive battle of Jonesboro, were fought exclusively by Logan. Of all the Union corps commanders engaged during this campaign, Logan contributed the most to bring about the final Federal victory.

Blair also performed competently, though he missed the first month of the campaign and often found himself in a supporting role. He maneuvered his corps quite well, displayed aggressive tendencies, followed orders, and provided inspiring leadership when necessary. At the battle of Atlanta, his efforts played a major role in saving the Army of the Tennessee from destruction. Throughout most of the campaign, his corps supported the Fifteenth Corps and was not engaged in battle on many occasions, but this resulted more from Confederate command decisions than from any failing on Blair's part.

The fall of Atlanta presented Sherman with a logistical and strategic quandary. His army was tied to a long, vulnerable supply line that stretched into Tennessee and required large numbers of troops to protect and repair. Garrisoning Atlanta also required substantial numbers of soldiers. At the same time, he had to worry about Hood's army, wounded but still dangerous. In the fall, Hood attempted to break the supply line by marching on Sherman's rear, a movement that forced Sherman to chase after Hood until the latter retreated into Alabama. Sherman now decided to abandon both his supply line and Atlanta. Sending Thomas with two corps to operate in Tennessee, Sherman determined to take sixty thousand men and march across Georgia to the sea, living off the land while seeking to destroy both the material resources of the region and Confederate morale.

Neither Blair nor Logan participated in the fall movements, as both went north to campaign for Lincoln in the 1864 election. Following Lincoln's victory, Blair returned to Atlanta and resumed command of the Seventeenth Corps, though Logan, for personal and political reasons, remained in the North. As a result, only Blair participated in Sherman's march from Atlanta to Savannah.

Early on the morning of November 15, Blair's corps moved south, forming the right wing of Sherman's army. The march to Savannah, as one officer later wrote, assumed "something of the character of an armed picnic on a grand scale, minus the bright eyes and enchanting smiles of women." The

Confederates, with Hood's army marching into Tennessee, offered no practical resistance, allowing the Federals to sweep through Georgia unopposed. On December 10, Sherman's army arrived at Savannah, capturing the city three days later. Blair bragged that "we had no fighting and very pleasant marching & have inflicted more damage upon the enemy then [*sic*] could be done by a dozen victories." They destroyed, he continued, four hundred miles of railroad and millions of dollars worth of cotton and "gobbled up enough provisions to have fed Lee's army for six months."[51]

At the end of December, Logan resumed command of the Fifteenth Corps, returning after nearly receiving command of Thomas's army in Tennessee. In mid-December, what remained of Hood's army stood outside of Nashville, protected by Thomas's superior force. Thomas, due to inclement weather, refused to attack, leading Grant to send Logan to Nashville with orders to replace Thomas if the latter had not attacked when he reached the city. Unfortunately for Logan's personal hopes, shortly before he arrived, Thomas assaulted and practically annihilated Hood's army, preventing the politician from assuming command of an army.[52]

After resting and refitting, Sherman moved into South Carolina at the end of January 1865, seeking to visit upon the Palmetto State the same destruction Georgia had suffered. Once again, the Union vandals, marching through the center of the state toward Columbia, met no resistance. Blair's corps successfully feinted toward Charleston, convincing the meager Rebel forces that Sherman intended to move toward the coast. There was little for the generals to do during the march, as illustrated by the events that transpired when the Army of the Tennessee approached the Augusta and Charleston Railroad. Howard and Logan stopped the advance to debate how best to proceed when an enlisted man, riding a white mule, cantered up to the two generals, saluted, and shouted, "Hurry up! Hurry up! We've got the railroad!" The army's foragers, moving rapidly in front of the army, not only had captured sections of the railroad but, as a veteran wrote, "were already throwing up defensive works to hold it, while the generals were planning for the attack."[53]

The Federal campaign through South Carolina visited horrific destruction upon the material resources of the state, including the controversial burning of Columbia. At Columbia, Logan, whose corps occupied the city, ordered his troops to put out the fire. Throughout the rest of the march, both Blair and Logan, though officially condemning unjustifiable devastation, made little effort to stop their troops from taking out their frustration on the state they blamed for starting the war. At the end of the campaign, when asked how much actual property was destroyed, Blair remarked, "Well, we left them the wells."[54]

As Sherman's army moved into North Carolina, they met reinforcements that included units commanded by Meagher that had arrived by sea at New Bern, North Carolina. In the fall of 1864, Meagher received command of a division in eastern Tennessee. In January 1865, his command was ordered to proceed to New York City for transport down the coast to North Carolina. Meagher hurried ahead of his two brigades and reached New York on January 23, but by this time the high command had redirected his troops to Annapolis. Despite the new orders, Meagher lingered in New York and then traveled to Baltimore, where accusations of drunkenness and complaints about his embarkation schedule soon swirled about, leading Halleck to order the division loaded onto transports with or without their commander. Meagher, Halleck complained to Grant, "seems to be ignorant of what troops he has, or where they are." Grant decided that Meagher's behavior provided the opportunity for doing what should have been "done long ago—dismissing him." Meagher was relieved of command on February 24, 1865, as his army career came to a humiliating end.[55]

At the beginning of March, Sherman's army entered North Carolina, and the wanton burning came to a sudden end. The soldiers seemed to have satisfied their bloodlust, and the generals took steps to once again enforce discipline. Foraging, Blair wrote, "is vicious and its results utterly deplorable," and since "there is no longer a necessity for it," unauthorized foraging and destruction should be ended. Sherman agreed and issued orders restricting the practice. At Bentonville, from March 19 to 21, the Federals skirmished with the tiny Confederate army commanded by Joseph Johnston scraped together by the Rebels. On March 21, Logan, supported by Blair's corps, opened an artillery barrage upon the Confederate lines and then sent units forward who easily routed the Rebel skirmishers and captured a line of rifle pits. Johnston, unable to recapture the pits, retreated during the night. This was the last major action in which either Logan or Blair participated. Less than a month later, the war in North Carolina ended.[56]

Nathaniel P. Banks

Francis P. Blair Jr.

Benjamin F. Butler

James Denver

(PHOTO NO. 111-B-3683)

John A. Dix

John C. Frémont

(PHOTO NO. 111-B-3756)

Stephen Hurlbut

John A. Logan

John A. McClernand

(PHOTO NO. 111-B-3868)

Thomas F. Meagher

(PHOTO NO. 111-B-5252)

Robert Schenck

(PHOTO NO. 111-B-3278)

Carl Schurz

(PHOTO NO. 111-BA-572)

James Shields

(PHOTO NO. 111-BA-1568)

Daniel Sickles

(PHOTO NO. 111-B-3464)

Franz Sigel

(PHOTO NO. 111-B-2200)

James S. Wadsworth

The
Eastern
Theater in 1864

As the decisive military campaigns in the West played out, equally important events occurred in the East that also featured political generals. On the battlefields of Virginia, Sigel, Butler, and Wadsworth participated in Grant's efforts to destroy the Army of Northern Virginia. Sigel and Butler both commanded small armies in the campaign, though Grant sought to neutralize their military liabilities by placing military professionals in their commands. Grant's concept collapsed, primarily because operations were hampered by constant feuding that erupted between political generals and West Point graduates, bickering that had a detrimental effect on the campaign. Both Sigel's and Butler's enterprises eventually ended in failure. These debacles resulted from their failed generalships and provided further proof that those citizen generals with little experience or competency could not be entrusted with independent commands.

In mid-March, Grant assumed command of the Union army and began preparing his grand design to win the war. The main push in the East would be made by the Army of the Potomac against Richmond and in the West by Sherman against Atlanta, each seeking to destroy the Rebel armies defending those points. Smaller armies would support these two drives. One force would attack Mobile, another would advance up the Shenandoah Valley, and a third would strike at Richmond from Fortress Monroe. The purpose of these expeditions was to draw off Rebel forces from the main enemy armies and prevent these armies from receiving reinforcements.[1]

Political generals commanded these smaller armies, a situation that Grant disliked. He could not remove these generals, but he intended to counterbalance their liabilities by placing West Pointers under their command to direct tactical operations or provide military advice. For instance, Grant planned for Banks to attack Mobile. The commanding general had no respect for Banks's military ability and no intention of allowing the political general to exercise complete authority over the Alabama expedition. Instead, he determined to place "some one near Banks, who can issue orders to him and see that they are obeyed." The failure on the Red River ended the need for such measures because it ruined Banks's military career and postponed the attack against Mobile, but Grant planned to apply the concept with Sigel, commanding the Department of West Virginia, and Butler, commanding the Department of the James.[2]

Both of these political generals controlled areas vital to Grant's Virginia campaign. As the Army of the Potomac struck at the Army of Northern Virginia, seeking to destroy Lee's army before it slipped into the defenses around Richmond, Grant expected Sigel and Butler to prevent reinforcements and supplies from reaching Lee's army. This was to be accomplished by advancing up the Shenandoah Valley and attacking Richmond, compelling the Rebels to commit forces to defend these points, thus weakening the main Confederate field army.

Sigel assumed command of West Virginia in March 1864 after using his political connections to obtain the position. Following his removal from command of the Eleventh Corps, Sigel was assigned to the Department of the Susquehanna, but he spent most of his time lobbying for an independent assignment. At the same time, his political allies from New York and West Virginia put pressure on the president to appoint the German general to the Mountain State. Lincoln, desperate to retain the support of the German community, many of whom seemed ready to embrace Frémont for president in the fall election, relented and assigned Sigel to command the Department of West Virginia. Col. David Strother, a department staff officer inherited by Sigel, commented that "the Dutch vote must be secured at all hazards for the Government and the sacrifice of West Virginia is a small matter." Despite this unfavorable opinion, Sigel worked day and night and, by the end of April, had managed to put the department into the best condition it had ever enjoyed.[3]

Grant, aware of Sigel's lackluster military record, had no respect for the German's military abilities and placed Gen. Edward O. C. Ord, a West Point graduate, in charge of the spring campaign's main effort in this department. Ord was ordered to prepare an expedition of ninety-five hundred men at Beverly, Virginia, with the intention of destroying the East Tennessee and Virginia Railroad. Sigel was to play a secondary role in the campaign. He was directed to advance southward from Harper's Ferry to Staunton with a large supply train guarded by a small force of infantry to meet Ord, allowing him to resupply and attack Lynchburg.[4]

Grant's scheme to neutralize Sigel fell apart upon Ord's arrival in the department. The two generals rubbed each other the wrong way and began feuding. Sigel, obviously jealous of Ord's assignment, complained that "all dispositions were made in such a manner as if I did not exist at all." For his part, Ord was "vexed at being placed *under*" the German general. These feelings led to several bitter arguments. Sigel promised to provide only sixty-five hundred of the requested ninety-five hundred troops, a decision that incensed Ord, who felt that the German was not obeying Grant's orders and ensuring the expedition's failure. The final break occurred when the two generals were discussing Sigel's intended enterprise to supply Ord at Staunton, a plan that Sigel torpedoed when he remarked, "I don't think I shall do it." Disgusted, Ord asked to be relieved in the middle of April.[5]

With Ord out and the start of the spring campaign approaching, Grant reluctantly turned to Sigel for a new plan. The German general proposed abandoning the movement from Beverly and advocated assembling a strong force under his own command to advance up the valley. Sigel intended to lead seven thousand men southward "to threaten the force of the enemy in the Shenandoah Valley, and to advance . . . as far as possible." Grant sent Lt. Col. Orville Babcock to consult with the political general and, when assured by Babcock that the plan was sound, agreed.[6]

Even as these plans were maturing, Sigel was losing the confidence of many of the American officers in his department. The German general, whose grasp of English was poor, basically barricaded himself in his headquarters, refused to see anyone but his staff, and soon stopped associating with his American staff members, preferring to confer with the Europeans on his staff. Most of these men, although dedicated to the Union cause, barely understood English or their American compatriots. These officers irritated the Americans, convincing them that Sigel's appointment was a mistake. At the end of April, Strother described the German general as "a military pedagogue . . . totally wanting in practical capacity."[7]

This state of affairs worsened as Sigel moved up the Shenandoah Valley. For one thing, he never understood what he was supposed to do and believed that he lacked sufficient forces to advance very far. As a result, the German general proceeded only in fits and starts. Moving south from Martinsburg on April 29, the Union army reached Winchester on May 1, where it remained for several days as Sigel drilled his troops and then staged two mock battles. The sham battles were a farce; units wandered across the battlefield with no purpose, foreign staff officers issued confusing and contradictory orders in poor English, and Sigel, after ordering one regiment to charge the enemy, forgot to recall the unit, forcing staff officers to bring it back. These examples of poor leadership angered the troops, who lost all respect for their commanding general. "There was never anything seen half so ridiculous," cried one soldier, "and it bred in everyone the most supreme contempt for General Sigel."[8]

Marching south on May 9, Sigel's advance continued to move slowly and then stalled completely. On May 11, Sigel scored a coup when he occupied Woodstock and captured Confederate dispatches. These letters reported that Gen. John C. Breckinridge had assembled a Rebel army of four thousand men at Staunton, two days south of an important gap in the Blue Ridge Mountains at New Market. Sigel was only a day's march north of this gap, a position that if captured would allow him to operate on Robert E. Lee's flank and rear. Instead of moving upon New Market, Sigel used the letters as an excuse to do nothing, arguing that he lacked sufficient force to proceed farther south. As rain descended on the valley, Sigel hunkered down at Woodstock, drilled his men, and allowed Breckinridge to seize the initiative.[9]

Over the next two days, Breckinridge moved north to New Market, where his lead units routed Federal cavalry scouting the area. Sigel now had to confront this threat. The German, who thus far had been indecisive, overly cautious, and slow, now committed an even greater blunder when he sent Col. Augustus Moor to New Market with twenty-three hundred men. Instead of meeting the Rebels with his entire army, Sigel divided his modest force and sent the smaller contingent south to feel for the enemy. As the sun went down on May 14, Moor engaged the Rebels. Sigel, who could hear the roar of cannons but had little idea what was happening, spent an anxious night.[10]

At dawn the next day, Sigel marched south to aid Moor at New Market. The day was hot, and the army, "all exhausted & drenched" from the previous three days of rain, became spread out along the road. Sigel, riding ahead of his main units, reached New Market at noon, just as Breckinridge was leaving the town to attack the Union forces, and ordered Moor's unit to take up defensive positions on a hill north of the city. He also issued orders for the rest of his scattered army to hurry forward, but committed a mistake when he forgot to order two regiments to New Market. Thus, he failed to concentrate his army. With Confederate forces overlapping both flanks, Sigel ordered his command to retreat and take up new positions along the road, hoping that the rest of his units would soon arrive.[11]

The day might still have been saved, but the political general continued to commit blunders that doomed Union hopes. In the heat of battle, Sigel began shouting orders in German, rendering his American staff members useless. He then failed to take advantage of a hole that opened in the center of the Rebel line, and Breckinridge was able close the gap. Instead, Sigel ordered a cavalry charge on his left, an assault that the Confederates shattered with artillery. The cavalry broke and ran, leaving the left flank in the air. With his left crumbling, the German general sought to retrieve the situation by directing three regiments to charge the now reinforced Rebel center. This "fatal charge," one eyewitness wrote, "did no good but cost them the lives of a hundred brave men."[12]

With his assault a failure and left flank annihilated, Sigel had no choice but to withdraw. The troops retreated in some disorder, but Sigel, after coming upon the two regiments that never received orders to march to New Market, tried to make one last stand at Rude's Hill. When he saw the Confederates approaching, the citizen general realized this position was untenable and ordered a final withdrawal to Mount Jackson. As the troops fell back, the Union army dissolved into "a perfect panic." There was, as one officer wrote, "an indiscriminate skeddadling [sic] of cavalry, infantry & artillery towards Mt. Jackson."[13]

The disaster at New Market left many Federals seething at the German general. "Our army was literally routed and defeated," one officer sadly commented. Strother wrote, "The campaign was conducted miserably by Sigel. . . . We can afford to lose such a battle as New Market to get rid of such a mistake as Major General Sigel." When Halleck told Grant that Sigel was in full retreat, he commented, "If you expect anything from him you will be mistaken. He will do nothing but run. He never did anything else."[14]

Such criticism was justified because Sigel conducted this campaign dreadfully. From the beginning, he undermined the enterprise by angering his staff officers and then lost the confidence of his men by holding ridiculous mock battles. Once the expedition was under way, the German general moved slowly, failed to take advantage of splendid intelligence, and not only divided his army but inexplicably sent the smaller part to confront the Rebel threat at New Market. Once the battle began, he failed to concentrate, reacted slowly to developing events, and ordered futile charges that doomed his cause. At New Market, Sigel proved conclusively that he was unfit for independent command.

Grant also came to this conclusion and ordered Gen. David Hunter to re-place Sigel, but this did not end the German general's military career. Hunter, hoping to take advantage of Sigel's "earnest patriotism," placed the political general in command of the department's reserve troops at Harper's Ferry. The position primarily involved the forwarding of soldiers and supplies to Hunter, who was marching down the valley to Lynchburg, where, on June 18, a Rebel force led by Gen. Jubal Early whipped him. Hunter compounded his defeat by retreating west into the mountains, allowing Early to advance unopposed up the Shenandoah, link up with Breckinridge, and on July 2 move against Sigel, then encamped at Martinsburg. Sigel retreated to Harper's Ferry. Instead of holding this position, he abandoned the town and fled across the Potomac River to Maryland Heights, where he finally dug in.[15]

This move obliterated what was left of the German general's military reputation and political support. Several of Lincoln's cabinet members berated Sigel. Attorney General Bates wrote that "he seems foredoomed to be whipped and laughed at—His reputation is good *for retreat.*" Gideon Welles commented that "General Sigel is beaten and not the man for the command given him." Grant also was fed up. "All of General Sigel's operations," he wrote, "from the beginning of the war have been so unsuccessful that I think it advisable to relieve him from all duty." After obtaining Lincoln's approval, Grant relieved the German, ending Sigel's military career.[16]

Sigel's defeat meant that Grant's concept to neutralize the military liabilities of one political general had failed, but he still hoped his plan might succeed with Butler. In November 1863, Butler assumed command of the Department of Virginia and North Carolina. His new command consisted of Fortress Monroe, Norfolk, Cape Hatteras islands, and some scattered outposts around Pamlico and Albemarle sounds. Butler received this command because throughout 1863 he spoke at numerous war rallies and increased his political standing, a fact noticed by Lincoln. As a result, the president returned Butler to active duty, though he made sure to assign the citizen general to what at the time was a relatively insignificant department, consisting of, on paper, forty thousand men, but in actuality only twenty-three thousand soldiers scattered about the command.[17]

Despite having held an army commission for two and a half years, the new department commander remained an untested general, one who had never led troops in combat. This inexperience was not important because his department, despite its proximity to Richmond, did not require vast military experience. For the first six months, Butler's duties revolved around administrative work. In his spare time, he began planning for a possible campaign to capture the Rebel capital. He believed this feat could be accomplished by ascending the

James River to Bermuda Hundred and City Point, occupying and fortifying these two positions, and finally using them as bases for a final advance against Richmond. The political general lacked the troops and resources to carry out such a campaign.[18]

Butler proposed this campaign to Grant in early April when the commanding general visited the politician at Fortress Monroe. Grant was impressed by the plan, since it coincided with his own thoughts on how to use Butler's forces, and decided not only to implement it but also to strengthen the citizen general's command by adding to it a corps from South Carolina. This mobile force, consisting of about thirty thousand men in two corps, was termed the Army of the James. With his army, Butler was ordered to capture City Point, entrench and concentrate his troops, and then operate against the Confederates, bearing in mind that "Richmond is to be your objective point." Grant also told Butler to be prepared to cooperate with the Army of the Potomac. As a result of this meeting, the untried Butler was no longer a passive player on the sidelines but now commanded an essential component of Grant's spring campaign.[19]

Unfortunately, Grant and Butler held differing conceptions of what these orders directed the citizen general to do. In these orders and subsequent missives, Grant impressed upon Butler that his primary objective was to aid the Army of the Potomac by capturing Richmond. Failing at this, Butler could fulfill other significant goals: occupy Petersburg or cut the Petersburg and Richmond Railroad; success at either would prevent supplies and reinforcements from reaching Lee's army. The campaign on the James was conceived by Grant as an effort to capture Richmond and sever Lee's lines of supply and communication, thereby crippling the Army of Northern Virginia.[20]

The political general arrived at a different interpretation of Grant's orders. First, Butler believed that his primary mission was to capture and fortify City Point and Bermuda Hundred, providing the Army of the Potomac with a base from which it could subsequently operate. Once this base was established, Butler decided that his second mission was to "regulate my movements by those of the Army of the Potomac, so as to co-operate with it." This goal could be achieved by moving against Richmond, attacking Petersburg, or cutting the railroad. If he advanced on Richmond, Butler thought that he was to make only a limited attack, since no "assault should be made upon Richmond, except in co-operation with the Army of the Potomac." The political general believed that his operation was one part of a pincer movement against the Rebel capital and he could expect the Army of the Potomac to arrive on the James River within ten days of the expedition's commencement. Thus, all of his actions during the campaign were regulated by this misconception of Grant's orders.[21]

Before their April conference, Grant had never met Butler and possessed considerable doubt about his military capability. Therefore, one reason the commanding general visited Fortress Monroe was to gauge whether Butler was qualified to lead the Army of the James. Impressed by what he saw and heard, Grant decided to retain Butler, though he determined to provide the untried political general with a "sufficient number of able Genls to render him all necessary aid to execute" the plan. Grant, worried about Butler's inexperience and lack of formal training, was not about to send the politician into battle without assistance from military professionals.[22]

To provide this assistance, Grant assigned West Pointers to command Butler's two corps. The most important of these men was Gen. William F. Smith, who received command of the Eighteenth Corps and specific instructions to aid Butler in the coming campaign. As Smith later recalled, "I was turned over to him [Butler] as an assistant and military mentor" in order to keep Butler "straight in military matters." Grant also assigned Quincy A. Gillmore to command the Tenth Corps. These two military academy graduates were expected to offset, with their superior military knowledge, what Grant perceived to be the novice political general's chief liability, namely, his lack of field experience.[23]

Once again, Grant's expectations were dashed, as the three generals proved unable to work together. Smith evidently thought that Grant contemplated placing him in command of Butler's army, was miffed when he found himself subordinated to the citizen general, an officer he suspected was incompetent, and viewed as absurd his unofficial position as Butler's military mentor. Holding an inflated view of his military capability, Butler refused to be mentored by Smith, believing that he possessed more than enough knowledge, ability, and experience to direct the campaign. As for Gillmore, he did not arrive in the department until the day before the expedition began. This mistake irritated Butler and made cooperation among the three generals difficult since they had never previously met and were unable to become acquainted with one another before the operation started. The clashes that occurred among these three officers severely undermined the Army of the James's operations.[24]

Problems began shortly after the expedition commenced on May 5. Butler's operation surprised the Rebels, allowing him to easily capture Bermuda Hundred and City Point. The political general then received intelligence from a spy that Richmond was undefended and ripe for the taking. Butler considered immediately advancing on the capital with the ten thousand men then ashore, a daring scheme but one that might work if the Confederates were as unprepared as the spy reported. Smith and Gillmore objected, and Butler, feeling that he could not carry out an operation without the cooperation of his corps commanders, abandoned the idea.[25]

Disagreements among Butler and the two West Pointers continued to plague operations. The army spent the next twenty-fours hours entrenching, but on May 6 Butler determined to strike the railroad only a few miles west of Bermuda Hundred and ordered Smith and Gillmore to destroy as much of this road as possible. The attempt failed because Smith moved too late in the afternoon and encountered unexpected opposition, while Gillmore, for reasons he deemed "good and sufficient," refused to advance at all. Gillmore's response incensed Butler, who retaliated by asking Henry Wilson, chairman of the Senate Military Affairs Committee, to reject Gillmore's pending nomination as a major general.[26]

The next day, Smith managed to destroy a small section of the railroad, but the operation was beginning to suffer from a lack of coherent direction from the top. Butler could not decide what to do with his army, fluctuating between attacking Richmond, destroying the railroad, moving on Petersburg, or simply holding at Bermuda Hundred. The troops spent the time entrenching for "fear of accident to the Army of the Potomac," as Butler wrote. The fortifications at Bermuda Hundred were formidable, but the time spent constructing them cost Butler the advantage of surprise and delayed his advance on Richmond, Petersburg, or any other objective. This mistake allowed the Confederates to rush reinforcements into the area.[27]

Two days later, on May 9, Butler ordered his two corps commanders to break the railroad and demonstrate toward Petersburg. This attempt was a success, as the Union forces captured a large section of the road and began tearing it up, until resistance offered by a small company of Rebels convinced Smith that he was facing substantial Confederate forces. Once again, the effort to destroy the railroad was abandoned. Moving south toward Petersburg, Smith and Gillmore confronted Rebel entrenchments guarding a railroad bridge at Swift Creek. After several hours of skirmishing, during which no assault was attempted, the corps commanders abandoned operations for the day.[28]

As the sun set on May 9, Butler and his corps commanders agreed to strike at Petersburg. Once out of Butler's presence, Smith and Gillmore decided that the plan was faulty and proposed a new scheme that involved building a bridge over the Appomattox River. Butler was outraged. He criticized the two West Pointers' "infirmity of purpose," berated them for their "vacillation," and refused to even consider their suggestions. The politician's response cowed the two corps commanders, and they stopped volunteering advice. The contemplated move on Petersburg was canceled, and the next day the army retreated to Bermuda Hundred. Despite these failures, Butler believed that his campaign was a success because he had "done all I agreed to do with Grant," that is, construct the fortifications at Bermuda Hundred and City Point.[29]

After wasting May 11, Butler finally decided to move on Richmond and, because he possessed no confidence in his corps commanders, personally lead the movement. This advance was just a demonstration. Butler maintained his viewpoint that he was not to attack Richmond until the Army of the Potomac arrived, and, because of the overly optimistic and faulty reports he was receiving from Stanton, he had good reason to think that Grant would soon drive Lee's army into Richmond. The political general, based on his interpretation of Grant's orders, hurried to the Rebel capital to fulfill his part of the plan.[30]

With his two corps, Butler marched northward, aiming to attack the Confederate defenses at Drewery's Bluff. On May 12, the Union forces assaulted the outer trenches, pushed the Rebels back in several places, and gained a foothold. The next day, the fighting resumed, with Smith attacking the Confederate center while Gillmore moved on the enemy's right flank, trying to flank their position. Though the Federals captured more ground, progress was slow, a result of Confederate resistance and more disagreement within the Union high command. Butler continually pressed for vigorous offensive action, but Smith was reluctant to move forward against what he considered to be strong Rebel positions. At one point, he refused to attack "unless I received orders to do so" from Butler. The citizen general failed to provide such orders, and no assault occurred.[31]

This detrimental feuding continued for the next several days, but the changing strategic and tactical situation soon ended Butler's campaign. Butler learned from Gen. Philip Sheridan, commanding the Army of the Potomac's cavalry then resting at Bermuda Hundred after a raid, that Grant's offensive against Lee had not been the success portrayed by Stanton, but instead had degenerated into a series of bloody battles. This information persuaded Butler to abandon the assault on Richmond and retreat to Bermuda Hundred in order to "carry out the branch of the plan agreed upon between Grant and myself, namely, to make him an impregnable base." The political general believed "it was my duty" to withdraw back into the entrenchments prepared a week earlier.[32]

The Confederates convinced Butler that this was the proper course of action on May 16 when Gen. P. G. T. Beauregard attacked the Union army. Some eighteen thousand Rebels charged through a fog that reduced visibility to a mere fifteen yards, striking the Federal right flank. As the Confederates drove into their lines, the Army of the James's high command continued to bicker. Gillmore sent Butler a dispatch that suggested he was retreating, which incensed the citizen general and caused an ugly spat between them. As they argued, Smith, confused by the fog, panicked and ordered his corps to retreat, an order he tried to countermand when the fog began to lift, only to realize that it was too late to stop his men. Soon the entire army was withdrawing, though, after reestablishing his line, in the afternoon Butler ordered a general advance to probe the new Rebel position. This assault lasted barely an hour, resulted in no serious action, and accomplished nothing.[33]

With the failure of this dismal action, Butler ordered the army back to Bermuda Hundred. The political general, who was so focused on Gillmore's supposed timidity that he failed to supervise Smith, could do nothing but accept the humiliating result. The troops castigated Butler for the failed campaign. One sergeant concluded that Butler "was fairly out-generalled by Beauregard." Another soldier wrote that "there is no confidence felt in" Butler and that he was "more likely to get *booted* than *cheered* by" the troops. These appraisals of Butler's military performance were harsh, but accurate. From May 5 to 16, Butler was indecisive, confused, and erratic. He misinterpreted Grant's orders; spent too much time entrenching; could not decide whether to attack Richmond, Petersburg, or the railroad; and argued constantly with his subordinates, who failed to provide Butler with the sound military advice expected by Grant. The feuding among Butler, Smith, and Gillmore undermined the expedition and almost guaranteed that it would fail.[34]

As Butler's enterprise on the James floundered, the Army of the Potomac, with Wadsworth commanding a division, moved against the Army of Northern Virginia. In the spring of 1864, Wadsworth, following his inspection of African Americans in the Mississippi Valley, returned to the Army of the Potomac. The political general was placed in command of the Fifth Corps' Fourth Division. All three of the army's corps commanders had requested Wadsworth's assignment to their corps, a sign of respect rarely granted to a political general by West Pointers. The oldest division commander in the army, Wadsworth was also one of the army's most popular generals, primarily because he served without pay, a decision that one soldier called "an extraordinary example of patriotism."[35]

Early on May 4, the Army of the Potomac crossed the Rapidan River and moved south through the Wilderness, seeking to pass through the tangled mass of woods and underbrush as quickly as possible. The Rebels had no intention of allowing the Army of the Potomac to march unopposed through this area and, on May 5, attacked. Proceeding south toward Parker's Store on the Orange Plank Road, the Fifth Corps swung west to meet the oncoming Rebels, a difficult maneuver in the woods that the corps failed to carry out effectively.[36]

Nevertheless, the corps was ordered to attack. Wadsworth formed a line of battle in an open field and then pushed his troops into the woods for about half a mile before encountering Confederate resistance. Several problems quickly developed. For one, Wadsworth advanced with no support on his left, leaving his flank exposed. Second, the woods disoriented the troops and broke

149

apart formations, separating Wadsworth's three brigades. The division was vulnerable to counterattack, an onslaught that came after an hour of fighting and caused the division to crumple like a house of cards as soldiers dashed for the rear and the Rebels took hundreds of prisoners. Fortunately, the woods also frustrated the Confederate attack, allowing Wadsworth to re-form what was left of his division. Near the end of the day, the political general, hoping to redeem his division's reputation, volunteered to lead an attack against the northern end of A. P. Hill's corps. Reinforced by a brigade, the assault met with initial success, but ground to a halt when darkness fell.[37]

The next day, Grant determined to renew his attacks on Lee's army. Wadsworth, reinforced by a second brigade, was directed to assault Hill's north flank while the Second Corps, which had formed to the south of the Fifth Corps, pushed into Hill's front. Once again, the attack met with initial success only to bog down after encountering Confederate resistance and the onrushing troops of the Second Corps, causing the Federal units to become entangled. The Rebels then counterattacked, driving Wadsworth's division back in confusion until two brigades arrived to reinforce the faltering line. Their appearance stopped the Rebel advance, but the political general's division had been severely depleted.[38]

Wadsworth managed to patch together a new line composed of units from several different divisions. The situation remained confused and was not helped when Wadsworth ordered a series of charges that failed to do anything save lose "a great many men." Later that morning, the Rebels launched an attack directly at Wadsworth's position that completely crumpled the Federal line. The citizen general tried to lead a counterattack, but quickly gave up the idea and, waving a sword over his head, attempted to rally the troops around him. At that moment, a bullet tore into the back of his head, knocking him to the ground as the Union soldiers retreated in disarray.[39]

Wadsworth was captured, but the wound proved fatal and he died on May 7, a loss mourned by many in the North. Lincoln was deeply affected, commenting that "no man has given himself up to the war with such self sacrificing patriotism as Genl. Wadsworth." Grant reportedly said that "he would rather have lost an entire infantry brigade than this brave and wise man." The *New York Times* wrote that his death "excites feelings of intense regret," and throughout New York State, towns passed resolutions praising Wadsworth and expressing sorrow at his passing.[40]

Most of this praise was deserved, though Wadsworth's performance in his last battle was erratic. Wadsworth's sense of duty, patriotism, devotion to his troops, and courage were above reproach, and for the most part he proved to be a steady battlefield commander. In the Wilderness, many of these traits were on display, but he also had difficulty maneuvering his division and struggled to understand what was occurring on the battlefield. Much of this was due to the terrain, which made it difficult for any general to function properly. His lack of military training led him to order hopeless charges and seek offensive action even when facing an overwhelming Rebel attack. Essentially, in this battle Wadsworth was too aggressive. Nevertheless, his death was a loss to the army.

Following the Wilderness, a contest that ended in a draw, Grant continued to push south, engaging Lee in a series of bloody battles that drained both armies of men. With Butler's army, in Grant's apt phrase, stuck at Bermuda Hundred "in a bottle strongly corked," the commanding general decided to obtain reinforcements by detaching Smith's corps from the Army of the James and moving it north to join the Army of the Potomac. This order, occurring near the end of May, prevented Butler from undertaking a planned attack against Petersburg because he now lacked sufficient troops.[41]

During the second week of June, the political general decided to attack Petersburg with what little force he had left. Instead of entrusting this assignment to Gillmore, whom Butler despised, he ordered Gen. Edward W. Hincks to launch simultaneous assaults against Petersburg from the north and south. Though ambitious, the scheme had a good chance to succeed because few Rebels manned the Petersburg entrenchments. As Butler and Hincks conferred at Butler's headquarters, Gillmore walked in and demanded that he, as the senior officer, command the expedition. Inexplicably, Butler relented, a decision he regretted and later scolded himself for making.[42]

As the campaign began on June 9, Butler was filled with foreboding and told his wife that "I think it will fail." This prediction was accurate. Gillmore marched his force to within sight of Petersburg, refused to attack because he feared the Rebel defenses were too strong, and then returned to Bermuda Hundred without firing a shot. Outraged at this "disgraceful failure," Butler relieved Gillmore from command and banished him to Fortress Monroe. This debacle ended Butler's hopes of capturing Petersburg with the small force he then possessed.[43]

As this farce was unfolding, Grant, following the defeat at Cold Harbor, decided to transfer the Army of the Potomac to Bermuda Hundred in an attempt to capture Petersburg. Essentially, he decided to adopt the strategy that Butler had been pursuing since the last week of May. The actual assault on Petersburg, while nominally under Butler's command, was directed by Smith, whose corps was the first to arrive at Bermuda Hundred. Butler's assignment was to occupy the railroad and prevent or delay Lee's army from reinforcing Petersburg. To accomplish this task, Grant increased the size of Butler's force by temporarily attaching the Sixth Corps, commanded by Gen. Horatio Wright, to the Army of the James.[44]

Once again, Butler's effort to capture Petersburg failed. Smith refused to launch an all-out assault against the city's entrenchments and provided the Rebels with enough time to send reinforcements and prevent the town's fall. As this occurred, Butler, who was again feuding with his subordinates, was unable to prevent part of Lee's army from marching to Petersburg's relief. Wright infuriated Butler by arriving at Bermuda Hundred later than expected. After Wright's corps took position, Butler ordered his forces to advance westward, but his corps commanders refused to move vigorously and quarreled with Butler throughout the entire operation. Butler and Wright spent as much time arguing between themselves as they did fighting the Rebels. By June 18, the attempt to capture Petersburg had failed, and the Union army settled in for a siege.[45]

Shortly thereafter, Grant returned Smith's corps to Butler's command, and strife immediately broke out between the two generals. Renewed controversy erupted over a scolding Butler gave Smith for marching too slowly, a reprimand that the West Pointer refused to accept. He demanded a court-martial. Taken aback by Smith's response, Butler tried to retract his statement, but discovered that it was too late because Smith refused to back down. The bad blood between the two generals continued to worsen. Col. Cyrus B. Comstock, one of Grant's aides, commented that neither Smith nor Butler "could get on well with any one, much less with each other."[46]

By July the political general was irritating most of the West Pointers in Grant's army. He had quarreled openly with Gillmore, Smith, and Wright, and the hostility was spreading. A French military observer was astonished to find that "I have never heard the name of Butler mentioned without an uncomplimentary epithet, and the most indulgent of the military [West Pointers] content themselves with saying that he is a *politician*, which is not exactly a compliment in the army." For his part, Butler complained about "West Pointism," a disease that he believed was "killing *both* sides."[47]

Fed up with the constant personal acrimony among his generals, Grant, who blamed Butler for causing all of the turmoil, finally decided to remove the politician. Grant believed that Butler was an excellent administrative officer and followed orders, but he was not competent enough to command troops in the field. The commanding general realized that his plan to provide Butler with the guidance of military professionals had failed. Therefore, Grant asked Halleck to draw up orders directing Butler to relinquish command, retire to Fortress Monroe, and appoint Smith to command of the Army of the James. Realizing that it was politically impossible to remove Butler completely, Grant wanted to give tactical control of the army to another general while Butler, carefully confined to Fortress Monroe, remained in charge of the Department of Virginia and North Carolina. Lincoln endorsed Grant's plan.[48]

Nothing came of this proposal because Grant suddenly changed his mind. The orders drawn up by the War Department created more confusion than clarity, and Grant's second proposal, to place Gen. William Franklin between Butler and Smith, was too unwieldy to work. In the end, Butler was left in command of the Army of the James, and, instead of firing Butler, Grant relieved Smith. This reversal of fortune was brought about by a series of critical remarks made by Smith that angered the commanding general. Smith castigated Meade, accused Grant of drunkenness, made hostile remarks about Grant's handling of the battle of Cold Harbor, wrote intemperate letters of advice, and wondered aloud how Grant could retain an incompetent like Butler. As a result, the commanding general saw Smith and not Butler as the root cause of the constant bickering in the army. On July 19, Smith was relieved, and Butler's authority over the Army of the James was confirmed.[49]

Some officers, convinced that Butler used his political connections to save himself and force Smith's removal, accused the citizen general of Machiavellian intrigues during this episode. Rather imaginatively, Smith believed that Butler somehow got Grant intoxicated and then used this incident to blackmail the commanding general. These colorful stories have no foundation in reality. In fact, Butler exerted little influence on the decision to retain him, a decision made in private by Grant, Halleck, and a few other key personnel.[50]

This settlement was based not on military considerations but on purely political grounds, for it was Butler's position as a Democrat that saved his military career. Even Grant could not relieve Butler and send the politician home. The only way to remove Butler was by politely shoving him aside, placing him in a position where he no longer commanded field troops yet still exercised authority over administration, but when that effort failed, Grant had no choice but to retain the political general. At the end of July, Lincoln expressed why Butler remained in the army. Butler, the president declared, "has my confidence in his ability and fidelity to the country and to me. And I wish him sustained in all his efforts in our great common cause." As long as Lincoln needed the support of prominent Democrats, Butler remained untouchable.[51]

After being nearly removed, Butler settled in as commander of the Army of the James, performing his duties competently throughout the fall campaign against Petersburg and Richmond. Grant was unable to batter his way into either city or break the rail connections that allowed Lee to supply his army. Stalemated, as autumn ended the Union army prepared for winter, though Grant still sought ways to strike at the Rebel army. He found one at Fort Fisher, located outside of Wilmington, North Carolina, a bastion that protected the last major Confederate port open to blockade runners.

In the fall of 1864, Grant decided to strike at this last Rebel coastal fortification with a joint army-navy operation. The commanding general entrusted the army component of the expedition to Gen. Godfrey Weitzel, a twenty-nine-year-old West Point graduate, and ordered him to prepare sixty-five hundred men from the Army of the James with the object of capturing Fort Fisher and, if possible, Wilmington. If he failed to take either, Grant instructed Weitzel to entrench and lay siege to Fort Fisher; retreat was an option only if he was unable "to effect a landing."[52]

As commander of the Army of the James, all of these orders passed through Butler, who saw this expedition as a chance to try out a new idea he was toying with. Butler had recently read of a gunpowder explosion in Erith, England, that devastated several miles of the surrounding countryside. This event convinced him that Fort Fisher could be destroyed by filling a vessel with explosives and detonating it several hundred yards from the fortress. On a visit to Washington, Butler pitched his idea to Lincoln and Gustavus Fox, the assistant secretary of the navy. The president was skeptical, but the navy endorsed the concept, including Adm. David Porter, commanding the naval contingent of the expedition, who encouraged the scheme because he "saw the road to success." Grant possessed no faith in the idea, believing that it "would have about the same effect on the fort that firing feathers from muskets would have on the enemy." Nonetheless, Grant allowed the scheme to go forward.[53]

What shocked Grant was Butler's decision to assume command of the enterprise. Butler took command because, he argued, Weitzel "was quite a young man" and thus unfit to lead the campaign. Grant later testified that he never "dreamed of [Butler] going with the expedition." Porter, who disliked Butler and had no respect for him, was also dumbfounded by this decision. The admiral believed the change occurred because, as he later wrote, Butler "was in the zenith of his power and seemed to do pretty much as he pleased." Neither Grant nor Porter could stop Butler, because the political general had the right to lead any attack that used troops from his army. Even the enlisted men saw ill tidings in Butler's decision. As one sergeant commented, "Old Butler is here and perhaps will command the expedition—in order to insure its failure."[54]

Butler's decision helped to turn a promising expedition into one of the most embarrassing Union defeats of the war. From the beginning, things went wrong. Despite proddings from Grant, Butler dallied at Fortress Monroe for a week, finally sailing on December 13 and arriving at the rendezvous point on December 15, only to discover an empty sea because the navy was still in port, loading the powder boat. Porter finally showed up on December 18, but rough seas prevented any attack for three days. By this time, the army transports were running out of fuel and water, forcing them to sail to Beaufort, North Carolina, for supplies. Early on the morning of December 24, Porter, without bothering to wait for the army to return, detonated the powder boat. The explosion had no effect on Fort Fisher, except to awaken the garrison.[55]

Butler returned to find the navy bombarding the bastion and decided to attempt a landing. On December 25, twenty-five hundred Union soldiers stormed ashore unopposed, established a beachhead, and waited for orders to assault the fortress. None ever came, because Butler, who had lost all enthusiasm for the expedition after his pet idea failed, was searching for an excuse to abandon the enterprise. He quickly discovered three. First, Weitzel reported that any assault on the fort "would be butchery," an opinion that coincided with Butler's own. Then, the citizen general learned that Rebel reinforcements from Virginia were due to arrive at any moment. Finally, officers reported that more bad weather was expected that could strand the troops on the beach if they were not promptly withdrawn. This last information convinced Butler, and he ordered his soldiers to withdraw and return to Fortress Monroe, ending the campaign.[56]

The debacle at Fort Fisher caused a firestorm of protest that swept Butler out of command. Grant began the debate, wiring Lincoln, "The Wilmington expedition has proven a gross and culpable failure. . . . Who is to blame I hope will be known." The blame fell on Butler. One sergeant wrote, "Everybody is disgusted. Officers and men express [the belief] that the fort was ours and that no one but Butler prevented them from taking it." Naval officers condemned Butler as "either a black-hearted traitor or an arrant coward." Furious over Butler's decision to retreat, several of the expedition's brigade commanders personally complained to Grant about the politician's inept handling of the operation. These complaints and Butler's report, which clearly showed he disobeyed orders, led Grant to request Butler's removal, a request that Lincoln, now safely reelected, granted on January 7, 1865.[57]

Ending Butler's military career for the bungling Fort Fisher expedition was justified, even if not all the blame for the defeat rested with the political general. An equal amount of the blame must go to the navy. Porter failed to arrive at the rendezvous point on time, detonated the powder boat before the army returned from Beaufort, and did not provide adequate cover fire for the troops on shore. Nevertheless, Butler cannot escape censure. He insisted on attempting a scheme that had dubious merits, delayed his departure, failed to communicate effectively with Porter, and then made no real effort to attack Fort Fisher. He clearly disobeyed orders when he landed troops and then failed either to attack the fort or to lay siege to it, as directed by his instructions. The successful storming of the fort on January 15, 1865, demonstrated that Butler's decision not to assault the bastion was a poor one.

Butler's removal was only partly motivated by this disaster. Grant clearly had come to dislike the politician. He had been searching for a way to rid himself of the citizen general's presence since July, and this episode merely provided the grounds that allowed him to relieve Butler. In February, his dislike of Butler led him to block an attempt to appoint the politician as provost marshal of Charleston, South Carolina. Lincoln accepted the decision because with the election of 1864 behind him and the war winding down, he no longer needed Butler's political support. Thus, Butler's Civil War career came to an end.[58]

The campaigns of 1864 demonstrated conclusively three trends that had been evident since early in the war. The first was that political generals with little command experience or who were proven failures should never have been allowed to lead independent armies. Banks, Butler, and Sigel all failed miserably in their respective expeditions primarily because they lacked the ability or experience to direct an army in the field. Their only claims to command were their political connections, claims that led Lincoln to place military incompetents in positions they clearly had no place holding. Grant tried to rectify this to some extent by assigning military professionals within these commands, but this plan failed because of petty feuding and the fact that these professionals were no more competent than the citizen generals. As a result, three campaigns that might have succeeded ended in failure, defeats that contributed to falling Union morale in the summer of 1864 and almost ruined Lincoln's hopes for reelection.

The second trend evident throughout 1864 was that political generals could make important contributions to victory when not advanced beyond their abilities. Many of the citizen generals who began their military careers commanding smaller units, either a regiment or a brigade, and worked their way up to higher commands, earning promotions through demonstrated competence, often proved to be good generals. Blair, Logan, and Wadsworth all earned the commands they held in 1864, and throughout the year proved at the very least to be capable, if not excellent, battlefield commanders. They had all learned, through practical experience, how an army functions, to direct units in the field, to communicate in the heat of battle, and to inspire troops. None of them, with the exception of Logan, could have directed an independent army, but they made significant contributions to Union victory.

Finally, the last trend to manifest itself was the poisonous relations that existed between citizen generals and West Point graduates. In every campaign throughout 1864, bickering between them occurred. This feuding was not always dangerous, as the case with Logan and Sherman illustrates, but it was present and often affected the conduct of operations. On the Red River, in the Shenandoah Valley, and wherever Butler appeared, these acrimonious disputes hindered operations and even played a role in bringing about Union disasters. No satisfactory solution to this problem was ever found, save to remove the general who appeared to be the most offensive.

Curiously, in 1864, politics did not play as a great a role in determining military appointments. Lincoln began the year by placing politically important individuals in significant military commands, but he was much more willing to sack failed generals than in previous years. Banks, Sigel, and Butler were all relieved or demoted, despite their political connections. This occurred for two reasons. First, Lincoln adopted a much more ruthless attitude toward winning the war, an attitude that made him less forgiving of military failure. And second, the support of these generals was not as politically necessary after Lincoln received the Republican nomination for president and then won the 1864 presidential election. He no longer needed to coddle incompetent generals in order to ensure their political support.

CHAPTER 9

Quasi-
Civil Support

One task that political generals seemed well suited to perform was military administration, what Lincoln called "quasi-civil support." Before the war, many of them had gained practical experience holding offices in local, state, and national governments, experience that appeared to make them perfect candidates to manage civil-military affairs in the North and South. At one time or another, Lincoln placed many of his political generals in command of military departments or districts, positions that involved martial law or military government. Their duties often required them to spend more time governing than fighting. Even citizen generals who commanded combat units on occasion had to deal with aspects of military administration. As a result, political generals exerted a great amount of influence over these aspects of the Union war effort.[1]

When Union armies occupied portions of the South, and on occasion when they operated in the border states, they had to assume the duties or help enforce the laws of the civil administration through either military government or martial law. Military government began when the army assumed control of the civil government; civilian officials often remained in office, but they served at the discretion of the military. It occurred in captured regions, served as a transitional phase between active military operations and the establishment of Unionist civilian control, and continued until a loyal civilian authority could be installed. During the Civil War, military government was used in the Confederacy, whereas in the border states Lincoln often declared martial law. This allowed military authorities to exercise temporary control over the civilian population in these states, but authority remained in the hands of the civilian government, with whom the army cooperated.[2]

Military administration encompassed a vast array of duties. Generals had to work with local authorities, assume police duties, tend to public utilities, establish commercial rules, deal with foreign consuls, and create charities for the poor, along with many other mundane matters. They also engaged in controversial activities, such as suppressing newspapers, confiscating property, and arresting suspected Rebels. These duties occupied the time of many generals from the moment the war began. In June 1861, Schenck commented that in Virginia he had to not only perform his military tasks but also "arrest & try secessionists or suspected traitors, restore wandering pigs, & act as a sort of police judge generally." As the war progressed and Lincoln looked to the postwar period, a few generals had to confront the issue of Reconstruction. This duty involved them in weighty questions such as citizenship, elections, and constitution making.[3]

The problems inherent in military administration were complicated by the Lincoln administration's failure to create a body of rules regulating it until April 1863. For two years, all Union generals were allowed to formulate their own policies. Butler later commented that he governed New Orleans without ever receiving "any direction or intimation from Washington" about how to "carry on the administration of the government." Even after the War Department issued General Orders 100 in April 1863, establishing the basic rules of military government, commanders were free, as Halleck told Hurlbut, to decide how to apply the new regulations. Throughout the conflict, therefore, commanders on the spot determined how to govern their departments. Unless specifically asked, Lincoln usually provided little direction, and as a result generals naturally developed a variety of rules and regulations; remarkably, they dealt with many problems of military government in similar manners, but on some questions there was a great amount of variety. More important, many of their choices and actions resulted in controversy since Americans disliked any form of military rule.[4]

While operating in the Confederacy, and even other states, one commonality among the department and district commanders was their determination to exercise control over their commands. Sherman explained this goal to a committee from Mississippi: "In war the Commander on the Spot is the judge, and may take your house, your fields, your everything, and turn you all out helpless to starve." Commanders used several different methods to impose their authority, such as arrests, suppression of newspapers, and confiscation of property. Regardless of their political persuasion, citizen generals also adopted these techniques.[5]

One method used by generals to maintain control over the populations in their districts and departments was to arrest suspected Rebels or citizens who aided the Confederacy. Since martial law applied to these regions, military commanders were free to incarcerate anyone deemed disloyal. For instance, while commanding the Mountain Department in 1862, Frémont arrested a minister for "having spoken publicly and privately against the [U.S.] Government." In 1864, Butler justified the detention of one individual in Virginia simply by stating, "He is a secessionist."[6]

Operating under martial law in Maryland during 1861, Banks and Dix engaged in wide-scale arrests of citizens, including members of the state legislature, to maintain order and prevent the state from seceding. In the summer, Banks commanded the military forces in eastern Maryland, including Baltimore, a city with many Confederate sympathizers. Secessionist strength, especially among the city's police, frightened the Lincoln administration into ordering Banks to arrest Chief of Police George Kane and the city police board. On June 27, the general tried to avoid antagonizing the city by apprehending only Kane, justifying the act by claiming that the chief of police was "the head of an armed force hostile" to the U.S. government. The next day, the city police board defiantly disbanded the entire force. Faced with this challenge, Banks incarcerated the police board on July 1 but brought no charges against them. These actions temporarily quieted the city.[7]

In August, Dix assumed command of the military forces in eastern Maryland, while Banks took charge of those in the western part of the state. Dix made numerous arrests, as he received authority to "make any arrest that you may consider necessary." During the fall, he jailed a newspaper editor for printing prosecession articles, an individual for forwarding recruits to the Confederate army, a gentleman for disloyalty, and one man for "raising a rebel flag on his home and applying to the rebels for arms to defend it." On one occasion in 1862, Dix ordered the arrest of a judge to be made in the judge's court "in order that the proceeding might be more marked." This action ensured that everyone understood who possessed authority in eastern Maryland. Many of these actions, Dix admitted, were done "without any warrant or authority whatever," but the general justified them by claiming that this was the only way to prevent Maryland from seceding.[8]

In mid-September, Banks and Dix received orders from the Lincoln administration to arrest prosecession members of the Maryland legislature before the legislature met at Frederick. The administration feared that the legislature might pass an ordinance of secession, an act that was to be prevented, McClellan wrote Banks, by imprisoning "the whole party." Acting swiftly, Banks arrested nine legislators in his department, and Dix rounded up another seven. The night of the arrests, Dix learned that a lawyer from the eastern shore of Virginia intended to obtain a writ of habeas corpus for their release. The general ordered the lawyer's detention and confinement until morning and then sent him back across the Chesapeake by steamer with instructions to the captain not to bring him back to Baltimore. This action, Dix commented, was "a summary and effective process; but it is not in the books."[9]

To further secure the state, in November the two generals jailed more men on the eve of Maryland's elections for the state legislature. Banks ordered the confinement of candidates opposed to the pro-Union ticket deemed too hostile to the government and of any "suspected persons," especially those just returned from the Confederacy. Dix also ordered the arrest of any suspected Rebels to prevent "their criminal attempt to convert their elective franchise into an engine for the subversion of the government." Both of these actions in the fall of 1861 helped to prevent Maryland from seceding, primarily by overpowering the opposition with the often arbitrary use of the power of arrest.[10]

Throughout the war, citizen generals used the power of arrest to assert Federal authority. In New Orleans in 1862, Butler did so when he seized, tried, and hanged William Mumford for tearing down the U.S. flag. To drive his point home about who was in control, shortly before Mumford was executed, Butler commuted a sentence of death to hard labor for six men convicted of raising a company for the Confederate army. Schenck, while commanding the Middle Department in 1863, an area that included northern Virginia, Maryland, Pennsylvania, and Delaware, imprisoned men for aiding Rebels, insulting the flag, declaring sympathy for the Confederacy, and violating their oath of allegiance. While in Missouri in August 1861, Hurlbut ordered the arrest of "prominent secessionists," including John McAfee, a former Speaker of the Missouri House of Representatives, whom he required "to dig trenches in the hot sun."[11]

Sometimes, the mere threat of incarceration was enough to quell a restless population. Butler understood this fact when he issued the controversial General Orders 28. Upon arriving in New Orleans, Union soldiers encountered a hostile population, especially from females who regularly insulted them, spit in their faces and on their uniforms, and made rude remarks and gestures. To put a stop to these "she adders," Butler ordered that any woman who insulted a Federal soldier "shall be regarded and held liable to be treated as a woman of the town plying her avocation." This order was condemned throughout the Confederacy and even in Europe, but it ended the mistreatment of his troops. As Butler wrote, "The order executed itself. No arrests were ever made under it or because of it."[12]

A second method used by department and district commanders to assert Federal authority was to suppress newspapers deemed hostile or disloyal. By doing so, they could to a limited extent control the flow of information within their departments, determine what news was reported, and shape editorial comments. Lincoln privately regretted such actions, believing that they stirred up more opposition, but publicly defended his commanders.[13]

Dix suppressed several newspapers while commanding eastern Maryland, but always with some reluctance and only after seeking approval from higher authority. The general believed that "we must get along with" freedom of the press and "let the newspapers publish what nonsense they please." To forestall the drastic step of shutting down a newspaper, he often met with the editor to explain what changes had to be made to avoid suppression, a tactic that worked successfully with the *Baltimore Sun*, a paper that "changed its tone" after Dix talked with the editor. Nevertheless, Dix was not afraid to close a newspaper if he had no other choice. In August 1861, he shut down the *Exchange, South*, and *Republican*, three of Baltimore's small but "rabid secession papers," and jailed the editor of the *Exchange* "to remove the incitement of his presence" from the city.[14]

In 1864, while commanding the Department of the East, headquartered in New York City, Dix's suppression of several newspapers aroused controversy. In mid-May, the *New York World* and the *Journal of Commerce* published a spurious presidential proclamation that called for the drafting of four hundred thousand men. Dix discovered that the papers were not responsible for the false proclamation and, upon realizing their mistake, published a bulletin announcing it was a fraud. Unfortunately, before receiving Dix's explanation, Stanton obtained an order from Lincoln to close the papers and arrest the editors because he feared that the bogus proclamation was a Confederate plot aided by Democratic newspapers. When Dix delayed enforcing the order, he received a rebuke from Stanton for delaying the execution of the president's directives. After receiving this telegram, Dix did as he was told.[15]

Stanton realized his error and told Dix to ignore the president's order, but Dix's suppression of the two papers caused problems with New York City authorities. Prodded by Democratic governor Horatio Seymour, the district attorney arrested Dix and four other officers for illegally seizing the papers and imprisoning the editors. In a cabinet meeting, Lincoln admitted "the act to be his" and "thought the government should protect Dix." Fortunately, the matter never went to trial because a grand jury refused to indict the general. The episode demonstrated that generals could not exercise as much authority in the North, where the normal process of civil government was not disrupted or threatened by rebellion, as they could in the border states and the South.[16]

Other political generals, especially those in the South, were not as squeamish as Dix about suppressing newspapers. Upon assuming control in New Orleans, Butler issued a proclamation that established rules governing what the local papers could publish. These regulations banned the publication of troop movements, unflattering comments about the Union, and anything that might influence the public against the U.S. government. Butler's rules were imprecise and open to interpretation, giving him considerable leeway in how he might deal with the press. The general interpreted these rules broadly. Within two weeks, Butler shut down four of the city's papers: the *True Delta* for refusing to publish a proclamation, the *Bee* for publishing a "covert argument in favor of the cotton burning mob," the *Daily Delta* for discussing the cotton question "in a manner which violates the terms" announced in his proclamation, and the *Crescent* because the owner was currently in arms against the Union. For the rest of his tenure in New Orleans, Butler continued to suppress papers. In each case, he allowed the paper to reopen within a week. These actions demonstrated his authority but also showed that his control was never complete because opposition newspapers continually ignored his orders, regardless of the consequences.[17]

Butler's successor, Banks, also shut down New Orleans newspapers. Initially, Banks tried to convince the newspapers to cooperate with him, arguing that he needed their support in order to establish a new government in Louisiana, but when the journals refused to heed his advice, the general suppressed them in an effort to assert his authority. He shut down the *Courier Français* for publishing pro-Confederate statements about the Atlanta campaign and the *Picayune* for printing a false presidential proclamation. Altogether, Banks suppressed five pro-Southern papers. He also distributed money to pro-Union papers on the stipulation that they submit to censorship and publish anything he submitted. When they refused, as the *Daily Delta* did, he closed them down. These actions showed Banks's determination to eradicate the "feeling on the part of publishers that they are irresponsible to the Military Authorities."[18]

Schenck engaged in the wholesale suppression of newspapers in the Middle Department, shutting down or banning the sale of twelve newspapers. The attempt to eliminate from his department every paper deemed disloyal led Schenck into a controversy in January 1863 when he closed the *Philadelphia Evening Journal*. The paper, the only Democratic sheet in Philadelphia, published an editorial that praised Jefferson Davis's annual message while referring to Lincoln's as "quite damaging to the intellectual capacity of the Federal president." Angered by this characterization of his friend, Schenck suppressed the journal and arrested the editor, jailing him illegally in Maryland. These actions brought protests from Democrats and even criticism from Republicans, including Pennsylvania governor Andrew Curtin. Schenck refused to back down until the editor apologized and promised not to publish any more like editorials, at which time he was released.[19]

Other generals did not engage in such wide-scale suppression of the press. For instance, Wadsworth shut down a few journals while commanding Washington, D.C., but only on orders from his superiors. In Missouri, Frémont closed only one newspaper. Sigel, while in charge of the Department of West Virginia in 1864, arrested only one editor and received harsh criticism from the state's governor for doing so. In Memphis, Hurlbut suppressed the distribution of only the *Chicago Times*, but he did so for essentially personal reasons: the paper attacked his friends Lincoln and Yates and censured Hurlbut's administration of Memphis. He not only banned the paper but also threatened fines and punishment to anyone carrying the *Times*. These orders brought a storm of protest that forced Grant to countermand Hurlbut's action.[20]

Yet another method of asserting authority was the confiscation of property. By threatening to or even taking an individual's property, generals sought to compel local populations to abide by their rules and recognize Federal authority. Confiscation, of course, was a tool adopted by field commanders for different reasons. As the war progressed, generals allowed their soldiers to take authorized items from Southern farms and towns to obtain food, forage, wood, and other goods deemed essential for an army's survival. By taking civilian property, they struck at the enemy's material resources and morale, hoping to weaken the Confederacy's ability to resist.[21]

Federal military policy toward civilian property changed slowly. In 1861 and into 1862, most commanders avoided confiscating civilian possessions, adopting a policy of conciliation in order to entice Southerners back into the Union. Conciliation ended with the issuing of the Emancipation Proclamation, initiating a period of pragmatism in which commanders attempted to distinguish among secessionist, neutral, and loyal individuals. By 1864, the Union had adopted a policy of hard war, focusing considerable military resources on confiscating or destroying civilian property such as farm products, factories, and businesses in an effort to weaken the Confederacy. The attitude of political generals toward civilian property followed this pattern, though some of them never accepted the notion of hard war.[22]

Throughout 1861 and into 1862, political generals issued orders regarding civilian property that sounded a similar theme. They all declared, as Butler wrote in Virginia, that the "rights of property . . . must be respected." Property could be seized only "when the exigencies of the service require[d]." In Missouri, Hurlbut said, "No depredations will be tolerated in property," and Frémont "strictly" forbade his troops "to take private property"; both decreed that only authorized officers could do so. Dix told one of his officers operating on the eastern shore of Virginia "to prevent any outrage upon persons or property" and ordered the arrest of any soldier who violated this command. These orders basically met the requirements of the Confiscation Act passed by Congress and signed into law by Lincoln in August 1861, which allowed for the seizure of property used in military aid of the rebellion.[23]

Beginning in the summer of 1862, many citizen generals adopted a pragmatic approach to confiscating Southern property. In New Orleans, Butler issued orders against the "plundering of public and private property," but seized several homes for the use of himself and his staff and twice forced wealthy individuals and businesses who aided the rebellion to pay large sums into a relief fund for the poor. While in charge of Memphis, Hurlbut began confiscating buildings and homes desired by the military for quarters and offices. These generals took property only when it benefited the Federal occupation forces, but this marked a definite shift from their attitude of a year before when they tried to avoid seizing private property.[24]

Not all political generals, especially Democrats, agreed with the policy of confiscating civilian property, particularly when it entailed large-scale confiscation that they believed amounted to plundering civilians. Denver, commanding a district in West Tennessee in the fall of 1862, allowed his troops to scour the country for food, but despised what he viewed as the "vandalism" of many soldiers. His troops engaged in wholesale plunder, stripping the land of everything and turning the army into an "undisciplined mob." By doing so, Denver complained, they "throw aside civilization, and become savages."[25]

In Virginia, Dix agreed with these sentiments. His department, he wrote in April 1863, had "been disgraced . . . by the most shameful pillage of unprotected families." To put a stop to it, Dix arrested and tried an officer for allowing his troops to kill poultry, but this only temporarily halted his soldiers' activities. By July, the general was unable to control them, as, he wrote, they "rob & plunder without the slightest regard to what I say." To Dix, there was nothing "so revolting in this war," and he promised to shoot anyone he caught stealing or destroying property. Though both Denver and Dix understood that confiscating some property was necessary in order to provide their troops with supplies, they deplored the slide of Federal policy toward hard war, a policy that these two conservative generals viewed as immoral and unwise.[26]

Several political generals commanding departments adopted the tactics of hard war. Schenck, as commander of the Middle Department, never hesitated to confiscate property if, even on the slightest pretext, the owners could be labeled Rebels. His troops, trying to prevent the trade of illegal goods between Virginia and Maryland, seized such items as pianos, ladies' hoops, bolts of cotton velvet, and pairs of women's Moroccan slippers. Butler, after he assumed command in Virginia and North Carolina in 1863, issued orders that allowed for a hard war. These directives forbade taking property except for use as shelter, transportation, fuel, or food unless it was seized "to prevent its use by the enemy." Troops could also destroy property "as a summary punishment" for a variety of offenses. Naturally, the soldiers under his command used the widest latitude when interpreting and applying these orders, and Butler made little effort to prevent abuses from occurring.[27]

As Union department and district commanders asserted control over their jurisdictions in the South, they often struggled with local civil governments and, later, military governors. Most generals had little patience for these local governments and regularly ignored them, left them temporarily vacant, or even placed army officers in them, preferring to administer their departments through military channels. They even ignored or feuded with Unionists and the military governors appointed by Lincoln as they sought to obtain mastery over their Southern commands.

When Butler arrived in New Orleans in 1862, he found a city government hostile to Union authority, but promised to allow the mayor, who though an unrepentant Confederate remained in office, freedom to run the city "so I should not have to occupy my time with such details." The honeymoon lasted just over two weeks. Shortly after Butler issued his Woman Order, the mayor publicly castigated the order and then signed a letter of protest. To Butler, these actions were a direct challenge to his authority, and he had the provost marshal haul the mayor down to his office. The mayor apologized, but shortly thereafter, cajoled by his advisers, he withdrew his apology. If Butler was angry before, he was now enraged. When he learned that the mayor had recently contributed twenty dollars to a secessionist group, the political general had the mayor, his secretary, and police officials arrested and imprisoned in Fort Jackson. The general then assumed control of the city's municipal government.[28]

In the summer of 1862, Lincoln named Brig. Gen. George Shepley military governor of Louisiana. Shepley was a good friend of Butler and owed his new position to his friend's patronage. The military governor had power over the provost marshals, parish police, juries, schools, court system, and basic state government functions. Butler and Shepley cooperated, but Banks's arrival ended the harmony that existed between the military governor and the commander of the Department of the Gulf. Banks, who believed that all of Butler's appointees worked against him in the hopes of returning Butler to command, sought to strip Shepley of his power and secure firm control over the state. In December 1862, Banks transferred jurisdiction over all nonmilitary court cases to a recently established provisional court, a month later he took control of the provost marshals, and at the end of 1863, he, not Shepley, began organizing a new state government by preparing to hold state elections. When this government was instituted, it received Shepley's remaining powers, and Shepley went home.[29]

In the fall of 1863, when Butler took command of the Department of Virginia and North Carolina, he sought to strip power from the loyal governor of Virginia, Francis H. Pierpont. Under the previous department commander, Pierpont had been allowed to govern with little interference, but Butler immediately began subverting the governor. The political general initiated an investigation of banks to determine if they smuggled funds to aid the Confederacy, looked into Norfolk's finances, and ordered his provost marshals to take control of the police and judicial functions in Norfolk and Portsmouth. These actions confounded Pierpont, and he complained to Lincoln, who suspended Butler's acts until the citizen general provided a written justification. In February, Butler submitted a long brief defending his conduct and subtly ridiculing Pierpont.[30]

The conflict simmered until June, when Butler seized the initiative and sought to replace Norfolk's civil government with a military government. The general called an election and asked the loyal residents to decide whether they wanted to continue the present civilian administration or submit to military rule. Supporters of Pierpont's government refused to participate, the few citizens who actually voted chose not to continue the government, and Butler ordered the civil government to cease functioning, threatening to arrest officials who tried to perform their jobs. Nearly every member of Lincoln's cabinet damned Butler's actions. Stanton called it "a high-handed measure," and Attorney General Bates declared it "barbarous government." Lincoln "said he was much perplexed to know what to do" but allowed Butler's action to stand.[31]

For a month, a tense stillness settled over the issue, but at the end of July the situation exploded when Virginia Circuit Court judge Edward Snead attempted to hold court in Norfolk. Snead, acting on the advice of Bates, deliberately sought to challenge and thereby embarrass Butler. Never one to back down, Butler arrested Snead and asked Lincoln to decide the matter, telling him that only the president could "sustain, uphold, protect, and defend" Pierpont's government. Lincoln, always reluctant to overrule his military commanders, did nothing and thus sustained Butler, probably because he disliked the idea of antagonizing the influential Democrat on the eve of the presidential election.[32]

Even as they struggled for control over their jurisdictions, Union department and district commanders invariably found themselves dealing with matters associated with municipal government. In the South, the arrival of Federal troops often led to a breakdown of civil government as Confederate authorities fled, local officials deferred to the occupiers, or the new authorities simply replaced the civil government. Dix, for example, encountered this situation in some Virginia counties, where he found "no civil magistrate in this country." As a result, the general was forced to undertake these duties himself. This was especially true in New Orleans, where Union military authorities under Butler, Banks, and Hurlbut ran the city for three years. Even in Maryland, where local and state governments functioned throughout the war, political generals often became involved in some aspects of municipal affairs.[33]

Maintaining law and order was the most important local governmental issue confronting political generals. In 1861, after arresting the Baltimore chief of police and city police board, Banks first assigned their duties to a Union officer and then appointed a loyal citizen chief of police "to administer the police law." Nevertheless, Banks and then Dix continued to run the Baltimore police force until March 1862, when Dix transferred control to a newly established police commission. Despite the transfer, Dix felt free, when trouble erupted in the city in May, to ask Stanton for authority "to assume control of the police." Peace was restored and the military did not assume control, but the episode demonstrated that military authorities believed they could in an emergency displace the local police to restore law and order.[34]

In New Orleans, Butler took control of both the police and the judicial functions. After imprisoning the mayor and the chief of police, Butler appointed a Union officer chief of police, who, because all but eleven of the city's police officers resigned after refusing to take a loyalty oath, recruited five hundred new policemen. The new police department, acting in conjunction with Federal troops, successfully maintained law and order. Similar action was taken in regards to the city's courts. Four of the five civil district court judges quit, and Butler closed the courts with criminal jurisdiction when he took control of the police. The Union army administered justice through two courts: a provost court to try misdemeanors and a military commission to hear cases punishable by death or ten or more years' imprisonment. In the fall, as overt hostility toward the Federal occupation diminished, Butler reopened a few civil courts, and Shepley, undoubtedly with Butler's approval, appointed the judges.[35]

After Banks took command, Lincoln created a United States Provisional Court for Louisiana to administer justice in the state, but its civilian judge quarreled with Banks over the issue of confiscation. The court seized large amounts of Rebel property, including foodstuffs the army needed, thus angering Banks. As a result of the Bobbin Boy's complaints, a regular U.S. district court was established. The major issue of who had authority over the courts was not solved, and Banks and the new district judge also wrangled over confiscation; at one point, Banks's chief of staff nearly arrested the judge. The controversy, which could have been resolved only by Lincoln, who refused to interfere, simmered for the rest of the war.[36]

Political generals also faced mundane municipal problems. When Butler jailed the mayor of New Orleans, he became the city's acting mayor, compelling him to deal with a wide range of issues. In order to forestall waves of typhoid, typhus, and yellow fever, for example, the political general ordered the regular cleaning of the streets, removal of garbage, and flushing of sewage ditches and also established a quarantine station for incoming ships. As a result, only two cases of the dreaded yellow fever occurred in 1862. To provide for the poor and destitute, Butler distributed captured foodstuffs, put men to work cleaning the streets and repairing levees, taxed wealthy individuals and businesses to create a fund for "providing employment and food for the deserving poor," and appointed a superintendent to administer the program. He also replaced the city's currency, ordering the banks to stop circulating Confederate notes and meet their obligations only with bank notes, U.S. Treasury notes, gold, or silver.[37]

Butler's successors in New Orleans maintained and even expanded many of these policies while creating some of their own. Banks added more public works programs to employ the poor and continued the system of relief, but paid for it by renting confiscated property. The former congressman also prohibited foreclosures on mortgages and forced sales of property until August 1864, when he allowed them "except in cases where it is against equity and justice." During the winter of 1863–64, owing to a shortage of coal, Banks regulated the price of the substance to prevent vendors from oppressing "the poor by unreasonable or extortionate charges." Hurlbut ordered the levees along the Mississippi River repaired and, during a flood in March 1865, impressed the entire male population of Algiers, a district near New Orleans, to repair the levee in front of the city.[38]

Some political generals dealt with problems unique to their commands or ones they created for themselves. In New Orleans, Butler became embroiled in disputes with foreign consuls representing nine European countries. He believed that all of the consuls had "aided the rebellion by every means," especially by transferring Confederate funds to Europe and buying arms and ammunition. To put a stop to this activity, Butler waged a personal vendetta against them. Within a week of assuming command, the political general learned that the British Guard, a militia company composed of British citizens, had voted to send their arms and uniforms to the Rebel army. Butler, over the protests of the British consul, expelled from the city every man who refused to turn in his arms and uniform to Union authorities.[39]

Thereafter, the struggle with the consuls escalated. On May 10, learning that the Netherlands' consul might be holding a large amount of Confederate money, Butler ordered the consul's office searched. When more than eight hundred thousand dollars was found, the consul was arrested and the money confiscated. By mid-June, Butler had wrangled with the consuls in nearly a dozen cases, precipitating complaints from foreign governments and forcing Washington to send Reverdy Johnson to investigate the merits of Butler's charges. In almost every case, Johnson ruled against Butler and restored seized property to its owners. Butler continued to feud with the consuls, causing further headaches for Secretary of State Seward and Lincoln that eventually played a role in the president's decision to remove the general from command.[40]

Dix confronted his own special problem in New York City when he was assigned in July 1863 to command the Department of the East, encompassing New Jersey, New York, and New England. In 1863, with few men volunteering for army service, Congress passed the Enrollment Act to stimulate volunteering. The act made all able-bodied males from twenty to forty-five eligible for the draft, though a draft was to be held only when the quota for volunteers was not met, as occurred in the summer of 1863. The draft was denounced by Democratic politicians and newspapers and particularly disliked by the working class, who believed that they bore the burden of the fighting and had no desire to wage a war to free black slaves. On July 13, these resentments set off the New York City draft riot. For four days, mobs of working-class, mostly Irish, men swept through the city, burning draft offices and homes of Republicans and lynching blacks. More than 120 people were killed in the worst riot in American history.[41]

With the draft suspended in New York City and relations strained between Lincoln and the city and state governments, both controlled by Democrats, the president needed a commanding officer in New York who was trusted and respected. Dix, a longtime native of the state and a Democrat, was a shrewd choice to command the Department of the East. With many friends in the state and local governments and among other prominent citizens, he was a known and respected figure, possessed important contacts, and could ease the doubts of those who opposed the draft. His chief goal was to uphold the law and peacefully resume the draft as quickly as possible by pursuing a policy of conciliation. This meant working with state and local authorities and using police and militia forces, not Federal troops, to enforce the draft. In the North, Dix had no authority to remove civilian officeholders or impose martial law, but he had the power to enforce all Federal laws, even if local officials refused to cooperate.[42]

Upon his arrival, Dix met with New York state and city officials to discuss how best to restart the draft and ascertain their willingness to help. He concluded that the mayor was hostile but that Tammany Hall, which Dix thought represented more than half of the democracy, and militia commanders would uphold the Federal draft law. In an interview with Governor Horatio Seymour and several subsequent letters, the general expressed his desire for goodwill and cooperation with the state authorities, but the governor had no intention of working with Dix. Instead, Seymour tried to prevent the draft from resuming by appealing directly to Lincoln to suspend the draft. The president refused and endorsed Dix's plan to resume the draft on August 19.[43]

As the draft approached, Seymour still refused to cooperate, and Dix, realizing that conciliation had failed, prepared to enforce the law with Federal troops. Seymour's opposition, Dix believed, had increased the chances "of collision." To meet this possible threat, he asked Stanton for ten thousand more troops (he already had five thousand) and Lincoln to federalize the New York militia to prevent Seymour from using it to protect citizens from the draft. Dix did not want to take these steps but believed they were the only way to overawe resistance. In response, Stanton dispatched to New York ten thousand troops and three batteries of artillery from the Army of the Potomac, and Lincoln sent the general a proclamation nationalizing the militia that Dix could use if necessary.[44]

The night before the draft commenced, Dix informed Seymour that he now possessed a force adequate to suppress all opposition to the draft. The governor, outmaneuvered and beaten, agreed to uphold the law, and, the next day, the New York City draft began. "The draft is progressing quietly," the general proudly boasted. No incidents marred the renewal of the draft, primarily because Dix's security measures compelled the opposition to admit defeat. Though his original policy of conciliation failed, the general was deft enough to switch tactics and thereby compel Seymour and other opponents to support, or not openly oppose, the draft.[45]

Few generals dealt with issues related to the draft, but regulating commerce in occupied areas posed a common problem for all department commanders. As generals settled into their new positions, they received demands to open their areas to commerce. There were immense profits to be made, especially in cotton, a commodity demanded by textile producers in both the North and Europe. Generals faced two related problems when confronting this topic. As the war progressed, an illicit traffic with the Confederacy sprouted in which the Rebels swapped cotton in return for war goods. Department commanders somehow had to prevent this trade from occurring or limit it as much as possible, but doing so was difficult because the lure of easy wealth attracted many unscrupulous characters and led to corruption. Complicating matters, the Treasury Department tended to ignore profiteering, pursuing a liberal policy of issuing permits for trade in occupied areas, but the treasury's haphazard system never worked and, because it was loosely administered, even encouraged contraband trade.[46]

Military commanders tried to solve commercial problems in a number of ways. They attempted to ban trade, but that choice was politically unpopular. Even Lincoln preferred that some trade occur, since he believed it benefited the North more than the South. Most political generals did not adopt a ban. Instead, they either advocated a system that amounted to free trade or tried to regulate commerce in order to curb its worst abuses. Two citizen generals took advantage of their situation and made enormous profits through enterprises that overwhelming circumstantial evidence suggests were illegal, though no general was tried and convicted in court for committing such acts. Regardless of how they dealt with the issue, trade was an aspect of military administration that dominated the time of those generals who commanded departments.[47]

While commanding the Department of Virginia, Dix's experiences demonstrated the problems created by the issue of commerce. Upon his arrival at Fortress Monroe in June 1862, Dix ended the ban on trade enforced by his predecessor. Both Stanton and Chase approved Dix's request to allow shipments into Norfolk carrying goods for use by destitute citizens. Officially, the federal government permitted only eight ships into Norfolk, but everyone realized that many more vessels docked at the city and engaged in traffic extending well beyond providing goods for the area's forty thousand inhabitants. Many of Dix's officers granted these vessels illegal permits to trade at Norfolk. Dix was not satisfied with the amount of trade and sought to open the port to free trade. In early September, he recommended that the blockade of Norfolk be ended and that he be allowed "to grant permits to vessels" to trade goods in Norfolk essential for the inhabitants' survival.[48]

The Union navy hoped to completely end all such commerce. Secretary of the Navy Welles wanted the blockade, which officially still applied to Norfolk, enforced and told the new naval commander of the North Atlantic Blockading Squadron, Rear Adm. Samuel Lee, to stop trade with Norfolk. He also reminded Lee that no army or naval officer had authority to issue permits for trade. Lee so informed Dix, telling the general that only vessels in the service of the army and navy would be allowed into Norfolk. Such a policy conflicted with Dix's proposal, and throughout the fall the general and admiral sparred over the issue. Dix's subordinates continued to issue permits to vessels, but the navy stopped these ships and once halted and searched Dix's own boat, inflaming the conflict between Dix and Lee.[49]

Undeterred by the navy, Dix simply outflanked both Lee and Welles. He wrote several petitions to Chase, Stanton, and Halleck, reiterating his proposal and asking for its immediate adoption, and traveled to Washington on three occasions to appeal in person. For a time, the cabinet remained divided. Chase and Stanton both agreed with Dix, Welles wanted to enforce the blockade, and Seward believed the question should not be answered until after the fall elections. Finally, on November 12, after the election, Lincoln issued orders granting everything that Dix requested.[50]

The opening of trade witnessed a massive surge in the number of permits, as merchants flocked to Dix and his officers seeking authority to trade in Norfolk. The result was an immense amount of corruption as Northern goods flowed into and out of the city and into the Confederacy in exchange for cotton and other staples. Despite Dix's promise "to prevent illicit traffic," the flow of goods became impossible to regulate. One witness estimated that perhaps eight million pounds of Northern bacon passed through Norfolk and into Robert E. Lee's army, meat that may have saved the Army of Northern Virginia from starvation during the winter of 1863. All efforts to end this illegal traffic failed, and the commerce persisted for the rest of the war.[51]

Dix did not personally benefit from this illegal commerce. Even Welles, who deplored the new policy, believed that Dix was "clear of pecuniary gain," but he feared the general was surrounded by a "set of bloodsuckers who propose to . . . enrich themselves." Dix either was blind to or simply turned his back on the illegal activities pursued by officers and merchants in his department, men willing to pay any price to trade with the enemy. Either way, the general's actions did his country a disservice.[52]

Another attempt to open trade in the South by a political general resulted in similar contraband commerce. When Butler arrived in New Orleans, he recommended that the blockade of the city be lifted and trade resumed, an action taken by Lincoln on May 12. This initiated an illegal trade between Northern merchants and Confederate agents, as cotton and sugar were traded for military items like salt, shoes, and provisions. As in Virginia, the North was indirectly supplying the Rebel army. Butler pursued a contradictory policy toward this trade. To treasury agent George Dennison, the general said that he "understood there should be no trade with the enemy," but six days later told Chase that "I have endeavored in every possible way to open trade in cotton through the rebel lines." Butler never attempted to reconcile these contradictory positions, realizing that officials in the government as well as Northern businessmen desired this illegal traffic to continue.[53]

Regardless of what policy he pursued, many people suspected that Butler was personally involved in the illicit trade and amassed an enormous fortune. These beliefs were encouraged by acts Butler took before he arrived in New Orleans. While organizing the expedition in New England, a New York hat manufacturer accused Butler of demanding a 10 percent kickback. So many rumors of illegalities swirled around the general that Governor Andrew complained that Butler's activities seemed designed "to afford means to persons of bad character to make money unscrupulously." Though one individual complained directly to Quartermaster Gen. Montgomery Meigs, no action was taken against Butler. Once in the Gulf, Butler made several questionable business deals that only increased the gossip. On one occasion, he shipped $60,000 worth of sugar, tar, and turpentine as ballast to Boston and New York. The proceeds from the sale of these goods went to the Federal government, but Meigs scolded Butler for making this questionable transaction.[54]

Even worse were the activities of his brother, Andrew Jackson Butler. Andrew engaged in numerous nefarious schemes, though just how involved the general was in his brother's plots is difficult to assess. In one instance, Butler banned liquor in the department, and Andrew went from store to store buying all illegal beverages at bargain prices, gaining control of the market. At that point, General Butler lifted the ban, allowing his brother to sell his stock at inflated prices and reap a huge profit. On another occasion, Andrew began importing flour and, with his brother's approval, seized the city bakery, giving him control of the city's bread supply. Andrew also engaged in the illicit trade with the Rebels and earned, according to treasury agent Dennison, "between one and two million dollars." Dennison believed that the political general was Andrew's "partner or agent," but offered no direct evidence of Butler's complicity in these illegal actions.[55]

It seems improbable that Butler was not involved in his brother's corrupt activities. Too many of Andrew's dealings required the general's active support, and, as the commander of the department, he must have been aware of his brother's schemes and a participant. The massive increase in his net worth certainly suggests this fact. In May 1862, Butler was worth about $150,000; by 1868, he was worth an estimated $3 million. He could never have amassed this enormous fortune in so short a time from his legitimate income sources: salaries as a general and congressman, legal fees, and dividends from stockholdings. The citizen general was far too shrewd to leave any direct evidence of his duplicitous actions, and no one was ever able to prove that he actually engaged in any criminal acts.[56]

The second political general to govern New Orleans, Banks, made greater efforts to regulate trade and was not implicated in any illegalities. The opportunity to enrich himself certainly existed. Immediately upon his arrival, Banks was offered a bribe of $100,000 if he would approve an illegal transaction of Rebel cotton for Union salt. The general refused, but the experience convinced him that "there has been open trade with the enemy." The general realized that not all trade could be banned, but he also understood that this commerce provided the Rebels with supplies. Thus, he had to find a solution to the problem of illicit commerce with the enemy that did not eliminate all trade.[57]

Banks's solution was to regulate the traffic in cotton as much as possible. In early January 1863, he approved the cotton trade inside Union lines and told planters to forward their products directly to New Orleans to be sold, thereby avoiding speculators and the army. He hoped to eliminate the commerce with the enemy and cut down on the amount of corruption in the department. The plan worked well but failed to provide the large amounts of cotton demanded by Northern textile mills, and, in order to obtain more of the valuable crop, Banks sought to extend the system to include cotton held outside of Federal lines. He proposed to allow cotton across the lines. Union officials would hold half the sale price to guarantee that the profits were not used to buy war matériel for the Confederacy. The plan was rejected by the Treasury Department, which sought to control and encourage the commerce in cotton.[58]

Undeterred by this rejection, the general formulated a new plan. He decided to simply seize all the cotton his army encountered as it marched through enemy territory. The idea did not work well. The Confederates usually burned cotton ahead of the approaching Federals, and the scheme brought protest from Treasury officials, who complained about the army seizing what little cotton was discovered.[59]

With his plan not working, Banks returned to his original idea to regulate the traffic in cotton. In the winter of 1863–64, he again proposed that privately owned cotton be allowed to pass through the lines, only now he suggested withholding only one-third of the proceeds to ensure that none of the profits aided the Rebels. The general also recommended allowing Confederate cotton through the lines, but the Federal government would hold all the proceeds, except eighteen cents a pound, until proof was offered that the revenue would not be used to aid the Confederacy. Neither of these proposals was adopted, primarily because of objections from the Treasury Department, and in March Banks abandoned all of his plans, admitting that his attempts to implement an adequate system for regulating the cotton trade had failed.[60]

As Banks struggled to regulate the cotton trade, Hurlbut sought to profit from it. Due to Memphis's location on the Mississippi River, the city was the center of an extensive network of illegal commerce, as Northern goods came down the river to be exchanged for Southern cotton; a large percentage of the Northern goods then ended up in the hands of Confederate troops and guerrillas. Grant and Sherman both tried to stop this extralegal commerce, but their efforts proved futile, as smuggling and bribery made a mockery of their regulations and the trade only grew in volume. When Hurlbut assumed command of the city, he received instructions from Grant to do all he could to halt this traffic, but the political general made little effort to enforce the regulations banning the cotton trade.[61]

Hurlbut's lack of enforcement was motivated by his desire to profit from smuggling. Shortly after arriving in Memphis, the general established a cotton ring with a number of nefarious associates. The group allowed speculators to engage in their profitable illicit trade in exchange for cash bribes. To provide cover for these acts, the general made an occasional arrest and complained about "the plundering and bribery that is going on," blaming the extensive corruption on the Treasury Department.[62]

These illegal activities remained profitable until the fall of Vicksburg. At that time, Hurlbut feared that Grant might discover his avarice, broke up the cotton ring, and attempted to resign his commission. Unfortunately for Hurlbut, both Lincoln and Halleck urged the general to withdraw his resignation. Faced with this pressure, Hurlbut remained in the army. He made no effort to renew his cotton scheme and instead focused on prison extortion, taking ransom to release smugglers, Rebel sympathizers, and Confederate military prisoners.[63]

Hurlbut managed to survive charges of corruption in the spring of 1864 and, following his relief from command of Memphis, found himself in the fall assigned to New Orleans. Gen. Edward Canby, commander of the Military Division of West Mississippi, had restricted trade since his arrival in May, and Hurlbut insisted to Lincoln that "rigid non intercourse should be kept." Hurlbut, who knew what he was talking about, explained to the president that "no man can deal in purchases of cotton without violating his allegiance to the country" or aiding the Confederacy. Shortly thereafter, Hurlbut ordered his officers to stop all commerce.[64]

What Hurlbut did not say was that he hoped to exploit the restriction of trade for his own profit. He again established a cotton ring to allow merchants to carry on illegal trading in exchange for bribes of ten thousand dollars. When merchants refused to pay, Hurlbut jailed them. These acts only hinted at the extent of the general's criminal activities in New Orleans. Shortly after arriving in the city, he ordered several prominent citizens to pay a tax or face imprisonment and confiscation of their property. On another occasion, he directed his provost marshal, Hurlbut's partner in all of his nefarious acts, to confiscate the remaining property of Christ's Church, which had been accused of disloyalty. The property was then sold on the New Orleans market, and Hurlbut and the provost marshal split the profits. A month later, the general ordered all of the church's property returned to the deacons. These illegal schemes, when combined with his previous acts in Memphis, branded Hurlbut as perhaps the most corrupt Federal general of the war.[65]

All of this crookedness did not go unnoticed, and in December 1864 Lincoln created a commission to investigate charges of corruption. In April 1865, the investigators convinced Hurlbut's provost marshal to testify against the general, whereupon Hurlbut perjured himself during his testimony before the commission. The evidence against the general was overwhelming, and the commission found him guilty; Canby arrested him, and both the commission and Canby recommended an early court-martial for the corrupt political general. Fortunately for Hurlbut, the end of the war saved him. Neither the new president, Andrew Johnson, nor the War Department desired a trial that might embarrass the government in its moment of triumph. Thus, Hurlbut was released and allowed to return home to Illinois.[66]

Elections were another matter that concerned political generals administering departments and districts. Supervising elections required generals to provide security at polling stations to ensure that secessionists did not disrupt the elections and Unionist candidates won. In Maryland Banks and Dix dealt with elections in 1861 and Schenck in 1863.

In early November 1861, Maryland held elections for the state legislature that were fraught with tension. Secessionists hoped to win control of the legislature and take the state into the Confederacy, while Unionists sought not only to retain control of Maryland but also to win, as Dix wrote, by "an overwhelming majority." To ensure this outcome, Banks and Dix allowed all the Maryland soldiers in their commands to vote, dispatched troops to polling places to protect loyal voters and arrest anyone suspected of treason, and sent detachments to the eastern shore to prevent residents of Virginia from illegally voting. Essentially, these two political generals used the military to secure a victory for the Union. Their efforts were successful, as the Union candidate for governor won by thirty-one thousand votes and the Union party secured a large majority in the legislature.[67]

Two years later, Schenck, as commander of the Middle Department, also involved himself directly in Maryland's elections. Although conditions in 1863 favored the Union and there was little chance of the state electing a secessionist legislature, Schenck issued orders that caused a controversy with Governor Augustus Bradford. On October 27, the Ohio general published General Order 53, establishing procedures for the election. He ordered provost marshals to arrest anyone near the polls who had supported the rebellion, require each voter to swear an oath of allegiance, and report "any Judge of an election who" refused to "aid in carrying out this order" or "require the oath of allegiance." Four days later, he determined that each voting precinct was to be guarded by at least ten soldiers.[68]

The order displeased Governor Bradford, who viewed it as a usurpation of his authority, and he complained to Lincoln. Bradford objected to both the presence of military personnel at the polls and the required loyalty oath. Lincoln, after discussing the situation with Schenck, essentially backed his general. The president saw no objection to a military presence at the voting precincts to protect Union voters. As for the loyalty oaths, the president believed that this was a "cheap enough" price to pay to ensure the loyalty of all the voters. Lincoln revoked the first section of General Order 53, inserting in its place the proviso that provost marshals were to arrest only those individuals who caused disturbances at the polls.[69]

Before Bradford received Lincoln's letter, the governor issued a proclamation that inflamed the controversy. Bradford condemned Schenck's order, declaring that it was "without justification." There was no need for military intervention, the governor argued, and the presence of the army would only provoke trouble. Schenck immediately moved to suppress this "most extraordinary proclamation." Orders were issued forbidding the telegraph to transmit the proclamation and newspapers to publish it, especially on the eastern shore. Then Schenck published his own address. In "To the Loyal People of Maryland," the general condemned Bradford's proclamation and defended his order as a necessary measure intended to exclude from participation only those individuals "hostile to the Government." He assured readers that his only goal was "to secure peace and good order at the polls."[70]

The election on November 4 went smoothly for the most part, though there were several prominent arrests. The army arrested one former governor and a former clerk of the Maryland Senate, in one county a nervous officer confined the election judge and closed the polls after only one person voted, and in Kent County an officer arrested several of the county's politicians. Though there were many complaints from individuals, the major newspapers either endorsed Schenck's policy or remained silent. Nevertheless, the political general was overzealous and forced Lincoln to intervene in a matter that should have been resolved without involving the president, especially since there was no real threat to Maryland's loyalty.[71]

Finally, a few political generals serving as department and district commanders in the South confronted the question of Reconstruction—how to bring the Rebel states back into the Union. The issue was politically explosive because what Reconstruction meant remained vague and open to various interpretations; thus, any action a citizen general took was likely to cause controversy. Further complicating the process was the fact that the president and Congress both claimed the right to direct Reconstruction. Such a situation made it nearly impossible for a general to please everyone. In 1862, Butler in New Orleans and Dix in Virginia tentatively addressed this question, but Banks dealt with it directly in 1864.

In December 1862, both Dix and Butler held elections in their commands designed to initiate Reconstruction. Dix, in Virginia, sought to elect a representative to Congress for the congressional district that included Norfolk, intending to return the area to its former allegiance to the Union. Lincoln offered no objections, and the election went forward. Only individuals who swore an oath of loyalty were allowed to vote, and, as a result, only 1,402 men cast ballots, but Dix considered it a success. The effort suffered from numerous faults. Few voters participated, the House of Representatives refused to seat the winner, no effort was made to organize new state and local governments, and Dix completely ignored the issues of slavery and black rights. Essentially, Dix sought to return the area to the Union as if secession had not occurred.[72]

In Louisiana, Butler also made a halfhearted attempt to reconstruct the state. From the moment that New Orleans fell, Lincoln was keenly interested in reorganizing Louisiana as a loyal state, but hoped that Louisiana Unionists would do the necessary work. Consequently, Butler accomplished nothing until the fall of 1862, when Lincoln pressed the general to hold elections for the House of Representatives. Moving quickly, in early December the political general held elections for two seats in Congress. Though the House eventually accepted both of the men elected, Butler's efforts provided only a halting beginning to Reconstruction in Louisiana and suffered from many faults: light voter turnout, no reorganization of the state and local governments, and failure to address the issues of slavery and black rights.[73]

One reason Lincoln replaced Butler with Banks in Louisiana was to speed up the progress of Reconstruction. The president hoped that Banks's considerable political experience, conciliatory approach, and moderate views would provide excellent tools for reconstructing the state along lines envisioned by Lincoln. For most of 1863, Banks accomplished little. He spent the first half of the year campaigning against Port Hudson and the fall operating along the Texas coast. Some Louisiana Unionists organized the Free State of Louisiana, a committee that sought to call a constitutional convention to write a new document and win readmission to the Union, but they made few real accomplishments. Not satisfied, in August, Lincoln wrote Banks seeking to push forward the constitutional convention. The president wanted "a new

Constitution recognizing the emancipation proclamation" and extending it to those parts of the state where it did not already apply. He left it to Banks, Shepley, and the Free State of Louisiana to work out the details.[74]

Despite Lincoln's prodding, Banks took no constructive action throughout the fall because he was focused on Texas and disliked Unionist Thomas Durant. An active member of the Free State of Louisiana, Durant was a utopian who wanted to completely restructure the state. His vision encompassed revolutionary economic change, the abolition of slavery, and social and political equality to blacks, which included extending suffrage to freed slaves. Working with Shepley, he began registering voters for a constitutional convention. Banks, who was not yet willing to upset the planters or grant blacks voting rights, refused to cooperate with Durant and obstructed all efforts to move forward on Reconstruction.[75]

The lack of progress angered Lincoln. In November, the president scolded Banks and urged the general "to lose no more time." Hurt by Lincoln's censure, Banks protested that he had done nothing because Washington had "exclusively committed" authority on the matter to Shepley. He assured Lincoln that, if given complete control, he could organize a new state government "in sixty days." Tired of the delays and desiring results, Lincoln apologized for not fixing who had authority over Reconstruction and stated, "You are master. . . . [G]ive us a free-state re-organization of Louisiana, in the shortest possible time."[76]

The president was anxious about Louisiana because he wanted it to be the test state for his recently announced Reconstruction program. In early December, he issued the Proclamation of Amnesty and Reconstruction, offering a full pardon and restoration of rights and property, except slaves, to all Rebels who took an oath swearing loyalty to the Constitution and pledging to obey all acts of Congress and presidential proclamations regarding slavery. The proclamation promised to readmit into the Union any state that formed a government supported by one-tenth of its 1860 voters who took the oath of allegiance. Lincoln took this step because authority over Reconstruction was in dispute, with both the president and Congress claiming the authority to direct the process, and he sought to seize control of Reconstruction before congressional Republicans, especially the Radicals, asserted their claim to direct it. Furthermore, the president hoped to admit some Southern states back into the Union in time for the presidential election, thereby securing greater support for his reelection.[77]

Banks, after receiving Lincoln's assurance that he was master, moved quickly to form a new state government. The general decided that the best way to proceed was to establish a free state government based on Louisiana's Constitution of 1852, excepting those features that related to slavery. That institution would "be declared . . . inoperative and void." To achieve this end, in early January Banks ordered an election for February 22, 1864, to choose a governor, lieutenant governor, and other state officers and a second election in April to select delegates to a constitutional convention. Only those citizens who took an oath of allegiance would be allowed to vote.[78]

Over the next six weeks, the political general threw himself into preparing the election. He attempted to bring as many parties in as possible, and eventually three candidates for governor appeared, representing the conservative, moderate, and radical factions of the Louisiana Unionists. Michael Hahn, the moderate, won Banks's support. Not everyone agreed with Banks's plan. Thomas Durant declared it "a great mistake," and Benjamin Flanders feared the result would not be favorable and called it "odious to the friends of Freedom," but, faced with a fait accompli, Flanders ran as the radical candidate for governor. Banks also worked hard to achieve a large voter turnout, trying to attain the 10 percent called for in Lincoln's proclamation. Ten days before the election, he promised the president that between ten and twelve thousand votes would be cast in February and nearly fifteen thousand in April.[79]

The February election went as Banks predicted, but after that his efforts met with less success. Eleven thousand ballots, double that required by Lincoln's proclamation, were cast, and Hahn easily secured the governorship. At the beginning of March, Hahn was inaugurated, and Banks could claim to have effectively initiated the Reconstruction of Louisiana. At the end of March, however, things began to go wrong when Banks held elections for the state constitutional convention, which met from April 6 to July 25. Many radicals boycotted the election, and the turnout was so small that the convention had no legitimacy. Meeting in New Orleans, the convention created a new constitution based on the one of 1852, but with some radical changes. Significant differences included authorizing public education for both races, abolishing slavery without compensation, and enrolling into the militia all able-bodied males regardless of race. The most contentious issue was whether to grant black males suffrage. After Banks applied pressure, the delegates voted to give the state legislature the power to enfranchise blacks.[80]

Banks next turned his attention to ratifying the new constitution. Hoping to secure a large voter turnout, Banks ordered his subordinates to register every voter possible. The results of the vote on September 5 fell far below the general's expectations. Although the constitution was ratified and three congressmen and a new state legislature elected, his predicted turnout of twenty thousand failed to materialize, as fewer than half that many ballots were cast, a result that satisfied Lincoln's 10 percent plan but also signaled a lack of popular support.[81]

In October, Banks returned to Washington to secure congressional acceptance of his new government. Some Radical Republicans disliked Banks because they felt that he had not struck with enough fervor against slavery and disapproved of the new Louisiana Constitution due to its failure to enfranchise blacks. Furthermore, they objected to the military forming governments, especially since it was done under Lincoln's direction and not their own. Banks did his best to win approval but ultimately failed, as the short winter session ended without Congress recognizing his government. Depressed by this failure, Banks remained in the North until spring, returning to New Orleans just as the war ended.[82]

Banks's Reconstruction efforts were partially constructive but ultimately fruitless. He managed to elect a new government, write and ratify a new constitution, and ensure that blacks received some advantages beyond mere freedom, such as education and militia service. The failure to achieve black suffrage was disappointing but understandable, considering the state's prevailing political climate. The major flaw in his attempt to reorganize the government was the inability to achieve widespread support, especially for the constitution, a failure that cast doubt on the legitimacy of the entire effort, without which the attempt could not succeed. The error was demonstrated vividly by the refusal of the Louisiana radicals to participate in the elections for the constitutional convention. As a result, the Radical Republicans, who already doubted Banks and his government, had a legitimate reason for refusing to ratify the government.

From 1861 to 1865, in the North and occupied South, political generals proved to be effective administrators of military departments and districts. They asserted Federal authority, influenced or managed municipal governments, and dealt with difficult issues such as trade, elections, and Reconstruction. The various generals who served as department and district commanders adopted similar policies in their commands, regardless of their political affiliation. Thus, all generals made arrests, suppressed newspapers, and confiscated property; they all reestablished Federal authority, and most of them feuded with local civil authorities. For the most part, they kept their departments in good order and prevented major outbreaks against Union governance.

Not every issue was dealt with well, especially the controversial problem of trade, for which no political general was able to formulate an effective solution. The demands of Northern textile mills and merchants, the large amount of money involved, and the inconsistent attitude of the Lincoln administration made the creation of any reasonable solution impossible. Regular army officers, such as Grant and Sherman, struggled just as futilely to stop the traffic in illegal goods with the Confederacy. Two political generals, Hurlbut and Butler, took advantage of their positions to enrich themselves, but aside from this corruption citizen generals were no more successful in halting illegal trade than West Point generals.

The actions of citizen generals often inflamed already controversial issues, compelling Lincoln to intervene. Butler was especially prone to involving himself in disputes, as occurred with the foreign consuls in Louisiana and Governor Pierpont in Virginia, which eventually landed on the president's desk. Dix, Schenck, Hurlbut, and Banks also engaged in feuds or activities that required Lincoln's intervention. These controversies tried the president's patience, as they consumed energy, time, and goodwill that could have been put to better use in more constructive pursuits. Political generals were not the only department and district commanders who involved Lincoln in such disputes. The arrest of Clement Vallandigham in 1863 by Gen. Ambrose Burnside, commander of the Department of the Ohio, was but one example of a professional soldier causing a controversy that required Lincoln's personal attention.[83]

Despite numerous problems, political generals tended to perform well in positions of military government. The only exception was Hurlbut, who was a failure. Other than Hurlbut, others demonstrated competence, resilience, and on occasion ingenuity when dealing with the problems they confronted. Citizen generals clearly performed best in this role, a fact recognized by Lincoln, who tried to exploit their experience in state and local governments by assigning several of these generals to positions as department commanders.

CHAPTER 10

Slavery, Freedom, and Black Soldiers

The most controversial issues that political generals confronted were slavery and the arming of blacks. How to deal with the peculiar institution was a question that the Lincoln administration struggled with throughout the war, and the president's political generals complicated that struggle. Throughout the conflict, political generals, especially those commanding departments, helped to shape the Union's policy toward black Americans, although all citizen generals had to contend with the institution. Not every one of Lincoln's political generals agreed with the policies adopted by their colleagues and the president, leading one general to resign his commission.

As the war began, Lincoln adopted a hands-off policy toward slavery. Essentially, the president meant to wage war without interfering with the peculiar institution and uphold all national and state slavery laws, which meant suppressing slave revolts, enforcing the Fugitive Slave Act, and leaving slavery alone. The policy was based on his inaugural pledge not to interfere with the institution where it already existed and his fear that any rash move against it might stampede the border slave states of Kentucky, Maryland, and Missouri into the Confederacy. Lincoln, as he stated in the spring of 1862, believed the institution "was wrong" and took significant steps against it, such as outlawing slavery in the territories. In early 1861, however, there would be no action against the institution where it already existed.[1]

The issue of runaway slaves furnished the first test of Lincoln's policy and enabled a political general, Butler, to influence the president's approach to slavery. Wherever Union armies went in the South, they attracted black Americans seeking freedom. The camps and posts of soldiers in blue uniforms provided sanctuaries for slaves escaping from bondage, and over the course of the war thousands of African Americans took advantage of this opportunity. By running away, they helped to hasten slavery's demise. Early in the war, the issue of runaway slaves posed a problem because, under the Fugitive Slave Act, the Lincoln administration was legally bound to return all escaped slaves to their masters. Doing so was not politically acceptable to many Northerners, and it made little military sense, since slavery benefited the South.

In late May 1861, Butler, while stationed at Fortress Monroe, Virginia, faced this question when three blacks, claiming that the Confederate army was using them to erect batteries, surrendered to his picket guards. Butler decided to detain the slaves and put them to work while informing their master that he held them. The next day, a Rebel officer arrived at the fort and demanded that Butler hand over the three slaves, pointing out that this was the general's constitutional obligation. Butler refused and enunciated a novel legal argument why he was not bound to return the slaves. He argued that since Virginia claimed to be a foreign power, the Fugitive Slave Act no longer applied and the blacks could be confiscated "as contraband of war, since they are engaged in the construction of your battery."[2]

Butler had never opposed slavery, and he based his argument entirely on practical, not moral, grounds. By declaring slave property contraband of war, Butler created legal grounds for Union forces to confiscate this property, providing Federal officers with a reasonable way of dealing with the slaves that continually streamed into their lines. Confiscating blacks also hurt the Confederacy, since the Rebels depended on slave labor to grow their food, build their fortifications, cook their meals, and perform a variety of other tasks, thus freeing white men to fight.[3]

The Lincoln administration and Congress both gave their consent to Butler's policy. The president approved of the contraband idea, referring to it as "Butler's fugitive slave law," and told Butler not to surrender any escaped slaves to their alleged masters. Less than two months later, Congress passed the First Confiscation Act, decreeing that all property, including slaves, used to aid the rebellion was subject to confiscation. Signed into law by Lincoln in August, the act gave legal sanction to Butler's policy.[4]

The contraband policy applied only to slaves who ran away from disloyal masters; the slaves of loyal masters still fell under the Fugitive Slave Act and had to be returned. This remained true after Lincoln signed the First Confiscation Act, which affected only slaves used to aid the rebellion. When Union forces advanced into the Confederacy, this posed few problems, since most slave owners there were disloyal. In the border slave states, Federal troops faced the difficult task of differentiating between loyal and disloyal masters. Each political general dealt with this problem in his own way.

In the late summer and fall of 1861, Dix, commanding in eastern Maryland, tried to avoid the entire controversy by simply excluding all slaves from his lines. Dix, though personally opposed to slavery, had never publicly spoken against it and believed that the Union should not "meddle with the slaves even of secessionists." As he wrote Secretary of War Simon Cameron, "We are neither negro-stealers nor negro-catchers," and he recommended that "we should send them away if they came to us." Therefore, Dix directed his officers not to allow any slaves within their lines unless the blacks had the consent of their masters, which Dix knew was an unlikely prospect. When runaway slaves came to his lines, Dix refused them entry. On occasion, he ordered his officers to search their camps to find an escaped slave alleged to be in Union lines.[5]

When Dix occupied Accomac and Northampton counties in Virginia, he continued his policy, even though he was now operating in a state that had seceded from the Union. Thus, Dix ignored the contraband policy, but he received no rebuke for his disobedience, as McClellan believed Dix's "view of the negro policy is right" and Lincoln refused to interfere. This policy angered Radical Republicans such as Thaddeus Stevens, who berated Dix for taking "special care . . . that nobody's slave should be liberated," and, in response to both Dix's policy and similar orders issued by Halleck in the Western Department, in March 1862 Congress passed a new article of war prohibiting officers from returning fugitive slaves.[6]

Wadsworth, as military governor of Washington in 1862, took the opposite position of Dix and in doing so helped to undermine the Fugitive Slave Act in the border slave states. At the beginning of the war, Wadsworth opposed only the extension of slavery but by 1862 had been persuaded that immediate emancipation was necessary. As military governor, Wadsworth allowed all slaves from Virginia into his lines, whether they came from loyal or disloyal masters. In regard to slaves from Maryland, the general officially tried to return the slaves of loyal masters, but distinguishing between loyal and disloyal owners was difficult. More often than not, he granted military protection to blacks regardless of the political sympathies of their masters. He essentially evaded enforcing the Fugitive Slave Act, even in areas still in the Union.[7]

Wadsworth's measures created a controversy with Ward Lamon, U.S. marshal for the District of Columbia. The political general's actions enraged Maryland slave owners, who clamored for the vigorous enforcement of the Fugitive Slave Act, and Lamon felt no compunction about enforcing the law. His deputies regularly arrested blacks throughout Washington, even entering a camp Wadsworth established for blacks and the regimental encampments of the city's army garrison. Infuriated, Wadsworth ordered his officers to release all African Americans imprisoned by Lamon in Washington's jail and, on at least two occasions, to arrest for kidnapping the marshal's deputies. Republican senators Henry Wilson, Benjamin Wade, Charles Sumner, and Zachariah Chandler encouraged Wadsworth, telling him to "pay no regard" to Lamon's demands unless ordered to by the president. In June, Lincoln met with both parties to try to work out a compromise. The effort failed, and, since Lincoln refused to resolve the impasse, the feud continued until Wadsworth was reassigned to a combat command in November 1862.[8]

Another officer who adopted a similar attitude to Wadsworth's was Sickles, who had never opposed slavery and in fact had been a solid defender of the South until secession. While commanding a brigade in Maryland early in 1862, Sickles stated flatly that "I do not hunt for runaway negroes." In March, when several owners looking for their escaped slaves entered Sickles's camp, the general ordered them to leave. The incident touched off a controversy with his division commander, Gen. Joseph Hooker, who previously had ordered that such civilians should be given access to the division's camps to find their property.[9]

McClernand, on the other hand, while stationed at Cairo, Illinois, in the fall of 1861, bent over backward to return fugitive slaves to their masters. On several occasions, he ordered his officers to allow slave owners to search army camps, telling one officer "to give prompt and personal attention to this matter." McClernand, who had never opposed slavery, assumed that all masters, who lived in Kentucky, were loyal and made every effort to aid them.[10]

As McClernand advanced into Tennessee in 1862, he changed his policy to meet the new situation and conform to the new article of war. He now encouraged the capture of black men because they could "relieve our men from" some of the "fatigue duty required of them." In March, hoping to avoid the problem, he proposed the creation of a civil commission to follow the army and deal with the issue, relieving "commanding officers from a duty not contemplated in the articles of war." Nothing came of his proposal. That same month, Congress enacted the new article of war that ordered officers to stop aiding in the capture or return of fugitive slaves. From now on, generals could either accept the slaves or exclude them from their lines. McClernand did both in 1863 during the Vicksburg campaign. He excluded all black women and children from his lines without his express permission, eventually shipped those allowed in to Memphis, and accepted the men, whom he put to work on projects around his camp and on local plantations. This remained his policy until he was relieved in June.[11]

As Union forces advanced farther into the Confederacy and the war dragged on, most political generals, like the majority of all Union officers, accepted the logic of allowing at least some escaped slaves into their lines. Logan exemplified the new attitude in the army when he proclaimed in the summer of 1863 that slavery was dead, and he refused to return escaped slaves to their former owners, including loyal owners. Union soldiers realized that by striking at slavery, they were weakening the rebellion and hastening the war to its conclusion. Thus, by 1863, Butler's contraband policy had been adopted by nearly all Federal generals operating in the South, but by then it had become national policy owing to congressional laws and Lincoln's Emancipation Proclamation.[12]

The first Union official to issue an emancipation order during the Civil War was Frémont, in late August 1861. At that time, the Pathfinder commanded the Western Department, headquartered in St. Louis, where he faced a chaotic situation. Confederate armies rampaged in southern Missouri, guerrillas swarmed through much of the state, and the general lacked adequate numbers of troops and supplies to solve these problems and garrison key points. To deal with this mess, on August 30, 1861, Frémont issued a proclamation declaring martial law throughout Missouri. Establishing martial law was not controversial—it had occurred in Maryland—but Frémont also decreed that anyone carrying arms within army lines would be tried by court-martial and shot and that "the property, real and personal," of anyone who took up arms against the United States would "be confiscated to the public use, and their slaves . . . are hereby declared freemen."[13]

In one order, Frémont repudiated Lincoln's declared policy of not interfering with slavery and thereby threatened to transform the struggle to preserve the Union into a war for freedom. Two reasons impelled Frémont to take this dramatic step. The first was military necessity. The general reasoned that only by threatening to shoot them and free their slaves could he possibly hope to intimidate and stop the guerrillas and Rebel sympathizers who plagued his command. By issuing this decree, he signaled his intention to inflict harsh penalties on anyone aiding the rebellion. Second, the Frémonts, both John and his wife, Jessie, viewed themselves as leaders of the antislavery cause.

Therefore, as the Republican Party's first presidential candidate, Frémont believed that he should act as the party's spokesman on slavery and issue the first proclamation on emancipation.[14]

Frémont's proclamation aroused a tremendous reaction from Unionists, much of it positive. Abolitionists and Radical Republicans embraced the order and Frémont, and the general remained their beloved hero for the rest of the war. The St. Louis press, regardless of its political affiliation, also praised the measure, calling it, in the words of the *Missouri Democrat*, a "bold step" and a "heavy blow" to the Rebels in the state. The Pathfinder's proclamation also stirred up passionate denouncements. Frank Blair Sr. decried it, writing that by "superseding the Constitution, the law and the President," Frémont had established a "dictatorship" and "proclaimed a new political issue by ignoring the President and giving manumitting paper to slaves." Powerful men such as the Blairs, Attorney General Bates, and Missouri governor Hamilton Gamble demanded that Lincoln repeal the proclamation.[15]

The man most disturbed by the proclamation was the president. Lincoln objected to Frémont's intention to shoot anyone for aiding the rebellion, a policy that certainly invited retaliation from the Confederacy; he ordered the Pathfinder not to execute anyone without his approval. More important, the president feared that freeing any slaves "will alarm our Southern Union friends, and turn them against us—perhaps ruin our rather fair prospect for Kentucky." In issuing his proclamation, Frémont threatened to hurry Kentucky into seceding and joining the Confederacy, a prospect that filled Lincoln with dread. As he wrote to Senator Browning, "I think to lose Kentucky is nearly the same as to lose the whole game." Finally, Lincoln privately seethed at Frémont because he believed that the political general had usurped a power granted to the president and Congress. Freeing slaves, Lincoln wrote to Browning, "is *purely political*, and not within the range of *military* law, or necessity."[16]

The president therefore asked Frémont to modify his proclamation so as to conform to the First Confiscation Act, but the political general compounded his troubles by refusing to modify the proclamation without orders from Lincoln. "If I were to retract it of my own accord," he wrote, "it would imply that I myself thought it wrong, and that I had acted without reflection. . . . But I did not. I acted with full deliberation, and upon the certain conviction that it was a measure right and necessary." Lincoln may have appreciated Frémont's passionate defense of his order, but he could not tolerate the general's refusal to heed his suggestions. He therefore ordered the proclamation modified as he requested.[17]

Frémont certainly overstepped his authority when he attempted to free Missouri's slaves. Worse, he violated good policy by rashly initiating a new approach toward a politically sensitive issue at a moment when any wrong step on that topic could damage the war effort by causing Kentucky to secede. Frémont, despite his claim, never considered the ramifications of freeing slaves. Fortunately, Lincoln understood the situation and acted accordingly. Nevertheless, Frémont's action helped to undermine the president's current slavery policy by increasing the clamor for emancipation. He also pointed the way for future action on this issue by Lincoln himself by basing this proclamation on military necessity, the same argument the president would make the next year to justify issuing the Emancipation Proclamation.[18]

That step was taken in the fall of 1862 when Lincoln issued the preliminary Emancipation Proclamation on September 22. For the first year and a half of the war, Lincoln pursued his policy of limited interference with slavery while trying to convince the border states to adopt some form of compensated emancipation. By the summer of 1862, two things had become clear to Lincoln. For one, the border states, no matter how much he implored them, were not willing to adopt any form of emancipation. At the same time, he came to "the conclusion that we must free the slaves or be ourselves subdued." The war, especially in the East, was not going well, and Lincoln decided that the Union must change policy to regain the initiative. He was persuaded by the defeats during the Seven Days battles; growing antislavery opinion; declining volunteers for the army, which some blamed on the failure to act against slavery; and the Second Confiscation Act. Passed in July, the new law declared that after sixty days, the slaves of Rebels would be "forever free of their servitude." To preempt this act, the president, after the Union victory at Antietam, issued the preliminary Emancipation Proclamation, promising to free the slaves of states in rebellion that had not returned to the Union by the end of the year.[19]

Lincoln signed the final proclamation on January 1, 1863. The document, an executive war measure designed to weaken the Confederacy by striking at its social structure and most valuable economic resource, declared all slaves in the states of the Confederacy free except those in territory occupied by Union forces. Thus, the slaves in Louisiana around New Orleans, Tennessee, West Virginia, and parts of northern and eastern Virginia were not affected. The proclamation also announced Lincoln's intention to enlist blacks into the Union army.[20]

Reaction from Lincoln's political generals to the proclamation ranged from support to hostility and usually depended on their political affiliation. Republican generals basically followed the sentiment expressed by Wadsworth: "I stand by Abraham Lincoln." Wadsworth endorsed the proclamation because it "strike[s] from this rebellion the support which it derives from the unrequited toil of the slaves." Schurz, who believed from the start of the war that "the wild malignity of the South" offered the opportunity to destroy slavery, enthusiastically endorsed emancipation. Other Republican generals, such as Banks, Blair, Hurlbut, and Schenck, also supported the proclamation as a war measure, if not on moral grounds.[21]

Among Democratic generals, there were a variety of opinions, not all of them favorable. Butler supported freeing the slaves because it made no sense to him to "end the war and not eradicate the cause." Logan, on the other hand, initially called the proclamation a "foolish message [that] does us no good" because many officers and soldiers might refuse to fight a war to free black slaves. By the spring of 1863, he had changed his mind and argued that emancipation offered an excellent way of hurting the rebellion. Dix believed that the war "doomed" slavery, but he argued that it should be left alone because any action against the institution might "divide the north and consolidate the south." Once emancipation became a fact, Dix may have represented one-third or more of Northern Democrats who continued to support the war effort but called the proclamation bad policy.[22]

Denver was so disgusted by the Emancipation Proclamation that he resigned his commission. His Civil War career had not amounted to much, as he failed to find an assignment until the summer of 1862 in Tennessee, when he assumed command of a brigade in Gen. William Sherman's division. Denver's dissatisfaction with both his career and the war only intensified after the politically charged issue of emancipation became a Union war goal. On January 10, 1863, the political general told his wife "not to be surprised to see me at home at any time." He explained to her that he had "entered the service to support the Constitution, and laws of the country—not to overthrow them and trample them underfoot. My obligations were to protect the government, not to revolutionize it."[23]

Though Denver never specifically mentioned the Emancipation Proclamation, the thrust of his tirade was clearly directed at that document, the only recent event that could be said to have revolutionized the war. Denver had no desire to fight, as his wife wrote, "for the everlasting nigger." Other factors also contributed to Denver's resignation in March 1863, such as the failure to secure a desirable command, petty politics, and neglected personal business, but his anger over the Emancipation Proclamation provided the most important reason for his leaving the army. Fortunately for Lincoln and the Union war effort, Denver's action was not repeated by a significant number of soldiers and officers.[24]

Even before Lincoln issued the proclamation, Butler had helped set Federal policy toward black labor. To a large extent, political generals, specifically Butler and Banks, determined the nature of black labor in the South. These two men commanded the Union military government in Louisiana, covering much of the southern part of the state, a vast area that included large numbers of slaves and numerous plantations, when compared to the limited pockets of Federal occupation of Virginia. Following the conquest of New Orleans, the region submitted to Union authority. The arrival of Federal forces led African Americans to run away from their plantations, complicating Lincoln's Reconstruction efforts since the president sought to renew planters' loyalty to the Union by reviving the plantation economy. This required workers, forcing Butler and Banks to create a labor plan that ensured the plantations continued to function and provided blacks with enough incentives to stay and work. Their solution was the contract labor system, which spread throughout the Mississippi Valley.[25]

As soon as Butler assumed control of New Orleans in May 1862, he confronted the problems posed by the disintegration of slavery. The general initially intended no additional interference with the institution in Louisiana. Slave owners within Union lines did not have their property confiscated; to do so, Butler realized, would destroy the economy, since the plantations depended on slave labor, but scores of blacks fled to the army camps seeking freedom and disrupting the system. Because of the article of war enacted in March 1862, the general could not return these slaves to their owners. So he ordered his officers to employ as many as possible and simply exclude the rest from army lines, "leaving them subject to the ordinary laws of the community." These fugitives would be rounded up by local law authorities and returned to the plantations. In fact, the president of the Jefferson Parish Police Jury suggested this policy. By adopting it, Butler hoped to maintain the slave system and keep the plantations working while not violating federal law.[26]

Unfortunately for the political general, one of his own officers upset this scheme. The officer was Brig. Gen. John Phelps, who commanded Fort Parapet, seven miles north of New Orleans. Phelps not only admitted all fugitive slaves into his camp and refused to return them to their masters but also allowed his soldiers to liberate blacks from local plantations. This infuriated planters because the remaining blacks refused to work, knowing that "they have only to go to the Fort to be free." They demanded that Butler stop Phelps. The political general sent aides and issued orders telling Phelps to desist and adopt the official policy, but his subordinate refused to comply. The standoff continued for three weeks, and then Butler dumped the dispute into Lincoln's lap.[27]

In early July, Stanton communicated the president's decision. The blacks could not be sent back to their masters and must be cared for by the army. Those who were able should be put to work and paid wages. The decision "was not setting any general rules, but dealing solely with the case at hand."

Although the president's decision was ambiguous, Butler believed it sustained Phelps. The decision also did not end the feud between Butler and Phelps. Phelps now refused to put the blacks to work, defiantly proclaiming that "I am not willing to become a mere slave driver," and their bickering, which eventually encompassed the question of arming blacks, led Phelps to resign in August.[28]

Nevertheless, Phelps's actions and Lincoln's response to them ruined Butler's original slavery scheme because they encouraged blacks to flee into Union lines and left the plantations without a labor force. By September 1, as Butler wrote to Halleck, blacks were "coming in by hundreds, nay thousands almost daily. Many of the plantations are deserted. . . . Crops of sugar-cane are left standing to waste." Much to his displeasure, the slave system was falling apart around him. The Lincoln administration provided little guidance. There seemed to be no way to continue his current policy. So Butler changed course.[29]

Two events caused him to adopt a new approach. Lincoln's preliminary Emancipation Proclamation (which did not apply to the area Butler controlled in Louisiana) signaled to Butler that the political winds on the slavery issue were blowing toward freedom, and the capture in the late summer of the Lafourche District, west of New Orleans, placed under Federal control a large number of abandoned plantations and freed blacks. The African Americans were free because their owners were declared disloyal, allowing Butler to confiscate the property of these whites. The Lafourche District provided the political general with a large area to experiment with a new labor system.[30]

In November, Butler issued General Order 91, adopting a system of contract labor in Lafourche already tentatively applied in two other districts. Butler ordered all former slaves to work ten hours a day for twenty-six days each month, prohibited planters from inflicting "cruel or corporal punishment," and promised to pay able-bodied males ten dollars a month, though three dollars was deducted for clothing. The wages of women and children were negotiable, and the planters had to supply proper food for the laborers and their dependents. Butler's order also provided army guards and patrols to maintain order on the plantations. His new plan was designed to preserve the plantation system, thereby ensuring that the economy did not collapse and planters remained content, while also providing blacks with incentives to remain and work on the plantations. This arrangement also freed the army from the responsibility of directly caring for blacks.[31]

The tentative experiment in free labor inaugurated by Butler's policy won the immediate attention of Lincoln, who asked his general for information on the new system. After only a month in operation, Butler declared it a success and sent the president the first sugar ever made by free black labor in Louisiana. The blacks, he boasted, have "gone willingly to work." He assured the president that, despite some planters who chose to abandon their plantations rather than use free labor, the system would work. Black labor, he proclaimed, can be "used, and made as profitable in a state of freedom as in slavery."[32]

194

In mid-December, Banks assumed command of the Department of the Gulf and inherited Butler's new labor system. Like Butler, Banks's primary concern was to ensure that the plantations continued to function. His first General Order stated that the Emancipation Proclamation was a "declaration of purpose only" that did not apply to Louisiana and admonished the slaves to remain on the plantations. Furthermore, he forbade his soldiers from encouraging blacks to desert their masters while suggesting that the planters compensate their laborers. Banks's order recognized that the war was destroying slavery but postponed freedom in Louisiana. The political general took no further action, hoping the situation would work itself out.[33]

By the end of January 1863, the situation was deteriorating and demanded firm action from Banks. Blacks continued to flee into army camps and could not be returned to their masters, burdening the military with the necessity of supporting them. Thousands of runaway slaves congregated around the army encampments and lived in terrible conditions that threatened public health. It was impossible to distinguish between blacks who remained slaves, those exempted by the Emancipation Proclamation because they resided within army lines on January 1, 1863, and free blacks, those who resided outside of army lines on January 1 but had since fled within army lines. As a result, the social and economic situation was chaotic. With the planting season fast approaching, Banks was forced to adopt Butler's contract labor system.[34]

Banks's plan, announced on January 30, was far more detailed than Butler's and set the basic guidelines followed for the rest of the war and immediate postwar period. Blacks, unless they had a job in town, must work on a plantation. They could choose their own employers but were required to sign a contract and work for one year with whomever they signed. Black laborers would receive up to ten dollars a month, though half the wages would be withheld until after the harvest, or they could adopt sharecropping if their employer agreed. Other benefits included rations, medical treatment, schooling for their children, quarters, fuel, and a garden plot of at least one acre. Furthermore, the regulations outlawed physical abuse of any kind and established the work period as dawn to dusk. In return, blacks had to supply "respectful, honest, [and] faithful labor"; not feign sickness, laziness, or another form of disobedience; and respect their employers. Banks appointed an army officer to supervise the system and ensure that it functioned as intended. None of these provisions established freedom for blacks, who found themselves trapped somewhere between slavery and freedom, but it did create a means for running the plantations and relieving the army from the burden of caring for the African Americans.[35]

The formulation of this policy filled Banks with immense pride, satisfaction, and unrealistic expectations, but it was heavily criticized. Banks bragged to his wife that "it is the best act of my life and within three months will solve all the troubles here about slavery." Three weeks later, he confidently told her that the blacks "are all going to work for wages" and the "planters are all delighted." Criticism of the policy came from a variety of different groups. Most blacks disliked the annual contracts and restrictions on their mobility, others griped about the low pay, and some discovered that their employers ignored the stipulations against corporal punishment. The planters also found reason to grumble, especially about the prohibitions against whipping and the fact that they now had to pay their slaves wages. Treasury agent Dennison reported to Chase that "labor is at once restored . . . and there is a fair prospect of a good crop," but he considered slavery "as completely re-established." Abolitionist Wendell Phillips complained that Banks's plan denied "every element of citizenship and freedom" to blacks and protested that it was better to accept "the bullet from . . . Jeff Davis than . . . serfdom from General Banks."[36]

Wadsworth, who toured the Mississippi Valley in the fall of 1863, offered an insightful critique of and alternative to Banks's labor plan. The War Department directed him to inspect black troops raised in the region and the condition of the entire black population and report on the best means of maintaining and employing African Americans. Traveling down the Mississippi River with his son, Wadsworth inspected camps along the river, some of which, his son wrote, were "very comfortable & healthy" but others of which were "in a deplorable condition." At the latter encampments, blacks "are dying off like sheep owing to bad management." These conditions angered the general, who berated the officers managing the camps.[37]

Returning north in early December, Wadsworth submitted his report. He described the miserable conditions prevailing in many of the African American camps, but blamed the "large slave holders" for this and exonerated Federal authorities. As for the contract labor system, despite some problems "the system has been practically successful." The former slaves seemed contented and worked hard, and plantation owners had done well. Nonetheless, the general recommended that a system of leasing land directly to blacks was preferable and should be "inaugurated to a moderate extent." He also believed that black children should be educated and arms given to the adults, methods that provided "the most efficient means of elevating" the black race.[38]

A month later, in testimony given to the American Freedmen's Inquiry Commission, Wadsworth admitted, "My report is in fact apologetic" on the matter of the contract labor system. In Louisiana, he found "a strong tendency, to make the negroes stay on the plantations." Provost marshals regularly arrested blacks not on plantations and forced them to work on the levee without wages. These actions and other aspects of Banks's system were helping to "establish a system of serfdom" that, once Reconstruction was over, would leave blacks "as serfs to the local authorities," who would then return the African Americans to slavery. Wadsworth believed that it was proper that the majority of blacks "become peasant cultivators," but it was important to prevent them from being reenslaved and ensure that some rights were protected. Wadsworth's testimony went unheeded, and his report was buried in the War Department, nullifying their potential impact on the labor system developing in the Mississippi Valley.[39]

The contract labor system created by Butler and Banks was a flawed system. It was probably not viable economically, for it seems that, at least in the case of the sugar industry, the new labor system failed to halt a precipitous fall in production. Socially, the new scheme had a mixed impact. For instance, blacks received some protection. They were removed from unhealthful camps; provided with rations, clothing, and shelter; granted opportunities to receive schooling; sheltered to some extent from abuse; and paid a small wage for their work, introducing them to the free labor system. Nevertheless, Banks's plan entrapped blacks in a system only slightly better than slavery. They were forced to work on plantations, had little freedom of movement, and had no ability to negotiate for better wages or living conditions. Furthermore, the army remained sympathetic to planters, and it relied on them to maintain order, limiting the army's protection of African Americans. Although some changes were implemented later, the contract labor system created by political generals placed blacks in a state of serfdom that continued after the conclusion of the war.[40]

A final aspect of Federal policy toward African Americans that political generals played an important role in developing and sustaining was the enlistment of blacks into the army. Again, Butler was in the forefront of this policy, though he was not the first general to enlist blacks. In the spring of 1862, Gen. David Hunter, commanding the Department of the South, began recruiting black troops in South Carolina, but Lincoln promptly stopped Hunter, stating that he "would employ all colored men as laborers, but would not promise to make soldiers of them." The president reiterated his opposition in July after Congress passed the Second Confiscation Act, which granted Lincoln the power to use blacks in "any military" capacity he thought necessary. Although Lincoln signed the act, he refused to enlist blacks into the army. The president was reluctant to touch a potentially explosive topic opposed by many Northerners.[41]

Butler shared Lincoln's doubts. Despite a severe shortage of soldiers in Louisiana, the general believed that "military necessity does not exist here for the employment of negroes in arms." Shortly after arriving in New Orleans, Butler made his feelings known when the city's free black militia regiment, the Native Guards, offered its services to the general. Organized in 1861 and enrolled in the Confederate Louisiana militia, the guards traced their origins to the free blacks who fought in the battle of New Orleans during the War of 1812. Butler rejected their offer.[42]

The issue lay dormant until the end of July, when Phelps, without authority, began forming three black regiments. As early as June, the Vermont general proposed enlisting African Americans as a way of advancing freedom. After his fugitive slave victory over Butler, Phelps asked his commander for equipment and arms "for three regiments of Africans which I propose to raise." Phelps's request violated both Butler's and Lincoln's policy, and the Massachusetts general lectured his subordinate that "you are [not] empowered to organize companies of Negroes, and drill them as a Military organization." Therefore, "you must desist from the formation of any Negro Military Organization." Phelps asked to resign, and Butler forwarded the matter to Washington, which rejected Phelps's request to arm slaves and accepted his resignation.[43]

Ten days after ordering Phelps not to arm blacks, Butler wrote his wife, "I shall arm the free Blacks, I think, for I must have more troops." His reversal in policy was brought about by military necessity. Shortly after the controversy with Phelps erupted, Confederate forces attacked Baton Rouge. Although Union forces held, the attack convinced Butler that he lacked enough troops to hold the ground he already occupied, let alone undertake offensive operations. He also feared that the Rebels might strike at New Orleans and was not certain if he could defend the city without reinforcements. Therefore, on August 14, he informed Stanton that he had decided to "use the services of the free colored men who were organized by the rebels." The decision to use the Native Guards was shrewd because it avoided the troubling issue of arming slaves, which conjured fears of slave rebellion. He was arming not slaves but free blacks that Louisiana's Confederate authorities had enlisted.[44]

After raising one regiment, Butler at the end of August requested "prompt approval" from the president, but Lincoln answered with silence. Butler took this as approval and continued his activities. The first regiment was mustered into the Union army at the end of September, a second regiment in October, and a third in November. The majority of officers in these regiments were black, a precedent not followed in the future. Butler claimed to be recruiting only free blacks, but recruiters did not probe too deeply into a potential soldier's slave status, and perhaps as many as half the recruits were runaway slaves. The regiments immediately went on active duty, though their work consisted of training or repairing railroads.[45]

The political general's actions helped convince Lincoln to adopt a policy of recruiting black soldiers, a policy the president undertook in 1863, as announced in the Emancipation Proclamation. Massachusetts senator Charles Sumner, Vice President Hannibal Hamlin, and Secretary of War Stanton also were instrumental in pushing Lincoln toward this decision. The president became an enthusiastic champion of black soldiers. "The colored population," Lincoln explained, "is the great *available* and yet *unavailed* of, force for restoring the Union." Anything that might shorten the war appealed to the president, and he pushed the raising of African American troops upon his commanders, seeking to exploit a resource that in one stroke strengthened the Union and weakened the Confederacy.[46]

When white soldiers voiced opposition to the new policy, some political generals rose to defend arming slaves. In the Army of the Tennessee, both Blair and Logan made such an effort. Blair, who initially opposed using black troops, now favored it as long as white officers commanded them. Logan cynically appealed to his soldiers' sense of self-preservation, telling them that they should be "willing even a colored man should shield you from rebel bullets. I know you are. So we'll unite on this policy, putting the one who is the innocent cause of this war, in the front rank and press on to victory." Both of these speeches helped to quiet the discontent expressed by white soldiers in their units when the government began enlisting blacks.[47]

One political general who refused to enlist blacks was Dix. Dix, who commanded the Department of Virginia and North Carolina from Fortress Monroe until July 1863, opposed arming escaped slaves, a policy he felt was immoral, and he hoped that "we shall conduct the war on principles of humanity." He also believed that blacks would make unreliable soldiers. To Dix, the Civil War was a white man's struggle being waged to restore the Union; black soldiers had no role to play in his war. Therefore, when Lincoln asked him if black troops could garrison Fortress Monroe, Dix did not openly oppose using them but stated that most African Americans in his department would not enlist and argued that "inferior" soldiers should be "employed in Services of secondary importance," implying that he wanted no black troops at Fortress Monroe. As long as Dix remained in command, no African American regiments were raised in his department.[48]

On the other hand, after assuming command of this department in the fall of 1863, Butler began recruiting black regiments. As before, a lack of troops compelled Butler to undertake the large-scale recruitment of African Americans. The government having decided to recruit black soldiers, he told his new command, "it is therefore the duty of every officer and soldier to aid in carrying out that purpose." He paid his new recruits a ten-dollar bounty, provided subsistence to their families, and appointed a superintendent of Negro affairs to supervise all the blacks in the department. Every African American male between the ages of eighteen and forty-five, save for mechanics and skilled laborers, was subject to military service. Butler sent out press gangs beyond his lines to collect as many blacks as possible, increasing his pool of potential recruits while also depriving the Rebels of workers.[49]

Other political generals commanding departments also began to recruit black troops, though not always with enthusiasm. Banks, for instance, inherited Butler's three African American regiments in Louisiana, but made only a limited effort to increase the number of black troops in his army, which, after two months in command, remained at just over thirty-two hundred men. Treasury agent Dennison stated that Banks "is evidently opposed to" arming blacks. The political general feared the loss of plantation laborers to the army, viewed the black troops as potentially disruptive to the rest of the African American population, and believed that the racism of his white troops would create a hostile environment and undermine army morale.[50]

In the spring of 1863, the Bobbin Boy changed his mind, primarily because Lincoln had decided to recruit blacks in large numbers, a point driven home when the president sent Gen. Daniel Ullmann to Louisiana to enlist a brigade of black troops. Banks disliked the idea of surrendering control of the project to Ullmann. To head off Ullmann, on May 1, Banks ordered the creation of the Corps d'Afrique and began to actively recruit black soldiers. He also used Butler's three regiments at the siege of Port Hudson. During the assault on May 27, these regiments fought well, earning glowing raves from Banks: "They fought splendidly! Splendidly! Every body is delighted that they did so well." The general immediately decided to recruit twenty regiments, a "corps de ar-mée" of infantry, artillery, cavalry, and engineer units. These efforts successfully fended off Ullmann, who, after struggling throughout the summer to organize five regiments, found himself in September placed directly under Banks. By the end of the war, Banks had formed twenty-five regiments and recruited more African American soldiers than any other general during the conflict.[51]

There were significant limitations to Banks's enthusiasm for black troops. Most of his regiments contained only five hundred men rather than the standard one thousand. He kept the regiments small because he believed that African Americans were "unaccustomed to military service," and it allowed him to recruit a large number of units while not draining the plantations of too many laborers. The general argued that he could not recruit the regiments to full strength until he captured enemy territory containing plentiful numbers of slaves. Furthermore, Butler's three regiments originally contained a large number of black officers, but Banks made a special effort to weed these men out and replace them with whites. Black officers, the Bobbin Boy argued, were a "constant source of embarrassment and annoyance" because their use "demoralizes both the white troops and the negroes." Finally, after Port Hudson, Banks made no effort to employ his African American troops in combat, preferring to use them as laborers.[52]

As a result of these decisions, morale in the black regiments was often low, a fact made worse by the presence of some incompetent white officers who mistreated their troops. The outcome was a mutiny on December 9, 1863, at Fort Jackson. The Fourth Regiment, Corps d'Afrique, was commanded by Lt. Col. A. C. Benedict, an officer who often used the lash and other severe punishments against the recently freed soldiers. Incensed by this treatment, the troops mutinied. The revolt was quickly suppressed, but it demonstrated the flaws in Banks's efforts to recruit and organize black troops. The failure to create full regiments, the decision not to use black officers, and the policy of relegating these units to fatigue duty all drove home to the African American troops the fact that whites considered them to be second-class soldiers. Banks tried to remedy these problems by attempting to eliminate incompetent officers and ordering an end to the practice of using black troops to perform most of the fatigue duty, requiring them only "to take their fair share of fatigue duty, with the white troops." Such efforts improved morale, but Banks never used his Corps d'Afrique in combat.[53]

Schenck's efforts, on the other hand, caused Lincoln headaches when the commander of the Middle Department began recruiting black soldiers in Maryland. In late June 1863, Schenck hired four thousand blacks to work as laborers, an effort that convinced him he could raise at least one African American regiment from among Maryland's black population. This was a potentially controversial project because, since the Emancipation Proclamation did not apply to Maryland, it was illegal to recruit slaves in this state without their masters' consent. Unfortunately, Schenck's recruiters in eastern Maryland sought to recruit slaves without obtaining consent from their masters, leading to complaints from owners and orders from the War Department to stop these actions.[54]

These orders did not end Schenck's activities, and by October he was sending troops into neighborhoods with directions to carry off all the able-bodied black men, regardless of whether they were free or slave. By doing so, the political general was engaging in forcible black recruitment, a scheme not approved by Lincoln. The president preferred that free African Americans volunteer and also understood that in Maryland slaves could not enlist without the consent of their masters. Predictably, the Ohio general's recruiting methods drew more anger that inevitably found its way to the White House when a delegation arrived in October to complain to Lincoln. Before the president could rebuke Schenck, more trouble arose. On occasion, Schenck's recruiting parties included black troops, which on October 21 led to violence and the death of one of these detachments' white lieutenants. After this embarrassment, Lincoln told his general to avoid sending blacks to recruit, though he did not repudiate the general's policy of forcefully enlisting African Americans. Schenck's resignation in November ended the controversy.[55]

Perhaps in no other area of the war effort did political generals make a greater contribution toward determining Union policy than in regards to slavery. Their actions on such questions as fugitive slaves, emancipation, black labor, and African American soldiers helped to push the Lincoln administration to make major policy decisions on these controversial issues. On many occasions, Lincoln adopted a scheme initiated by a political general. Such generals as Butler and Frémont took the lead, whereas others, such as Banks, Logan, Wadsworth, and Blair, supported, defended, and even advanced a particular plan when it became apparent that Lincoln had decided to adopt that policy.

Several factors shaped political generals' thinking toward slavery and African Americans. Military necessity underlay most of the plans adopted by these citizen generals. Butler's actions, for instance, on fugitive slaves, black labor, and African American soldiers all had their rationale in the need to formulate an answer to these problems that would aid the war effort. Politics also played an important role. By the late summer of 1862, Butler understood that the political winds were blowing in the direction of some form of emancipation and changed his policies to meet the new situation. In August 1861, Frémont's order freeing the slaves of Rebels was motivated in part by political considerations. Nearly every decision that Banks made was calculated to secure his authority in Louisiana or to win political support in the North, and he spent much of the last year of the war defending his policies to Northern voters. Finally, some generals, such as Logan, accepted emancipation and black soldiers simply because they saw them as new tools in the war against the rebellion.

On the other hand, several political generals cared little for Lincoln's policies toward African Americans. Dix disliked the solution to the fugitive slave issue, believed emancipation to be a mistake, and opposed arming blacks. He never openly challenged Lincoln on any of these decisions but, at least in the case of African American soldiers, tried to some extent to obstruct the president's policy. Denver, on the other hand, despised the Emancipation Proclamation so much that he resigned his commission, refusing to fight a war to free slaves. Not surprisingly, both of these men were conservative Democrats with a prewar history of supporting the South and, on the issues of slavery, freedom, and black soldiers, among the least influential of all citizen generals.

CHAPTER 11

Exerting
Political Influence

T he most important reason Lincoln commissioned politicians was to generate political support to restore the Union and win the war. These men were expected to persuade their constituents to enlist in the army, vote for the administration at the polls, and generally support the cause. Politics encompassed a variety of different activities. Citizen generals constantly engaged in political intrigue, trying to influence the president and other politicians in order to advance their careers, while congressmen and private citizens also petitioned Lincoln on behalf of their favored general. Running for office, stump speaking during elections, and writing letters and giving speeches defending the war were all aspects of politics practiced by political generals. All of these actions affected the war in many different ways, some for good and others for ill.

Political intrigue was a fact of life during the Civil War. Most generals recognized the need to curry the favor of politicians in order to increase their chances of advancing in rank or achieving a conspicuous command. The necessity for such assistance was expressed by Gen. Orlando Willcox, a West Point graduate from Detroit, who begged Senator Zachariah Chandler for help in obtaining a promotion. "Other officers are exerting political influence from their own states," Willcox wrote, "& it might be important in my case to prevent being crowded out." Military ability was important, but by seeking the patronage of politicians, officers hoped to increase their chances of advancing up the chain of command.[1]

The relationship between Grant and Illinois representative Elihu Washburne illustrated that even capable soldiers needed political aid. Washburne acted as Grant's "political manager." At the beginning of the war, he secured for Grant a commission as colonel of an Illinois infantry regiment, shortly thereafter he ensured that the former captain became one of Illinois' first six brigadier generals, and for the rest of the war he watched over the general. Without his guardian angel, Grant, who disliked asking politicians for help, might have remained in Galena, Illinois, or been assigned to a nondescript department in the Midwest. Grant's case was not unique. Other West Point graduates who benefited from similar political patronage included McClellan, Burnside, and Sherman.[2]

Though all generals sought the aid of politicians, citizen generals did so more frequently than West Pointers. Most of them already had strong political ties with a governor, congressman, senator, member of the cabinet, and even the president, and they sought to exploit these advantages. They also had little compunction about employing these connections to further their careers. Many citizen generals, though motivated in part by a desire to suppress the rebellion or destroy slavery, also joined the army in hopes of advancing their postwar political careers. Success in the present conflict, if history was any guide, almost guaranteed success in postwar politics. As a friend of Banks told the general in July 1861, "Our next president will be one of the military men of this war." Not all political generals nursed presidential ambitions, but most of them hoped to receive political rewards for their wartime service, rewards that required military success.[3]

The one politician nearly all citizen generals sought aid from was Lincoln, who, as the commander in chief, was best positioned to aid them. Regardless of their political affiliation, these men hoped the president would promote their careers; asked him to help their friends, relatives, or business associates; and bombarded him with advice on a variety of topics. The president brought many of these petitions on himself by telling at least three generals, Butler, Schurz, and McClernand, to write him whenever they desired. The fact that communicating directly with their commander in chief violated army regulations did not concern these men, who tended to ignore the few reprimands they received for doing so. As a result, the president received an unending flood of often unnecessary and distracting correspondence from his political generals.[4]

Many citizen generals complained to Lincoln about their rank and current assignment, hoping to obtain a promotion or more prominent command. On two occasions, Butler asked Lincoln to promote him to major general in the Regular army, a request that the president refused. McClernand was equally as blatant in his attempts to gain an independent command. Throughout 1861 and 1862, he sent a steady stream of letters and individuals to Washington begging the president for "a field of independent action." These efforts bore fruit when Lincoln finally assigned the former congressman to a command on the Mississippi River. As McClernand sought his command, Schenck also campaigned for promotion to major general and his own independent assignment. Schenck sent letters to Lincoln and Stanton and dispatched his friend Donn Piatt to Washington, who hounded the president and secretary of war through much of the spring of 1862. This persistence paid off when, in the fall, Lincoln promoted the Ohio politician and placed him in command of the Middle Department.[5]

Meanwhile, Dix also harassed Lincoln with complaints about his assignments. In early 1862, the New Yorker held a subordinate position in the Department of Pennsylvania, an arrangement he found distasteful and degrading for a general of his rank. He asked the president to assign him the task of capturing Charleston, South Carolina, but Lincoln believed that Dix was too old for a field command and instead created the Middle Department for him. Shortly thereafter, Dix was incensed when he was transferred to Fortress Monroe, Virginia, an appointment that placed him under McClellan, then conducting the peninsular campaign. Lincoln realized that Dix "was a little hurt" and tried to find him a new independent command, but it was not until August, when McClellan abandoned the peninsula, that the situation was resolved. Dix was left at Fortress Monroe.[6]

Hoping to influence the war effort, political generals sent the president advice, suggestions, and comments on a variety of topics. Sigel, from January to March 1863, sent Lincoln four separate papers presenting thoughts on several subjects. The German offered a plan of campaign for the Army of the Potomac to undertake in North Carolina, ideas for creating a reserve cavalry division, a scheme for reorganizing the War Department's bureaus, and an outline for a presidential military staff. In the late summer of 1863, Blair dispatched to Lincoln a letter explaining why the Mississippi River should be opened to commerce. In 1864, Sickles offered advice on how to stimulate recruiting and complained about a proclamation issued by Andrew Johnson, then military governor of Tennessee, which Sickles believed was harsh and vindictive. Lincoln ignored all of these unsolicited missives.[7]

If the president merely disregarded their advice, he was at times downright irritated when political generals pressed him to deal with private concerns that had little bearing on the war effort. Early in 1863, Wadsworth asked the president to transfer his son to his staff. In June 1863, as Robert E. Lee raided Maryland and Pennsylvania, Schenck, who commanded the department Lee was moving through, took time out from the emergency to beg Lincoln to grant his nephew an appointment to Annapolis. Dix, who in between his military duties served as president of the Union Pacific Railroad, pestered Lincoln with appeals to provide aid for his company. In all of these cases, Lincoln declined to intervene. From time to time the president did oblige a general, as when he fulfilled Shields's request to commission one of the Irishman's friends.[8]

On most occasions, Lincoln managed to suppress his irritation with these pleas, but one appeal from Sickles was too much for the president. Sickles asked him to settle a question regarding the Panoche Grande, a California land-grant case involving the general as counsel for one of the claimants. Lincoln refused to intervene, asking the political general to "point me to the law which assigns any duty to the President in the case." Sickles ignored this brush-off and continued to press Lincoln for help. In the fall, he sent the president a second letter and even visited the White House, imploring Lincoln to intervene, but nothing came of these appeals, and Sickles eventually dropped the matter. By tolerantly putting off Sickles, Lincoln kept the influential New York Democrat involved in the war effort.[9]

The political general who badgered Lincoln with the most requests, advice, and appeals was Schurz. Acting on Lincoln's wish that he write "whenever anything occurred to me," the German dashed off dozens of letters to the White House. The deluge began in mid-June 1862, only two days after he began his first military duty under Frémont, when Schurz sent the president a letter defending the Pathfinder's conduct during the recent Shenandoah campaign.[10]

Schurz's letters covered a variety of topics, from politics to requests for promotion, but he eventually wore out the president's patience. In November 1862, he blamed the Republicans' losses in the fall elections on Lincoln, lecturing the president that he had appointed the wrong men, namely, Democrats, to command. The two men exchanged a series of letters on this topic, as the president put up with, and perhaps even enjoyed, the young general's intemperance. In early 1863, Schurz bombarded Lincoln with petitions designed to win him a promotion to major general, messages that ranged from disingenuous to impudent and self-aggrandizing to whining. No record of the president's responses to these letters remains, but in March Schurz received his promotion. By 1864, a frustrated Lincoln tried to avoid communicating with the general. When the German demanded a pass to visit Washington and discuss politics, the president refused and instead sent his private secretary, John Nicolay, to confer with the general in New York. Lincoln had grown tired of Schurz's constant lecturing and self-promotion and hoped to evade him if possible.[11]

Schurz's relationship with Lincoln demonstrated that political generals were willing to spend significant time and effort trying to influence the president. They all hoped to advance their careers; provide advice on military, administrative, and political matters; and seek his aid in resolving their private concerns. When their requests might strengthen the war effort, Lincoln happily complied, something that happened most often when they sought promotions or better commands. Although their constant pestering could be aggravating, the president frequently agreed to these demands, believing that by appeasing these generals he would cement their loyalty to his administration.

Lincoln was far less forgiving on other matters. He routinely ignored their advice on military and administrative questions not involving their commands, since he had appointed other individuals to deal with these issues. When it came to personal matters, the president on occasion lost his patience. Though he might bow to an occasional request and appoint a general's friend to a position, he preferred to ignore these issues altogether and disliked being hounded about them. Political generals irritated the president on many occasions, and from time to time he must have wondered if keeping some political generals in the army was worth all the headaches that they caused.

Political generals not only sought the president's aid but also solicited help from cabinet members and members of Congress. All citizen generals had prewar ties with politicians from both parties and now exploited these connections to advance their careers. They hoped to take advantage of a politician's relationship with Lincoln or other influential figures. In January 1865, Schurz openly expressed this motive to Washburne when explaining why he was seeking the congressman's help: because Grant is "your General, and you are undoubtedly in continual correspondence with the man who does things." For a variety of reasons, politicians were willing to help citizen generals, regardless of their political affiliation. They often had the same goals, sought to ride the coattails of successful military leaders, hoped a general could advance a particular political cause, and believed they could shore up their political support by aiding popular commanders. Whatever the reason, citizen generals and politicians in the cabinet and Congress formed alliances, though these alliances often shifted and met with varying degrees of success.[12]

Seeking the aid of cabinet members was a high priority. These men wielded great power because they controlled branches of the executive department and had frequent contact with Lincoln. By gaining the support of a cabinet member, a political general wanted to have his requests filled, influence the president, and advance his career. Of course, it was much easier for cabinet members to fill small demands. For instance, in the fall of 1861, Dix beseeched Secretary of State Seward to help him add two additional officers to his staff, a request the War Department had refused. In less than a week, Seward cut through the red tape, and Dix received his two staff officers. Shields was not as fortunate when he asked Seward to help him obtain the War Department's approval for a plan of campaign he originally wrote for McClellan, who ignored the scheme. Shields hoped to circumvent the commanding general by going through Seward. The secretary of state dutifully presented the proposal to Secretary of War Simon Cameron, but the plan was tabled and forgotten.[13]

Butler proved to be particularly adept at gaining the support of cabinet members. In 1861, his primary contact was Postmaster Gen. Montgomery Blair. They found common cause in their dislike of Gen. Winfield Scott, who Butler felt was deliberately hindering his command and Blair believed was too old and feeble to conduct a vigorous war. While Butler served at Fortress Monroe in the summer of 1861, Blair defended Butler's controversial decision to classify slaves as "contraband of war," worked to increase the size of the Democrat's forces, and advised the novice general to rely on Regular army officers. Following the victory at Hatteras Inlet, Blair helped Butler obtain command of the Department of the East. After Butler assumed control of New Orleans in the spring of 1862, their alliance withered because the general began advocating war measures such as arming African Americans, ideas Blair had little sympathy with.[14]

As his association with Blair ended, Butler turned to Secretary of the Treasury Chase. Chase, the most radical member of Lincoln's cabinet, held presidential ambitions he hoped to further partly by winning the support of former slaves, support he believed could be found in a reconstructed Louisiana. Butler's efforts to create units of black soldiers also intrigued the secretary, who supported arming former slaves. In the summer of 1862, Chase began writing flattering letters to Butler, informing the Democrat that Lincoln was moving slowly on antislavery issues and encouraging him to adopt a radical approach toward slavery to improve his political standing. Butler eagerly took advantage of Chase's patronage, using the secretary as a courier to convey his letters directly to the president. Following the citizen general's removal from Louisiana, Chase worked to return the ousted general to New Orleans.[15]

Though his effort failed, Chase continued to champion Butler. The two men wrote and saw each other throughout 1863, and the secretary came to "wish [that] the President would make him General in Chief." This appointment never happened, but Chase implored Lincoln to grant Butler another command. Finally, in the fall, Lincoln caved under the pressure and assigned

Butler to command the Department of Virginia and North Carolina. In the end, the Butler-Chase alliance benefited Butler, gaining him an assignment that provided him with the chance to win a military victory.[16]

Political generals were also adept at seeking the aid of members of both houses of Congress. These politicians proved perfectly willing to assist generals, especially if they were residents of the same state. For instance, Banks communicated frequently with George Boutwell, a friend from Massachusetts who in 1862 won election as a Republican representative. While Banks was in Louisiana, Boutwell served as the former governor's intermediary with Lincoln, urging the president to send reinforcements to the Gulf Department and discussing Banks's concerns over Reconstruction and the extent of his authority in Louisiana. Hurlbut, following his removal from command of the Sixteenth Corps, successfully exploited his ties with Illinois congressmen, especially Senator Trumbull, whom Hurlbut pleaded with for help to persuade Lincoln to appoint the general commander of New Orleans. McClernand sought the aid of most of Illinois' congressmen, constantly asking them for help in obtaining better military commands. These congressmen, all of whom recognized the influence he wielded in Egypt, sought to help him, but their aid had its limits, as ultimately Lincoln did not grant McClernand the independent command he cherished. The president was not going to allow political considerations to override sound military policy.[17]

Political generals also petitioned congressmen from various regions of the country for aid, a tactic that ethnic generals, especially Germans, were adept at. German settlements could be found in almost every Northern state, with large concentrations in New York, Pennsylvania, Ohio, Indiana, Missouri, and Wisconsin, thus giving German generals influence with a large number of congressmen. For instance, in early 1863, when seeking his promotion to major general, Schurz solicited the aid of Massachusetts senator Sumner and Washburne. The general who best exploited this situation was Sigel.[18]

In the winter of 1863–64, Sigel, then stationed at Reading, Pennsylvania, effectively used his German heritage to lobby a variety of congressmen to gain an independent command. The campaign began at the end of 1863, when he beseeched newly elected Missouri representative Sempronius Boyd for "something better to do than to sit here in the Coal Region." Several weeks later, Sigel again asked Boyd for help, complaining that there was an "unjust and infamous system . . . against foreigners." Prejudice against German generals, Sigel claimed, was especially strong. Over the next two months, the Yankee Dutchman enlisted the support of an impressive array of congressmen, cabinet members, and other political figures, including Representatives Robert Schenck (Ohio), Isaac Arnold (Illinois), and Kellian Whaley (West Virginia), and William Seward, Simon Cameron, and Thurlow Weed. This powerful coalition, representing six states with large numbers of German voters, was too much for Lincoln to resist, and the president, who needed to secure the German vote, appointed Sigel to the command of West Virginia.[19]

As these examples attest, winning the support of cabinet members or congressmen did not always provide a political general with enough leverage to achieve his goals. In the end, Lincoln made appointments based on his own calculations of a citizen general's political value and military necessity. If the president concluded that military necessity dictated refusing a general's requests, no amount of political pressure would help that man's cause. McClernand discovered this unpleasant fact on several occasions. The president was susceptible to suasion, but only if it coincided with his own evaluation of the situation. Thus, Lincoln, under political pressure, reinstated Butler in 1863 and Sigel in 1864 to command, but only because he believed that placing these men in new assignments aided the war effort.

Political generals did not always instigate the pressure brought upon Lincoln on their behalf. Throughout the war, politicians, interest groups, and private individuals all petitioned the president to grant their favored general some preference. Such pressure often proved to be effective, especially when a large number of groups, newspapers, and politicians worked toward the same goal (though not always in concert), because it provided evidence that promoting or appointing a citizen general would bring political benefits. Lincoln, especially early in the war, was susceptible to these petitions, as demonstrated by two cases in the winter of 1862 involving Frémont and Sigel.

Lincoln's decision in October 1861 to remove Frémont from command of the Western Department produced a political firestorm that caused the president headaches for the next five months. Abolitionists and Radical Republicans were furious that Frémont had been fired; he was "the only general that has done anything," as one irate correspondent wrote Senator Benjamin Wade. Enthused by Frémont's order to emancipate the slaves of Rebels, they now jumped to his defense. In New York City at the end of November, Sumner praised the Pathfinder at a mass meeting held at the Cooper Institute, and, from the halls of Congress, Thaddeus Stevens thundered to his fellow Radicals, "Where are you that you let the hounds run down your friend Frémont?"[20]

The howls of protest coalesced into a powerful political force that created the Committee on the Conduct of the War (CCW). Many factors led to the formation of this committee, including the military defeats of Bull Run, Wilson's Creek, and Ball's Bluff and political considerations such as fears of disloyalty and lack of action against slavery, but it was Frémont's removal that finally pushed Congress to create the investigative body composed of members of both houses. In the middle of December, a bipartisan coalition voted to form the CCW, empowering it to investigate every aspect of the war effort. The committee quickly became dominated by the Radicals, particularly Wade, Chandler, and Representative George W. Julian.[21]

Among the committee's goals was to publicize generals sympathetic to emancipation and a hard war against Rebels, a goal that led it to make Frémont's case a priority. Finding generals of "right principle," as one of Chandler's friends put it, was the CCW's overriding objective; a general's military qualifications were of secondary consideration. Chandler, for instance, had visited St. Louis and observed the Western Department while the Pathfinder was in command. "Frémont is a failure" was the senator's harsh judgment. Despite this opinion, Chandler still became one of the citizen general's chief defenders. Frémont's military abilities mattered little to Chandler, Wade, and Julian, who were all close friends of the Pathfinder, agreed with his political positions, and hoped to force Lincoln to reappoint the citizen general and perhaps even have their hero replace Democrat George McClellan, whom they all despised.[22]

The CCW's investigation of Frémont's conduct in the West was a sham, since it was evident that the only goal was to rehabilitate the general. In January 1862, the Pathfinder appeared before the committee three times, during which he read a prepared statement and answered easy questions designed to elicit responses favorable to his defense. Even before the political general finished his testimony, Wade declared that "every charge against Mr. Frémont [was] exploded." Nevertheless, the CCW dutifully called several more witnesses. Most of them were friendly to Frémont, with the exceptions of Montgomery Blair, Frank Blair, and Gen. David Hunter, all of whom were treated with hostility and sarcasm. Not surprisingly, the committee's conclusions exonerated Frémont of all wrongdoing.[23]

Armed with Frémont's testimony, throughout February and early March the committee and other Radicals badgered Lincoln to reappoint the Pathfinder. In early February, several CCW members visited Stanton and requested that he give the political general a second command. Stanton, who was also being pestered by newspaper editor Charles Dana, told Dana that "if General Frémont has any fight in him, he shall have a chance to show it." When no appointment arrived, in March, Horace Greeley published Frémont's testimony in the *New York Daily Tribune* and, in the House, Schuyler Colfax of Indiana, John Shanks of Indiana, and Stevens gave speeches defending the Pathfinder. Under such pressure, the president bowed to the Radicals and on March 11 created for Frémont the Mountain Department.[24]

At the same time, Sigel's actions ignited a controversy that caused the president more political agony. In mid-November 1861, Sigel, then commanding Union forces at Rolla, Missouri, took a thirty-day leave of absence to recuperate from an illness. Over the next month, reports of insubordination, poor discipline, and other irregularities among the troops at Rolla filtered into St. Louis, where Halleck, now commanding the Western Department, worried about this crucial outpost. With Sigel still on leave, Halleck resolved the growing problem by assigning Gen. Samuel Curtis to command of the Southwestern District of Missouri. This infuriated Sigel, who, upon his return to Rolla at the end of December, submitted his resignation. Halleck realized that the Yankee Dutchman was too popular among the German troops to be allowed to resign and persuaded Sigel to withdraw his resignation, promising him that he would play an important role in the upcoming campaign.[25]

Unfortunately for Lincoln, a wave of protest erupted from German Americans. Many Germans saw Sigel as a symbol of their community and its commitment to the war and perceived any attack on him as an attack on all Germans. Thus, they rallied to his defense. One German soldier termed Sigel's resignation a calamity, and others swore they would refuse to fight if the Yankee Dutchman was not restored to command. Mass meetings occurred across the country protesting Sigel's treatment and demanding that he be provided with an active command. German newspapers referred to Halleck as a nativist and urged Sigel's promotion to major general. Sigel committees sprang up all over the North, there were calls for a congressional investigation, and selling portraits of Sigel became a profitable enterprise in the Midwest.[26]

The outcry from the German community caused a corresponding action from American newspapers and politicians. *The New York Herald* referred to Sigel as "too good an officer to be set aside." One of Trumbull's constituents begged him to "exert your influence with the administration in this matter." In a letter to Frank Blair, then in Congress, that Blair passed on to Lincoln, P. A. Ladue wrote that "we cannot really afford to lose his services. . . . The whole German element among us clings to and adores him." Illinois representative Isaac Arnold formed a pro-Sigel group that submitted a petition to Lincoln asking him to make the Yankee Dutchman a major general. After Sigel's return to the army, the common demand was that he be promoted.[27]

All of this political pressure fell squarely on the president's shoulders. In January, Lincoln dispatched to St. Louis his friend Gustave Koerner to investigate the matter. Koerner talked with Halleck and Sigel, laid the blame for the entire episode on Halleck, and recommended Sigel's promotion to major general. The president took no further action and instead waited for an appropriate opportunity to promote the German general, an opportunity that came in March following the victory at the battle of Pea Ridge. At the end of the month, in an obvious bow to the German community, Lincoln promoted Sigel to major general.[28]

Lincoln may have bent to the demands of the Radicals and Germans on these occasions, but he was able to resist their and others' appeals when he believed that a general had outlived his usefulness. After Frémont's resignation in June 1862, the Radicals again called for the president to find another assignment for the Pathfinder. In February 1863, Stevens asked Lincoln to grant Frémont "a fair command. It will greatly encourage your friends." A month later, Julian saw Lincoln in the White House and demanded that Frémont be given a new post, arguing that "his restoration to duty would stir the country." The president fended off Julian's argument by pointing out that "it would stir the country on one side, and stir it the other way on the other. It would please Frémont's friends, and displease the conservatives; and that is all I can see in the stirring argument."[29]

Despite Lincoln's statement, in April, the release of the CCW's report on Frémont's Western Department led the Radicals to renew their clamoring for the Pathfinder. The report praised the political general's conduct, especially his emancipation order, and ignored his many failures. Once again, Lincoln was besieged with demands to restore Frémont to active service. The president fended off these requests by offering to place Frémont in command of ten thousand United States Colored Troops, an offer Frémont declined. He also pleaded, as he told Sumner, that "I can not now give . . . [Frémont] a Department, because I have not spare troops to furnish a new Department; and I have not, as I think, justifiable ground to relieve the present commander of any old one." These tactics quieted the Radicals, and in the middle of August the Pathfinder resigned his army commission.[30]

Throughout the war, Lincoln received petitions on behalf of nearly all of his political generals and dealt with most of these with his usual tact and patience. Most he politely turned down or ignored, but, on occasion, these appeals tried Lincoln's patience. In January 1865, a group of Kentuckians visited the White House and implored Lincoln to place Butler in charge of their state. This was too much for the president. "You howled when Butler went to New Orleans," he complained in an uncharacteristic outburst. "Others howled when he was removed from that command. Somebody has been howling ever since at his assignment to military command. How long will it be before you . . . will be howling to me to remove him?" Experience had demonstrated to Lincoln that assigning a political general to command created as much controversy as harmony. In this and many other cases, the president decided that, regardless of the political consequences, it was often best to ignore these petitions and let a citizen general remain on the sidelines.[31]

Lincoln was willing to endure considerable political intrigue if the citizen generals he appointed aided the war effort on the battlefield and at the polls. The major rationale behind the president's policy of commissioning politicians was to bind these men to the war effort with the hope that they would convince their electorates and friends to support the Union cause and quiet the criticism of the Lincoln administration. Of all the political generals, only Dix articulated this idea in his wartime correspondence. "I have labored," he wrote in September 1862, "by all the means in my power to bring to the support of President Lincoln all the influence of my democratic friends, and begged them to postpone the questioning of errors of administration to the close of the war." Such influence was brought to bear throughout the entire conflict and expressed in speeches, letters, and running for elective office. These generals gave many speeches and wrote dozens of letters, but their efforts failed on occasion, worked at cross-purposes, sometimes opposed the president, and often did more harm than good.[32]

For the first year of the war, there was little partisan political conflict, as the majority of Republicans and Democrats sought to support the war. The Republicans attempted to bury party activity, arguing that all loyal men should rally around the president in order to suppress the rebellion. Stephen Douglas, the democracy's ostensible leader in April 1861, aided the Republicans in their efforts. He declared, in one of his last speeches, that "whoever is not prepared to sacrifice party and organizations and platforms on the altar of his country, does not deserve the support or countenance of honest people."[33]

During the next year, several Democratic political generals echoed these sentiments. McClernand, Douglas's political ally, argued in a letter to Ohio representative Samuel S. Cox that it was impossible to manufacture "a political movement which can be distinguished from hostility to the government and the war." Butler aided the ultimately futile attempts to organize the "No Party" movement in Massachusetts. In a series of letters to various Democratic officials, Dix expressed his belief that it was impossible to create "a political movement which can be distinguished from hostility to the government and the war."[34]

For many Democrats, these notions crumbled during the first year of the conflict, causing the democracy to fracture over the question of partisanship. The process began with the death of Douglas in June 1861. His demise left the Democrats with no one man who could set the party's agenda and define its responses to Lincoln's policies. As a result, the party broke into three factions. The War Democrats supported the war and the Lincoln government, opposed the revival of party competition, and formed coalitions with the Republicans. By 1864, many of them had united with the Republicans to establish the Union Party. Such generals as Butler, Dix, Logan, McClernand, Meagher, and Sickles were counted in their ranks, but, as one of Lincoln's secretaries observed, "nobody knows how large a part of the old-time Democracy" joined the Union Party, which the Republicans dominated.[35]

The other two factions were the Regular and Peace Democrats. Regular or Conditional Democrats supported the war, but attacked the Republicans' racial plans, military ineptitude, and assaults on civil liberties, such as controversial political arrests, suspension of habeas corpus, and suppression of opposition newspapers. These Democrats damned all efforts to ally with the Republicans and revived party competition. Denver and Shields fell within this group, although neither of them actively participated in political campaigns, and McClernand became one in 1864. Finally, the Peace Democrats composed the last faction. Also called Copperheads, they denounced Republican Party policies, sympathized with the South, and opposed the war. No general in this study was a Peace Democrat.[36]

As for the Republicans, they split into three factions, though there was some blurring among them. The Radicals despised slavery, demanded immediate emancipation, advocated the confiscation of Rebel property, and called for the use of black soldiers, and a few spoke of granting civil and political equality to African Americans. Always a minority within the party, Radicals were vocal, active, and tenacious and exercised more influence over the party, congressional actions, and military decisions than their numbers suggested. Such generals as Frémont, Schurz, Sigel, and Wadsworth fell within their ranks.[37]

Opposing them were the Moderate and Conservative Republicans. These men also disliked slavery and opposed its extension, but they resisted outright emancipation except as a wartime measure, instead seeking gradual, compensated emancipation, and some favored the colonization of blacks. The Conservatives opposed upsetting the South's social system and initially resisted enlisting African Americans. The main belief of both groups was that the preservation of the Union came first and should govern all other considerations. Banks, Hurlbut, and Schenck could be classed as Moderates, whereas Blair was a Conservative.[38]

Throughout the war, many political generals made speeches or published pamphlets supporting the war effort. They did not voice approval of all of Lincoln's policies, although they usually remained silent on aspects of policy they disagreed with, but they always argued for the continuation of the war until the Confederacy was defeated. The speeches and pamphlets of political generals of both parties provided important support for the war effort and offered to their constituents arguments concerning what the war was about and why it should continue.

Dix provided some of the most important public support for Lincoln be-

cause he defended controversial policies. Initially, he tried to avoid addressing
the public, but in 1863 he realized that opposition to the war was growing
and that he had to speak out against it and sustain the administration. In the
spring, Dix joined the Loyal Union League, a New York organization designed
to promote support for the war, and in the fall he published several letters that
defended some of Lincoln's controversial policies. In a message to the War
Democracy of Wisconsin, he argued that the Emancipation Proclamation, even
if it was bad policy, should be supported, explained why political arrests were
necessary, and justified the draft. To a Union Ratification meeting at the Cooper
Institute, the old general reiterated his pledge to convince as many Democrats
as possible to provide the government with their unqualified support.[39]

During the election of 1864, Dix publicly supported the president and
his war policies. In September, before an audience in Ohio, he assailed any
peace effort and argued that the Union could be preserved only by "a steady,
persistent, and unremitting prosecution of the war." A month later, in a published letter to Philadelphia Democrats, the New Yorker condemned the Peace
Democrats and McClellan and asked the people to give their "earnest support
to the war." Finally, at the end of October, he helped organize a convention
of War Democrats at the Cooper Institute and endorsed Lincoln.[40]

Another prominent Democrat to defend Lincoln and his war policies was
Butler. Throughout the spring of 1863, he gave a series of speeches on the
East Coast, culminating on April 2 in an address at the Academy of Music in
New York City. Declaring himself "an old-fashioned Andrew Jackson Democrat," the general explained that he had adopted a Radical stance because, by
leaving the Union, Southerners had created a revolution and were now "alien
enemies." As a result, he exclaimed, "I am not for the Union as it was." Instead,
Unionists must "build it up with all the modern improvements," which meant
confiscating and distributing Southern land to loyal men and freeing and
arming the slaves. Butler's Academy of Music address, distributed throughout
the North by the Loyal Publication Society, created a storm of controversy
as Democrats denounced and Republicans praised it. The general followed
the speech with further addresses and then, in the fall, campaigned for the
Republicans in New Hampshire.[41]

Unlike Dix and Butler, who never publicly wavered in their support of
Lincoln, McClernand eventually abandoned the president. Following his removal from command of the Thirteenth Corps, the general returned to Illinois,
where he was inundated with requests to speak. His speeches tended to avoid
controversial issues such as emancipation, the draft, and the suppression of
civil liberties and instead focused on appeals to save the Union, castigations
of the rebellion's leaders, and condemnations of the peace movement. In one

address, he "declared that the peace cry meant the surrender of our dignity, our honor and our rights to the rebellion" as well as an end to free commerce on the Mississippi. Instead, McClernand called for "teaching the rebels a lesson that they would not forget for a century."[42]

The political general's speeches may not have been ringing endorsements of Lincoln's policies, but they nonetheless supported the war effort. In the fall, McClernand expanded his speaking schedule. He gave addresses in Wisconsin, Indiana, Ohio, and New York that touched on themes expressed in his Illinois speeches. At the end of November, he chaired a Northwestern Convention of War Democrats meeting at Chicago, called, as he said, "to place the Democratic party in a position of supporting the Government in its efforts to put down the rebellion." The convention passed two sets of resolutions, one endorsing a Radical agenda, essentially demanding an end to slavery, and a second that made no mention of slavery and declared that the preservation of the Union was the paramount objective. McClernand signed the second resolution, indicating his dislike of Lincoln's emancipation policies and growing disenchantment with the president.[43]

During the election of 1864, McClernand renounced Lincoln and supported McClellan. McClernand refused to endorse the president because he resented the shabby way Lincoln had treated him since his removal from command during the Vicksburg campaign. Instead, he canvassed throughout Illinois for McClellan, arguing that the democracy's nominee "would preserve the Union at all hazards." McClernand's switch had no adverse effect for Lincoln since the Republicans carried Illinois.[44]

Of all the Democrats, Logan provided Lincoln with the most dramatic and important public support. Beginning in the summer of 1863, while on leave from the army, he made a series of addresses in Illinois that created great enthusiasm. On July 31, at Duquoin, the general defended the Lincoln administration and denounced the peace movement. The war, Logan declared, was a constitutionally sanctioned conflict undertaken to suppress a "most damnable" rebellion. In order to destroy this rebellion, the government had the right to create an army, enforce the draft, confiscate enemy property, and arrest and detain citizens who opposed the war. As for emancipation, he denied that he was an abolitionist, but he also avowed that the institution was dead. The general called for a hard peace, arguing that the rebellion's leaders should never be allowed "to have the same constitutional rights as they had before." He spent more time lashing out at the peace movement, charging that these men would ruin the country. He concluded by asking the people to "quit your quarreling. Be for your Government . . . [and] assist the soldier."[45]

Logan's speech met with wild excitement and spurred the general to speak throughout Illinois, culminating in an address in Chicago on August 10 that was virtually a replica of the Duquoin lecture. Both the Duquoin and the Chicago speeches were quickly published and used as campaign literature by Union candidates in the fall elections. Even the *New York Times* took notice of Logan's efforts, praising his "able and eloquent" speeches. As a result, influential Republicans begged the president to extend the former congressman's leave so he could continue drumming up support for the war. Lincoln granted the request, commenting that "John Logan was acting so splendidly now, that he absolved him in his own mind for all the wrong he ever did & all he will do hereafter." The general remained in the state until the end of August, giving more speeches, and then returned to the army.[46]

During the election of 1864, Logan continued to offer the president enthusiastic support. At the personal request of Lincoln, Logan obtained leave and returned to Illinois to stump for the Republicans. After consulting with Republican leaders, the general agreed to give sixteen speeches in Illinois, primarily in Egypt. He made clear that he stood by the president, endorsed all the Illinois Republican candidates, attacked the Democratic Party, and announced that he was prepared to use all means to destroy the rebellion, but he avoided controversial issues such as emancipation, the draft, and the suppression of civil liberties. On the eve of the election, Washburne assured Lincoln that "Logan is carrying all before him in Egypt."[47]

Several ethnic generals also actively supported the Lincoln administration and the war effort. In 1863, Meagher spoke to primarily Irish audiences in both the United States and Ireland, attempting to explain what the war was about and why the Irish should stand by the Union. In two letters published in a pamphlet, he argued that the North waged war to destroy a rebellion undertaken "against the spirit and institutions of Democracy" by "the territorial oligarchy of the South" seeking "not independence, but domination." The general did not shy away from controversial topics such as slavery. The war was essentially being fought to reassert the national authority, but he contended that "the emancipation of the slaves in the revolted States became a military necessity." He finished by praising the thousands of Irishmen in the North who had taken up arms to destroy the rebellion.[48]

Meagher attempted to reach out to non-Irish audiences, but these efforts met with less enthusiasm. In the fall of 1863, he sent a public letter to the Union Committee of Ohio, endorsing the Union Party's gubernatorial candidate, John Brough, and attacking the Democratic nominee, the Peace Democrat Clement Vallandigham. "Electing Mr. Brough, Ohio vindicates and fortifies the National Government," but, Meagher warned, electing Vallandigham would place a government in Ohio that would "be in conflict with the policy and action of the Government at Washington." The general's views elicited a harsh reaction from the *Irish American*, a newspaper that typically defended Meagher. The editor declared that the general's stance was one that "can only be regarded with pain by his friends, and with malignant triumph by his enemies." Defending Lincoln and the war was beginning to cost Meagher the support of many Irishmen.[49]

In the election of 1864, Meagher was the only prominent Irishman to come out in favor of Lincoln, but his diatribes against the Irish who remained loyal to the democracy led to a backlash. In a letter to a friend published in October 1864, he castigated "the great bulk of Irishmen" who had been "bamboozled" because of their blind allegiance to the Democrats, a "selfish and conscience-less faction" that would "cripple the national power." Such rhetoric lost him many Irish friends. The *Irish American* blasted Meagher for "his unprovoked attack upon our people" and lamented "an act that has gone so far to darken the whole record of a life." Meagher's actions probably cost Lincoln what few Irish votes he hoped to obtain.[50]

A second ethnic general who spoke in support of the war was Sigel. In October 1863, Sigel, at the request of Republicans who believed that the general "could do great good if he were to . . . address our German population," campaigned for thirty days throughout Pennsylvania, Ohio, and New York. His speeches dwelled exclusively on the peace movement, attacking the Copperheads as a "national calamity" and an "immortal shame to the Republic." Fervent crowds greeted the inexperienced speaker wherever he went.[51]

During the election of 1864, Schurz campaigned for Lincoln and other Republican candidates. As early as February, Schurz offered to campaign for the president in the fall elections, but it was not until August that Lincoln told the German to "go in." The general canvassed vigorously in New York, Pennsylvania, and Wisconsin. The speeches he gave criticized any peace effort as foolish and naive, described the Democrats as "fair-weather" patriots "ready to give up the country in the hour of misfortune," called for continuing the war until the rebellion was crushed, and defended emancipation. His lectures generated great enthusiasm and were published and distributed throughout the North.[52]

Blair also made several public speeches. His efforts were aimed at both shoring up support for the war and attacking his opponents, specifically the Radicals in Missouri and their chief ally in Lincoln's cabinet, Secretary of the Treasury Chase. In one speech in 1863, Blair argued that all questions about emancipation should be put off until the end of the war, railed against a harsh peace toward the South, and criticized Chase's trade policies on the Mississippi. Blair concluded by calling for a broad-based Union Party to replace the Republican Party. The speech set out several themes he would expand on when he returned to Congress in the winter of 1864, but offered little aid to Lincoln and the war effort because it inflamed the division within the Missouri Republican Party.[53]

In their speeches and pamphlets, political generals offered different opinions on a variety of topics, but they all voiced support for the war. The only other issue they all agreed on was the peace movement, which every one of them castigated and portrayed as a threat to the nation. There was great disagreement on several topics. Emancipation, naturally enough, was the most controversial. Some generals, such as Dix and McClernand, obviously disagreed with this policy, but made no outright public repudiation of Lincoln's proclamation. Others, such as Butler, Blair, Logan, and Meagher, offered varying degrees of support. Disagreement also surrounded the issue of Reconstruction. Butler and Logan called for a hard peace, whereas Blair argued for leniency. With such a variety of political and ethnic backgrounds, differences of opinion were inevitable. For the most part, these generals exhorted their audiences to stand by the administration regardless of their opinions on the specific policies adopted by Lincoln, arguing that preserving the Union was more important than the methods used to win the war.

Another way in which political generals tried to support the war effort was by running for political office. Of course, these politicians-turned-generals had selfish reasons for seeking office, but by pursuing elective office they turned their elections, at least in part, into referenda on the war, the policies of the Lincoln administration, and the appeal of Lincoln's opponents. These would have been major issues anyway, but the presence of a political general, who was an important symbol of the war effort, enhanced these issues. Of those political generals who ran for office, Wadsworth sought the governorship of New York, Schenck and Blair ran for seats in the House of Representatives, and several political generals either ran or almost ran against Lincoln in the 1864 presidential election.

For the 1862 New York gubernatorial election, the Republicans nominated Wadsworth. In September, Horace Greeley forcefully pushed for both the political general and an emancipation platform. Still military governor of Washington, Wadsworth replied that he would become a candidate on one condition: the platform must endorse emancipation. This fitted in perfectly with Greeley's aspirations, and at the convention, meeting two days after Lincoln issued the Emancipation Proclamation, he secured Wadsworth's nomination on the first ballot. In his acceptance letter, Wadsworth pledged to sustain the national government, suppress the rebellion, and support the Emancipation Proclamation. After releasing this statement, Wadsworth remained in Washington, sitting out most of the campaign except for two speeches he made near its end. In these, he strongly endorsed emancipation, declaring, "Let the rebellion be crushed, and . . . let Slavery also be crushed with it."[54]

The Republican Party faithful fought for his election in a campaign dominated by several national issues. The Republicans argued that Wadsworth would best support the Lincoln administration, accused the Democrats of disloyalty, praised emancipation, and defended the administration's suppression of civil liberties. The Democrats nominated Regular Democrat Horatio Seymour. They fended off claims that they were disloyal, voiced their support for the war, and bitterly attacked what they perceived to be the Republicans' revolutionary program, denouncing emancipation and the suspension of the writ of habeas corpus. They also launched an ugly personal assault against Wadsworth. The *New York World* asserted that he was hostile to McClellan, insubordinate, unfit for any official position, and spent his time haunting the taverns of Washington.[55]

In a stunning reversal, Wadsworth lost to Seymour. In 1860, Lincoln had carried the state by 50,000 votes, and Edwin Morgan won the governorship by 63,000 ballots. Two years later, the final tally gave Seymour a 10,700–vote majority. Wadsworth blamed the result on Seward, claiming that the secretary of state was always against him. Some agreed with the general, while others pointed to the lack of progress on the battlefield and the fact that large numbers of Republicans were in the army and could not vote. The Regular Democrats argued that it was a sweeping denunciation of both emancipation and the Lincoln administration in particular.[56]

Some of these explanations had merit. The lack of significant success on the battlefield disenchanted voters, leading many to voice their displeasure by voting for Seymour or, in the case of some Republicans, not voting at all. More than 100,000 New Yorkers were disenfranchised because they were in the army, the majority of whom would probably have voted for Wadsworth. Finally, Wadsworth's failure to canvass and almost single-minded focus on emancipation hindered his campaign because he did not address significant questions—the suppression of civil liberties, military failures, and how his election would aid the war effort—that concerned voters. He basically failed to give many voters a reason to cast ballots for him.[57]

As Wadsworth stumbled toward defeat, Schenck was the beneficiary of a successful struggle for Ohio's Third Congressional District. His opponent was the despised Vallandigham, a man the Lincoln administration wanted out of Congress. At the personal urging of Lincoln and Chase, Schenck agreed to run. The Ohio general, still in Washington recuperating from the wound he received at Second Bull Run, played no role in the campaign; he did not even bother to return to the state. Instead, local Republicans canvassed for him. They waved the flag, appealing to patriotism and condemning the Democrat as a traitor while extolling Schenck's military record. These efforts, and the Ohio legislature's gerrymandering of the district to favor the Republicans, allowed Schenck to defeat Vallandigham by 600 votes.[58]

In St. Louis, Blair waged a struggle to retain his seat in Congress. The state Republican Party was fracturing into two increasingly hostile wings over the question of emancipation and what to do with the former slaves. Blair advocated Lincoln's original slavery policy: compensated, gradual emancipation and the colonization of blacks. The growing Radical wing of the party also endorsed gradual emancipation but rejected colonization. After Lincoln issued the Emancipation Proclamation (which did not affect Missouri's slaves), Blair accepted the change in policy as necessary to crush the rebellion. He parted with the Radicals because he argued for compensated emancipation for loyal slave owners, continued to promote colonization, and strenuously opposed enlisting blacks into the army. The two camps became locked in a contest for control of the state party.[59]

As the 1862 elections approached, the Radicals decided to oust Blair and, when they were unable to prevent his nomination at the state Union convention, broke from the party and chose their own candidate. St. Louis attorney Samuel Knox received the nod on a platform that endorsed emancipation, rejected colonization, and advocated enlisting freed blacks. The Democrats selected former Whig Lewis V. Bogy, but he was never a factor, as the election became a clash between Knox and Blair. The ensuing campaign was bitter, focusing on two issues: emancipation and Frank Blair. The Radicals attacked him as "a liar, a drunkard, an intriguer, a conservative, and a traitor." In the end, Blair prevailed because he shored up his political base and attracted sufficient numbers of Democrats to offset the defection of the Radicals. The margin of victory was a meager 153 votes, and Knox challenged the result.[60]

During the 1864 presidential election, several political generals either sought office or were mentioned as possible candidates. Despite some opposition, Lincoln won the Republican or Union Party nomination. During the election, many political generals actively campaigned for Republican or Union Party candidates, several were suggested for vice president, two made veiled attempts for the White House, and Frémont almost ran against Lincoln on a third-party ticket. In the end, Lincoln's sole opponent was Democrat George McClellan, nominated on a peace platform, though in his letter of acceptance the general pledged to continue the war.

In the months leading up to the election, several generals were considered as vice presidential candidates, and at least one was offered the post.

Democrats Dix and Butler were both suggested as possible running mates for Lincoln, but the president appears to have considered only Butler. Alexander McClure later wrote that Butler was "Lincoln's first selection," and after the war the political general claimed that in March Simon Cameron, acting on the president's behest, came to Fortress Monroe and offered him the position. Butler declined, preferring to remain in the army. Logan was mentioned as a potential vice presidential candidate for both Frémont and McClellan.[61]

At least two political generals, Banks and Butler, made unsuccessful informal bids for the presidency. It was no secret that they both harbored presidential ambitions, and at various points during the year each made some effort to win a nomination. Banks supported a scheme to use his military success on the Red River, a campaign he and his supporters expected to end triumphantly in May, a few weeks before the Republican convention convened in June, to win the Republican presidential nomination. The entire affair, including Banks's role, remains murky and came to nothing, since the failure in Louisiana, as a disappointed supporter wrote, "spoiled everything."[62]

Butler's bid was more serious because he had the backing of several important politicians. As early as January 1863, Weed wished that the Democrat was president and, between then and August 1864, Adam Gurowski, Boutwell, Wendell Phillips, Wade, Stevens, and Greeley all voiced a desire to see the general in the White House. Even Lincoln believed, at least for a time, that there was a movement to make Butler president. Butler kept out feelers, but realized that none of this talk translated into actual support. In the late summer of 1864, as the war looked increasingly bad for the Union, a flurry of activity occurred in his favor. Many Radicals feared that the Union was heading for disaster and, if the Democrats nominated a Peace candidate, proposed calling a convention, inviting the War Democrats and nominating Butler for president. In the end, nothing came of this scheme, as the Radicals reluctantly backed Lincoln and Butler abandoned his presidential hopes.[63]

Only Frémont made an open bid for the presidency. In May 1864, a group of disaffected Radical Republicans and abolitionists, including Schuyler Colfax, Wendell Phillips, and Frederick Douglass, who were determined to prevent Lincoln's reelection, met in Cleveland and nominated Frémont for president. The Pathfinder, still angry over the way Lincoln treated him in 1861 and 1862, accepted the nomination. Some of his strongest supporters came from the German community in Missouri, which rallied around him because they believed Lincoln was moving too slowly on emancipation and discriminated against Germans in military appointments. The general failed to arouse any large following, and the Lincoln administration initially thought little of this insurgency.[64]

By the late summer, Frémont's campaign posed a serious threat to Lincoln's reelection hopes. Republican Party leaders realized that Frémont, though having no chance to win himself, might take enough votes away from Lincoln to allow McClellan to win the presidency. September witnessed efforts to convince the Pathfinder to abandon his presidential campaign. Frémont, whose goal was to ensure the election of an acceptable antislavery president, detested McClellan even more than he disliked Lincoln and was persuaded to drop out of the race on the condition that Lincoln remove Montgomery Blair from the cabinet. Thus, on September 22, Frémont withdrew from the race, and the next day Lincoln announced Blair's resignation.[65]

The elections of 1864 ended in complete victory for Lincoln and the Republican Party, but political generals had only a tangential effect on this result. Republican generals played minor roles in the campaign and thus had no impact on its outcome. Among ethnic generals, Schurz's efforts shored up support among the German population, but Meagher probably cost Lincoln any votes with the Irish. Immediately following the election, Dix eagerly wrote Lincoln claiming that "the number of votes drawn off from McClellan by the meeting of the War Democrats at the Cooper Institute was much greater than the majority for the Union ticket." Despite this assertion, the War Democrats exercised very little influence on the election, except perhaps among elite opinion. Amid the rank and file, there was no major defection away from the democracy: in 1860, the party polled 44.7 percent of the Northern popular vote and in 1864, 45 percent.[66]

The only exception to this pattern occurred in southern Illinois, where Logan helped convince Egypt to vote Republican. In 1860, Logan won the Thirteenth Congressional District with 79 percent of the vote, and Douglas beat Lincoln by nearly fourteen thousand ballots, but in 1864 the Republican congressional candidate squeaked out a slender victory (by just under a thousand votes), and Lincoln also narrowly captured the region. The *New York Times* praised Logan for this accomplishment, writing, "The solid Democratic column has been broken into by a grand flank movement under General Logan." The credit for much of this remarkable transformation did lie with Logan, whose switch from partisan Democrat to active Unionist convinced enough of his constituents to abandon the democracy for the Republicans and enable Lincoln and his party to carry Egypt.[67]

Only Blair served in Congress while also still in the army, a constitutionally dubious position that caused Lincoln far more trouble than it was worth. At the beginning of 1864, Blair arrived in Washington to assume his seat in the House of Representatives. It was unconstitutional to hold an army commission above the rank of colonel and serve in Congress, but Lincoln asked the general to come to Washington and "put his military commission in my hands," that is, give the president his resignation with the understanding that Blair could revoke it when desired. Lincoln wanted Blair to help organize the House and perhaps win election as its Speaker, hoping to secure a body friendly to his Reconstruction plan. If Blair were not elected Speaker, Lincoln told him to return to the army, where "he can serve both the country and himself more profitably than he could as a member of congress." Unfortunately, Blair failed to arrive before the House was organized. He was tied up by the Chattanooga campaign, and Schuyler Colfax, a Radical, was elected Speaker.[68]

Ignoring Lincoln's advice, the citizen general took his seat in Congress, seeking to destroy his enemies, Chase and the Missouri Radicals. The fiery congressman also wanted to defend Lincoln's Reconstruction plan and reelection hopes, goals that he could accomplish by destroying Chase's presidential ambitions and patronage policies in Missouri. Chase sought to become the Radicals' leader and use their backing to catapult himself into the White House. In order to increase his support in Missouri, the secretary allied with the Radical faction opposed to Blair, awarded them patronage, especially trade permits on the Mississippi River, and excluded Blair's allies from these posts. This infuriated Blair, who saw it as an attack on his political existence and believed that Chase was abusing his authority to advance his presidential ambitions. He wanted to shut down Chase's patronage machine to strengthen his political position in Missouri. Thus, by helping Lincoln, Blair would also help himself.[69]

Over the next three months, Blair and the Radicals waged a brutal battle. On February 5, Blair rose for the first time in the House and attacked the Radicals' Second Confiscation Act. Defending the president's Reconstruction plan, the general lashed out at the Radicals, arguing that their plan assailed Unionists and Rebels alike, and then blasted his Missouri opponents. They countered with their own speech that castigated Blair while praising Chase. Blair retaliated on February 27. In a bitter address, Blair laid out his entire case against the Missouri Radicals and Chase, accusing them of conspiring to unseat Lincoln and damning Chase's administration of the Treasury Department. Blair claimed that "the whole Mississippi valley is rank and fetid with the fraud and corruption practiced there by [Chase's] agents." Even before Blair finished speaking, Lincoln received hurriedly scribbled notes warning him that the political general's address was "so far from a benefit to you" as to be "disastrous."[70]

Blair's strident rhetoric did him no good since the Radicals controlled the House. They refused to place him on any important committees, blocked his efforts to create a special five-man committee to investigate Chase's policies in the Mississippi Valley, and brought forth scurrilous charges that he had trafficked in illegal alcohol and tobacco during the Vicksburg campaign. Out-maneuvered, the congressman decided to return to the army, but not before unleashing one last broadside against his enemies. On April 23, he launched a diatribe against Chase. Despite repeated interruptions by Speaker Colfax declaring him out of order, he defended himself against the false accusations made by the "dogs" set loose by Chase, charged that in 1861 the secretary favored abandoning Fort Sumter and letting the South go, again blasted Chase's patronage practices, attacked his congressional opponents for not investigating these activities, and accused Chase of still seeking the presidency. Shortly after concluding, Blair visited Lincoln, retrieved his military commission, and left Washington to join Sherman's army.[71]

As soon as he heard about the speech, Lincoln realized that "another beehive was kicked over." The Radicals were furious. They believed that Blair spoke with the full approval of Lincoln and scampered out of town after the president rewarded him by returning his army commission. The president's action was "a stretch of power and construction" that even the conservative Welles disliked. James Garfield, one of Chase's chief House supporters, railed that it was a "flagrant outrage against the rights of the Senate and the House, against the Constitution and the army." Two members of the Ohio congressional delegation called on Lincoln for an explanation, but left satisfied that the president had not conspired with Blair or had prior knowledge of the speech.[72]

The Radicals were not ready to drop the matter and continued to torment Lincoln and attack Blair. They considered Lincoln's handling of Blair's resignation to be both unconstitutional and unethical. As a result, the House demanded a written explanation of the entire matter, and Lincoln duly complied with their request. In June, it rebuked the president by concluding that because Blair had held his army commission until January, he had disqualified himself from assuming the office of representative. The Senate also passed a resolution condemning the president's actions. As for Blair, the Radicals investigated his disputed election. The House Elections Committee, dominated by the Radicals, voted to award the seat to Knox, and the full House accepted this decision, ending Blair's career in that body.[73]

Blair's stay in Congress helped neither himself nor Lincoln and caused political grief for both of them. In his attempt to aid the president, the most that Blair could claim was that he played a small role in undermining Chase's presidential ambitions. The secretary's allies unwittingly did the most damage to his candidacy by publishing the so-called Pomeroy Circular, a document that tried to block Lincoln's renomination and promote Chase as the Republican candidate. The circular caused such outrage that Chase apologized to

Lincoln and abandoned his presidential hopes. Otherwise, Blair only made trouble for the president. His three speeches led to a backlash that forced Blair out of office, stirred up further hostility toward Lincoln among the Radicals, and inspired some congressmen to mutter threats of impeachment. Both the president and Blair acted badly in this matter. Lincoln never should have asked Blair to submit a patently false resignation, and Blair should have stayed in the army.[74]

The activities of citizen generals in the political arena were a mixed blessing to the war effort. The worthy deeds they performed in elections and stump speaking were often canceled out by their constant harassing of Lincoln and other politicians, the seemingly endless petitions submitted by congressmen and others on their behalf, and the controversies that sometimes entangled them. Some generals were more of a problem than others. Butler, Frémont, and Sigel caused more trouble than they were worth. Others, such as Blair, McClernand, Meagher, Schenck, Schurz, Sickles, and Wadsworth, managed to offset their political deficiencies somewhat. Some were just harmless: Banks, Denver, Hurlbut, and Shields caused few political difficulties while contributing nothing positive. Only Dix and Logan offered effective political support while also not stirring up too many hornets' nests.

Lincoln's expectation that these generals would bring support to the war effort was not completely fulfilled, as few of their constituents rallied to the cause because a politician had become a general. With the exception of Logan in Egypt, they had little effect on the way citizens voted. More important issues, such as the conduct of the war, emancipation, civil liberties, and party loyalty, determined how people voted during the Civil War, not whether a particular general supported the cause. These generals, however, did help to explain the issues, perhaps clarified for some citizens exactly what the war was about, and thus had an indirect effect on voters. A few, such as Meagher and Wadsworth, more than likely had a negative impact, hurting the war effort.

Conclusion

As the Civil War began in 1861, President Abraham Lincoln needed generals to command his rapidly growing armies of volunteer soldiers. With only a limited number of professional officers available to fill these positions, out of necessity and following American tradition, the president proceeded to grant commissions to civilians and specifically to politicians. Many of these men lacked both a military education and experience and seemed to possess no qualifications other than their political prominence. Despite their lack of preparation, Lincoln appointed these men to high command. Thus, wrote General William Averell, a West Point graduate, "now hastened the heedless untowardness of making generals of politicians without the least military experience." Averell criticized Lincoln's policy, describing the performance of political generals as "largely a record of blunders and disasters."[1]

Many others both during and after the war repeated Averell's criticism, but at the time Lincoln believed he had to give politicians important positions. The president thought that it was impossible to fight the war without the services of political generals. Granting Republicans generals' commissions was a logical source of patronage, helped to build the party, and ensured that prominent party members supported the president. Lincoln also needed to ensure that the war was a national undertaking, a goal that could be partly secured by giving generals' commissions to Democrats and members of important ethnic groups such as the Germans and Irish.

Several other equally important factors also influenced Lincoln's decision. There simply were not enough professional officers to command the huge volunteer army. The North secured the services of only 754 of the approximately 1,700 available West Point graduates, a number far too small to lead the sixteen armies, forty-three corps, and more than two thousand cavalry and infantry regiments and artillery batteries eventually organized by the Union. Necessity alone dictated that civilian officers fill many of these positions and civilian generals command some of the brigades, divisions, corps, and armies. The president also could draw on historical precedent to buttress his decision, as politicians had secured important commands in both the War of 1812 and the Mexican War. Many Americans also distrusted West Point, viewing it as a bastion of aristocracy that produced elitist officers unfit to lead citizen soldiers. Traditional fears of a standing army mixed with a belief that talented citizens could properly direct military units convinced many people that the nation must look to civilians to command units within the army.[2]

Moreover, there was no reason to believe that politicians or any civilians would not make good generals. Throughout the young nation's military history, civilian commanders with little or no professional experience had performed well, demonstrating to many Americans that a military education was not a prerequisite for good generalship. From the Revolution, Americans could point to Nathanael Greene and Henry Knox, from the War of 1812 to Andrew Jackson and William Henry Harrison, and from the Mexican War to John A. Quitman and Alexander Doniphan. As the Civil War began, there was no way of determining who would become a capable general, since no one, regardless of their prewar profession or education, had any experience commanding the large armies or corps that dominated the war. Politicians, with their experience in administering local, state, and federal governments, seemed to possess some of the necessary requirements for managing such forces. In the end, the only way to determine who might succeed as a general was through the test of battle.

The battlefield generalship of political generals in this study was mixed, as some excelled, others were adequate, and a few were failures. Logan proved to be an excellent general who demonstrated leadership and tactical ability at every level of command from regiment to army. Both Blair and Wadsworth were good battlefield generals; they proved to be first-rate and inspiring leaders but on occasion made mistakes. On the other hand, Banks, Butler, Frémont, and

Sigel were poor commanders, especially when placed in charge of independent armies. They suffered from many of the same liabilities: they hesitated, did not act decisively, allowed their forces to become strung out, failed to reconnoiter, and struggled to understand the complex situations that developed on the battlefield.

The majority of political generals fell somewhere between mediocre and competent, often depending on how much responsibility they held. McClernand, Sickles, Schurz, Schenck, and Shields all displayed varying degrees of competence as brigade or division commanders, making some mistakes, following orders, acting aggressively, and sometimes proving to be good leaders. On the other hand, Hurlbut and Meagher, though brave and occasionally competent, were on the whole mediocre commanders who suffered from alcoholic binges that limited their effectiveness.

As corps commanders, McClernand, Sickles, and Schurz fared less well. Each made significant errors—McClernand at Champion's Hill failed to properly engage the enemy, Sickles at Gettysburg advanced his troops to a position they could not hold, and Schurz at Gettysburg allowed a gap to grow in the Union lines. At the corps level, these political generals often acted hesitantly, betraying their lack of experience and inadequate understanding of military concepts. Though competent brigade and division commanders, they were mediocre corps leaders.

How successful a political general was on the battlefield was often determined by the size of his first unit. Those generals who started the war as commanders of regiments or brigades usually, though not always, capably led these units. At these levels, they were able to learn how to organize, supply, maneuver, and lead troops while dealing with a relatively small number of soldiers. They could build gradually on their limited experience. Not all of them demonstrated competence for higher command or received promotions beyond brigades, but those who became division commanders usually proved to be capable commanders at that level.

The jump to corps command proved beyond the ability of most political generals, because their lack of education and training left them unprepared for the complexities of leading such a large unit. Only Blair and Logan served well at this level, and Logan alone demonstrated that he could lead an army. Though both possessed military ability and worked hard, the main reason they succeeded as corps commanders was that they served under one or both of the Union's two best generals, Grant and Sherman.

This fact pointed to a major reason that citizen generals usually served capably in regiment, division, and corps commands: they were placed under West Point generals. Though many U.S. Military Academy graduates proved to be inferior generals, the majority of them performed well, and the Union army's best leaders almost all graduated from the academy. These officers, who had spent varying amounts of time in the Regular army, usually possessed the basic knowledge and experience required to operate units of different sizes, and some did well managing an army. Thus, they supervised their less experienced subordinate commanders and allowed these men to develop as officers.

One inescapable fact was that every political general who commanded an independent army failed. These included Banks in the Shenandoah Valley, at Cedar Mountain, and on the Red River; Frémont in Missouri and the valley; Butler outside of Richmond and Petersburg and at Fort Fisher; and Sigel in the valley. Except for Sigel, none of them led smaller units under West Pointers early in the war, but instead were thrust immediately into command of independent forces. Sigel had military training and experience but lacked ability, whereas the other three generals did not have the experience, knowledge, or ability necessary to command an army, and Lincoln promoted these men to positions beyond their competence. Lacking the guiding hand of a military professional, their faults became magnified and resulted in humiliating Union defeats. Early in the war, with few experienced generals to choose from, it was understandable that Lincoln allowed these men to lead armies, but, as the war progressed and these generals demonstrated their incompetence, they should have been denied further chances to direct an army. Command of an independent army was one position that no citizen general should have held.

Political generals, as Lincoln and others recognized, could carry out other martial duties credibly, especially the administration of military departments and districts. The president assigned many of his citizen generals to these positions precisely because he believed that their experience in local, state, and federal governments made them particularly qualified to undertake military administration. As a result, Banks, Butler, Denver, Dix, Frémont, Hurlbut, Schenck, Sigel, and Wadsworth found themselves at one time or another in command of a department or district that often entailed more administrative than combat duties. In these positions, citizen generals made some of their best contributions to the Union war effort.

As commanders of military departments and districts, political generals tended to excel. Banks, Butler, Dix, Schenck, and Wadsworth were particularly effective, managing affairs in Maryland, Louisiana, New York, and eastern Virginia. These officers sometimes stirred up controversy, but the nature of their work, administering military government or martial law in a nation historically suspicious of the military, almost guaranteed some conflict. More important, they administered their departments efficiently, imposed Federal authority in the South and the border states, prevented anti-Union outbreaks from occurring, conducted elections, worked (in New York and Maryland) with civilian officials, carried out Federal policy in occupied areas, and attempted to deal with difficult and contentious issues such as trade and Reconstruction. Not all of their efforts succeeded, but they tended to carry out their duties credibly. The only exception to this trend was Hurlbut, who was a failure. The success of several citizen generals as administrators should have persuaded Lincoln to place these men in such positions permanently, especially those who had failed as battlefield commanders. The president did this with Dix, Hurlbut, and Schenck, but political considerations prevented him from adopting such a prudent policy with Banks, Butler, and Sigel (though, after the near disaster on the Red River, he finally relegated Banks to such a position).

The influence of political generals on the war effort was especially important in regards to slavery, black freedom, and African American soldiers. Citizen generals often acted first on these issues, forcing Lincoln and Congress to react to their policies. One example of this was Butler's "contraband policy" in May 1861, which provided a solution to the issue of runaway slaves in the South that Lincoln approved of and Congress sanctioned with the First Confiscation Act. There were several other instances when the actions of political generals influenced Federal policy. Frémont's emancipation order at the end of August 1861, though repudiated by the president, demonstrated to Lincoln that such a policy could be based on military necessity. In Louisiana, Butler and Banks developed the contract labor system that was adopted throughout the Mississippi River valley. Their labor policy had an impact on Reconstruction, as Federal officials and planters continued to use it in the immediate postwar years. Finally, Butler played an important role in the Union's decision to enlist black soldiers. Not all of these actions were beneficial to blacks, especially the contract labor system that placed African Americans in a state of serfdom, but they all helped to shape Federal policy.[3]

A last contribution political generals made was with the political support they provided the war effort. Every general in this study except Denver and Shields made efforts to campaign on behalf of the war, giving speeches or writing letters urging their constituents to support the conflict. They participated in elections where most of them implored voters to elect prowar candidates (Republicans or War Democrats) to office. By doing so, these generals provided Lincoln with the visible political support the president expected when he commissioned them. The support of these political generals did not necessarily mean that their constituents enlisted in the army or voted for war candidates. This fact was especially true for the Democratic generals, since the rank and file of that party remained loyal to the democracy. The only exception to this trend occurred in southern Illinois, where Logan's efforts swayed just enough

Democrats to vote Republican in 1864 to allow Lincoln and his party to carry that Democratic bastion.

Thus, political generals made substantial contributions to the Union war effort in military administration, shaping Federal policy in regards to slavery and black freedom, and creating political support for the conflict. The tendency among some historians to focus almost exclusively on the battlefield obscures these important activities and the accomplishments that many citizen generals made. Although not as dramatic as the campaigns, these activities had to be carried out with skill and care if the war was to be fought to a successful conclusion. Many political generals possessed the abilities and experience necessary to perform these duties, credentials that their West Point–trained colleagues often lacked. As a result, citizen generals often executed these tasks with admirable proficiency, although not without making mistakes and causing controversy.

Given their numbers and widespread employment, political generals also created many problems. One of the most important was the conflict that often occurred between citizen generals and West Point officers. Discord occurred in virtually every campaign and, though they rarely had a decisive impact on the course of events, fashioned an uneasy atmosphere that made cooperation difficult. This was only one problem that Lincoln created by continuing the American tradition of putting politicians in uniform. Many of these civilian generals spent too much time promoting their own careers as they sought higher rank and prestigious commands, worried too much about their own political fortunes, and were promoted to positions they were not qualified for by training, experience, or (as became clear as the war progressed) competence. Finally, the major flaw in the policy, Lincoln gave several of them too many chances after they demonstrated their incapability, especially on the battlefield. Other generals should have been chosen or other deserving officers promoted.

Some generals were more troublesome than others, usually depending on their rank, how much responsibility they held, and how long they remained in service. Notably, Banks, Butler, Hurlbut, McClernand, Sickles, and Sigel, all of whom served for at least three years, were particularly difficult officers for many reasons. Most of them were failures on the battlefield, especially those who held independent or corps commands, though some performed adequately when in charge of divisions or brigades. Two were corrupt. Most of them feuded with West Pointers, and nearly all of them engaged in continual political scheming. Several of these men made important contributions to the war effort, but the controversy and trouble they caused must have made Lincoln wonder whether their appointments were worth it. The president added to the problems by giving these generals too many chances, even after they demonstrated their incompetence to either command large field forces or, in the case of Hurlbut, administer a department. Political considerations convinced Lincoln that he had to keep these officers in some military position.

Other officers caused less trouble. Frémont was a controversial, polarizing, and difficult figure but served for less than one year; Schenck, who could be a contentious and barely competent battlefield commander, resigned his commission after a little more than two years of service; Schurz constantly pestered Lincoln and, though an adequate division leader, performed poorly as a corps commander but served in the field for less than two years; and Blair caused political troubles, yet these could be overlooked due to his battlefield success. These generals all made other important contributions and, save for Frémont, provided Lincoln with satisfactory service.

Only three political generals created few difficulties for Lincoln. Logan was an excellent battlefield commander, spoke out in support of both the war effort and Lincoln, worked well with West Pointers, and engaged in almost no political intrigue. Dix, though never given a chance on the battlefield, excelled as an administrator and wrote letters and gave speeches defending the war effort. Wadsworth was a good general and a capable military governor of Washington, D.C., and defended Lincoln during his failed bid for the New York governorship. All three officers did yeoman service for the Union cause, providing the president with the kind of generalship and support he hoped to obtain from all of his citizen generals.

Several generals caused few problems because they played little role in the war at all. From the fall of 1861 through the spring of 1862, Denver found himself bounced around the country as the War Department tried to find a position for him. He was finally assigned to command a brigade in western Tennessee, but spent his time administering a district and resigned in the spring of 1863 without making any noticeable impact on the war effort. Shields participated without distinction in the 1862 Shenandoah campaign, but then was assigned to California, where he resigned his commission in the spring of 1863 after leaving no appreciable impression on the conflict. Meagher commanded a brigade in several major battles in the East and also wrote some letters defending the war, which actually may have cost Lincoln the support of some Irish, but he too did little to aid the Union effort, and his career essentially ended in the summer of 1863.

Despite the problems and controversies, the policy of using political generals demonstrated Lincoln's leadership skills and his remarkable ability to mold public opinion. Lincoln appointed members of both political parties and various ethnic groups to high command to forge a national coalition to wage the Civil War. Although partisanship remained and an antiwar element existed in the North, the majority of Northerners supported the president's policies, even as he adopted radical war measures such as emancipation. The use of political generals was one way that Lincoln retained the support of the Northern majority. They provided visible evidence that key members of the political class stood by the president, despite the changing nature of the war, and thus played a role in ensuring that the president's national coalition survived the defeats, setbacks, and other turmoils that racked the nation during the four-year conflict.

As a result, Lincoln carried on with his policy of using political generals, regardless of battlefield defeats and controversies, because he realized their service made significant contributions to restoring the Union. Never once did he repudiate his policy, though in 1864, following his nomination for the presidency and then reelection, he was more willing to permanently remove generals who failed on the battlefield, as occurred with Banks, Butler, and Sigel. The president continued the policy because it worked, providing the Union with a number of general officers that made important contributions to the Federal war effort. Of course, not every general was a success, but most of them provided capable and necessary service, leading troops on the battlefield, administrating districts and departments, defending and explaining the war, or striking at slavery and enlisting black soldiers. Such service more than justified Lincoln's use of political generals.

Notes

Abbreviations

B&L   *Battles and Leaders of the Civil War.* Edited by Robert Johnson and Clarence Buel. 4 vols. New York: Thomas Yoseloff, 1956.

BC   *Private and Official Correspondence of General Benjamin F. Butler, during the Period of the Civil War.* 5 vols. Norwood, Mass.: Plimpton Press, 1917.

BFP   Blair Family Papers. Manuscript Division, Library of Congress, Washington, D.C.

BLCU   Butler Library. Columbia University, New York.

CW   *The Collected Works of Abraham Lincoln.* Edited by Roy Basler. 8 vols. New Brunswick, N.J.: Rutgers University Press, 1953.

FSP   Franz Sigel Papers. Western Reserve Historical Society, Cleveland, Ohio.

ISHL   Illinois State Historical Library. Springfield, Illinois.

JMP   John A. McClernand Papers. Illinois State Historical Library, Springfield, Illinois.

JWFP   James Wadsworth Family Papers. Manuscript Division, Library of Congress, Washington, D.C.

LC   Library of Congress. Manuscript Division, Washington, D.C.

NYSL   New York State Library. Albany, New York.

OR   *War of the Rebellion: A Compilation of the Official Records of the Union and Confederate Armies.* 128 vols. Washington, D.C.: Government Printing Office, 1880–1901.

PAL   Papers of Abraham Lincoln. Manuscript Division, Library of Congress, Washington, D.C.

PES   Papers of Edwin Stanton. Manuscript Division, Library of Congress, Washington, D.C.

PJL Papers of John A. Logan. Manuscript Division, Library of Congress, Washington, D.C.

PLT Papers of Lyman Trumbull. Manuscript Division, Library of Congress, Washington, D.C.

PUG *The Papers of Ulysses S. Grant.* Edited by John Y. Simon. 22 vols. Carbondale: Southern Illinois University Press, 1967–.

RSP Robert C. Schenck Papers. Archives, Miami University, Oxford, Ohio.

SCW *Sherman's Civil War: Selected Correspondence of William T. Sherman, 1860–1865.* Edited by Brooks D. Simpson and Jean V. Berlin. Chapel Hill: University of North Carolina Press, 1999.

SOR *Supplement to the Official Records of the Union and Confederate Armies.* 100 vols. Wilmington, N.C.: Broadfoot Publishing, 1994.

SU Syracuse University. Syracuse, New York.

WPL William R. Perkins Library. Duke University, Durham, North Carolina.

WSP William Seward Papers. Ruch Rhees Library, University of Rochester, Rochester, New York.

Chapter 1: The Necessity of the Time

1. Jacob D. Cox, Military Reminiscences of the Civil War, 2 vols. (New York: Charles Scribner's Sons, 1900), 1:170–71.

2. James Spencer, *Civil War Generals: Categorical Listings and a Biographical Directory* (New York: Greenwood Press, 1986), 121–38; Ezra Warner, *Generals in Blue: Lives of the Union Commanders* (Baton Rouge: Louisiana State University Press, 1964), xix.

3. Bruce Catton, "Lincoln's Mastery in the Use of Volunteer Soldiers and Political Generals," *Lincoln Herald* 57, no. 3 (1955): 9–10; Bruce Catton, *America Goes to War: The Civil War and Its Meaning Today* (New York: Hill and Wang, 1958), 42; James McPherson, *Ordeal by Fire: The Civil War and Reconstruction* (New York: McGraw-Hill, 1992), 175–76; James McPherson, *Battle Cry of Freedom: The Civil War Era* (1988; reprint, New York: Ballantine Books, 1989), 328–29; James McPherson, *Abraham Lincoln and the Second American Revolution* (New York: Oxford University Press, 1991), 70–71; Brooks D. Simpson, "Lincoln and His Political Generals," *Journal of the Abraham Lincoln Association* 21 (Winter 2000): 76–77 (emphasis is in the original).

4. Thomas J. Goss, *The War within the Union High Command: Politics and Generalship during the Civil War* (Lawrence: University Press of Kansas, 2003), xii, xx.

Chapter 2: Hunting for Generals

1. George T. Ness, *The Army on the Eve of the Civil War* (Manhattan, Kans.: MA/AH Publishing, 1983). See the chapter "The Plumed Hats," discussing the general officer corps in 1860.

2. William Osborn Stoddard, *Inside the White House in War Times: Memoirs and Reports of Lincoln's Secretary,* edited by Michael Burlingame (Lincoln: University of

Nebraska Press, 2000), 12; Herman Hattaway and Archer Jones, *How the North Won: A Military History of the Civil War* (Urbana: University of Illinois Press, 1983), 30; Lincoln to Edwin Stanton, December 18, 1863, in *CW,* 7:79.

3. Hattaway and Jones, *How the North Won,* 9–10.

4. T. Harry Williams, *Lincoln and His Generals* (New York: Alfred A. Knopf, 1952), 4.

5. Polk quoted in Richard Bruce Winders, *Mr. Polk's Army: The American Military Experience in the Mexican War* (College Station: Texas A&M University Press, 1997), 34, 36, 49, 48.

6. *New York Times,* June 10, 1861; *New York Tribune* and *Harper's Weekly* in Harry Williams, "The Attack upon West Point during the Civil War," *Mississippi Valley Historical Review* 25 (March 1939): 492, 500.

7. *Harper's Weekly,* January 17, 1863, quoted in Williams, "Attack upon West Point," 491, 500; W. Y. Wheaton to Lyman Trumbull, January 9, 1862, PLT, Microfilm Reel #12.

8. Don E. Fehrenbacher and Virginia Fehrenbacher, eds., *Recollected Words of Abraham Lincoln* (Stanford: Stanford University Press, 1996), 400; Gerald J. Prokopowicz, "Military Fantasies," in *The Lincoln Enigma: The Changing Faces of an American Icon,* edited by Gabor Boritt (New York: Oxford University Press, 2001), 67.

9. Harry J. Carman and Reinhard H. Luthin, *Lincoln and the Patronage* (New York: Columbia University Press, 1943), 150–53; T. W. Higginson, "Regular and Volunteer Officers," *Atlantic Monthly* 14 (September 1864): 354; Stanton to John A. Dix, June 11, 1861, in Morgan Dix, *Memoirs of John Adams Dix,* 2 vols. (New York: Harper and Brothers, 1883), 2:18.

10. Lincoln to Richard Yates and William Butler, April 10, 1862, in *CW,* 7:145.

11. James G. Hollandsworth Jr., *Pretense of Glory: The Life of General Nathaniel P. Banks* (Baton Rouge: Louisiana State University Press, 1998), 3, 11, 22, 40.

12. David Davis to Lincoln, November 19, 1860, PAL; George Boutwell to Lincoln, December 17, 1860, ibid.; Isaac Arnold to Lincoln, December 29, 1860, ibid.; Lincoln to Hannibal Hamlin, December 8, 1860, in *CW,* 4:147; Hollandsworth, *Pretense of Glory,* 43.

13. William Sturges to Lincoln, May 27, 1861, PAL; Salmon P. Chase to Simon Cameron, May 1861, in *The Salmon P. Chase Papers,* edited by John Niven (Frederick, Md.: University Publications of America, 1987), Microfilm Reel #15; Hollandsworth, *Pretense of Glory,* 45; Francis B. Heitman, *Historical Register and Dictionary of the United States Army,* 2 vols. (1903; reprint, Urbana: University of Illinois Press, 1965), 1:28.

14. Andrew Rolle, *John Charles Frémont: Character as Destiny* (Norman: University of Oklahoma Press, 1991), 4, 136; William Seward to Lincoln, December 25, 1860, in *CW,* 4:164; Lincoln to Seward, December 29, 1860, ibid., 4:164; Lincoln to Seward, March 11, 1861, ibid., 4:281; Seward to Lincoln, March 11, 1861, PAL.

15. Gustave Koerner, *Memoirs of Gustave Koerner, 1809–1896,* edited by Thomas J. McCormick (Cedar Rapids, Iowa, 1909), 152, 162; Isaac Sherman to Francis P. Blair

Sr., May 29, 1861, BFP, Microfilm Reel #12; William Ernest Smith, *The Francis Preston Blair Family in Politics*, 2 vols. (New York: Macmillan, 1933), 2:53–54.

16. Allan Nevins, *Frémont: Pathmarker of the West* (New York: Longmans, Green, 1955), 475; Chase to Cornelius S. Hamilton, November 21, 1861, in *The Salmon P. Chase Papers*, edited by John Niven, 5 vols. (Kent, Ohio: Kent State University Press, 1993), 3:111; Heitman, *Historical Register*, 20.

17. James R. Therry, "The Life of General Robert Cummings Schenck" (Ph.D. diss., Georgetown University, 1968), 7–8, 16, 33, 47, 103, 140, 169–71.

18. Ibid., 179–80; Robert Schenck to Lincoln, March 30, 1861, RSP; Lincoln to John G. Nicolay, November 3, 1860, in *CW*, 4:136; Benjamin F. Wade and Thomas Corwin to Lincoln, January 20, 1861, PAL; Therry, "General Schenck," 188.

19. Schenck to Merriam Dennison, May 9, 1861, ibid.; Schenck to Lincoln, May 18, 1861, PAL; Therry, "General Schenck," 190; Chase to Henry B. Carrington, June 17, 1861, in *Chase Papers*, edited by Niven, Microfilm Reel #15; Cameron to Schenck, June 5, 1861, RSP.

20. Jeffrey N. Lash, "Stephen Augustus Hurlbut: A Military and Diplomatic Politician, 1815–1882" (Ph.D. diss., Kent State University, 1980), 21, 54, 67, 80.

21. Ibid., 103, 108.

22. Ibid., 116–21; Memorandum, April 30, 1861, in *CW*, 4:349; Yates to Stephen Hurlbut, May 29, 1861, in *Between Peace and War, a Report to Lincoln from Charleston, 1861: In the Midst of War, a Letter from Shiloh, 1862*, edited by Stephen A. Hurlbut II (Charleston, S.C.: St. Albans Press, 1953), 15; Elihu Washburne to Lincoln, June 11, 1861, PAL; Yates to Hurlbut, May 29, 1861, in *Between Peace and War*, edited by Hurlbut, 15.

23. Warner, *Generals in Blue*, 532 (see chap. 1, n. 2); Charles A. Dana, *Recollections of the Civil War, with the Leaders at Washington and in the Field in the Sixties* (1898; reprint, Lincoln: University of Nebraska Press, 1996), 2; Wayne Mahood, *General Wadsworth: The Life and Times of Brevet Major General James S. Wadsworth* (Cambridge, Mass.: Da Capo Press, 2003), 57.

24. Carman and Luthin, *Lincoln and the Patronage*, 35; Dana, *Recollections of the Civil War*, 2.

25. Henry Greenleaf Pearson, *James S. Wadsworth of Geneseo, Brevet Major-General of United States Volunteers* (New York: Charles Scribner's Sons, 1913), 62–64; Union Defense Committee to James S. Wadsworth, August 20, 1861, JWFP; Pearson, *James S. Wadsworth*, 81.

26. William E. Parrish, *Frank Blair: Lincoln's Conservative* (Columbia: University of Missouri Press, 1998), 38, 60.

27. Smith, *Blair Family*, 2:121–28.

28. Ibid., 2:142, 145–46; Parrish, *Frank Blair: Lincoln's Conservative*, 154.

29. Joel H. Silbey, *A Respectable Minority: The Democratic Party in the Civil War Era, 1860–1868* (New York: W. W. Norton, 1977), 19; Lincoln to Carl Schurz, November 10, 1862, in *CW*, 5:494; Albert G. Riddle, *Recollections of War Times: Reminiscences of Men and Events in Washington, 1861–65* (New York: G. P. Putnam's Sons, 1895), 65–66.

30. Dix, *Memoirs*, 1:65; Warner, *Generals in Blue*, 125–26; Dix, *Memoirs*, 1:347, 371.

31. Edwin Morgan to Dix, March 9, 1861, John A. Dix Papers, BLCU; Dix to Chase, May 29, 1861, ibid.; Dix to Cameron, May 24, 1861, John A. Dix Papers, NYSL; Lincoln to Cameron, June 14, 1861, in *CW*, 4:407; Heitman, *Historical Register*, 1:28.

32. Richard S. West Jr., *Lincoln's Scapegoat General: A Life of Benjamin F. Butler, 1818–1893* (Boston: Houghton Mifflin, 1965), 35–37, 45.

33. Dick Nolan, *Benjamin Franklin Butler: The Damnedest Yankee* (Novato, Calif.: Presidio Press, 1991), 60; Benjamin F. Butler, *Autobiography and Personal Reminiscences of Benjamin F. Butler* (Boston: A. M. Thayer, 1892), 170; Henry Greenleaf Pearson, *The Life of John A. Andrew, Governor of Massachusetts, 1861–1865*, 2 vols. (Boston: Houghton Mifflin, 1904), 2:184; Heitman, *Historical Register*, 1:28.

34. Richard Kiper, *Major General John Alexander McClernand: Politician in Uniform* (Kent, Ohio: Kent State University Press, 1999), 1–2; John A. McClernand to Lincoln, April 10, 1861, JMP.

35. Kiper, *McClernand*, 22; Yates to Lincoln, May 15, 1861, JMP; Lincoln to McClernand, in *CW*, 4:381; Edward G. Longacre, "The Rise of John A. McClernand: Congressman Becomes General," *Civil War Times Illustrated* 21 (November 1982): 32.

36. Orville Hickman Browning, July 27, 28, 1861, in *The Diary of Orville Hickman Browning*, edited by Theodore Pease and James Randall, 2 vols. (Springfield: Illinois State Historical Library, 1925), 1:487, 490; Lincoln to Lorenzo Thomas, September 27, 1861, in *CW*, 4:527; Jesse K. Dubois to Lincoln, June 8, 1861, PAL; Lincoln to McClernand, August 7, 1861, in *CW*, 4:477; Kiper, *McClernand*, 24.

37. Warner, *Generals in Blue*, 120; George C. Barns, *Denver, the Man: The Life, Letters, and Public Papers of the Lawyer, Soldier, and Statesman* (Wilmington, Ohio: George C. Barns, 1949), 15, 17.

38. James Denver to P. H. Harris, January 26, 1861, in *Denver*, by Barns, 267; Denver to the editors of the *Union*, October 24, 1861, ibid., 274; "Untitled Summary of James W. Denver's Civil War Career," n.d., James W. Denver Papers, Western History Collection, Division of Manuscripts, University of Oklahoma, Norman, Oklahoma.

39. Thomas Keneally, *American Scoundrel: The Life of the Notorious Civil War General Dan Sickles* (New York: Doubleday, 2002), 11, 209–10.

40. Ibid., 212; Daniel Sickles to Cameron, April 15, 1861, in *OR*, ser. 3, vol. 1, p. 72; Sickles to Cameron, May 8, 1861, ibid.; Thurlow Weed to Seward, May 21, 1861, WSP, Microfilm Reel #64; Weed to Lincoln, May 23, August 18, 1861, PAL.

41. W. A. Swanberg, *Sickles the Incredible* (New York: Charles Scribner's Sons, 1956), 116–18.

42. James P. Jones, *"Black Jack": John A. Logan and Southern Illinois in the Civil War Era* (Tallahassee: Florida State University Press, 1967), 8, 16.

43. John A. Logan to I. N. Haynie, January 1, 1861, PJL; Jones, *"Black Jack,"* 73; Ulysses S. Grant, *Memoirs and Selected Letters: Personal Memoirs of U. S. Grant, Selected Letters, 1839–1865*, 2 vols. (New York: Library of America, 1990), 1:162; Logan to

Mary Logan, July 25, 1861, PJL; Gary Ecelbarger, *Black Jack Logan: An Extraordinary Life in Peace and War* (Guilford, Conn.: Lyons Press, 2005), 82.

44. Grant to Washburne, February 22, 1862, in *PUG*, 4:274–75; Lincoln to Stanton, March 3, 1862, in *CW*, 5:142.

45. William L. Burton, *Melting Pot Soldiers: The Union's Ethnic Regiments* (Ames: Iowa State University Press, 1988), 15–16, 24; David H. Donald, *Lincoln* (London: Jonathan Cape, 1995), 242.

46. Ella Lonn, *Foreigners in the Union Army and Navy* (Baton Rouge: Louisiana State University Press, 1951), 41, 43, 46, 48.

47. Stephen D. Engle, *Yankee Dutchman: The Life of Franz Sigel* (Fayetteville: University of Arkansas Press, 1993), 2, 4, 42, 52.

48. Ibid., 55; Charles Sumner to Lincoln, 1861, PAL; Weed to Seward, July 5, 1861, WSP, Microfilm Reel #64.

49. Hans L. Trefousse, *Carl Schurz: A Biography* (Knoxville: University of Tennessee Press, 1982), 3, 23, 71, 94.

50. John Hay, April 27, 28, 1861, in *Inside Lincoln's White House: The Complete Civil War Diary of John Hay*, edited by Michael Burlingame and John R. Turner (Carbondale: Southern Illinois University Press, 1997), 13; Carl Schurz, *The Reminiscences of Carl Schurz*, 3 vols. (New York: McClure, 1907), 2:229; Lincoln to Schurz, May 13, 1861, in *CW*, 4:368.

51. Schurz, *Reminiscences*, 2:327–28; Chase to Henry Wilson, March 10, 1862, in *The Life and Public Services of Salmon Portland Chase*, by J. W. Schuckers (1874; New York: Da Capo Press, 1970), 434.

52. William W. Hassler, "The Irrepressible James Shields," *Lincoln Herald* 81 (Fall 1979): 187–89.

53. Memorandum, July 1861, in *CW*, 4:418; Judith M. Curran, "The Career of James Shields, an Immigrant Irishman in Nineteenth Century America" (Ph.D. diss., Columbia University Teachers College, 1980), 185; Lincoln to Cameron, August 19, 1861, in *CW*, 4:492; James Shields to Winfield Scott, October 14, 1861, James Shields Papers, ISHL.

54. Adjutant General's Office, "Military History of James Shields," May 10, 1878, ibid.; Shields to Amador County, California, Breckinridge Club, October 10, 1860, PAL; F. B. Murdock to Lincoln, December 10, 1861, ibid.; Ira P. Rankin to Cameron, December 10, 1861, ibid.; Rankin to Cameron, December 18, 1861, with newspaper clipping from the *Sacramento Union* dated December 17, 1861, ibid.; Seward to the Republican General Committee of the State of California, January 7, 1862, WSP, Microfilm Reel #68.

55. Burton, *Melting Pot Soldiers*, 10; Michael Cavanagh, *Memoirs of Gen. Thomas Francis Meagher* (Worcester, Mass.: Messenger Press, 1892), 367–68.

56. Cavanagh, *Memoirs of Meagher*, 369; John Hughes to Seward, August 12, 1861, WSP, Microfilm Reel #65; *Irish American* quoted in Joseph G. Bilby, *The Irish Brigade in the Civil War: The 69th New York and Other Irish Regiments of the Army of the Potomac* (Conshohocken, Pa.: Combined Publishing, 1998), 20; Cavanagh, *Memoirs of Meagher*, 429.

Chapter 3: The Opening Campaigns

1. Scott to Denver, September 17, 1861, in *OR*, ser. 1, vol. 50, pt. 1, p. 624 (all *OR* citations are to series 1 unless otherwise indicated); William C. Kibbe to Simon Cameron, September 6, 1861, ibid., 607–9; Barns, Denver, 282–83 (see chap. 2, n. 37); Diary of Captain August V. Kautz, February 12, 1862, in *SOR*, pt. 1, vol. 1, p. 359.

2. William Rosecrans to George McClellan, February 7, 1862, in *OR*, vol. 51, pt. 1, p. 527; Barns, *Denver*, 285; James Lane and Samuel Pomeroy to Lincoln, April 24, 1862, PAL.

3. Dix to Lincoln, March 13, 1862, ibid.; Dix to Edward Pierrepont, July 17, 1861, John A. Dix Papers, SU.

4. Dix to Lincoln, March 13, 1862, PAL; Dix to Pierrepont, July 17, 1861, June 10, 1862, Dix Papers, SU; Stoddard, *Inside the White House*, 25 (see chap. 2, n. 2).

5. Alpheus S. Williams to daughter, December 7, 1861, Alpheus S. Williams, *From the Cannon's Mouth: The Civil War Letters of General Alpheus S. Williams*, edited by Milo M. Quaife (Detroit: Wayne State University Press and the Detroit Historical Society, 1959), 40.

6. G. H. Gordon to Banks, October 6, 1861, Nathaniel P. Banks Papers, LC; McClernand to Logan, November 17, 1861, JMP; John Rawlins to McClernand, February 25, 1862, ibid.

7. Swanberg, *Sickles the Incredible*, 129 (see chap. 2, n. 41); McClernand to Grant, January 11, 1862, JMP; McClernand to Grant, January 12, 1862, *PUG*, 4:39; William S. Hillyer to McClernand, January 12, 1862, JMP.

8. Trefousse, *Carl Schurz: A Biography*, 110 (see chap. 2, n. 49); Fred H. Harrington, *Fighting Politician: Major General N. P. Banks* (1948; reprint, Westport, Conn.: Greenwood Press, 1970), 55; Jones, *"Black Jack,"* 106 (see chap. 2, n. 42); Kiper, *McClernand*, 38 (see chap. 2, n. 34); Keneally, *American Scoundrel*, 227 (see chap. 2, n. 39); Butler, *Autobiography*, 865, 868 (see chap. 2, n. 33); Engle, *Yankee Dutchman*, 3 (see chap. 2, n. 47); Bilby, *Irish Brigade in the Civil War*, 33 (see chap. 2, n. 56).

9. Wadsworth to Chase, October 11, 1861, in *Chase Papers*, edited by Niven, Microfilm Reel #17 (see chap. 2, n. 13); McClernand to P. B. Fouke, October 6, 1861, JMP; John F. Krumwiede, *"Old Waddy's Coming": The Military Career of Brigadier General James S. Wadsworth* (Baltimore: Butternut and Blue, 2002), 8; George Ruggles to McClernand, October 10, 1861, JMP.

10. T. Harry Williams, *Hayes of the Twenty-third: The Civil War Volunteer Officer* (New York: Alfred A. Knopf, 1965), 20, 23.

11. McClernand to Logan, November 17, 1861, JMP; Jones, *"Black Jack,"* 106; James Wadsworth, "Untitled Paper Describing His First Year in the Service," n.d., JWFP; Swanberg, *Sickles the Incredible*, 133.

12. Henry B. Smith to John C. Frémont, September 3, 1861, JMP; McClernand to Frémont, September 8, 1861, ibid.; Grant to McClernand, September 8, 1861, *PUG*, 2:210.

13. A. Schwartz to McClernand, October 9, 1861, JMP; Military Commission to

McClernand, October 9, 1861, ibid.; General Order No. 5, October 9, 1861, ibid.; General Order No. 22, November 24, 1861, ibid.; McClernand to A. O. Millington, December 5, 1861, ibid.

14. James Long to Trumbull, July 13, 1861, PLT, Microfilm Reel #11; Joseph Medill to Trumbull, July 13, 1861, ibid.; Lash, "Stephen Hurlbut," 129, 132, 136 (see chap. 2, n. 20).

15. Orville H. Browning to Lincoln, September 11, 1861, PAL; Lincoln to Browning, September 22, 1861, in *CW*, 4:533; Browning to Lincoln, September 30, 1861, PAL; Lash, "Stephen Hurlbut," 143.

16. Scott to Butler, May 18, 1861, in *OR*, vol. 2, p. 641; Butler to Scott, May 29, 1861, in *BC*, 1:117; West, *Lincoln's Scapegoat General*, 87 (see chap. 2, n. 32).

17. Report of Butler, June 10, 1861, in *OR*, vol. 2, p. 77; General Butler's Orders for Attack on Big Bethel, in *BC*, 1:133.

18. Report of Brig. Gen. E. W. Pierce, June 12, 1861, in *OR*, vol. 2, pp. 84–85; Report of Col. Frederick Townsend, June 12, 1861, ibid., 87.

19. Report of Butler, June 16, 1861, ibid., 82; Edward Baker to Lincoln, June 16, 1861, PAL; *New York Times*, May 31, June 12, 14, 1861; Special Orders No. 214, August 9, 1861, in *BC*, 1:207.

20. James B. Fry to Schenck, June 17, 1861, in *OR*, vol. 2, p. 125.

21. Reports of Schenck, n.d., June 18, 1861, ibid., 126–28; Memorandum: Defeat at Vienna, Virginia, July 15, 1861, in *CW*, 4:449.

22. *New York Times*, June 19, 1861; Memorandum, July 15, 1861, in *CW*, 4:449.

23. *New York Times*, June 12, 1861; *New York Evening Post*, quoted in *Washington, D.C., Daily National Intelligencer*, June 14, 1861; *Boston Daily Advertiser*, quoted in ibid., July 1, 1861.

24. Ethan S. Rafuse, *A Single Grand Victory: The First Campaign and Battle of Manassas* (Wilmington, Del.: Scholarly Resources, 2002), 120; Report of Schenck, July 23, 1861, in *OR*, vol. 2, pp. 357–59; Report of Brig. Gen. Daniel Tyler, July 27, 1861, ibid., 349.

25. Report of Maj. Gen. Irvin McDowell, August 4, 1861, ibid., 323–24.

26. John Wool to Butler, August 25, 1861, in *BC*, 1:226; West, *Lincoln's Scapegoat General*, 107.

27. John C. Frémont, "In Command in Missouri," in *B&L*, 1:278.

28. Jessie Benton Frémont to Montgomery Blair, July 28, 1861, in *Letters of Jessie Benton Frémont*, edited by Paula Herr and Mary Lee Spence (Urbana: University of Illinois Press, 1993), 256; Frémont to Montgomery Blair, July 1861, ibid., 257–58; Frémont to Lincoln, July 30, 1861, in *OR*, vol. 3, pp. 416–15.

29. Frémont to Montgomery Blair, July 13, 1861, BFP, Microfilm Reel #21; Nevins, *Frémont*, 476 (see chap. 2, n. 16); E. D. Townsend to Frémont, July 18, 1861, in *OR*, vol. 3, p. 399.

30. William G. Piston and Richard W. Hatcher III, *Wilson's Creek: The Second Battle of the Civil War and the Men Who Fought It* (Chapel Hill: University of North Carolina Press, 2000), 103–4; Report of Sigel, July 11, 1861, in *OR*, vol. 3, pp. 17–19.

31. Nathaniel Lyon to E. D. Townsend, July 17, 1861, in *OR*, vol. 3, pp. 397–98.

32. Piston and Hatcher, *Wilson's Creek*, 133; Nevins, *Frémont*, 483; Frémont to Scott, August 2, 1861, in *OR*, vol. 3, p. 420; Frémont, "In Command in Missouri," in *B&L*, 1:280–82.

33. Frémont, "In Command in Missouri," in *B&L*, 1:281; Frémont to Scott, August 2, 1861, in *OR*, vol. 3, p. 420; Frémont to John Nicolay, August 6, 1861, ibid., 427.

34. John M. Schofield, *Forty-six Years in the Army* (1897; reprint, Norman: University of Oklahoma Press, 1998), 40 (emphasis in the original).

35. Nathaniel Lyon to Frémont, August 9, 1861, in *OR*, vol. 3, p. 57; Report of Maj. John M. Schofield, August 20, 1861, ibid., 58; Piston and Hatcher, *Wilson's Creek*, 177.

36. Schofield, *Forty-six Years in the Army*, 43.

37. Report of Sigel, August 18, 1861, in *OR*, vol. 3, pp. 86–87; Franz Sigel, "The Flanking Column at Wilson's Creek," in *B&L*, 1:304–5.

38. Engle, *Yankee Dutchman*, 75; Piston and Hatcher, *Wilson's Creek*, 250; Report of Sigel, August 18, 1862, in *OR*, vol. 3, p. 87; Sigel, "The Flanking Column at Wilson's Creek," in *B&L*, 1:305.

39. Sigel, "The Flanking Column at Wilson's Creek," in *B&L*, 1:305; Report of Sigel, August 18, 1861, in *OR*, vol. 3, p. 87; Piston and Hatcher, *Wilson's Creek*, 255, 260.

40. E. F. Ware, *The Lyon Campaign in Missouri, Being a History of the First Iowa Infantry* (1907; reprint, Iowa City: Press of the Camp Pope Bookshop, 1991), 336–37; Schofield, *Forty-six Years in the Army*, 47–48.

41. *Janesville (Wisc.) Daily Gazette*, August 13, 1861, quoted in *Yankee Dutchman*, by Engle, 82; Schofield to Halleck, February 13, 1862, in *OR*, vol. 3, p. 95.

42. Frémont to Lincoln, August 14, 1861, in *OR*, vol. 3, p. 441; Frémont to Montgomery Blair, August 19, 21, 1861, BFP, Microfilm Reel #21; Frémont, "In Command in Missouri," in *B&L*, 1:283.

43. Frémont to Lincoln, August 17, 1861, PAL; Frémont, "In Command in Missouri," in *B&L*, 1:284.

44. Frémont to Grant, August 28, September 5, 1861, in *OR*, vol. 3, p. 142.

45. Frémont to Lincoln, September 8, 1861, ibid., 478.

46. Frémont to Jefferson C. Davis, September 13, 1861, ibid., 173; Frémont to Samuel Sturgis, September 14, 1861, ibid., 175; John Pope to Frémont, September 16, 1861, ibid., 176.

47. Smith, *Blair Family*, 2:62 (see chap. 2, n. 15); *New York Times*, September 24, 1861; Edward Bates to Hamilton Gamble, September 27, October 3, 1861, in *SOR*, pt. 3, vol. 1, pp. 59, 71.

48. John Pope, *Military Memoirs of General John Pope*, edited by Peter Cozzens and Robert I. Girardi (Chapel Hill: University of North Carolina Press, 1998), 11; Samuel R. Curtis to Lincoln, October 12, 1861, PAL.

49. Pope, *Military Memoirs*, 10, 11, 32; Nevins, *Frémont*, 493; William T. Sherman, *Memoirs of General William T. Sherman*, 2 vols. (1875; reprint, New York: Library of America, 1990), 1:212–13; Rolle, *John Charles Frémont*, 202 (see chap. 2, n. 14).

50. *New York Times*, September 24, 1861; Lorenzo Thomas to Cameron, Oct 21, 1861, in *OR*, vol. 3, pp. 540–43; Nevins, *Frémont*, 509; Frank Blair Jr. to Montgomery Blair, September 6, 1861, Frank Blair Jr. to Frank Blair Sr., October 23, 1861, BFP, Microfilm Reel #2; Proclamation, August 30, 1861, in *OR*, vol. 3, p. 466; Lincoln to Frémont, September 11, 1861, ibid., 485.

51. Lincoln to David Hunter, September 9, 1861, in *CW*, 4:513; Lorenzo Thomas to Cameron, October 21, 1861, in *OR*, vol. 3, p. 544.

52. Nicolay to Lincoln, October 17, 1861, PAL; Ward H. Lamon to Lincoln, October 21, 1861, ibid.

53. Lincoln to Curtis, October 7, 1861, in *CW*, 4:549; Curtis to Lincoln, October 12, 1861, PAL; Lincoln to Curtis, October 24, 1861, in *CW*, 4:562.

54. Frémont, "In Command in Missouri," in *B&L*, 1:287; Nevins, *Frémont*, 534–35; Frémont to Lincoln, October 27, 1861, in *OR*, vol. 3, p. 249.

55. Ware, *Lyon Campaign*, 248.

56. Chauncey McKeever to Grant, November 1, 1861, in *OR*, vol. 3, p. 267; Nathaniel C. Hughes Jr., *The Battle of Belmont: Grant Strikes South* (Chapel Hill: University of North Carolina Press, 1991), 45, 53.

57. Grant, *Memoirs*, 1:179 (see chap. 2, n. 43); Report of McClernand, November 12, 1861, in *OR*, vol. 3, pp. 278–79; Report of Logan, November 11, 1861, ibid., 288.

58. Grant, *Memoirs*, 1:180; Report of McClernand, November 12, 1861, in *OR*, vol. 3, p. 280; Jones, *"Black Jack,"* 113.

59. Report of Grant, November 17, 1861, in *OR*, vol. 3, p. 271; Grant to Jesse R. Grant, November 8, 1861, in *PUG*, 3:138; Report of McClernand, November 12, 1861, in *OR*, vol. 3, p. 282.

60. Report of Logan, November 11, 1861, ibid., 289.

Chapter 4: The Campaigns of 1862

1. Engle, *Yankee Dutchman*, 90 (see chap. 2, n. 47); William L. Shea and Earl J. Hess, *Pea Ridge: Civil War Campaign in the West* (Chapel Hill: University of North Carolina Press, 1992), 14.

2. Franz Sigel, "The Pea Ridge Campaign," in *B&L*, 1:317; Report of Curtis, April 1, 1862, in *OR*, vol. 8, p. 197; Report of Sigel, March 15, 1862, ibid., 209.

3. Report of Sigel, March 15, 1862, in *OR*, vol. 8, p. 210; Sigel, "The Pea Ridge Campaign," in *B&L*, 1:320; Shea and Hess, *Pea Ridge*, 69, 76.

4. Report of Curtis, April 1, 1862, in *OR*, vol. 8, pp. 200–201; Report of Sigel, March 15, 1862, ibid., 213.

5. Report of Sigel, March 15, 1862, ibid., 214–15.

6. Engle, *Yankee Dutchman*, 118; Shea and Hess, *Pea Ridge*, 279–80; Reports of Curtis, March 9, April 1, 1862, in *OR*, vol. 8, pp. 192, 203; Curtis quoted in Shea and Hess, *Pea Ridge*, 278.

7. Field Order No. 1, February 5, 1862, in *OR*, vol. 7, p. 125.

8. McClernand to Grant, February 6, 1862, JMP; McClernand to Logan, January 8, 1862, PJL.

9. Grant to McClernand, February 5, 1862, in *PUG*, 4:152.

10. McClernand to Grant, February 6, 1862, ibid., 4:159; McClernand to Lincoln, February 8, 1862, PAL.

11. Grant to Halleck, February 6, 1862, in *OR*, vol. 7, p. 124; McClernand to Grant, February 9, 1862, JMP; Lew Wallace, *An Autobiography*, 2 vols. (New York: Harper and Brothers, 1906), 1:377.

12. Report of McClernand, February 28, 1862, in *OR*, vol. 7, pp. 171, 174; Benjamin Franklin Cooling, *Forts Henry and Donelson: The Key to the Confederate Heartland* (Knoxville: University of Tennessee Press, 1987), 281, 283.

13. Grant, *Memoirs*, 1:198; Brooks D. Simpson, *Ulysses S. Grant: Triumph over Adversity, 1822–1865* (New York: Houghton Mifflin, 2000), 114.

14. Lew Wallace, "Capture of Fort Donelson," in *B&L*, 1:411; Grant, *Memoirs*, 1:201.

15. Grant to George Cullum, February 15, 1862, in *PUG*, 4:213; Cooling, *Forts Henry and Donelson*, 168.

16. Kiper, *McClernand*, 80 (see chap. 2, n. 34); Report of McClernand, February 28, 1862, in *OR*, vol. 7, p. 175.

17. Report of McClernand, February 28, 1862, in *OR*, vol. 7, pp. 175–76; Wallace, *Autobiography*, 398; Cooling, *Fort Henry and Donelson*, 183; Report of McClernand, February 28, 1862, in *OR*, vol. 7, p. 176.

18. John A. Logan, *The Volunteer Soldier of America* (Chicago: R. S. Peale, 1887), 655–56; Cooling, *Forts Henry and Donelson*, 175.

19. Cooling, *Forts Henry and Donelson*, 180–82; Wallace, *Autobiography*, 412–13.

20. *Illinois State Journal*, February 27, 1862, quoted in Kiper, *McClernand*, 88.

21. Grant to Edwin Stanton, March 14, 1862, in *OR*, vol. 10, pt. 2, p. 35; Grant to Washburne, February 22, 1862, in *PUG*, 4:274–75.

22. Field Order No. 145, February 17, 1862, JMP; McClernand to Lincoln, February 18, 27, 1862, PAL; Grant to N. H. McLean, April 21, 1862, in *OR*, vol. 7, p. 170.

23. Larry J. Daniel, *Shiloh: The Battle That Changed the Civil War* (New York: Simon and Schuster, 1997), 109; Lucius W. Barber, *Army Memoirs of Lucius W. Barber* (Chicago: J. M. W. Jones Stationery and Printing, 1894), 45–46.

24. Simpson, *Ulysses S. Grant*, 129, 131; Grant, *Memoirs*, 1:246; McClernand to Grant, March 27, 1862, JMP.

25. Sherman, *Memoirs*, 1:257–58 (see chap. 3, n. 49); Report of McClernand, April 24, 1862, in *OR*, vol. 10, pt. 1, pp. 115–16.

26. Report of Hurlbut, April 12, 1862, ibid., 203–4; Daniel, *Shiloh*, 192.

27. Report of McClernand, April 24, 1862, in *OR*, vol. 10, pt. 1, p. 117; Sherman, *Memoirs*, 1:258.

28. Report of McClernand, April 24, 1862, in *OR*, vol. 10, pt. 1, pp. 119–20.

29. Sherman, *Memoirs*, 1:258.

30. Barber, *Army Memoirs*, 57.

31. Grant, *Memoirs*, 1:246.

32. West, *Lincoln's Scapegoat General*, 126, 131 (see chap. 2, n. 32).

33. George B. McClellan, "The Peninsular Campaign," in *B&L*, 2:164; Robert G. Tanner, *Stonewall in the Valley: Thomas J. "Stonewall" Jackson's Shenandoah Valley Campaign, Spring 1862* (Garden City, N.Y.: Doubleday, 1976), 100–101.

34. Sheldon Colton to Delia Colton, March 3, 1862, in *The Colton Letters: Civil War Period, 1861–1865*, edited by Betsey Gates (Scottsdale: McLane Publications, 1993), 78; Nathan Kimball, "Fighting Jackson at Kernstown," in *B&L*, 2:303.

35. Report of Shields, March 29, 1862, in *OR*, vol. 12, pt. 1, p. 339; Kimball, "Fighting Jackson at Kernstown," in *B&L*, 2:305.

36. Tanner, *Stonewall in the Valley*, 128–31.

37. Banks to S. Williams, March 25, 31, 1862, in *OR*, vol. 12, pt. 3, pp. 18, 33; Stanton to Banks, April 25, 1862, ibid., 105; Banks to Stanton, April 30, May 2, 1862, ibid., 118, 129; Morris Copeland to Banks, May 21, 1862, Banks paper, LC.

38. Frémont to Stanton, March 30, 1862, PES, Microfilm Reel #2; Nevins, *Frémont*, 554–55 (see chap. 2, n. 16).

39. Report of Brig. Gen. Robert H. Milroy, May 14, 1862, in *OR*, vol. 12, pt. 1, p. 465.

40. Report of Schenck, May 14, 1862, ibid., 462–63.

41. Banks to Stanton, May 22, 1862, ibid., 524; Stanton to Banks, May 16, 1862, ibid., 522.

42. Banks to Stanton, May 24, 1862, ibid., 526; Banks to P. H. Watson, May 24, 1862, ibid., 526; Banks quoted in George H. Gordon, *Brook Farm to Cedar Mountain in the War of the Great Rebellion, 1861–62* (Boston: James R. Osgood, 1883), 193.

43. Banks to Lincoln, May 24, 1862, in *OR*, vol. 12, pt. 1, p. 527; John D. Imboden, "Stonewall Jackson in the Shenandoah," in *B&L*, 2:289; Banks quoted in Hollandsworth, *Pretense of Glory*, 63–64 (see chap. 2, n. 11).

44. Report of Banks, June 1862, in *OR*, vol. 12, pt. 1, pp. 549–50; Williams to daughter, May 27, 1862, in Williams's *From the Cannon's Mouth*, 81–82 (see chap. 3, n. 5); Banks to Lincoln, May 26, 1862, in *OR*, vol. 12, pt. 1, p. 530.

45. Lincoln to Frémont, Lincoln to Irvin McDowell, May 24, 1862, in *CW*, 5:230–31, 232.

46. Shields to Stanton, June 2, 1862, in *OR*, vol. 12, pt. 3, p. 322.

47. Frémont to Lincoln, May 28, 1862, in *OR*, vol. 12, pt. 1, p. 645; Lincoln to Frémont, May 29, 1862, in *CW*, 5:247.

48. Frémont to Lincoln, May 29, 31, 1862, in *OR*, vol. 12, pt. 1, pp. 647, 649; Frémont to Stanton, June 2, 1862, ibid., 650.

49. Robert K. Krick, *Conquering the Valley: Stonewall Jackson at Port Republic* (New York: William Morrow and Company, 1996), 154, 218; Frémont to Stanton, June 9, 1862, in *OR*, vol. 12, pt. 1, p. 654.

50. Frémont to Stanton, June 12, 1862, ibid., 657–58; Report of Schenck, June 12, 1862, ibid., 666–67; Krick, *Conquering the Valley*, 236.

51. Shields to Carroll, June 4, 1862, in *OR*, vol. 12, pt. 3, p. 335; Krick, *Conquering the Valley*, 299.

52. Bilby, *Irish Brigade in the Civil War*, 42 (see chap. 2, n. 56); Report of Sickles, June 7, 1862, in *OR*, vol. 11, pt. 1, pp. 822–23; Report of Brig. Gen. Joseph Hooker, June 8, 1862, ibid., 820.

53. Stephen W. Sears, *To the Gates of Richmond: The Peninsula Campaign* (New York: Ticknor and Fields, 1992), 183.

54. Report of Sickles, July 7, 1862, in *OR*, vol. 11, pt. 2, pp. 134–35; Sears, *To the Gates of Richmond*, 184, 187.

55. Sears, *To the Gates of Richmond*, 210–11.

56. Report of McClellan, August 4, 1863, in *OR*, vol. 11, pt. 1, p. 57; quoted in Sears, *To the Gates of Richmond*, 248.

57. Report of Meagher, July 6, 1862, in *OR*, vol. 11, pt. 2, p. 71; Robert G. Athearn, *Thomas Francis Meagher: An Irish Revolutionary in America* (Boulder: University of Colorado Press, 1949), 112; Report of Sickles, July 9, 1862, in *OR*, vol. 11, pt. 2, p. 138.

58. Report of Meagher, July 2, 1862, ibid., 73; Report of Sickles, July 9, 1862, ibid., 140–41.

59. Frémont to Stanton, June 27, 1862, in *OR*, vol. 12, pt. 3, p. 437.

60. John Pope to Henry Halleck, August 25, 1862, in *OR*, vol. 12, pt. 2, p. 12; Sigel's comments on Pope, n.d., FSP; Pope to Banks, June 28, July 14, 1862, in *OR*, vol. 12, pt. 3, pp. 440, 472.

61. Report of Pope, January 27, 1863, in *OR*, vol. 12, pt. 2, p. 25; Engle, *Yankee Dutchman*, 132; Pope, *Military Memoirs*, 136 (see chap. 3, n. 48).

62. Report of Pope, January 27, 1863, in *OR*, vol. 12, pt. 2, pp. 25–26; Pope's orders quoted in W. J. Wood, *Civil War Generalship: The Art of Command* (Westport, Conn.: Greenwood Press, 1997; reprint, United States of America: Da Capo Press, 2000), 52–53.

63. Hollandsworth, *Pretense of Glory*, 74–75; Banks to Pope, August 9, 1862, in *OR*, vol. 12, pt. 2, p. 55.

64. Banks to Pope, August 9, 1862, in *OR*, vol. 12, pt. 2, p. 55; Gordon, *Brook Farm to Cedar Mountain*, 290; Hollandsworth, *Pretense of Glory*, 76.

65. Wood, *Civil War Generalship*, 68–69; Hollandsworth, *Pretense of Glory*, 76–78.

66. Banks to Wife, August 16, 1862, Banks Papers, LC; quoted in Hollandsworth, *Pretense of Glory*, 81.

67. Pope to Sigel, August 23, 1862, in *OR*, vol. 12, pt. 2, p. 61; John J. Hennessy, *Return to Bull Run: The Campaign and Battle of Second Manassas* (New York: Simon and Schuster, 1993), 105; Pope to Halleck, August 25, 1862, in *OR*, vol. 12, pt. 3, p. 653.

68. Hennessy, *Return to Bull Run*, 147–48.

69. Report of Sigel, September 16, 1862, in *OR*, vol. 12, pt. 2, p. 266; Report of Schurz, September 16, 1862, ibid., 297–98; Report of Schenck, September 17, 1862, ibid., 280.

70. Report of Sigel, September 16, 1862, ibid., 266–67; Report of Schurz, September 16, 1862, ibid., 298.

71. Kearny quoted in Hennessy, *Return to Bull Run*, 221–22; Sigel's comments on Kearny, March 10, 1867, FSP; Report of Schurz, September 16, 1862, in *OR*, vol. 12, pt. 2, pp. 298–99.

72. Report of Schenck, September 27, 1862, ibid., 282; Report of Sigel, September 16, 1862, ibid., 269; Hennessy, *Return to Bull Run*, 435.

73. Lincoln quoted in Schurz, *Reminiscences*, 2:381 (see chap. 2, n. 50); Therry, "General Schenck," 261 (see chap. 2, n. 17).

74. Report of Brig. Gen. Winfield S. Hancock, September 20, 1862, in *OR*, vol. 19, pt. 1, p. 277; Report of Meagher, September 30, 1862, ibid., 293–94.

75. Report of Meagher, September 30, 1862, ibid., 294–95; Report of Hancock, September 20, 1862, ibid., 279; Stephen W. Sears, *Landscape Turned Red: The Battle of Antietam* (New York: Ticknor and Fields, 1983), 243–44.

76. Report of Maj. Gen. Edwin V. Sumner, October 1, 1862, in *OR*, vol. 19, pt. 1, p. 276; Report of McClellan, August 4, 1863, ibid., 58; reporter quoted in Burton, *Melting Pot Soldiers*, 123 (see chap. 2, n. 45).

77. George C. Rable, *Fredericksburg! Fredericksburg!* (Chapel Hill: University of North Carolina Press, 2002), 231; Meagher quoted in Cavanagh, *Memoirs of Meagher*, 467 (see chap. 2, n. 55); Report of Meagher, December 20, 1862, in *OR*, vol. 21, pp. 241–42.

78. Report of Meagher, December 20, 1862, in *OR*, vol. 21, p. 242.

79. Villard quoted in Burton, *Melting Pot Soldiers*, 125; Report of Hancock, December 25, 1862, in *OR*, vol. 21, p. 228.

80. Lincoln quoted in *New York Tribune*, August 13, 1862, attached to Banks to Wife, August 16, 1862, Banks Papers, LC.

81. Joseph R. Ward Jr., *An Enlisted Soldier's View of the Civil War: The Wartime Papers of Joseph R. Ward, Jr.* (West Lafayette, Ind.: Belle Publications, 1989), 28; Adjutant General's Office, Military History of James Shields, May 10, 1878, Shields Papers, ISHL.

Chapter 5: The Vicksburg Campaign

1. Grant to Hurlbut, October 3, 4, 1862, in *PUG*, 6:105, 114; E. O. C. Ord to Grant, October 5, 1862, in *OR*, vol. 17, pt. 1, p. 302.

2. Jeffrey N. Lash, *A Politician Turned General: The Civil War Career of Stephen Augustus Hurlbut* (Kent, Ohio: Kent State University Press, 2003), 101–2.

3. William S. Hillyer to William T. Sherman, October 29, 1862, in *PUG*, 6:180; Grant to Horatio G. Wright, October 28, 1862, ibid., 6:302.

4. McClernand to S. S. Cox, December 4, 1861, JMP; Logan to McClernand, December 27, 1861, ibid.; Logan to McClernand, January 14, 1862, ibid.; McClernand to Logan, January 8, 1862, PJL.

5. Kiper, *McClernand*, 135 (see chap. 2, n. 34); McClernand to Lincoln, September 28, 1862, PAL.

6. Richard Yates et al. to Lincoln, September 26, 1862, ibid.

7. Gideon Welles, July 31, 1863, in *Diary of Gideon Welles, Secretary of the Navy under Lincoln and Johnson*, edited by Howard K. Beale, 3 vols. (New York: W. W. Norton, 1960), 1:387; September 27, 1862, in *Chase Papers*, edited by Niven, 1:404 (see chap. 2, n. 16).

8. Stanton to McClernand, October 21, 1862, in *OR*, vol. 17, pt. 2, p. 282.

9. Halleck to John Schofield, September 20, 1862, in *OR*, vol. 13, p. 654; September 28, 1862, in *Chase Papers*, edited by Niven, 1:406.

10. Grant to Halleck, November 10, 1862, in *PUG*, 6:288; Halleck to Grant, November 11, 1862, ibid., 6:288.

11. Grant, *Memoirs*, 1:285 (see chap. 2, n. 43).

12. Ibid., 1:287; Grant to Sherman, December 8, 1862, in *PUG*, 6:407.

13. Browning to McClernand, December 2, 1862, JMP.

14. Stanton to McClernand, December 17, 1862, in *OR*, vol. 17, pt. 2, p. 420; Williams, *Lincoln and His Generals*, 218–19 (see chap. 2, n. 4).

15. Halleck to Grant, December 18, 1862, *OR* vol. 17, pt. 2., p. 425; Welles, January 5, 1863, in *Diary*, 1:217.

16. Blair to Montgomery Blair, October 1862, November 13, 1862, BFP, Microfilm Reel #2; Lincoln to Blair, November 17, 1862, in *CW*, 5:498; Grant, *Memoirs*, 1:385; Sherman to John Sherman, December 20, 1862, in *SCW*, 348.

17. Sherman, *Memoirs*, 1:312 (see chap. 3, n. 49).

18. Report of Blair, December 30, 1862, in *OR*, vol. 17, pt. 1, pp. 655–56.

19. Report of Brig. Gen. Frederick Steele, January 3, 1863, ibid., 652.

20. Blair to Montgomery Blair, January 6, 1862, quoted in Smith, *Blair Family*, 2:155 (see chap. 2, n. 15); Parrish, *Frank Blair: Lincoln's Conservative*, 160 (see chap. 2, n. 26); Report of Blair, December 30, 1862, in *OR*, vol. 17, pt. 1, p. 656; George Morgan to J. H. Hammond, January 4, 1863, ibid., 657; Sherman to J. H. Hammond, January 4, 1863, ibid., 657.

21. Sherman to Ellen Sherman, January 24, 1863, in *SCW*, 362; Sherman to John A. Rawlins, January 4, 1863, in *OR*, vol. 17, pt. 1, p. 612; Sherman, *Memoirs*, 1:319; David Porter, *Incidents and Anecdotes of the Civil War* (New York: D. Appleton, 1885), 131.

22. McClernand to Grant, January 8, 1863, in *OR*, vol. 17, pt. 2, p. 546.

23. Report of McClernand, January 11, 1863, in *OR*, vol. 17, pt. 1, pp. 703, 706–8; Sherman, *Memoirs*, 1:324.

24. Sherman to John Sherman, January 17, 1863, in *SCW*, 361; Lincoln to McClernand, January 22, 1863, in *CW*, 6:70.

25. Grant to Halleck, January 11, 1863, in *PUG*, 7:209; Halleck to Grant, January 12, 1863, ibid., 7:210; Grant to McClernand, January 11, 1863, ibid., 7:210.

26. McClernand to Grant, January 16, 1863, in *OR*, vol. 17, pt. 2, p. 567; McClernand to Lincoln, January 16, 1863, PAL; Lincoln to McClernand, January 22, 1863, in *CW*, 6:70; Sherman to Grant, January 17, 1863, in *SCW*, 360.

27. Grant to Halleck, January 20, 1863, in *PUG*, 7:234; Grant, *Memoirs*, 1:294; Williams, *Lincoln and His Generals*, 222.

28. McClernand to Grant, January 30, 1863, PAL; McClernand to Grant, February 1, 1863, ibid.; McClernand to Lincoln, February 1, 1863, ibid.; Grant to J. C. Kelton, February 1, 1863, in *PUG*, 7:274.

29. McClernand to Lincoln, February 2, 14, March 15, 1863, PAL; McClernand to Yates, March 15, 1863, quoted in Kiper, *McClernand*, 207.

30. Sherman, *Memoirs*, 1:330; Grant, *Memoirs*, 1:294; Dana, *Recollections of the Civil War*, 32–33 (see chap. 2, n. 23).

31. Smith, *Blair Family*, 2:152; Sherman to Blair, February 1, 1863, in *OR*, vol. 17, pt. 2, pp. 581–82; Blair to Sherman, February 1, 1863, ibid., 582–86; Sherman to Thomas Ewing Sr., March 7, 1863, in *SCW*, 415.

32. James Wilson, *Under the Old Flag: Recollections of Military Operations in the War for the Union, the Spanish War, the Boxer Rebellion, Etc.*, 2 vols. (1912; reprint, Westport, Conn.: Greenwood Press, 1971), 1:323; Sherman to Ewing, March 7, 1863, in *SCW*, 415; Dana to Stanton, July 12, 1863, in *Recollections of the Civil War*, by Dana, 67–68.

33. Sherman to Ellen Sherman, April 29, 1863, in *SCW*, 465; Dana, *Recollections of the Civil War*, 32–33; Wilson, *Under the Old Flag*, 1:159; Simpson, *Ulysses S. Grant*, 183–84 (see chap. 4, n. 13).

34. Dana to Stanton, April 25, 27, 29, 1863, in *OR*, vol. 24, pt. 1, pp. 80–83; Edgar L. Erickson, ed., "With Grant at Vicksburg: From the Civil War Diary of Captain Charles E. Wilcox," *Journal of the Illinois State Historical Society* 30 (January 1938): 465; Wilson, *Under the Old Flag*, 1:174.

35. Grant to Halleck, May 3, 1863, in *OR*, vol. 24, pt. 1, p. 32; Report of McClernand, June 17, 1863, ibid., 143–45; James R. Arnold, *Grant Wins the War: Decision at Vicksburg* (New York: John Wiley and Sons, 1997), 103, 108–9.

36. Report of McClernand, June 17, 1863, in *OR*, vol. 24, pt. 1, p. 145; Arnold, *Grant Wins the War*, 112; Kiper, *McClernand*, 226.

37. Report of Logan, May 26, 1863, in *OR*, vol. 24, pt. 1, p. 643.

38. McClernand to Lincoln, May 1, 1863, PAL; Dana to Stanton, May 5, 1863, in *OR*, vol. 24, pt. 1, p. 84; Stanton to Dana, May 5, 1863, ibid., 84; Wilson, *Under the Old Flag*, 1:174–76.

39. Grant, *Memoirs*, 1:327–28.

40. McClernand to Grant, May 10, 1863, in *OR*, vol. 24, pt. 3, p. 289; Grant to McClernand, May 10, 1863, ibid.

41. Arnold, *Grant Wins the War*, 132; Report of Logan, May 26, 1863, in *OR*, vol. 24, pt. 1, p. 645.

42. Report of Logan, May 26, 1863, in *OR*, vol. 24, pt. 1, pp. 645–46; Jones, *"Black Jack,"* 162 (see chap. 2, n. 42).

43. Grant, *Memoirs*, 1:333.

44. Ibid., 1:339; McClernand to Blair, May 15, 1863, in *OR*, vol. 24, pt. 3, p. 313.

45. Report of McClernand, June 17, 1863, in *OR*, vol. 24, pt. 1, pp. 148–49.

46. McClernand to A. P. Hovey, May 16, 1863, in *OR*, vol. 24, pt. 3, p. 316; McClernand to Grant, May 16, 1863, ibid., 316–17.

47. Grant, *Memoirs,* 1:345; Grant to McClernand, May 16, 1863, in *OR,* vol. 24, pt. 3, pp. 317–18.

48. Report of Logan, May 26, 1863, in *OR,* vol. 24, pt. 1, pp. 645–46; Grant, *Memoirs,* 1:346.

49. Grant to McClernand, May 16, 1863, in *OR,* vol. 24, pt. 3, p. 318.

50. Kiper, *McClernand,* 245–46; Albert O. Marshall, *Army Life: From a Soldier's Journal* (Joliet, Ill.: Albert O. Marshall, 1883), 213.

51. Report of McClernand, June 17, 1863, in *OR,* vol. 24, pt. 1, p. 152.

52. Grant, *Memoirs,* 1:355; McClernand to Grant, May 20, 1863, in *OR,* vol. 24, pt. 3, p. 332.

53. Report of Blair, May 24, 1863, in *OR,* vol. 24, pt. 2, pp. 257–58; Arnold, *Grant Wins the War,* 250.

54. Report of McClernand, June 17, 1863, in *OR,* vol. 24, pt. 1, pp. 154–55; McClernand to Grant, May 22, 1863, ibid., 172.

55. Report of Grant, July 6, 1863, ibid., 56; Sherman, *Memoirs,* 1:352; Simpson, *Ulysses S. Grant,* 204.

56. Grant to Halleck, May 22, 1863, in *OR,* vol. 24, pt. 1, p. 37.

57. Grant to Halleck, May 24, 1863, ibid., 37; Report of Grant, July 6, 1863, ibid., 56.

58. Grant to Halleck, May 24, 1863, ibid., 37; Dana to Stanton, May 23, 24, 1863, ibid., 86–87.

59. Grant to Halleck, May 24, 1863, ibid., 37; Dana to Stanton, May 23, 1863, ibid., 86; Dana to Stanton, May 24, 1863, ibid., 87.

60. McClernand to Yates, May 28, 1863, JMP; *New York Times,* June 28, 1863; McClernand to Lincoln May 29, 1863, PAL.

61. McClernand to Grant, June 4, 1863, in *OR,* vol. 24, pt. 1, pp. 165–66.

62. Wilson, *Under the Old Flag,* 1:182–83; General Orders No. 72, May 30, 1863, in *OR,* vol. 24, pt. 1, pp. 159–61.

63. Sherman to Rawlins, June 17, 1863, ibid., 162; McPherson to Grant, June 18, 1863, ibid., 164; Grant to Lorenzo Thomas, June 26, 1863, ibid., 159.

64. McClernand to Lincoln, June 23, 1863, ibid., 158; McClernand to Halleck, June 27, 1863, ibid., 165; McClernand to Stanton, June 27, 1863, ibid., 167; Yates to Lincoln, June 30, 1863, ibid., 168.

65. Smith, *Blair Family,* 2:162; Blair to Montgomery Blair, June 23, 1863, BFP, Microfilm Reel #2; Sherman to John Sherman, May 29, 1863, in *SCW,* 473.

66. Grant, *Memoirs,* 1:365; Blair to Grant, May 31, 1863, in *OR,* vol. 24, pt. 2, p. 436.

67. Grant, *Memoirs,* 1:385; Dana to Stanton, July 12, 1863, in *Recollections of the Civil War,* by Dana, 66–68.

Chapter 6: Battles in the West and the East

1. Harrington, *Fighting Politician*, 85–86 (see chap. 3, n. 8); Hollandsworth, *Pretense of Glory*, 84–85 (see chap. 2, n. 11).

2. Halleck to Banks, November 9, 1862, in *OR*, vol. 15, p. 590.

3. Banks to Lincoln, December 19, 1862, PAL; Banks to Halleck, December 18, 1862, in *OR*, vol. 15, p. 614.

4. Lawrence L. Hewitt, *Port Hudson, Confederate Bastion on the Mississippi* (Baton Rouge: Louisiana State University Press, 1987), 37–38; Banks to Mary Banks, January 15, 1863, Banks Papers, LC; Banks to Halleck, January 7, 1863, in *OR*, vol. 15, p. 640; Richard Irwin, "The Capture of Port Hudson," in *B&L*, 3:588.

5. Banks to Halleck, January 7, 1863, in *OR*, vol. 15, p. 639; Halleck to Banks, February 27, 1863, ibid., 690.

6. Banks to Halleck, February 12, 1863, ibid., 240–41; Report of Banks, March 21, 1863, ibid., 252–53; Richard B. Irwin, *History of the Nineteenth Army Corps* (New York: G. P. Putnam's Sons, 1892), 79.

7. Report of Banks, March 21, 1863, in *OR*, vol. 15, pp. 252–53; Hollandsworth, *Pretense of Glory*, 104.

8. Hewitt, *Port Hudson*, 96; soldier quoted in Hollandsworth, *Pretense of Glory*, 107.

9. Irwin, "The Capture of Port Hudson," in *B&L*, 3:590; Irwin, *Nineteenth Army Corps*, 129–30; Banks to Grant, April 10, 1863, in *OR*, vol. 15, p. 296.

10. Hewitt, *Port Hudson*, 108; Smith quoted in Harrington, *Fighting Politician*, 120.

11. Irwin, *Nineteenth Army Corps*, 85–86; Banks to Halleck, April 10, 1863, in *OR*, vol. 15, p. 294.

12. Banks to Halleck, April 17, 1863, ibid., 296–97; Irwin, "The Capture of Port Hudson," in *B&L*, 3:590–91; Irwin, *Nineteenth Army Corps*, 94, 100.

13. Banks to Lincoln, April 17, 1863, PAL; Banks to Halleck, April 17, 1863, in *OR*, vol. 15, p. 297; Hollandsworth, *Pretense of Glory*, 115.

14. Irwin, *Nineteenth Army Corps*, 149; Banks to Lincoln, May 10, 1863, PAL; Banks to Grant, May 3, 1863, in *OR*, vol. 15, p. 309.

15. Halleck to Banks, May 23, 1863, in *OR*, vol. 26, pt. 1, p. 500 (emphasis in the original).

16. Report of Banks, April 6, 1865, ibid., 12; Banks to Halleck, May 12, 1863, in *OR*, vol. 15, pp. 314–15, 317; Hewitt, *Port Hudson*, 125.

17. Irwin, "The Capture of Port Hudson," in *B&L*, 3:593; Irwin, *Nineteenth Army Corps*, 163.

18. Special Orders No. 123, May 26, 1863, in *OR*, vol. 26, pt. 1, pp. 508–9.

19. Banks to Halleck, May 30, 1863, ibid., 44; Banks to Godfrey Weitzel, May 27, 1863, ibid., 509–10; Edward Cunningham, *The Port Hudson Campaign, 1862–1863* (Baton Rouge: Louisiana State University Press, 1963), 57; Irwin, *Nineteenth Army Corps*, 176.

20. Irwin, *Nineteenth Army Corps*, 177; Hollandsworth, *Pretense of Glory*, 124–25.

21. Wickham Hoffman, *Camp, Court, and Siege: A Narrative of Personal Adventure and Observation during Two Wars* (New York: Harper and Brothers, 1877), 70, 71; Banks to Halleck, May 30, 1863, in *OR*, vol. 26, pt. 1, p. 45; Joseph T. Glatthaar, *Forged in Battle: The Civil War Alliance of Black Soldiers and White Officers* (New York: Free Press, 1990), 123, 128–29.

22. Irwin, *Nineteenth Army Corps*, 192–95.

23. Henry T. Johns, *Life with the Forty-ninth Massachusetts Volunteers* (Pittsfield, Mass.: C. A. Alvord, 1864), 287; Hollandsworth, *Pretense of Glory*, 127–28; Special Orders No. 140, June 13, 1863, in *OR*, vol. 26, pt. 1, pp. 554–55.

24. John W. De Forest, *A Volunteer's Adventures: A Union Captain's Record of the Civil War* (New Haven: Yale University Press, 1946), 145; Philemon H. Fowler, *Memorials of William Fowler* (New York: Anson D. F. Randolph, 1875), 45; Johns, *Life with the Forty-ninth*, 302 (emphasis in the original).

25. Lincoln to Banks, August 5, 1863, in *CW*, 6:364.

26. Darius N. Couch, "The Chancellorsville Campaign," in *B&L*, 3:159.

27. Sigel to Lieutenant-Colonel Dickinson, February 12, 1863, in *OR*, vol. 25, pt. 2, p. 70; Engle, *Yankee Dutchman*, 156–58 (see chap. 2, n. 47); Schurz, *Reminiscences*, 2:405 (see chap. 2, n. 50).

28. Ernest B. Furgurson, *Chancellorsville, 1863: The Souls of the Brave* (New York: Alfred A. Knopf, 1992), 150; Keneally, *American Scoundrel*, 261 (see chap. 2, n. 39).

29. Oliver O. Howard, "The Eleventh Corps at Chancellorsville," in *B&L*, 3:191, 195.

30. Report of Sickles, May 20, 1863, in *OR*, vol. 25, pt. 1, p. 386.

31. Couch, "Chancellorsville Campaign," in *B&L*, 3:163; J. H. Van Allen to Howard and Henry Slocum, May 2, 1863, in *OR*, vol. 25, pt. 2, pp. 360–61.

32. Report of Schurz, May 12, 1863, in *OR*, vol. 25, pt. 1, p. 652; Schurz, *Reminiscences*, 2:415–16; Oliver O. Howard, *Autobiography of Oliver Otis Howard*, 2 vols. (New York: Baker and Taylor, 1907), 1:369.

33. Schurz, *Reminiscences*, 2:416–18.

34. Report of Schurz, May 12, 1863, in *OR*, vol. 25, pt. 1, pp. 652–53; Schurz, *Reminiscences*, 2:418–20; Furgurson, *Chancellorsville*, 158–59.

35. Report of Sickles, May 20, 1863, in *OR*, vol. 25, pt. 1, pp. 386–87; Alfred Pleasonton, "The Successes and Failures of Chancellorsville," in *B&L*, 3:179; Furgurson, *Chancellorsville*, 155.

36. Howard, "The Eleventh Corps at Chancellorsville," in *B&L*, 3:197; Report of Schurz, May 12, 1863, in *OR*, vol. 25, pt. 1, pp. 654–55; Schurz, *Reminiscences*, 2:423.

37. Report of Schurz, May 12, 1863, in *OR*, vol. 25, pt. 1, p. 657; Schurz, *Reminiscences*, 2:426–27.

38. Report of Sickles, May 20, 1863, in *OR*, vol. 25, pt. 1, pp. 387–88.

39. Ibid., 389–90; Furgurson, *Chancellorsville*, 210–11.

40. Furgurson, *Chancellorsville*, 218–19.

41. Report of Sickles, May 20, 1863, in *OR*, vol. 25, pt. 1, pp. 391–93.

42. Howard, *Autobiography*, 1:379; Couch, "Chancellorsville Campaign," in *B&L*, 3:171.

43. *New York Times*, May 5, 1863; *New York Herald*, May 6, 1863, quoted in Trefousse, *Carl Schurz: A Biography*, 134–35 (see chap. 2, n. 49); Schurz to Howard, May 21, 1863, in *OR*, vol. 25, pt. 1, p. 659; Halleck to Schurz, June 4, 1863, ibid., 661; Trefousse, *Carl Schurz: A Biography*, 135.

44. Noah Andre Trudeau, *Gettysburg: A Testing of Courage* (New York: HarperCollins, 2002), 6; Edwin B. Coddington, *The Gettysburg Campaign: A Study in Command* (1968; reprint, Dayton: Morningside Bookshop, 1979), 9.

45. Krumwiede, *"Old Waddy's Coming,"* 18–19 (see chap. 3, n. 9); Rufus R. Dawes, *Service with the Sixth Wisconsin Volunteers* (Marietta, Ohio: E. R. Alderman and Sons, 1890), 129.

46. Report of Wadsworth, July 4, 1863, in *OR*, vol. 27, pt. 1, p. 266; Coddington, *Gettysburg Campaign*, 268.

47. Report of Wadsworth, July 4, 1863, in *OR*, vol. 27, pt. 1, p. 266; Krumwiede, *"Old Waddy's Coming,"* 46; Journal of Major-General Abner Doubleday, July 1, 1863, in *SOR*, pt. 1, vol. 5, pp. 89, 91–92.

48. Wadsworth to Doubleday or Howard, July 1, 1863, in *OR*, vol. 27, pt. 3, p. 463; Harry W. Pfanz, *Gettysburg—the First Day* (Chapel Hill: University of North Carolina Press, 2001), 216; Report of Schurz, August 20, 1863, in *OR*, vol. 27, pt. 1, p. 727.

49. Report of Schurz, August 20, 1863, in *OR*, vol. 27, pt. 1, p. 727; Trefousse, *Carl Schurz: A Biography*, 136; Henry Hunt, "The First Day at Gettysburg," in *B&L*, 3:278; A. Wilson Greene, "From Chancellorsville to Cemetery Hill: O. O. Howard and Eleventh Corps Leadership," in *Three Days at Gettysburg: Essays on Confederate and Union Leadership*, edited by Gary W. Gallagher (Kent: Kent State University Press, 1999), 56–57; Pfanz, *Gettysburg—the First Day*, 140; Journal of Doubleday, July 1, 1863, in *SOR*, pt. 1, vol. 5, p. 95.

50. Report of Schurz, August 20, 1863, in *OR*, vol. 27, pt. 1, p. 728; Schurz, *Reminiscences*, 3:9; Greene, "From Chancellorsville to Cemetery Hill," 59–60.

51. Report of Schurz, August 20, 1863, in *OR*, vol. 27, pt. 1, p. 729; Greene, "From Chancellorsville to Cemetery Hill," 61–63; Pfanz, *Gettysburg—the First Day*, 323; Coddington, *Gettysburg Campaign*, 305.

52. Report of Wadsworth, July 4, 1863, in *OR*, vol. 27, pt. 1, p. 266; Coddington, *Gettysburg Campaign*, 286, 307; Pfanz, *Gettysburg—the First Day*, 323.

53. Krumwiede, *"Old Waddy's Coming,"* 72–74; Report of Schurz, August 20, 1863, in *OR*, vol. 27, pt. 1, p. 730; Schurz, *Reminiscences*, 3:15.

54. Report of Maj. Gen. George Meade, October 1, 1863, in *OR*, vol. 27, pt. 1, p. 116; George Meade, *The Life and Letters of George Gordon Meade*, 2 vols. (New York: Charles Scribner's Sons, 1913), 2:67, 70.

55. Swanberg, *Sickles the Incredible*, 197–98 (see chap. 2, n. 41); Trudeau, *Gettysburg*, 109–10; Meade to Sickles, June 29, 30, 1863, in *OR*, vol. 27, pt. 3, pp. 399, 421; William G. Robertson, "The Peach Orchard Revisited: Daniel E. Sickles and the Third Corps

on July 2, 1863," in *Three Days at Gettysburg*, edited by Gallagher, 136–38; Harry W. Pfanz, *Gettysburg—the Second Day* (Chapel Hill: University of North Carolina Press, 1987), 43.

56. Keneally, *American Scoundrel*, 277; Daniel Sickles, "Reply by Daniel E. Sickles," in *B&L*, 3:417.

57. Sickles, "Reply by Sickles," in *B&L*, 3:417–18; Robertson, "Peach Orchard Revisited," 140; Coddington, *Gettysburg Campaign*, 354.

58. Meade, *Life and Letters*, 2:70; Henry Hunt, "The Second Day at Gettysburg," in *B&L*, 3:301–2; Swanberg, *Sickles the Incredible*, 211; Pfanz, *Gettysburg—the Second Day*, 102–3.

59. Hunt, "Second Day at Gettysburg," in *B&L*, 3:302; Coddington, *Gettysburg Campaign*, 355; Pfanz, *Gettysburg—the Second Day*, 147–48.

60. Coddington, *Gettysburg Campaign*, 355; Pfanz, *Gettysburg—the Second Day*, 147–48.

61. Meade, *Life and Letters*, 2:72–73, 79; Trudeau, *Gettysburg*, 319; Pfanz, *Gettysburg—the Second Day*, 140; Meade quoted in Swanberg, *Sickles the Incredible*, 212; Coddington, *Gettysburg Campaign*, 345.

62. Swanberg, *Sickles the Incredible*, 214–15.

63. Keneally, *American Scoundrel*, 288.

64. Krumwiede, *"Old Waddy's Coming,"* 74–76; Harry W. Pfanz, *Gettysburg—Culp's Hill and Cemetery Hill* (Chapel Hill: University of North Carolina Press, 1993), 213; Report of Schurz, August 20, 1863, in *OR*, vol. 27, pt. 1, p. 731; Schurz, *Reminiscences*, 3:25; Pfanz, *Gettysburg—Culp's Hill and Cemetery Hill*, 263, 272.

65. Pearson, *James S. Wadsworth*, 229 (see chap. 2, n. 25); Schurz, *Reminiscences*, 3:42.

66. Pfanz, *Gettysburg—the Second Day*, 141.

67. Schurz to Howard, July 11, 1863, in *OR*, vol. 27, pt. 3, p. 650; Peter Cozzens, *The Shipwreck of Their Hopes: The Battles for Chattanooga* (Urbana: University of Illinois Press, 1994), 90.

68. Schurz, *Reminiscences*, 3:62; Report of Schurz, October 31, 1863, in *OR*, vol. 31, pt. 1, p. 110.

69. Schurz, *Reminiscences*, 3:63–64.

70. Report of Schurz, December 22, 1863, in *OR*, vol. 31, pt. 1, p. 382.

71. Report of Sherman, December 19, 1863, ibid., 570; Sherman quoted in Smith, *Blair Family*, 2:168 (see chap. 2, n. 15).

72. Report of Hooker, November 6, 1863, in *OR*, vol. 31, pt. 1, pp. 94–95; Schurz, *Reminiscences*, 3:92.

73. Athearn, *Thomas Francis Meagher*, 125 (see chap. 4, n. 57); Krumwiede, *"Old Waddy's Coming,"* 81.

Chapter 7: The Western Theater in 1864–65

1. Sherman, *Memoirs*, 1:416–17, 422 (see chap. 3, n. 49); Margie R. Bearss, *Sherman's Forgotten Campaign: The Meridian Expedition* (Baltimore: Gateway Press, 1987), 13; Sherman to Ellen Sherman, January 28, 1864, in *SCW*, 593.

2. Bearss, *Sherman's Forgotten Campaign*, 140; Sherman to Hurlbut, February 12, 1864, in *OR*, vol. 32, pt. 2, p. 383.

3. Sherman, *Memoirs*, 1:420; Report of Sherman, March 7, 1864, in *OR*, vol. 32, pt. 1, p. 176; Bearss, *Sherman's Forgotten Campaign*, 190, 192.

4. Sherman to James McPherson, April 6, 1864, in *OR*, vol. 32, pt. 3, p. 276; Sherman to Ellen Sherman, April 22, 1864, in *SCW*, 626; Sherman to Grant, April 2, 1864, ibid., 611; McPherson to Sherman, April 8, 1864, in *OR*, vol. 32, pt. 3, p. 298; Grant to Sherman, April 15, 1864, in *PUG*, 10:284.

5. Halleck to Banks, August 10, 1863, in *OR*, vol. 26, pt. 1, p. 661; William R. Brooksher, *War along the Bayous: The 1864 Red River Campaign in Louisiana* (Washington, D.C.: Brassey's, 1998), 27; Report of Banks, April 6, 1865, in *OR*, vol. 34, pt. 1, p. 194.

6. Ludwell H. Johnson, *Red River Campaign: Politics and Cotton in the Civil War* (Baltimore: Johns Hopkins University Press, 1958), 13–14, 47.

7. Sherman to Ellen Sherman, March 10, 1864, in *SCW*, 607.

8. Irwin, *Nineteenth Army Corps*, 283 (see chap. 6, n. 6); Brooksher, *War along the Bayous*, 34.

9. Brooksher, *War along the Bayous*, 34; Hollandsworth, *Pretense of Glory*, 175 (see chap. 2, n. 11); Harrington, *Fighting Politician*, 152 (see chap. 3, n. 8).

10. Brooksher, *War along the Bayous*, 50; Richard B. Irwin, "The Red River Campaign," in *B&L*, 4:349; Report of Banks, April 6, 1865, in *OR*, vol. 34, pt. 1, pp. 196–97.

11. Hollandsworth, *Pretense of Glory*, 180; Report of Banks, April 6, 1865, in *OR*, vol. 34, pt. 1, pp. 214–15; Irwin, *Nineteenth Army Corps*, 292.

12. Hoffman, *Camp, Court, and Siege*, 87 (see chap. 6, n. 21); Brooksher, *War along the Bayous*, 75; Porter to Sherman, April 16, 1864, in *OR*, vol. 34, pt. 3, pp. 171–72; Report of Banks, April 6, 1865, in *OR*, vol. 34, pt. 1, p. 198.

13. Report of Banks, April 6, 1865, in *OR*, vol. 34, pt. 1, p. 198; Irwin, *Nineteenth Army Corps*, 300; Brooksher, *War along the Bayous*, 75.

14. Report of Banks, April 6, 1864, in *OR*, vol. 34, pt. 1, p. 199; Hollandsworth, *Pretense of Glory*, 184–85; Irwin, *Nineteenth Army Corps*, 300–301.

15. Brooksher, *War along the Bayous*, 80; Banks to Halleck, April 13, 1864, in *OR*, vol. 34, pt. 1, p. 181; J. Schuyler Crosby to A. L. Lee, April 7, 1864, in *OR*, vol. 34, pt. 3, p. 72.

16. Irwin, "The Red River Campaign," in *B&L*, 4:352; Report of Banks, April 6, 1865, in *OR*, vol. 34, pt. 1, pp. 199–200; Irwin, *Nineteenth Army Corps*, 303.

17. Report of Banks, April 6, 1865, in *OR*, vol. 34, pt. 1, p. 200; George Drake to Richard Irwin, April 11, 1864, in *OR*, vol. 34, pt. 3, pp. 127–28; Irwin, "The Red

River Campaign," in *B&L*, 4:353; Frank McGregor to Susan Brown, April 12, 1864, in McGregor's *Dearest Susie: A Civil War Infantryman's Letters to His Sweetheart*, edited by Carl E. Hatch (New York: Exposition Press, 1971), 87 (emphasis in the original).

18. Report of Banks, April 6, 1865, in *OR*, vol. 34, pt. 1, p. 200; Irwin, *Nineteenth Army Corps*, 306; Brooksher, *War along the Bayous*, 104.

19. Brooksher, *War along the Bayous*, 107; Hollandsworth, *Pretense of Glory*, 190; Banks to Halleck, April 13, 1864, in *OR*, vol. 34, pt. 1, p. 183.

20. Brooksher, *War along the Bayous*, 110; William S. Burns, "The Red River Expedition," in *Battles and Leaders of the Civil War*, edited by Peter Cozzens (Urbana: University of Illinois Press, 2002), 581; Report of Banks, April 6, 1865, in *OR*, vol. 34, pt. 1, pp. 201–2; Report of Capt. Maschil Manring, April 14, 1864, ibid., 293; Report of Maj. Gen. A. J. Smith, September 26, 1865, ibid., 309.

21. Report of Banks, April 6, 1865, in *OR*, vol. 34, pt. 1, p. 202; Brooksher, *War along the Bayous*, 135.

22. Franklin quoted in Hollandsworth, *Pretense of Glory*, 193.

23. William Wiley, April 9, 1864, in *The Civil War Diary of a Common Soldier: William Wiley of the 77th Illinois Infantry*, edited by Terrence J. Winschel (Baton Rouge: Louisiana State University Press, 2001), 107; McGregor to Brown, April 19, 1864, in McGregor, *Dearest Susie*, 92; Hoffman, *Camp, Court, and Siege*, 97.

24. Porter to Sherman, April 14, 1864, in *OR*, vol. 34, pt. 3, p. 154; Porter, *Incidents and Anecdotes*, 238 (see chap. 5, n. 21); Hollandsworth, *Pretense of Glory*, 199.

25. Halleck to Banks, January 22, 1864, in *OR*, vol. 34, pt. 2, p. 123; Special Orders No. 53, March 1, 1864, ibid., 474; McClernand to Dwight, April 28, 1864, in *OR*, vol. 34, pt. 3, p. 318; McClernand to Banks, April 30, 1864, JMP; Kiper, *McClernand*, 290 (see chap. 2, n. 34).

26. Welles, April 26, 28, 1864, in *Diary*, 2:18–19 (see chap. 5, n. 7); Jonathan Sturgis to Banks, May 6, 1864, Banks Papers, LC; *New York Times*, May 16, 1864.

27. Grant to Halleck, April 25, 1864, in *OR*, vol. 34, pt. 3, p. 279; Grant to Halleck, April 22, 1864, ibid., 252–53; Halleck to Grant, April 23, 1864, ibid., 253; Halleck to Grant, April 29, 1864, ibid., 334.

28. Hollandsworth, *Pretense of Glory*, 206–7; Banks to Mary Banks, May 30, 1864, Banks Papers, LC.

29. Grant, *Memoirs*, 2:477–78, 489 (see chap. 2, n. 43).

30. Sherman, *Memoirs*, 2:496, 499–500; Jones, *"Black Jack,"* 195–96 (see chap. 2, n. 42); William Shanks, *Personal Recollections of Distinguished Generals* (New York: Harper and Brothers, 1866), 309–10.

31. Report of Logan, September 13, 1864, in *OR*, vol. 38, pt. 3, pp. 91–94.

32. Sherman, *Memoirs*, 2:512–14.

33. Report of Logan, September 13, 1864, in *OR*, vol. 38, pt. 3, pp. 95–96; Ecelbarger, *Black Jack Logan*, 173–74 (see chap. 2, n. 43).

34. Albert Castel, *Decision in the West: The Atlanta Campaign of 1864* (Lawrence: University Press of Kansas, 1992), 301, 304, 307; Logan, *Volunteer Soldier*, 683 (see chap. 4, n. 18).

35. Logan, *Volunteer Soldier*, 683–84; Reports of Logan, June 28, September 13, 1864, in *OR*, vol. 38, pt. 3, pp. 85, 99.

36. Castel, *Decision in the West*, 360.

37. Report of Logan, September 10, 1864, in *OR*, vol. 38, pt. 3, p. 22; Report of Blair, 1864, ibid., 544; Sherman, *Memoirs*, 2:547; Castel, *Decision in the West*, 383.

38. Report of Logan, September 10, 1864, in *OR*, vol. 38, pt. 3, pp. 24–25; Parrish, *Frank Blair: Lincoln's Conservative*, 199 (see chap. 2, n. 26); Jones, *"Black Jack,"* 214–15.

39. Report of Blair, 1864, in *OR*, vol. 38, pt. 3, pp. 546–47.

40. Report of Logan, September 10, 1864, ibid., 25–26; Jones, *"Black Jack,"* 216; Castel, *Decision in the West*, 408.

41. Report of Logan, September 10, 1864, in *OR*, vol. 38, pt. 3, p. 28.

42. Cox, *Military Reminiscences*, 2:308–9 (see chap. 1, n. 1); Sherman to Halleck, July 27, 1864, in *SCW*, 673; Jones, *"Black Jack,"* 218–19; Sherman, *Memoirs*, 2:558–59.

43. Logan to Mary Logan, August 6, 1864, PJL; Cox, *Military Reminiscences*, 2:309; Sherman to Logan, July 27, 1864, in *SCW*, 675.

44. Warner, *Generals in Blue*, 237–39 (see chap. 1, n. 2).

45. Sherman, *Memoirs*, 2:561; Report of Oliver Howard, September 17, 1864, in *OR*, vol. 38, pt. 3, pp. 40–41; Reports of Logan, July 29, September 13, 1864, ibid., 86, 104; Castel, *Decision in the West*, 428; Howard, *Autobiography*, 2:22 (see chap. 6, n. 32).

46. Report of Logan, September 13, 1864, in *OR*, vol. 38, pt. 3, p. 104; Logan, *Volunteer Soldier*, 691; Logan to Mary Logan, July 31, 1864, PJL.

47. Report of Logan, September 13, 1864, in *OR*, vol. 38, pt. 3, p. 105; Report of Howard, September 17, 1864, ibid., 41–42.

48. Sherman, *Memoirs*, 2:577–78; Report of Howard, September 17, 1864, in *OR*, vol. 38, pt. 3, pp. 43–44; Report of Logan, September 17, 1864, ibid., 108.

49. Report of Logan, September 17, 1864, in *OR*, vol. 38, pt. 3, p. 109.

50. Sherman, *Memoirs*, 2:583.

51. William P. Carlin, "The March to the Sea, an Armed Picnic," in *Battles and Leaders*, edited by Cozzens, 563; Blair to Frank Blair Sr., December 16, 1864, BFP, Microfilm Reel #2.

52. Grant, *Memoirs*, 2:659.

53. Parrish, *Frank Blair: Lincoln's Conservative*, 213; *The Story of the Fifty-fifth Regiment Illinois Volunteer Infantry in the Civil War, 1861–1865* (1887; reprint, Huntington, W.Va.: Blue Acorn Press, 1993), 405.

54. Marion B. Lucas, *Sherman and the Burning of Columbia* (College Station: Texas A&M University Press, 1976), 95, 97; Jones, *"Black Jack,"* 246; Blair quoted in Smith, *Blair Family*, 2:181 (see chap. 2, n. 15).

55. Bilby, *Irish Brigade in the Civil War*, 140 (see chap. 2, n. 56); Halleck to R. N. Scott, February 4, 1865, in *OR*, vol. 47, pt. 2, p. 305; Halleck to Grant, February 5, 1865, ibid., 306; Grant to Halleck, February 6, 1865, ibid., 318; Special Orders No. 13, February 24, 1864, ibid., 561.

56. Blair to Howard, March 7, 1865, ibid., 717; Cox, *Military Reminiscences*, 2:455–56; Smith, *Blair Family*, 2:181; Parrish, *Frank Blair: Lincoln's Conservative*, 220; Jones, *"Black Jack,"* 255.

Chapter 8: The Eastern Theater in 1864

1. Grant, *Memoirs*, 2:477–78, 489 (see chap. 2, n. 43).

2. Grant to Halleck, in *OR*, March 28, 1864, vol. 33, p. 753.

3. Engle, *Yankee Dutchman*, 168–69 (see chap. 2, n. 47); David H. Strother, *A Virginia Yankee in the Civil War: The Diaries of David Hunter Strother*, edited by Cecil E. Eby Jr. (Chapel Hill: University of North Carolina Press, 1961), 213; William C. Davis, *The Battle of New Market* (Garden City, N.Y.: Doubleday, 1975), 13.

4. Grant to E. O. C. Ord, March 29, 1864, in *OR*, vol. 33, p. 758; Grant to Sigel, March 29, 1864, ibid., 765–66; Grant to Sigel, April 4, 1864, ibid., 799; Franz Sigel, "Sigel in the Shenandoah Valley in 1864," in *B&L*, 4:487.

5. Sigel quoted in Davis, *New Market*, 22; Ord to Stanton, May 23, 1864, PES, Microfilm Reel #7; Ord to Seward, May 23, 1864, in *OR*, vol. 37, pt. 1, p. 526. The emphasis is in the original.

6. Grant to Sigel, April 17, 1864, in *OR*, vol. 33, p. 893; Sigel to Grant, April 18, 1864, ibid., 901; Orville E. Babcock to Grant, April 18, 1864, ibid., 901; Grant to Sigel, April 19, 1864, ibid., 911; Sigel, "Sigel in the Valley," in *B&L*, 4:487.

7. Engle, *Yankee Dutchman*, 172; Davis, *New Market*, 22–23; Strother, *Virginia Yankee*, 221–22.

8. Sigel to Grant, May 2, 1864, in *OR*, vol. 37, pt. 1, pp. 368–69; Soldier quoted in Davis, *New Market*, 42–43.

9. Sigel to Adjutant-General, May 13, 1864, in *OR*, vol. 37, pt. 1, pp. 446–47; Davis, *New Market*, 57–58.

10. Sigel, "Sigel in the Valley," in *B&L*, 4:488; Engle, *Yankee Dutchman*, 185–86; Michael Graham to S. Cole, May 17, 1864, FSP.

11. Alexander Neil, "The Leg That Broke Loose: Recollections of the Battle of New Market," edited by Richard R. Duncan, in *Civil War Times Illustrated* 19 (January 1981): 44; Davis, *New Market*, 99; Sigel, "Sigel in the Valley," in *B&L*, 4:489.

12. Strother, *Virginia Yankee*, 226; Davis, *New Market*, 129, 131; Neil, "Leg That Broke Loose," 44.

13. Engle, *Yankee Dutchman*, 192; Neil, "Leg That Broke Loose," 44.

14. Neil, "Leg That Broke Loose," 44; Strother, *Virginia Yankee*, 229–30; Halleck to Grant, May 17, 1864, in *OR*, vol. 36, pt. 2, p. 840.

15. David Hunter to Stanton, May 23, 1864, in *OR*, vol. 37, pt. 1, p. 524; Engle, *Yankee Dutchman*, 203–6.

16. Edward Bates, July 3, 1864, in *The Diary of Edward Bates*, edited by Howard K. Beale (New York: American Historical Association, 1933), 382; Welles, July 6, 1864, in *Diary*, 2:68 (see chap. 5, n. 7); Grant to Halleck, July 7, 1864, in *OR*, vol. 37, pt. 2, p. 98. The emphasis is in the original.

17. West, *Lincoln's Scapegoat General*, 219 (see chap. 2, n. 32); Edward G. Longacre, *Army of Amateurs: General Benjamin F. Butler and the Army of the James, 1863–1865* (Mechanicsburg, Pa.: Stackpole Books, 1997), 8.

18. Butler, *Autobiography*, 622 (see chap. 2, n. 33).

19. Grant, *Memoirs*, 2:480; Butler, *Autobiography*, 627; Grant to Butler, April 2, 1864, in *OR*, vol. 33, p. 795; Simpson, *Ulysses S. Grant*, 270–71 (see chap. 4, n. 13).

20. Grant to Butler, April 16, 1864, in *OR*, vol. 33, pp. 885–86; Report of Grant, July 22, 1865, in *OR*, vol. 36, pt. 1, p. 17; Grant, *Memoirs*, 2:479, 490.

21. Butler, *Autobiography*, 629, 631, 638; Longacre, *Army of Amateurs*, 63–64.

22. Grant, *Memoirs*, 2:479–80; Babcock to William F. Smith, April 29, 1864, in *PUG*, 10:365.

23. William F. Smith, *Autobiography of Major General William F. Smith, 1861–1864* (Dayton: Morningside, 1990), 84, 118.

24. Ibid., 84, 118–19; Babcock to Smith, April 29, 1864, in *PUG*, 10:235; William F. Smith, *From Chattanooga to Petersburg under Generals Grant and Butler* (Boston: Houghton Mifflin, 1893), 5; Butler to Quincy Gillmore, May 4, 1864, in *OR*, vol. 36, pt. 2, p. 392; Longacre, *Army of Amateurs*, 64–65.

25. Butler, *Autobiography*, 640–41; William G. Robertson, *Back Door to Richmond: The Bermuda Hundred Campaign, April–June 1864* (Newark: University of Delaware Press, 1987), 69–70.

26. Butler, *Autobiography*, 643; Smith to Butler, May 6, 1864, in *OR*, vol. 36, pt. 2, p. 475; Gillmore to Smith, May 6, 1864, ibid.; Butler to Henry Wilson, May 7, 1864, in *BC*, 4:171.

27. Butler to Stanton, May 7, 1864, in *OR*, vol. 36, pt. 2, p. 517.

28. Butler to Gillmore, May 8, 1864, ibid., 555; Robertson, *Back Door to Richmond*, 108–9, 112–15; Longacre, *Army of Amateurs*, 80–81.

29. Smith and Gillmore to Butler, May 9, 1864, in *OR*, vol. 36, pt. 2, p. 35; Butler to Smith and Gillmore, May 9, 1864, ibid.; Smith, *Autobiography*, 86; Butler to Sarah Butler, March 11, 1864, in *BC*, 4:192.

30. Butler, *Autobiography*, 651; Butler to Smith, May 11, 1864, in *OR*, vol. 36, pt. 2, p. 113.

31. Butler, *Autobiography*, 651; Robertson, *Back Door to Richmond*, 147; Report of Smith, June 8, 1864, in *OR*, vol. 36, pt. 2, pp. 113–15.

32. Butler, *Autobiography*, 656, 664.

33. Report of Smith, June 8, 1864, in *OR*, vol. 36, pt. 2, p. 116; Butler to Gillmore, May 16, 1864, in *BC*, 4:224; Robertson, *Back Door to Richmond*, 204; Longacre, *Army of Amateurs*, 97–99.

34. John A. Porter, *76th Regiment Pennsylvania Volunteer Infantry, Key Stone Zouves: Personal Recollections, 1861–1865, of Sergeant John A. Porter, Company B*, edited by James A. Chisman (Wilmington, N.C.: Broadfoot Publishing, 1988), 50, 53; James Horrocks, *My Dear Parents: The Civil War Seen by an English Union Soldier*, edited by A. S. Lewis (New York: Harcourt Brace Jovanovich, 1982), 85. The emphasis is in the original.

35. Krumwiede, *"Old Waddy's Coming,"* 86 (see chap. 3, n. 9); Charles E. Davis Jr.,

Three Years in the Army: The Story of the Thirteenth Massachusetts Volunteers from July 16, 1861, to August 1, 1864 (Boston: Esten and Lauriat, 1894), 329.

36. Gordon C. Rhea, *The Battle of the Wilderness, May 5–6, 1864* (Baton Rouge: Louisiana State University Press, 1994), 104–5, 109.

37. Fred T. Locke to Wadsworth, May 5, 1864, in *OR*, vol. 36, pt. 2, p. 420; Report of Capt. Frank H. Cowdrey, November 3, 1864, in *OR*, vol. 36, pt. 1, pp. 614–15; Rhea, *Battle of the Wilderness*, 157, 231.

38. Gouvenear Warren to Wadsworth, May 6, 1864, in *OR*, vol. 36, pt. 2, p. 458; May 6, 1864, Journal of Gouvenear Warren, in *OR*, vol. 36, pt. 1, p. 540; Rhea, *Battle of the Wilderness*, 292, 307–8; Krumwiede, *"Old Waddy's Coming,"* 103.

39. Report of Cowdrey, November 3, 1864, in *OR*, vol. 36, pt. 1, p. 615; Report of Brig. Gen. Alexander S. Webb, May 3–12, 1864, ibid., 437–38; C. A. Stevens, *Berdan's United States Sharpshooters in the Army of the Potomac, 1861–1865* (Dayton: Morningside Bookshop, 1972), 316, 404.

40. Hay, May 14, 1864, in *Inside Lincoln's White House*, edited by Burlingame and Turner, 196 (see chap. 2, n. 50); Grant quoted in Anna Atwood, "Our Heroes," 15, JWFP; *New York Times*, May 11, 1864; Public Meeting of the Citizens of Geneseo, May 10, 1864, JWFP.

41. Report of Grant, July 22, 1865, in *OR*, vol. 36, pt. 1, pp. 20–21; Butler, *Autobiography*, 671; Sarah Butler to Butler, May 29, 1864, in *BC*, 4:285.

42. Butler, *Autobiography*, 672, 677.

43. Butler to Sarah Butler, June 9, 11, 1864, in *BC*, 4:328, 337.

44. Longacre, *Army of Amateurs*, 155.

45. Nolan, *Benjamin Franklin Butler*, 289 (see chap. 2, n. 33); Hay, June 21, 1864, in *Inside Lincoln's White House*, edited by Burlingame and Turner, 209–10; Longacre, *Army of Amateurs*, 160.

46. Butler to Smith, June 21, 1864, in *BC*, 4:426; Smith to Butler, June 21, 1864, ibid., 4:427; Butler to Smith, June 21, 1864, ibid.; Cyrus B. Comstock, July 2, 1864, in *The Diary of Cyrus B. Comstock*, edited by Merlin E. Sumner (Dayton: Morningside, 1987), 278.

47. Hay, June 21, 1864, in *Inside Lincoln's White House*, edited by Burlingame and Turner, 209–10; July 23, 1864, F. V. A. de Chanal, "A Frenchman with Meade," edited by Lee B. Kennett, *Civil War Times Illustrated* 10 (January 1972): 42; Butler to Sarah Butler, June 22, 1864, in *BC*, 4:435. The emphasis in both documents is in the originals.

48. Dana to Stanton, July 1, 1864, in *OR*, vol. 40, pt. 1, p. 28; Grant to Halleck, July 1, 6, 1864, in *PUG*, 11:155, 176; Bruce Catton, *Grant Takes Command* (Boston: Little, Brown, 1968), 327–28.

49. Grant to Halleck, July 10, 1864, in *PUG*, 11:205–6; Longacre, *Army of Amateurs*, 178–80; Catton, *Grant Takes Command*, 326–35; Comstock, July 17, 1864, in *Diary*, 282.

50. Theodore Lyman, July 20, 1864, in *Meade's Headquarters, 1863–1865: Letters of Colonel Theodore Lyman from the Wilderness to Appomattox*, edited by George R. Agassiz

(Boston: Atlantic Monthly Press, 1922), 192–93; Smith to Solomon Foote, July 30, 1864, quoted in Smith, *From Chattanooga to Petersburg*, 174–75; Simpson, *Ulysses S. Grant*, 349, 358.

51. Lincoln quoted in J. W. Shaffer to Butler, July 27, 1864, in *BC*, 4:548.

52. Grant to Butler, December 6, 1864, in *OR*, vol. 42, pt. 1, pp. 971–72; Jno. Turner to Weitzel, December 6, 1864, ibid., 972–73.

53. Butler, *Autobiography*, 775; Porter, *Incidents and Anecdotes*, 269 (see chap. 5, n. 21); Grant to Sherman, December 3, 1864, in *PUG*, 13:56; Testimony, February 11, 1865, ibid., 13:401.

54. Butler, *Autobiography*, 783; Testimony, February 11, 1865, in *PUG*, 13:402; Porter, *Incidents and Anecdotes*, 262, 367; Rod Gragg, *Confederate Goliath: The Battle of Fort Fisher* (1991; reprint, New York: HarperPerennial, 1992), 43; Edward Wightman to Bro, December 11, 1864, Edward K. Wightman, *From Antietam to Fort Fisher: The Civil War Letters of Edward King Wightman, 1862–1865*, edited by Edward G. Longacre (Cranbury, N.J.: Associated University Press, 1985), 219.

55. Report of Butler, January 3, 1865, in *OR*, vol. 42, pt. 1, pp. 966–67; Longacre, *Army of Amateurs*, 253.

56. Report of Weitzel, December 31, 1864, in *OR*, vol. 42, pt. 1, p. 986; Gragg, *Confederate Goliath*, 88–89.

57. Grant to Lincoln, December 28, 1864, in *PUG*, 13:177–78; Wightman to Bro, December 28, 1864, Wightman, *From Antietam to Fort Fisher*, 226; Gragg, *Confederate Goliath*, 97; Longacre, *Army of Amateurs*, 257; Grant to Stanton, January 4, 1865, in *PUG*, 13:223.

58. Grant to Stanton, February 23, 1864, PES, Microfilm Reel #8.

Chapter 9: Quasi-Civil Support

1. Lincoln to John J. Astor, November 9, 1863, in CW, 7:5.

2. Peter Maslowski, *Treason Must Be Made Odious: Military Occupation and Wartime Reconstruction in Nashville, Tennessee, 1862–65* (Millwood, N.Y.: KTO Press, 1978), 26; Joseph G. Dawson, *Army Generals and Reconstruction: Louisiana, 1862–1877* (Baton Rouge: Louisiana State University Press, 1982), 2; John W. Chambers, ed., *The Oxford Companion to American Military History* (New York: Oxford University Press, 1999), 125, 421.

3. Schenck to Sally Schenck, June 25, 1861, RSP.

4. Butler, *Autobiography*, 386 (see chap. 2, n. 33); Halleck's views in Frank Freidel, "General Orders 100 and Military Government," *Mississippi Valley Historical Review* 32 (March 1946): 553.

5. Sherman to H. W. Hill, September 7, 1863, in *SCW*, 538; Robert J. Futrell, "Federal Military Government in the South, 1861–1865," *Military Affairs* 15 (Winter 1951): 181.

6. Futrell, "Federal Military Government," 186; Francis Kenrick to Lincoln, May 20, 1862, PAL; Butler to Lincoln, March 9, 1864, ibid.

7. Scott to Banks, June 24, 1861, in *OR*, ser. 2, vol. 1, p. 621; Proclamation, June 27, 1861, in *OR*, vol. 2, p. 141; Banks to Seward, July 9, 1861, PAL.

8. Cameron to Dix, September 11, 1861, Dix Papers, BLCU; McClellan to Dix, September 18, 1861, in *OR*, ser. 2, vol. 2, p. 71; Dix to Seward, November 26, 1861, ibid., 152; Dix to Silas Stilwell, November 6, 1861, Dix Papers, BLCU.

9. McClellan to Banks, September 12, 1861, in George B. McClellan, *The Civil War Papers of George B. McClellan*, edited by Stephen W. Sears (New York: Ticknor and Fields, 1989), 99; Banks to R. B. Marcy, September 20, 1861, in *OR*, vol. 5, p. 195; Dix to Cameron, September 13, 1861, PAL; Dix to Stilwell, November 6, 1861, Dix Papers, BLCU.

10. W. Veirs Bowie, William Brewer, and Isaac Young to Banks, September 23, 1861, Banks Papers, WPL; Harrington, *Fighting Politician*, 60 (see chap. 3, n. 8); Dix quoted in Charles B. Clark, *Politics in Maryland during the Civil War* (Chestertown, Md.: n.p., 1952), 76.

11. Butler, *Autobiography*, 437–38; General Orders No. 50, October 12, 1863, RSP; Therry, "General Schenck," 272 (see chap. 2, n. 17); Hurlbut to Loomis, August 1, 1861, PAL; J. T. K. Hayward to Frémont, August 10, 1861, in *OR*, ser. 2, vol. 1, p. 204.

12. Butler to O. C. Gardner, June 10, 1862, in *BC*, 1:582; General Orders No. 28, May 15, 1862, ibid., 1:490; Butler, *Autobiography*, 419.

13. Mark Neely Jr., *The Fate of Liberty: Abraham Lincoln and Civil Liberties* (New York: Oxford University Press, 1991), 28.

14. Dix, *Memoirs*, 2:31 (see chap. 2, n. 9); Dix to Montgomery Blair, August 22, 1861, BFP, Microfilm Reel #21; Dix to McClellan, August 16, 1861, in *OR*, vol. 5, p. 563; Arrests for Disloyalty, in *OR*, ser. 2, vol. 2, p. 779.

15. Dix, *Memoirs*, 2:97; Dix to Stanton, May 18, 1864, in *OR*, ser. 3, vol. 4, p. 389; Lincoln to Dix, May 18, 1864, ibid., 388; Stanton to Dix, May 18, 1864, ibid., 390; Neely, *Fate of Liberty*, 105; Ernest A. McKay, *The Civil War and New York City* (Syracuse: Syracuse University Press, 1990), 248–49.

16. Welles, July 5, 1864, in *Diary*, 2:67 (see chap. 5, n. 7); Martin Lichterman, "John Adams Dix: 1798–1879" (Ph.D. diss., Columbia University, 1952), 583–86.

17. Butler, *Autobiography*, 381, 377; Special Orders No. 37 and 39, May 13, 1862, in *BC*, 1:476; Chester G. Hearn, *When the Devil Came Down to Dixie: Ben Butler in New Orleans* (Baton Rouge: Louisiana State University Press, 1997), 100.

18. Banks to the Editors of the *New Orleans Picayune*, March 21, 1864, Banks Papers, LC; Banks to James Bowen, May 24, 1864, ibid.; Banks to Bowen, May 25, 1864, ibid.; Harrington, *Fighting Politician*, 96; Banks to C. A. Christensen, August 12, 1864, Banks Papers, LC.

19. James Darr to Schenck, May 25, 1863, RSP; James Hikin to Schenck, June 22, 1863, ibid.; Therry, "General Schenck," 278–79; Arnold Shankman, "Freedom of the Press during the Civil War: The Case of Albert D. Boileau," *Pennsylvania History* 42, no. 4 (1975): 307, 309–10, 313; Neely, *Fate of Liberty*, 132.

20. Stanton to Wadsworth, March 17, 1862, in *OR*, ser. 2, vol. 2, p. 269; *New York World*, October 2, 1862; Neely, *Fate of Liberty*, 33; Engle, *Yankee Dutchman*, 176 (see chap. 2, n. 47); Lash, "Stephen Hurlbut," 175–76 (see chap. 2, n. 20).

21. Futrell, "Federal Military Government," 187.

22. Mark Grimsley, *The Hard Hand of War: Union Military Policy toward Southern Civilians, 1861–1865* (New York: Cambridge University Press, 1995), 2–3.

23. Order, May 26, 1861, in *BC*, 1:110; Hurlbut to Colonel Smith, July 14, 1861, in *OR*, ser. 2, vol. 1, p. 185; General Orders No. 23, October 20, 1861, in *OR*, vol. 3, p. 540; Dix to Henry Lockwood, November 11, 1861, in *OR*, vol. 5, p. 425; McPherson, *Ordeal by Fire*, 266 (see chap. 1, n. 3).

24. General Orders No. 15, May 1, 1862, in *OR*, vol. 6, p. 717; West, *Lincoln's Scapegoat General*, 155 (see chap. 2, n. 32); Peggy Robbins, "Union Soldiers and Confederate Civilians Mingled Together . . . When the Yankees Held Memphis," *Civil War Times Illustrated* 16 (January 1978): 34.

25. Denver to Louise Denver, December 27, 1862, Kansas Collection, University of Kansas Libraries, Lawrence; Edward M. Cook, *Justified by Honor: Highlights in the Life of General James William Denver* (Falls Church, Va.: Higher Education Publications, 1988), 97–98.

26. Dix to Seward, April 15, 1863, WSP, Microfilm Reel #77; Dix to Catherine Dix, July 3, 1863, Dix Papers, BLCU.

27. William Rice to Edward Bates, March 7, 1863, RSP; Therry, "General Schenck," 272–74; General Orders No. 10, January 16, 1864, in *BC*, 3:298.

28. Butler, *Autobiography*, 378; West, *Lincoln's Scapegoat General*, 146.

29. Futrell, "Federal Military Government," 195; Harrington, *Fighting Politician*, 101–2; Dawson, *Army Generals and Reconstruction*, 14.

30. West, *Lincoln's Scapegoat General*, 264–65; Stanton to Butler, January 18, 1864, in *CW*, 7:135; Butler to Lincoln, February 23, 1864, in *BC*, 3:450–59.

31. Special Orders No. 50, June 22, 1864, in *BC*, 4:587; Welles, July 19, 1864, in *Diary*, 2:81; cabinet members and Lincoln quoted in Bates, July 20, 1864, in *Diary*, 386–87 (see chap. 8, n. 16).

32. Butler to Lincoln, August 1, 1864, in *BC*, 4:582–83; West, *Lincoln's Scapegoat General*, 272.

33. Dix to Halleck, January 3, 1863, in *OR*, vol. 18, p. 503.

34. To the People of Baltimore, July 10, 1861, Banks Papers, WPL; Dix to Police Commissioners, City of Baltimore, March 17, 1862, in *OR*, vol. 5, p. 765; Dix to Stanton, May 25, 1862, in *OR*, vol. 12, pt. 3, p. 231.

35. Joy J. Jackson, "Keeping Law and Order in New Orleans under General Butler, 1862," *Louisiana History* 34 (Winter 1993): 55, 57; West, *Lincoln's Scapegoat General*, 147; Hearn, *When the Devil Came Down to Dixie*, 93, 133; Thomas W. Helis, "Of Generals and Jurists: The Judicial System of New Orleans under Union Occupation, May 1862–April 1865," *Louisiana History* 29 (Spring 1988): 146–47, 151.

36. Hearn, *When the Devil Came Down to Dixie*, 154, 157–59.

37. Ibid., 96, 179; General Order No. 25, May 9, 1862, in *BC*, 1:458; Butler to George Shepley, June 4, 1862, ibid., 1:554; General Orders No. 55, August 4, 1862, ibid., 2:152–53; Special Order No. 166, July 2, 1862, ibid., 2:162; General Orders No. 30, May 19, 1862, ibid., 1:505.

38. Harrington, *Fighting Politician*, 99; General Orders No. 15, February 8, 1863, in *OR*, vol. 15, p. 1099; General Orders No. 113, August 22, 1864, Banks Papers, LC; General Order, December 28, 1863, ibid.; Hurlbut to C. T. Christensen, January 3, 1865, in *OR*, vol. 48, pt. 1, p. 402; Hurlbut to Christensen, March 16, 1865, ibid., 1191.

39. Butler to Stanton, June 17, 1862, in *BC*, 1:595; Butler to Seward, May 8, 1862, ibid., 1:450.

40. Manfred C. Vernon, "General Benjamin Butler and the Dutch Consul," *Civil War History* 5 (September 1959): 266; West, *Lincoln's Scapegoat General*, 195; Butler, *Autobiography*, 426.

41. McPherson, *Ordeal by Fire*, 353, 357–58; McKay, *Civil War and New York City*, 196–98.

42. Eugene C. Murdock, "Horatio Seymour and the 1863 Draft," *Civil War History* 11 (June 1965): 123, 131; Lichterman, "John Adams Dix," 557; Dix to James B. Fry, July 24, 1863, in *OR*, ser. 3, vol. 3, p. 566.

43. Dix to Stanton, July 25, 1863, PES, Microfilm Reel #5; Dix, *Memoirs*, 2:76; McKay, *Civil War and New York City*, 212; Dix to Seymour, July 30, August 8, 1863, in *OR*, ser. 3, vol. 3, p. 592, 652–54; Dix to James Fry, August 10, 1863, ibid., 665.

44. Dix to Fry, August 12, 1863, ibid., 671; Dix to Stanton, August 12, 1863, PAL; Dix, *Memoirs*, 2:85; Stanton to Dix, August 15, 1863, ibid., 2:86–87.

45. Dix to Seymour, August 18, 1863, Dix, *Memoirs*, 2:83; Dix to Halleck, August 19, 1863, in *OR*, ser. 3, vol. 3, p. 693.

46. McPherson, *Ordeal by Fire*, 381.

47. Ibid., 384.

48. Ludwell H. Johnson, "Blockade or Trade Monopoly? John A. Dix and the Union Occupation of Norfolk," *Virginia Magazine of History and Biography* 93 (January 1985): 56, 62, 65; Dix to Stanton, September 4, 1862, in *OR*, vol. 18, pp. 382–83.

49. Johnson, "Blockade or Trade Monopoly?" 63; Samuel Lee to Dix, September 18, 1862, in *OR*, vol. 18, p. 394; Lichterman, "John Dix," 510.

50. Welles, October 24, 1862, in *Diary*, 1:177–78; John Tucker to Dix, November 12, 1862, in *OR*, vol. 18, p. 452.

51. Dix to Lee, January 20, 1863, ibid., 523; Welles, January 23, 1863, in *Diary*, 1:226–27; Johnson, "Blockade or Trade Monopoly?" 76.

52. Welles, October 10, 18, 1862, in *Diary*, 1:166, 177; Lichterman, "John Adams Dix," 506–7.

53. West, *Lincoln's Scapegoat General*, 187; McPherson, *Ordeal by Fire*, 382; Dennison to Chase, October 16, 1862, in *BC*, 2:378; Butler to Chase, October 22, 1862, ibid., 2:395.

54. Andrew quoted in Ludwell H. Johnson, "The Butler Expedition of 1861–1862: The Profitable Side of War," *Civil War History* 11 (September 1965): 231–33, 236; Butler, *Autobiography*, 384–85; Hearn, *When the Devil Came Down to Dixie*, 181.

55. Hearn, *When the Devil Came Down to Dixie*, 183, 186; Dennison to Chase, October 10, 1862, in *BC*, 2:356.

56. Hearn, *When the Devil Came Down to Dixie*, 196, 223.

57. Banks to Mary Banks, January 15, 1863, Banks Papers, LC; Banks to William Emory, July 22, 1863, ibid.; Banks to Lincoln, December 24, 1862, PAL.

58. General Orders No. 8, January 1, 1863, in *OR*, vol. 15, p. 644; Banks to Halleck, May 5, 1863, ibid., 310; Harrington, *Fighting Politician*, 135–36; Hollandsworth, *Pretense of Glory*, 160 (see chap. 2, n. 11).

59. Hollandsworth, *Pretense of Glory*, 160; Dennison to Chase, May 9, 1863, in *Chase Papers*, edited by Niven, 4:24–25 (see chap. 2, n. 16).

60. Banks to Lincoln, February 2, 1864, in *OR*, ser. 3, vol. 4, pp. 68–70; Harrington, *Fighting Politician*, 139.

61. Joseph H. Parks, "A Confederate Trade Center under Federal Occupation: Memphis, 1862 to 1865," *Journal of Southern History* 7 (August 1941): 292–93, 294; Rawlins to Hurlbut, January 2, 17, 1863, in *OR*, vol. 17, pt. 2, p. 522; Lash, "Stephen Hurlbut," 170.

62. Lash, "Stephen Hurlbut," 182; Hurlbut to Rawlins, March 7, 1863, in *OR*, vol. 24, pt. 3, p. 92.

63. Hurlbut to Lincoln, July 10, 1863, PAL; Lincoln to Hurlbut, July 31, 1863, in *CW*, 6:358; Halleck to Hurlbut, July 30, 1863, in *OR*, vol. 24, pt. 3, p. 564; Jeffrey N. Lash, "The Federal Tyrant at Memphis: General Stephen A. Hurlbut and the Union Occupation of West Tennessee, 1862–64," *Tennessee Historical Quarterly* 48 (Spring 1989): 22; Lash, "Stephen Hurlbut," 195–97.

64. Hurlbut to Lincoln, September 26, 1864, PAL; Hurlbut to Benton, October 26, 1864, in *OR*, vol. 41, pt. 4, p. 246.

65. Lash, "Stephen Hurlbut," 230–32, 213, 222.

66. Ibid., 233, 239–41, 247.

67. Dix to McClellan, October 25, 1861, in *OR*, vol. 5, pp. 628–29; Proclamation, November 1, 1861, in *OR*, ser. 2, vol. 1, pp. 609–10; Dix to H. E. Paine, November 4, 1861, in *OR*, vol. 5, p. 641; Clark, *Politics in Maryland*, 74–76, 80.

68. General Orders No. 53, October 27, 1863, RSP; Instructions, October 31, 1863, ibid.

69. Augustus Bradford to Lincoln, October 31, 1863, in *CW*, 6:556; Lincoln to Bradford, November 2, 1863, ibid., 6:556–57.

70. Proclamation by the Governor, November 2, 1863, RSP; Schenck to Lincoln, November 2, 1863, ibid.; Schenck to American Telegraph Company and Editors of the *Baltimore American*, November 2, 1863, in *OR*, ser. 3, vol. 3, p. 983; "To the Loyal People of Maryland," November 3, 1863, RSP.

71. Therry, "General Schenck," 299; Clark, *Politics in Maryland*, 111.

72. Dix to Lincoln, October 28, 1862, PAL; Proclamation, December 8, 1862, ibid.; Dix to Lincoln, December 31, 1862, ibid.

73. Donald, *Lincoln*, 485 (see chap. 2, n. 45); Hearn, *When the Devil Came Down to Dixie*, 216–17.

74. Hollandsworth, *Pretense of Glory*, 164–65; Lincoln to Banks, August 5, 1863, in *CW*, 6:364–65.

75. Joseph G. Tregle Jr., "Thomas J. Durant, Utopian Socialism, and the Failure of

Presidential Reconstruction in Louisiana," *Journal of Southern History* 45 (November 1979): 504–5, 507–8.

76. Lincoln to Banks, November 5, 1863, in *CW*, 7:1; Banks to Lincoln, December 6, 1863, ibid., 90–91; Lincoln to Banks, December 24, 1863, ibid., 89–90.

77. Donald, *Lincoln*, 471–72, 487–88.

78. Banks to Lincoln, December 30, 1863, January 11, 1864, PAL; To the People of Louisiana, January 11, 1863, in *OR*, ser. 3, vol. 4, pp. 22–23.

79. Banks to Lincoln, January 22, 1864, PAL; Thomas Durant to Chase, January 16, 1864, in *Chase Papers*, edited by Niven, 4:258; Benjamin Flanders to Chase, January 9, February 21, 1864, ibid., 4:248; Banks to Lincoln, February 12, 1864, PAL.

80. Banks to Lincoln, February 25, 1864, PAL; Hollandsworth, *Pretense of Glory*, 171, 208; Harrington, *Fighting Politician*, 148; Banks to Lincoln, July 25, 1864, Banks Papers, LC.

81. Banks to A. P. Dostie, August 23, 1864, ibid.; Harrington, *Fighting Politician*, 149; Banks to Lincoln, September 6, 1864, PAL.

82. Donald, *Lincoln*, 489; Hollandsworth, *Pretense of Glory*, 214; Harrington, *Politician in Uniform*, 165.

83. McPherson, *Ordeal by Fire*, 346.

Chapter 10: Slavery, Freedom, and Black Soldiers

1. Lincoln quoted in Donald, *Lincoln*, 342 (see chap. 2, n. 45).

2. Butler to Scott, May 25, 1861, in *OR*, vol. 2, p. 650; Butler, *Autobiography*, 257 (see chap. 2, n. 33).

3. Butler to Scott, May 27, 1861, in *BC*, 1:113.

4. Lincoln quoted in Montgomery Blair to Butler, May 29, 1861, ibid., 1:116; Cameron to Butler, May 30, 1861, ibid., 1:119; Stephen B. Oates, *With Malice toward None: The Life of Abraham Lincoln* (New York: Harper and Row, 1977), 239–40; Louis S. Gerteis, *From Contraband to Freedman: Federal Policy toward Southern Blacks* (Westport, Conn.: Greenwood Press, 1973), 16.

5. Dix to Cameron, August 8, 1861, in *OR*, ser. 2, vol. 1, p. 763; Dix to McClellan, August 25, 1861, ibid., 766.

6. Dix to Augustus Morse, October 14, 1861, ibid., 773; Dix, *Memoirs*, 2:40 (see chap. 2, n. 9); McClellan's view was expressed in Stanton to Dix, August 14, 1861, Dix Papers, BLCU; Remarks on Fugitive Slaves in Congress, December 11, 1861, in Thaddeus Stevens, *The Selected Papers of Thaddeus Stevens*, edited by Beverly W. Palmer, 2 vols. (Pittsburgh: University of Pittsburgh Press, 1997), 1:231; McPherson, *Battle Cry of Freedom*, 498 (see chap. 1, n. 3).

7. Wadsworth to Horace Greeley, September 14, 1862, JWFP; Wadsworth Testimony before the American Freedmen's Inquiry Commission, January 1864, in *Freedom: A Documentary History of Emancipation, 1861–1867*, edited by Ira Berlin (New York: Cambridge University Press, 1990), ser. 1, vol. 3, p. 492; Pearson, *James S. Wadsworth*, 139 (see chap. 2, n. 25); Mahood, *General Wadsworth*, 91–92 (see chap. 2, n. 23).

8. Pearson, *James S. Wadsworth*, 137, 139; Henry Wilson et al. to Wadsworth, May 14, 1862, JWFP; Browning, June 11, 1862, in *Diary*, 1:550 (see chap. 2, n. 36).

9. Sickles to Henry Wikoff, January 30, 1862, Daniel Sickles Papers, LC, Microfilm Reel #1; John Toler to J. L. Palmer, March 27, 1862, in *OR*, ser. 2, vol. 1, p. 813; Hooker to Brigade and Regimental Commanders, March 26, 1862, ibid., 813–14.

10. McClernand to Colonel Marsh, September 30, 1861, JMP.

11. McClernand to Grant, February 18, 1862, ibid.; Gerteis, *From Contraband to Freedman*, 22; McClernand to Grant, March 29, 1862, JMP; Special Order No. 217, February 12, 1863, ibid.; McClernand to Grant, April 1, 1863, ibid.; Hurlbut to Rawlins, February 25, 1863, in *OR*, vol. 24, pt. 3, p. 68.

12. John A. Logan, *Speech of Major-General John A. Logan on Return to Illinois after Capture of Vicksburg* (Cincinnati: Caleb Clark, Printer, 1863), 10.

13. Frémont Proclamation, August 30, 1861, in *OR*, vol. 3, pp. 466–67.

14. Nevins, *Frémont*, 500–501 (see chap. 2, n. 16); Vernon L. Volpe, "The Frémonts and Emancipation in Missouri," *Historian* 56 (Winter 1994): 344–45.

15. *Missouri Democrat* quoted in ibid., 347; Francis Blair, Sr. to John Bigelow, October 26, 1861, in *Retrospections of an Active Life*, by John Bigelow, 5 vols. (New York: Baker and Taylor, 1909–1913), 1:376.

16. Lincoln to Frémont, September 2, 1861, in *CW*, 4:506; Lincoln to Browning, September 22, 1861, ibid., 4:531–32 (emphasis in the original).

17. Frémont to Lincoln, September 8, 1861, in *OR*, vol. 3, p. 477; Lincoln to Frémont, September 11, 1861, in *OR*, ser. 2, vol. 1, p. 768.

18. Dudley T. Cornish, *The Sable Arm: Negro Troops in the Union Army, 1861–1865* (New York: Longmans, Green, 1956), 12–14; Williams, *Lincoln and His Generals*, 36–37 (see chap. 2, n. 4); Oates, *With Malice toward None*, 260–61, 308–9; Donald, *Lincoln*, 316, 363.

19. Donald, *Lincoln*, 362, 364–65.

20. McPherson, *Ordeal by Fire*, 296, 627.

21. Pearson, *James S. Wadsworth*, 160; *New York Times*, October 6, 1862; Hay, May 10, 1861, in *Inside Lincoln's White House*, edited by Burlingame and Turner, 22 (see chap. 2, n. 50).

22. Butler to Edward Pierce, August 15, 1861, in *BC*, 1:216; Jones, *"Black Jack,"* 145–47, 155 (see chap. 2, n. 42); Dix to Francis P. Blair Sr., December 4, 1861, Dix Papers, BLCU; John A. Dix, *Letter from John A. Dix to the War Democracy of Wisconsin* (New York: n.p., 1863), 4–5.

23. Denver to Louise Denver, January 10, 1863, in *Denver*, by Barns, 315 (see chap. 2, n. 37).

24. Louise Denver to Denver, January 6, 1863, Kansas Collection, University of Kansas Libraries, Lawrence; Cook, *Justified by Honor*, 103 (see chap. 9, n. 25).

25. Gerteis, *From Contraband to Freedman*, 66; C. Peter Ripley, *Slaves and Freedmen in Civil War Louisiana* (Baton Rouge: Louisiana State University Press, 1976), 2.

26. Butler to Stanton, May 25, 1862, in *BC*, 1:518; Ripley, *Slaves and Freedmen*, 27.

27. Edward Page to Butler, May 27, 1862, in *BC*, 1:525; Butler to Captain Haggerty, May 27, 1862, ibid., 1:521; Butler to Phelps, May 28, 1862, ibid., 1:524; Butler to Stanton, June 18, 1862, ibid., 614–15.

28. Stanton to Butler, July 3, 1862, ibid., 2:41; Butler to Mrs. Butler, July 25, 1862, ibid., 2:109; Phelps to Butler, July 31, 1862, ibid., 2:126.

29. Butler to Halleck, September 1, 1862, ibid., 2:242–43.

30. Ripley, *Slaves and Freedmen*, 36–38.

31. Ibid., 38; Gerteis, *From Contraband to Freedman*, 72.

32. Lincoln to Butler, November 6, 1862, in *CW*, 5:487; Butler to Lincoln, November 28, 1862, in *BC*, 2:447.

33. General Orders No. 116, December 24, 1862, Banks Papers, LC.

34. Banks to William Garrison, January 30, 1865, Banks Papers, ISHL; Gerteis, *From Contraband to Freedman*, 74–75.

35. Harrington, *Fighting Politician*, 105 (see chap. 3, n. 8); Hollandsworth, *Pretense of Glory*, 92–93 (see chap. 2, n. 11); Gerteis, *From Contraband to Freedman*, 75; Ripley, *Slaves and Freedmen*, 48.

36. Banks to Mary Banks, January 30, February 24, 1863, Banks Papers, LC; Hollandsworth, *Pretense of Glory*, 93–94; Dennison to Chase, March 31, 1863, in *Chase Papers*, edited by Niven, 3:416 (see chap. 2, n. 16); Phillips quoted in Harrington, *Fighting Politician*, 106.

37. E. D. Townsend to Wadsworth, October 9, 1863, in *OR*, ser. 3, vol. 3, p. 872; J. W. Wadsworth to Nelie Wadsworth, October 29, 1863, JWFP.

38. Report of Wadsworth, December 16, 1863, in *Freedom*, edited by Berlin, ser. 1, vol. 3, pp. 757–62.

39. Wadsworth's Testimony, January 1864, ibid., 492, 494–95, 497–99, 508.

40. Gerteis, *From Contraband to Freedman*, 88.

41. Donald, *Lincoln*, 430; Cornish, *Sable Arm*, 46–47, 95; Oates, *With Malice toward None*, 331.

42. Butler to Stanton, May 25, 1862, in *BC*, 1:519; Howard C. Westwood, "Benjamin Butler's Enlistment of Black Troops in New Orleans in 1862," *Louisiana History* 26 (Winter 1985): 13–14; Glatthaar, *Forged in Battle*, 8 (see chap. 6, n. 21); Cornish, *Sable Arm*, 57–58; Noah Andre Trudeau, *Like Men of War: Black Troops in the Civil War, 1862–1865* (1998; reprint, Edison, N.J.: Castle Books, 2002), 24.

43. Phelps to R. S. Davis, June 16, 1862, in *OR*, vol. 15, p. 489; Phelps to Davis, July 30, 1862, in *BC*, 2:125; Butler to Phelps, August 2, 1862, ibid., 2:143; Westwood, "Butler's Enlistment," 11.

44. Butler to Mrs. Butler, August 12, 1862, in *BC*, 2:131; Butler to Stanton, August 14, 1862, ibid., 2:192; Butler to Halleck, August 27, 1862, in *OR*, vol. 15, pp. 555–57; Cornish, *Sable Arm*, 65–66; Trudeau, *Like Men of War*, 26.

45. Butler to Halleck, August 27, 1862, in *OR*, vol. 15, p. 557; Westwood, "Butler's Enlistment," 15, 17, 19; Trudeau, *Like Men of War*, 27–29.

46. Lincoln quoted in Donald, *Lincoln*, 430–31; Oates, *With Malice toward None*, 331 (emphasis in the original).

47. Parrish, *Frank Blair: Lincoln's Conservative*, 165 (see chap. 2, n. 26); Logan quoted in Jones, *"Black Jack,"* 155.

48. Dix to Charles Frickman, January 18, 1862, Dix Papers, SU; Dix to Lincoln, January 15, 1863, PAL; Lichterman, "John Adams Dix," 514–15 (see chap. 9, n. 16).

49. General Order No. 46, December 5, 1863, in *BC*, 3:183–87; West, *Lincoln's Scapegoat General*, 219 (see chap. 2, n. 32).

50. Banks to L. Thomas, February 12, 1863, in *OR*, ser. 3, vol. 3, p. 46; Dennison to Chase, March 7, 1863, in *Chase Papers*, edited by Niven, 3:395; Harrington, *Fighting Politician*, 110; Trudeau, *Like Men of War*, 29.

51. Lincoln to Banks, March 29, 1863, in *CW*, 6:154; Banks to Mary Banks, May 30, 1863, Banks Papers, LC; Hollandsworth, *Pretense of Glory*, 152–53; Cornish, *Sable Arm*, 126–28; Trudeau, *Like Men of War*, 33–34.

52. Banks to Lincoln, August 17, 1863, PAL; Banks to Lincoln, August 16, 1863, in *OR*, vol. 26, pt. 1, p. 689; Trudeau, *Like Men of War*, 33–34.

53. Banks to Halleck, December 11, 1863, in *OR*, vol. 26, pt. 1, p. 456; General Order No. 108, August 5, 1864, Banks Papers, LC; Glatthaar, *Forged in Battle*, 114; Trudeau, *Like Men of War*, 397–98.

54. Schenck to Lincoln, June 30, 1863, in *OR*, vol. 27, pt. 3, p. 432; Lincoln to Schenck, July 4, 1863, in *CW*, 6:317; C. W. Foster to Schenck, September 2, 1863, in *OR*, ser. 3, vol. 3, p. 761.

55. Lincoln to Schenck, October 21, 1863, in *CW*, 6:530; Lincoln to Schenck, October 22, 1863, ibid., 6:532; Schenck to Lincoln, October 1, 1863, in *OR*, vol. 29, pt. 2, p. 364; Hay, October 22, 1863, in *Inside Lincoln's White House*, edited by Burlingame and Turner, 97.

Chapter 11: Exerting Political Influence

1. Orlando Willcox to Zachariah Chandler, December 1, 1862, Zachariah Chandler Papers, LC, Microfilm Reel #1.

2. John Y. Simon, "From Galena to Appomattox: Grant and Washburne," *Illinois State Historical Society* 58 (Spring 1965): 188; Goss, *War within the Union High Command*, 52 (see chap. 1, n. 4).

3. J. H. Jordan to Banks, July 1, 1861, Banks Papers, WPL.

4. Allen T. Rice, ed., *Reminiscences of Abraham Lincoln by Distinguished Men of His Time* (New York: North American Review, 1888), 141; Lincoln to McClernand, January 8, 1863, in *CW*, 6:48; Schurz, *Reminiscences*, 2:341 (see chap. 2, n. 50).

5. Butler to Lincoln, November 9, 1861, in *BC*, 1:274; Butler to Lincoln, May 17, 1864, ibid., 4:228; McClernand to Lincoln, November 22, December 3, 1861, March 31, June 20, 1862, PAL; Schenck to Lincoln, January 4, 1862, ibid.; Schenck to Stanton, March 4, 1862, RSP; Therry, "General Schenck," 220–22 (see chap. 2, n. 17).

6. Dix to Lincoln, March 13, 1862, PAL; Dix to Pierrepont, June 20, 1862, Dix Papers, SU; Lincoln to McClellan, June 15, 1862, in *CW*, 5:272.

7. Sigel to Lincoln, January 17, 29, March 17 (2), 1863, PAL; Blair to Lincoln, September 9, 1863, ibid.; Sickles to Lincoln, January 11, October 13, 1864, ibid.

8. Wadsworth to Lincoln, March 12, 1863, ibid.; Schenck to Lincoln, June 13, 28, 1863, ibid.; Dix to Lincoln, November 23, 1863, October 4, 1864, ibid.; Shields to Lincoln, January 20, 1862, ibid.

9. Sickles to Lincoln, August 15, 1863, ibid.; Lincoln to Sickles, August 22, 1863, in *CW*, 6:402; Swanberg, *Sickles the Incredible*, 230–31 (see chap. 2, n. 41).

10. Schurz, *Reminiscences*, 2:341; Schurz to Lincoln, June 16, 1862, PAL.

11. Schurz to Lincoln, November 8, 1862, ibid.; Schurz to Lincoln, February 14, 1863, Carl Schurz Papers, LC, Microfilm Reel #2; Schurz to Lincoln, March 11, 1863, PAL; Schurz to Lincoln, February 29, 1864, ibid.; Nicolay to Lincoln, March 30, 1864, ibid.

12. Schurz to Washburne, January 18, 1865, Elihu Washburne Papers, LC (emphasis in the original).

13. Dix to Seward, October 28, November 2, 1861, WSP, Microfilm Reel #66; Seward to Cameron, January 14, 1862, Shields Papers, ISHL; Shields to McClellan, January 10, 1862, ibid.

14. Blair to Butler, May 29, 1861, in *BC*, 1:116; Blair to Cameron, June 22, 1861, ibid., 1:155; Blair to Butler, June 25, 1861, ibid., 1:159–60; Blair to Butler, August 20, 1861, ibid., 1:221.

15. John Niven, *Salmon P. Chase: A Biography* (New York: Oxford University Press, 1995), 316–17, 319; Chase to Butler, July 31, 1862, in *Chase Papers*, edited by Niven, 3:233–37 (see chap. 2, n. 16); Chase to Butler, December 14, 1862, in *BC*, 2:541.

16. Chase to Kate Chase, June 29, 1863, in *Chase Papers*, edited by Niven, 4:72; Chase to Butler, October 9, 1863, in *BC*, 3:120.

17. Boutwell to Lincoln, November 20, 1863, PAL; Boutwell to Banks, December 21, 1863, Banks Papers, LC; Hurlbut to Trumbull, May 15, 1864, PLT, Microfilm Reel #15.

18. Lonn, *Foreigners in the Union Army*, 8–11 (see chap. 2, n. 46); Schurz to Charles Sumner, February 13, 1862, Schurz Papers, LC, Microfilm Reel #2; Schurz to Washburne, January 29, 1863, Washburne Papers, LC.

19. Sigel to Sempronius Boyd, December 14, 1863, January 1, 1864, FSP; Schenck to Sigel, March 2, 1864, ibid.; Isaac Arnold to Sigel, March 4, 1864, ibid.; George Lyon to Sigel, March 12, 1864, ibid.

20. L. V. Birny to Benjamin Wade, November 1, 1861, Benjamin Wade Papers, LC, Microfilm Reel #3; Stevens quoted in Nevins, *Frémont*, 547 (see chap. 2, n. 16).

21. Bruce Tap, *Over Lincoln's Shoulder: The Committee on the Conduct of the War* (Lawrence: University Press of Kansas, 1998), 21–24, 85; T. Harry Williams, "Frémont and the Politicians," *Journal of the American Military Foundation* 2 (Winter 1938): 184–85.

22. William Doubleday to Chandler, December 6, 1861, Chandler Papers, LC, Microfilm Reel #1; Chandler to Wife, October 12, 1861, ibid.; Williams, "Frémont and the Politicians," 185; T. Harry Williams, *Lincoln and the Radicals* (1941; Madison: University of Wisconsin Press, 1965), 105.

23. Tap, *Over Lincoln's Shoulder*, 88–91; Jessie Frémont to Frederick Billings, January 21, 1862, in *Letters of Jessie Frémont*, edited by Herr and Spence, 309 (see chap. 3, n. 28).

24. Jessie Frémont to Billings, February 7, 1862, in *Letters of Jessie Frémont*, edited by Herr and Spence, 311; Stanton quoted in Dana, *Recollections of the Civil War*, 6 (see chap. 2, n. 23); Tap, *Over Lincoln's Shoulder*, 93; Williams, *Lincoln and the Radicals*, 109.

25. Earl J. Hess, "Sigel's Resignation: A Study in German-Americanism and the Civil War," *Civil War History* 26 (March 1980): 7; Engle, *Yankee Dutchman*, 90–91 (see chap. 2, n. 47); Halleck to Sigel, January 2, 1862, PAL; Sigel to Halleck, January 10, 1862, ibid.

26. Engle, *Yankee Dutchman*, 93–95, 101–2; L. Ledergerber to Trumbull, January 9, 1862, PLT, Microfilm Reel #12; Hess, "Sigel's Resignation," 9; New York City Citizens to Lincoln, January 16, 1862, PAL.

27. Newspaper quoted in Hess, "Sigel's Resignation," 10; Adam Klipper to Trumbull, January 13, 1862, PLT, Microfilm Reel #12; P. A. Ladue to Blair, January 6, 1862, PAL; Engle, *Yankee Dutchman*, 95.

28. Koerner, *Memoirs*, 197, 202 (see chap. 2, n. 15); Koerner to Lincoln, January 26, 1862, PAL.

29. Thaddeus Stevens to Lincoln, February 19, 1863, in Stevens, *Selected Papers of Thaddeus Stevens*, 1:370 (see chap. 10, n. 6); George W. Julian, *Political Recollections, 1840 to 1872* (1884; reprint, New York: Negro University Press, 1970), 230 (emphasis in the original).

30. Williams, *Lincoln and the Radicals*, 279; Lincoln to Sumner, June 1, 1863, in *CW*, 6:243; Frémont to Sumner, June 9, 1863, PAL.

31. Lincoln's Reply to a Delegation of Kentuckians, January 2, 1865, in *CW*, 8:195.

32. Dix to unknown, September 17, 1862, Dix Papers, SU.

33. Silbey, *Respectable Minority*, 39–41 (see chap. 2, n. 29); Douglas quoted in Christopher Dell, *Lincoln and the War Democrats: The Grand Erosion of Conservative Tradition* (Cranbury, N.J.: Associated University Presses, 1975), 59.

34. McClernand quoted in Silbey, *Respectable Minority*, 56; Dell, *Lincoln and the War Democrats*, 120; Dix to Pierrepont, August 10, 1862, Dix Papers, SU.

35. David E. Long, *The Jewel of Liberty: Abraham Lincoln's Re-Election and the End of Slavery* (Mechanicsburg, Pa.: Stackpole, 1994), 40; Silbey, *Respectable Minority*, 59; Stoddard, *Inside the White House*, 72 (see chap. 2, n. 2).

36. Long, *Jewel of Liberty*, 41, 44; Dell, *Lincoln and the War Democrats*, 161; Silbey, *Respectable Minority*, 100.

37. Williams, *Lincoln and the Radicals*, 6; Long, *Jewel of Liberty*, 21.

38. Williams, *Lincoln and the Radicals*, 5; Long, *Jewel of Liberty*, 22–23; Donald, *Lincoln*, 262, 331–33 (see chap. 2, n. 45).

39. Lichterman, "John Dix," 567; Sidney D. Brummer, *Political History of New York State During the Period of the Civil War* (New York: AMS Press, 1967), 299; Dix, *Letter*

from John A. Dix, 4–5, 6–11 (see chap. 10, n. 22); John A. Dix and Thomas F. Meagher, *The Voice of the War Democracy: Patriotic Letters of Gen. John A. Dix and Gen. Thomas Francis Meagher* (n. p.: 1863), 3.

40. John A. Dix, *The Presidency: Letter of General Dix to the Committee of the Mass Meeting in Philadelphia, October 1864* (n.p., 1864), 4; Dell, *Lincoln and the War Democrats*, 303.

41. Benjamin Butler, *Character and Results of the War: A Thrilling and Eloquent Speech* (New York: William C. Bryant, 1863), 7, 9, 10; Dell, *Lincoln and the War Democrats*, 233.

42. R. F. Stevens to McClernand, July 25, 1863, JMP; *New York Times*, August 14, 1863.

43. Kiper, *McClernand*, 274 (see chap. 2, n. 34); Dell, *Lincoln and the War Democrats*, 252; *New York Times*, December 6, 1863.

44. Arthur C. Cole, *The Era of the Civil War, 1848–1870* (1919; reprint, Urbana: University of Illinois Press, 1987), 327; McClernand quoted in Kiper, *McClernand*, 291.

45. Logan, *Speech of Logan*, 5, 7, 10, 24, 31 (see chap. 10, n. 12).

46. John A. Logan, *Great Union Speech*, August 10, 1863, PJL; *New York Times*, August 9, 1863; Jesse K. Dubois to Stanton, August 10, 1863, PES, Microfilm Reel #15; Hay, August 22, 1863, in *Inside Lincoln's White House*, edited by Burlingame and Turner, 75 (see chap. 2, n. 50).

47. Logan to Sherman, February 18, 1883, in Mary Logan, *Reminiscences of the Civil War and Reconstruction*, edited by George W. Adams (Carbondale: Southern Illinois University Press, 1970), 101; Logan quoted in Jones, *"Black Jack,"* 234–36 (see chap. 2, n. 42); Washburne quoted in ibid., 238.

48. Thomas F. Meagher, *Letters on Our National Struggle* (New York: Loyal Publication Society, 1863), 2, 3.

49. Dix and Meagher, *Voice of the War Democracy*, 3–4; *Irish American* quoted in Athearn, *Thomas Francis Meagher*, 129 (see chap. 4, n. 57).

50. Burton, *Melting Pot Soldiers*, 125 (see chap. 2, n. 45); *New York Times*, October 9, 1864; *Irish American* quoted in Athearn, *Thomas Francis Meagher*, 134.

51. Edward Wallace to Lincoln, September 24, 1863, PAL; Sigel quoted in Engle, *Yankee Dutchman*, 164.

52. Schurz to Lincoln, February 29, 1864, PAL; Lincoln quoted in Schurz, *Reminiscences*, 3:104–5; "Speech of Maj.-Gen. Carl Schurz," September 16, 1864, Schurz Papers, LC.

53. Smith, *Blair Family*, 2:166 (see chap. 2, n. 15); Parrish, *Frank Blair: Lincoln's Conservative*, 179 (see chap. 2, n. 26).

54. Wadsworth to Greeley, September 14, 1862, JWFP; *New York World*, September 24, 1862; *New York Times*, September 29, October 6, November 1, 1862.

55. Brummer, *Political History of New York*, 228–41; *New York World*, October 18, 1863.

56. Brummer, *Political History of New York*, 97, 249; Pearson, *James S. Wadsworth*,

164 (see chap. 2, n. 25); Adam Gurowski, January 24, 1863, *Diary, November 18, 1862 to October 18, 1863* (New York: Carleton, 1864), 102–3; Pierrepont to Wadsworth, November 5, 1862, JWFP.

57. Silbey, *Respectable Minority*, 145; Long, *Jewel of Liberty*, 43–44.

58. Frank L. Klement, *The Limits of Dissent: Clement L. Vallandigham and the Civil War* (Lexington: University Press of Kentucky, 1970), 103–5, 111; n.a., Robert C. Schenck, U.S.A., Major General of Volunteers, 1862, RSP.

59. Parrish, *Frank Blair: Lincoln's Conservative*, 146–48; *New York Times*, October 18, 1862.

60. Parrish, *Frank Blair: Lincoln's Conservative*, 151; Smith, *Blair Family*, 2:213.

61. Martin Ryerson to Lincoln, April 18, 1864, PAL; Alexander K. McClure, *Abraham Lincoln and Men of War-Times: Some Personal Recollections of War and Politics during the Lincoln Administration* (Lincoln: University of Nebraska Press, 1997), 118; Benjamin Butler, "Vice-Presidential Politics in '64," *North American Review* 141 (October 1885): 331–34; Butler, *Autobiography*, 633 (see chap. 2, n. 33); *New York Times*, September 12, 1864; Logan to Mary Logan, June 8, 1864, PJL.

62. Edward Hamilton to Banks, January 20, 1864, Banks Papers, LC; J. Brisbin to Banks, June 17, 1864, ibid.

63. Weed to Bigelow, January 16, 1863, in *Retrospections of an Active Life*, by Bigelow, 1:596 (see chap. 10, n. 15); Horace White to William P. Fessenden, November 7, 1861, William P. Fessenden Papers, LC, Microfilm Reel #2; J. W. Shaffer to Butler, August 17, 1864, in *BC*, 5:68; John C. Waugh, *Reelecting Lincoln: The Battle for the 1864 Presidency* (New York: Crown Publishers, 1997), 270–72.

64. Rolle, *John Charles Frémont*, 230 (see chap. 2, n. 14).

65. Ibid., 231–32.

66. Dix to Lincoln, November 12, 1864, PAL; Silbey, *Respectable Minority*, 19, 149.

67. Jones, "*Black Jack*," 62–63, 238; *New York Times*, November 20, 1864.

68. Lincoln to Montgomery Blair, November 2, 1863, in *CW*, 6:555; Blair to Montgomery Blair, December 20, 1863, BFP, Microfilm Reel #2.

69. Smith, *Blair Family*, 2:235; Burton J. Hendrick, *Lincoln's War Cabinet* (Boston: Little, Brown, 1946), 394–96.

70. Parrish, *Frank Blair: Lincoln's Conservative*, 188–89; Frank Blair, "The Jacobins of Missouri and Maryland," February 27, 1864, BFP, Microfilm Reel #13; C. M. Hawley to Lincoln, February 27, 1864, PAL.

71. Parrish, *Frank Blair: Lincoln's Conservative*, 186, 188, 192, 194; Frank Blair, "Speech of Hon. F. P. Blair, of Missouri," April 23, 1864, Francis Preston Blair Papers, Missouri Historical Society, St. Louis, Missouri.

72. Lincoln quoted in Riddle, *Recollections of War Times*, 275, 277 (see chap. 2, n. 29); Welles, April 28, 1864, in *Diary*, 2:20 (see chap. 5, n. 7); Garfield quoted in Hendrick, *Lincoln's War Cabinet*, 429–30 (emphasis in the original).

73. Lincoln to the House of Representatives, April 28, May 2, 1864, in *CW*, 7:319–20, 326–27; House of Representatives, "Military Appointment of Hon. F. P. Blair, Jr.,"

BFP, Microfilm Reel #13; Smith, *Blair Family*, 2:259; Parrish, *Frank Blair: Lincoln's Conservative*, 195–96.

74. Long, *Jewel of Liberty*, 36–37; Smith, *Blair Family*, 2:259.

Conclusion

1. William W. Averell, *Ten Years in the Saddle: The Memoirs of William W. Averell*, edited by Edward K. Eckert and Nicholas J. Amato (San Rafael, Calif.: Presidio Press, 1978), 276, 349.

2. Hattaway and Jones, *How the North Won*, 10 (see chap. 2, n. 2).

3. Eric Foner, *Reconstruction: America's Unfinished Revolution, 1863–1877* (New York: Harper and Row, 1988), 56, 164.

Index

285

DAVID WORK has published articles in *Southwestern Historical Quarterly*, *Journal of Arizona History*, *Gulf South Historical Review*, *Vermont History*, and *Western Historical Quarterly*.

The University of Illinois Press
is a founding member of the
Association of American University Presses.

Composed in 10/13.5 Janson Text
with Arabesque Ornaments display
by Jim Proefrock
at the University of Illinois Press
Designed by Dennis Roberts
Manufactured by Thomson-Shore, Inc.

University of Illinois Press
1325 South Oak Street
Champaign, IL 61820-6903
www.press.uillinois.edu